THE THREE ORDERS

GEORGES DUBY

THE THREE ORDERS

FEUDAL SOCIETY IMAGINED

Translated by Arthur Goldhammer
With a Foreword by Thomas N. Bisson

THE UNIVERSITY OF CHICAGO PRESS
CHICAGO AND LONDON

THE UNIVERSITY OF CHICAGO PRESS, CHICAGO 60637
THE UNIVERSITY OF CHICAGO PRESS, LTD., LONDON
© 1980 by the University of Chicago
All rights reserved. Published 1980
Phoenix edition 1982
Printed in the United States of America
89 88 87   4 5 6

Originally published as *Les trois ordres ou l'imaginaire du féodalisme*.
© 1978 by Editions Gallimard.

LIBRARY OF CONGRESS CATALOGING IN PUBLICATION DATA

Duby, Georges.
The three orders.

Translation of Les trois ordres.
Includes index.
1. Feudalism—France. 2. France—Social conditions. I. Title.
HN425.D78313   321.3′0944   80-13158
ISBN 0-226-16771-2 (cloth)
        0-226-16772-0 (paper)

CONTENTS

FOREWORD

This is a book about the political and cultural uses of a social idea. It comes on as a doubly original book: first, because it appears to be—astonishing though this may seem—the first book ever devoted to the history of what became the paradigmatic image of the ancien régime; and second, because it seeks to explain the appearance and early diffusion of that image as expressions of the strategies of threatened or innovating elites. One may search in vain in McIlwain, the Carlyles, or other standard manuals of political theory for more than passing mention of the three orders of medieval society, an idea which, when it does appear, is represented (correctly enough from one point of view) as the commonplace and inert projection of observed social order. Here the idea is restored to life.

It will never, of course, seem the same again. One soon recognizes that the originality of this book is by no means confined to its engaging treatment of a neglected theme. It lies chiefly in Georges Duby's perception—with debts here, generously acknowledged, to Dumézil and Le Goff—that the tripartite conception of society is one of those collective "imaginings" (one cannot quite translate *l'imaginaire*) of which the records should be read not only in the light of historical actuality but also to reveal those structural (or systemic) articulations of human experience, with their continuities and interruptions, which inform a cultural history running, in this case, from Indo-European antiquity to the French Revolution. Accordingly, this history of the three orders is not only a remarkable essay on the Middle Ages but also a showcase for a new methodology in social history which insists upon the bonds between the mental, the ritual, the imaginary, and the material. In the formative generations of Capetian history Duby seeks "to grasp," as he urged in his inaugural lecture before the Collège de France in 1970, "the real connecting links to be found in a larger whole."

The implications of this approach will not be overlooked in the discussions of *The Three Orders* that are only just beginning. But one considerable point already seems clear. Whatever the interest of this work for interdisciplinary research, the result is unmistakably an achievement of *historical* scholarship. Here the sources, not the concepts, are sovereign. Here there is dialogue and debate with the scientists of society, culture, and language, not subservience to them. A scholar bent on proving willy-nilly the ideological force of trifunctionality would have told a much tidier story of the early twelfth century than does Georges Duby. What he shows, on the contrary, is that the schema reanimated by the bishops of old *Francia* was clustered with other hierarchical images and polarities of diverse ancestry and pertinence, and of which the political resonance varied according to historical circumstances that are evoked after the fashion of a masterly *explication de textes*. If I am not mistaken, social scientists should find here a rich harvest of new historical data for the analysis of societal structure, power, and process.

The underlying historical argument, while less original to this book, is nonetheless also largely Duby's own. The conception of a profound transformation in the early eleventh century was heralded in *La société aux XIe et XIIe siècles dans la région mâconnaise* (1953), gained independent support from the work of other scholars (notably J.-Fr. Lemarignier), and was elaborated in the author's *The Early Growth of the European Economy* (first published in French in 1973) and other publications. It represents a fundamental revision of Marc Bloch's chronology in "two feudal ages." The old monarchical-ecclesiastical order, persisting, however battered, down to ca. 1000, was not yet a feudal order, for the proliferation of vassals, fiefs, castles, and the exploitative domination of peasants cannot generally be found to antedate the years 980–1030. The old order then collapsed in a "feudal revolution" which precipitated other changes against which the old guard vainly protested with an imagined order of social stability. As for the "resurgent" monarchical regime under Philip Augustus, much that had been introduced in the author's *Le dimanche de Bouvines* (1973) and in new research on the noble family (see also his *Medieval Marriage*, 1978) is brought into resourceful new focus in the final chapters of the present book.

In short, *The Three Orders* provides a brilliant elaboration of what may now be called the "Duby thesis," perhaps the most incisive and coherent explanation of medieval social change yet propounded, even as it opens a stunning new perspective for historical research. Moreover, it is a book of enticing stylistic vigor, its French prose balanced in flowing periods, crackling staccato, and finely modulated quotations, a prose so wrought, it would seem, as to defy translation. Yet the effect and meaning alike come through admirably in Arthur Goldhammer's rendering, an achievement in its own right that should do much to bring this book to the wide readership it merits.

THOMAS N. BISSON

ACKNOWLEDGMENTS

In December of 1970, I began teaching in Paris, and I made efforts to gather together a number of my fellow researchers. In this I had the assistance of Jacques Le Goff. The seminar was organized. Together, we chose to consider the primitive expressions of the trifunctional image of society. For three years, in this group as well as in the one I continued to lead at Aix-en-Provence, papers were read and discussions held—fruitful ones—revolving around this problem. In March 1973, Georges Dumézil kindly consented to hear a presentation of our conclusions in a final session of the course. I have tried to bring together the scattered results of our investigation, to put them in order and complete them, and this book is the result of that attempt. Care has been taken to give credit to the authors whose contributions were most crucial. But it has not been possible to mention the names of all those who, sometimes with a single sentence, helped shed light on one point or another in this obscure area. They will recognize how much this work is in their debt. I have to say that, in large part, it is theirs.

G. D.

THE FIELD OF INQUIRY

"Some are devoted particularly to the service of God; others to the preservation of the State by arms; still others to the task of feeding and maintaining it by peaceful labors. These are our three orders or estates general of France, the Clergy, the Nobility, and the Third Estate."

This statement is among those which open the *Traité des Ordres et Simples Dignitez* published in 1610 by the Parisian Charles Loyseau, a work immediately recognized as highly useful and continually reissued throughout the seventeenth century. These words serve to define the social order, i.e., the political order, i.e., order itself. Here we are confronted with three "estates," three fixed and stable categories, three levels of a hierarchy. It is like a school, that model society where the child learns to remain seated and quiet in orderly rows, to obey, to be classified; it is the class: the older children, those of intermediate age, the youngest; the first, the second, the "third" estate. Or, rather, three "orders"—for that is clearly the word preferred by Loyseau. The members of the highest order turn their attention heavenwards, while those of the two others look to the earth, all being occupied with the task of upholding the state [in French, Loyseau uses *Estat* for both *estate* and *state,* but capitalizes it in the latter case—trans.]. The intermediate order provides security, the inferior feeds the other two. Thus we have three functions, mutually complementing one another. The whole has a triangular solidity, with a base, an apex, and most importantly that ternarity which in some mysterious way bestows a feeling of equilibrium on the construction.

For when Loyseau comes subsequently to talk about the nobility (on page 53 of the 1636 edition), he states clearly that this social body is diverse, with various layers and ranks superimposed on one another. Among the nobility, everything is a matter of rank and precedence, and men will sometimes fight

1

to decide who will be the first to cross a threshold, sit down, or don his hat. Loyseau's concern is thus to introduce some order into this complex situation. He chooses to divide these many gradations into three categories. Why three? No tradition, custom, or authority dictates a tripartite division in this instance. "Because," says Loyseau, "the most perfect division is that into three species." "The most perfect"—that is what is in question—perfection itself. What matters is to seek, in the disorderly jumble of the sublunary world, the proper bases for a harmonious and reasonable construction which would appear to reflect the intentions of the Creator.

Indeed, if the monarchy of the ancien régime thought of itself as established on a threefold foundation of estates general or orders, this was because the fitting of social relations into ternary structures made it possible to integrate these into global structures, which extended over the entire visible and invisible universe. Loyseau makes this point in a long preliminary discussion. This prologue should not be read as a bravura exercise. It is essential; it justifies the whole argument.

"There must be order in all things, because it is seemly that it should be so, and so that these things may be given direction." So that each "thing" may be assigned its proper rank and so that all may be governed. Consider, for example, the hierarchy of created beings, with its three levels. At the lowest level are the inanimate objects: these are obviously classified according to their degree of perfection. Dominating the rest are the "celestial intelligences," the angels: as we know, these are arranged in an immutable order. Between the two are the animals, made subject to man by God. As for men, the concern of the *Traité,* they live a less stable existence, being free to choose between good and evil; nevertheless, "they cannot subsist without order"; hence they must be ruled. The key idea is thus one of a necessary "direction," and consequently a necessary submission. Some are made subject to others. The former must obey. Loyseau here makes use of a military analogy; he speaks of the "orders" which proceed from the regiment to the company and thence to the squad, which must be carried out without hesitation or question. Discipline is the source of an army's strength. It is also the source of the strength of the state. The world's solidity depends on it.

Next, it is argued that discipline requires inequality. "We cannot live together with equality of condition, hence some must command and others obey. Those who command comprise several orders, ranks, and degrees." Order comes from above. It is propagated through a hierarchy. The arrangement of the ranks, one above the other, insures that order will spread throughout the whole. "The sovereign lords have command over all within their State, giving their orders to the great, who pass them on to those of intermediate rank, who pass them on to the small" (we notice that a ternary hierarchy has come into being of its own accord among the agents of sovereign power, under its sole authority), "and the small pass the orders on to the people. And the people, who obey all those mentioned" (on this point, let us be quite precise in marking the real dividing line: between the "smallest" of those who command, and the whole of the people, which must mutely obey; between the officers and the troops; between the state apparatus and its—good or bad—subjects), "are further divided into several orders and ranks so that each of the latter has its superiors, who answer for the actions of the whole order to the magistrates, who do the same to the sovereign lords. Thus by means of manifold divisions and subdivisions of this kind, several orders are made into one general order (this is the inflection which leads to the three functions) and several estates into one well-governed State, in which there is a proper harmony and consonance and a correspondence among relationships from the lowest to the highest level; in the end, there is an orderly progress from an innumerable order toward unity."

According to this theory, order is based on the plurality of orders, on a sequence of binary relations, in which some give orders to others, who execute or convey them. This first assertion is coupled with another less evident one: that this sequence tends ineluctably to take on a ternary character, that the three functions, i.e., the three "orders," come to superimpose themselves upon the innumerable links in the chain. Why? How? In a way which is, frankly, mysterious, or in any case unexplained. Inexplicable, perhaps? A gap appears at this point in the argument. Despite his concern with proof, Loyseau does not seek to prove that this superimposition is necessary. He merely observes that some are particularly devoted to one duty, others to another, and still others to a third. Trifunctionality is self-evident. It is a part of the order of things.

Nevertheless, Loyseau does feel the need to marshal an additional argument to bolster the assumption on which the whole *Traité* is built. As a conclusion to the Prologue, therefore, he adds a Latin text taken from the Decretum of Gratian, "the last canon of the eighty-ninth distinction." He does not suspect—or at least he shows no sign of suspecting—that at the time he is writing this text is more than a thousand years old. It is the preamble to a letter sent by Pope Gregory the Great to the bishops of Chilperic's kingdom in August of 595, urging them to recognize the primacy of the bishop of Arles in questions of ecclesiastical discipline.[1] "Providence has established various degrees [*gradus*] and distinct orders [*ordines*] so that, if the lesser [*minores*] show deference [*reverentia*] to the greater [*potiores*], and if the greater bestow love [*dilectio*] on the lesser, then true concord [*concordia*] and conjunction [*contextio*: the word evokes a fabric or weave in a very concrete way] will arise out of diversity. Indeed, the community [*universitas*] could not subsist at all if the total order [*magnus ordo*] of disparity [*differentia*] did not preserve it. That creation cannot be governed in equality is taught us by the example of the heavenly hosts; there

3

are angels and there are archangels, which are clearly not equals, differing from one another in power [*potestas*] and order [*ordo*]." Everything is here. Not, of course, an explanation of trifunctionality, but at least its justification. Because heaven and earth are related by homology, the structures of human society necessarily reflect those of a more perfect society; in an imperfect way, they reproduce the hierarchies, the inequalities, which establish order in the society of angels.

It is quite natural to introduce an essay on the trifunctional model with a citation from the *Traité des Ordres*. More surprising in such a context is the following statement: there are only "three courses open to young men, the priest's, the peasant's, and the soldier's. . . . The religious estate, because it incorporates, at a higher and purer level, all the soldier's virtues. . . . Labor on the land, because by placing man in continuous contact with nature and its creator, it inculcates the virtues of endurance, patience, and perseverance and thus naturally fosters the heroism needed on the battlefield." Here we find the three "estates" (the word appears in the quotation), three functions (the same ones we have seen already: to serve God, preserve the state by arms, and extract food from the earth), arranged hierarchically in the same way. There is one additional detail: those to whom Loyseau refers as "some" and "others" are here defined as "men," by which "adult males" is clearly meant; women are not involved in this sort of classification. And there are two differences. Here we find no "orders" but rather "courses," paths, which are chosen, vocations of sorts—although they are clearly stages in an ascent, since the same individual can and should take first the third path, then the second, and finally the first, thus taking up each of the three missions in turn in the course of his life, in order to "raise" himself by degrees from earth to heaven, from "nature" to its "creator." These are thus successive stages of a progress towards perfection or "purification." We have a scale of virtues, in a discourse which is less political than it is moral; what is really being proposed is a kind of ascesis. These three "courses," moreover, are not the only ones. They are merely the good ones. Of the others this Manichaean disquisition says nothing. This is because it condemns them. An entire portion of social life is here cursed, spurned, reduced to nothing. What is being proclaimed is that only the priest, the soldier, and the peasant avoid going astray; only they answer God's call. In this way a close agreement is established between Loyseau's statement and this much more recent one, which can be found in a work published in Paris in 1951: *Notre beau métier de soldat, suivi d'un Essai de portrait moral du chef,* by a M. de Torquat.

A quite similar image of the perfect society is set forth in two statements which echo one another, two Latin sentences which may be translated as follows: (1) "Triple then is the house of God which is thought to be one: on Earth, some pray [*orant*], others fight [*pugnant*], still others work [*laborant*]; which three are joined together and may not be torn asunder; so that on the function [*officium*] of each the works [*opera*] of the others rest, each in turn assisting all." (2) "He showed that, since the beginning, mankind has been divided into three parts, among men of prayer [*oratoribus*], farmers [*agricultoribus*], and men of war [*pugnatoribus*]; he gives clear proof that each is the concern of both the others."

Three functions then, the same three, and similarly conjoined. But this time the pronouncement issues from the depths of the ages. Six hundred years before Loyseau, nine hundred and fifty before M. de Torquat, it was put forward in the third decade of the eleventh century by Adalbero, bishop of Laon, and Gerard, bishop of Cambrai.

In juxtaposing these citations, my point is to show that an image of the social order endured in France for a millennium. In erecting their mental image of a society one and triune like the divinity who had created and would ultimately judge it, wherein mutually exchanged services unified the diversity of human actions, the bishops of the year 1000 took for their foundation a triangular figure in no respect different from the one that provided symbolic underpinning for a theoretical justification of the subjection of the regimented populace to the absolute monarchy of Henry IV—a theory which the newly born human sciences wasted no time in challenging. Even today, in certain circles no doubt diminished in importance but not yet extinct, it is to this same triangular image that the yearning for a regenerated humanity clings, the yearning for a humanity that would at last be purged of the twin infections, white and red, that breed in the big city, a humanity that would have rid itself at the same time of both capitalism and the working class. Thirty or forty successive generations have imagined social perfection in the form of trifunctionality. This mental representation has withstood all the pressures of history. It is a structure.

A structure encased within another that is deeper and more ample, which envelops it—namely, that similarly trifunctional system whose place among the modes of thought of the Indo-European peoples has been elucidated by the admirable work of Georges Dumézil. In countless texts patiently collected everywhere from the Indus to Iceland and Ireland, three functions are found: the first, in the name of heaven to lay down the rules, the law that institutes order; the second, brutally, violently, to enforce obedience; the third, finally, of fecundity, health, plenty, pleasure, to guide the "peaceful labors" discussed by Charles Loyseau to achievement of their ends; between these three functions and this same Loyseau's three "orders," M. de Torquat's three "courses," and the priests, warriors, and peasants of the bishops of Cambrai and Laon, the relationship is clear. So clear that there is no reason to make a point of it, other than to clarify the outlines of the investigation whose results this book will set down.

At the confluence of thought and language, closely associated with the structures of a language (I reiterate: a language—the linguists were the first to notice the functional triangle in written expression, and it must be acknowledged that it is not easy to detect a similar ternarity in symbolic modes of expression not involving words), there exists a form, a manner of thinking, of speaking the world, a certain way of putting man's action on the world—which is indeed what Dumézil has in mind when he speaks of trifunctionality: three constellations of virtues with which gods and heros are endowed. When a warrior chieftain, sovereign, or mistress has to be celebrated in panegyric rather than ritual, it is natural to reach for this classificatory implement, which is ready at hand. This is often the route by which the trifunctional model is transferred from heaven to earth, from imagination to experience: it is a way of organizing praise bestowed on an individual. Traces of its use in this manner abound in countless biographies, both real and fictitious. In contrast, this model is rarely applied in an explicit way to the body social. The "tripartite ideology" that Dumézil has always described as "an ideal and, at the same time, a means of analyzing, of interpreting the forces which are responsible for the course of the world and human life"[2] is the backbone of a value system; overt use is made of it in myth, epic, and flattery; but ordinarily it remains latent, unformulated; only rarely is it brought into the open in the shape of imperious statements as to the proper ideal of society, order, i.e., power. But all the citations above support statements of precisely this kind. In them trifunctionality is laid out as a framework for an ideal classification of the kinds of men. It serves as a justification of certain normative utterances, certain imperatives—whether calls to action in order to bring about a transformation or restoration of society, or reassuring homilies, justifications. I am thinking of a sort of trifunctionality that serves an ideology, a "polemical discursive formation through which a passion seeks to realize a value by exercising a power over society."[3] Precisely stated, the problem is this: Why, of all the simple, equally instrumental images, was that of the three functions chosen? "The human mind is constantly making choices among its latent riches. Why? How?" The question was raised by Dumézil himself.[4] As a historian, I will broaden it somewhat to include two further questions: Where? And when?

The first of these I shall evade by limiting the scope of the investigation to the region where the various statements cited above were made, namely, France, confining my attention more particularly to northern France, whose political, social, and cultural configuration remained for a long time quite distinct from that of the countries to the south of Poitou, Berry, and Burgundy. Indeed, as a matter of correct method it seems to me that ideological

6

systems must be studied within a homogeneous cultural and social formation, all the more so if the aim is to date the transformations occurring
within such systems. Hence I shall deliberately remain within the bounds of
this area. It may appear tiny. Its peculiar advantages should be noted: it is a
province with a particularly abundant literature, and in addition the place
where the Frankish monarchy took root. Now it happens that this form, this
manner of classification, of self-classification, whose early history I have
chosen to study, is first revealed to us by literature; it is closely associated,
moreover, with the concept of sovereignty.

The properly historical problem, that of chronology, remains. Within the
region thus circumscribed, I have tried to collect and date all traces of an
ideology based on social trifunctionality. Written traces—the only material
we have. Which leaves a good deal to be desired. Once we move away from
the vicinity of the present, we find that a vast portion of what was written
has been lost irremediably: what remains comes virtually exclusively under
the head of writing for solemn occasions. Official documents. Never does
the historian have anything other than remains to paw over, and such scarce
debris as he does have come virtually without exception from monuments
that power has caused to be erected; not only does all life's spontaneity
escape him, but also all that is of popular origin; only a few men manage to
make themselves heard: those who controlled the apparatus of what
Loyseau calls the State. As we are discussing chronology, it should therefore
be borne in mind that such few dates as can (sometimes with great difficulty)
be established indicate nothing other than the moment of emergence, the
point in time at which a certain mental representation gains access to the
highest levels of written expression. More than that, those emergences
whose traces have fortuitously been preserved are not necessarily the oldest,
as it behooves us not to forget. Clearly, the margin of uncertainty is quite
large.

At least one fact appears certain, so that I may rely on it from the outset:
no text in northern France prior to those containing the statements of Adalbero of Laon and Gerard of Cambrai makes mention of a trifunctional view
of society. This is beyond doubt: much care has been devoted to the search,
by Georges Dumézil himself, and after him by Jean Batany, Jacques Le Goff,
Claude Carozzi, and others. In vain: the rich harvest of writings—
theoretical writings—left by the Carolingian renaissance yielded nothing.
The two Latin sentences I cited above seem to have burst upon silence. In
any case, it is with them that the history of a trifunctional representation of
society begins in this tiny part of the world. But if the date of the original
utterance has been established, the chronology of the reception, acceptance,
and diffusion of the model remain to be constructed. All that has been said
about trifunctionality in medieval society is imprecise. Consider Marc
Bloch, for instance: "a theory at that time very widely current represented

the human community as being divided into three orders."[5] "At that time":
when? During the "first feudal age," i.e., according to the great medievalist,
in the centuries prior to the mid-eleventh century? "Very widely current":
what is meant by this? Consider Jacques Le Goff, who was the first to
formulate the problem in appropriate terms: "around the year 1000, Western literature represented Christian society according to a new model which
immediately enjoyed a considerable success." What is meant by "around,"
"new," "immediately," "considerable"? Are we sure of all this? By carrying the investigation forward into the eleventh and twelfth centuries,
pursuing it until the allusions to the three social functions, the three
orders, proliferate, until it becomes certain that the "theory" is "quite widespread," that the "model" enjoyed "a considerable success," I would like to
dispel the ambiguity as far as possible.

I would particularly like to answer Dumézil's question: why, how was
this choice among latent structures made? For this I think it necessary to be
precise about the location of the research. The trifunctional figure, as I have
said, is a form. Traces of it may be found in quite a few documents. I am not
bent on flushing out every one of them. This book's central character, the
trifunctional figure, will concern us only where it functions as a major cog in
an ideological system. Which it does in Loyseau's dissertation. Thus if we
are to grasp the why and the how, it will be essential to avoid isolating the
formulations of the trifunctional theme from their context—as has nearly
always been done. They should rather be left in their proper place within the
whole in which they are articulated. What matters is to reconstruct the
global character of that whole, to investigate the circumstances surrounding
the construction of the ideological system in which trifunctionality is embedded, and to ask what problems and contradictions had to be faced before
it could brought forward, promulgated, flaunted as a banner. For if it is
correct to contest the notion that the trifunctional schema was "constructed",[7] if, as a latent structure, it stands outside history, it is nevertheless
beyond doubt that the systems incorporating it as a supporting member
belong, for their part, to history. They form and are deformed. And by
closely observing their genesis and dismemberment we have some chance of
finding out why and how the trifunctional schema was chosen at a certain
time and place.

Having thus specified the object of the research, we come to another
category of problems. The model of three social functions—this postulate,
this axiomatic truth, whose existence is never proved, never evoked but in
relation to a cosmology, a theology, and certainly a morality, and on which
one of those "discursive polemical formations" known as ideologies is
founded, thereby providing a power with a simple, ideal, abstract image of
the social organization—how is this model connected with the concrete
relationships within society? Ideology, we are well aware, is not a reflection

of real life, but a project for acting on it. If this action is to have any likelihood of success, the disparity between the imaginary representation and the "realities" of life should not be too great. This being the case, and supposing that the ideological discourse does not go unnoticed, new attitudes may then crystallize, changing the way men look upon the society to which they belong. To observe the system in which the model of the three "orders" is embodied as it comes to light in France, to attempt to follow its course through success and misfortune from 1025 to 1225, is to confront one of the central questions now facing the sciences of man: the question of the relationship between the material and the mental in the evolution of societies.

And what is more, to confront that question in circumstances that are not hopelessly unfavorable. True, as has already been mentioned, to take so remote a period for our "terrain" is to condemn ourselves to working with mere shreds of information, and to paying heed only to intellectuals, cut off from the rest of society even more than intellectuals nowadays by the peculiarities of their vocabulary and their mode of thought. But at least the documentary resources are relatively limited. It is not impossible to take them all in with a single glance. More, we are liberated by the fact that our interest is focussed on so far distant a past: feudalism's contradictions no longer concern us sufficiently that we are loath to demystify the ideology that did its best to reduce or veil them.

The difficulty lies elsewhere. How are we to compare the imaginary and the concrete? How are we to sever the "objective" study of human behavior from investigation of the symbolic systems that dictated the conduct in question and justified it in men's eyes?[8] Is it within the power of the historian to strip away entirely the ideal garb in which the societies of the past cloaked themselves? Can he see them other than as they dreamed of, as they spoke of, themselves? As medievalists, let us ask ourselves. If to us "feudal society" seems composed of three orders, is it not true that the primary reason for this is that the two sentences cited above still obsess us as they once obsessed our mentors? Are we not ourselves slaves to that ideology that I am presumptuous enough to want to demystify? It was in any case a force powerful enough to have led us (I say us because I am one of the guilty) into certain blunders, such as dating knighthood's constitution as an "order" a century and a half too early. If for no other reason than this, for its role in the development of historical research, the trifunctional model deserves to be examined very closely, and held up for comparison with all that we are capable of seeing in the world that gradually adopted it for its own.

The time has now come to examine the words that for the first time in the "sources" stemming from northern France gave clear voice to this model.

9

PART ONE

REVELATION

I

FIRST FORMULATIONS

We begin, then, with two sentences: "Here below, some pray, others fight, still others work . . . "; "from the beginning, mankind has been divided into three parts, among men of prayer, farmers, and men of war." Three types of action: *orare, pugnare, agricolari-laborare.* Two speakers.

They are important personages. Hence not all memory of what their lives were like has been lost.[1] Adalbero, the elder of the two, is also the more famous for the role that he played—that of traitor—in the transfer of the French crown from the Carolingians to the Capetians. Nephew of Adalbero, the archbishop of Rheims, and cousin-german of the dukes of Lorraine, he belonged to a very powerful family with representatives throughout the vast province of Lotharingia, where it had gained control of a goodly number of counties and bishoprics. It was a family of the highest nobility: Adalbero knew himself to be of royal blood, a descendant of Charlemagne's ancestors. In this lineage, the name he bore was given to boys destined to become bishops. It was customary that they bide their time in the cathedral chapter of Metz until an episcopal vacancy should appear. Adalbero seems to have completed his education at Rheims, where his uncle, the great prelate of the family, was archbishop. In any case, Lothar, the Carolingian king of western France, soon made him his chancellor and in 977 established him in the see of Laon.

Gerard was born of the same stock. Recent marriages, moreover, had tied his family more closely to Adalbero's: the latter was cousin-german of Gerard's mother.[2] Gerard, too, studied at Rheims. He made his career, however, not in the western kingdom but in the east. In the chapel at Aix he joined the group of well-born ecclesiastics who served the emperor Henry II. With the support of Adalbero's cousins, that sovereign was endeavoring to restore the power of the German kings in Lotharingia. In 1012, the bishop of Cambrai, a town on the border of the French kingdom, lay dying. Even before he had drawn his last breath, Henry granted his bishopric to Gerard, thus forestalling the count of Flanders, who wanted to replace the dying man with one of his relatives. Along with the bishopric went the title of count, an adjunct it had acquired some five years earlier. All this was given to Gerard—a young man, perhaps, but a trustworthy one.

Thus the two men who, so far as we know, were the first to make use of the theme of social trifunctionality were close cousins. Both had been educated at Rheims. In that metropolitan town, in the presence of the archbishop to whom both were suffragans, they met frequently: they spoke together, or at least within each other's hearing. Members of the Lotharingian aristocracy used by the French king against the German and vice versa, Adalbero and Gerard were caught up in the vicissitudes of a common political situation. Their roles were identical. And if both of them spoke of the three functions, the reason was first of all that both were bishops.

On the threshold of the eleventh century, it was amid the vestiges of a Roman town that a bishop's see, or throne (*cathedra*), was to be found. From the city his power extended as far as the frontiers of the *civitas*, boundaries originally laid down in the late Empire, which separated the various dioceses. Within each of these territories, the bishop was the pastor, responsible for his flock. The true God had entrusted his faithful to him. The bishop presided over the celebration of the mysteries on behalf of the entire populace. His hands dispensed the sacred. Two centuries earlier, barring mischance, he would have been regarded a saint; he would have continued his good works after death, appearing in dreams, preaching, giving warning, issuing reprimands; from his tomb he would have distributed curses and benedictions. By the year 1000, times had changed. Yet it remained important that the biship be a nobleman, that his blood carry the charismas which predestined him to play the role of intercessor. The fact that all the bishops of Metz and Rheims were named Adalbero and were offspring of the house of Ardennes had more to do with magic than with family politics: only certain lineages were thought to possess the power of communicating with the invisible.

Still, this potential power had to be activated by a rite: the rite of unction, anointment. The bishop was a sacred personage, a Christ, the Lord's Anointed; passing through his skin, mixing with, penetrating his entire body, the chrism impregnated him forever with divine power. In particular, he was able to delegate the sacerdotal function to others by anointing them with consecrated oil. He ordained them. Under the bishop's control, men ordained by him exorcised demons in the villages of the diocese. Within its boundaries, no one made sacrifices, no one performed rituals, no one uttered propitiatory formulas that he himself had not instituted. The bishop begat the clergy (*clerus*). Over it he held the authority of a father. By spiritual filiation, the sacramental acts emanated from his own hands.

Anointment brought with it another gift: *sapientia,* a gaze capable of penetrating behind the veil of appearances to reach hidden truths. Only the bishop possessed the keys to the truth. This was a priceless privilege, whose concomitant obligation was to disseminate that truth, to teach it to those who knew it not, to punish those who strayed from the true path—by means of the word. The bishop was master of the word, and in particular of language of a very special kind. The language he used was a very old one, incomprehensible to most other men, but which by virtue of translation had become the language of Holy Scripture some seven centuries earlier in an Imperial Rome at long last converted to Christianity. Because the bishop was the interpreter of the word of God, and because, in this part of the world, that word was couched in the noble Latin of the fourth century, the bishop was the repository of classical culture. In his dwelling-place amidst antique ruins, what survived, in the year 1000, of the ordered and regular language of books, of pure Latin, was preserved, beleaguered on all sides by rustic barbarism. From the episcopal see a continual renaissance of Latinity flowed forth. This cultural labor was carried out in the school, that workshop that stood alongside the cathedral—there, a small crew of men of all ages set themselves to copying texts, to analyzing sentences, to dreaming up etymologies, endlessly exchanging what they knew with one another, constantly working over that most precious raw material, that treasure of homilies and incantations, the words of God.

One of those Latin words, the verb *orare,* summed up both aspects of the episcopal mission: to pray and to preach—which amounted to the same thing. Anointment had placed the bishop right at the point where heaven and earth were joined, between the visible and the invisible. His words were addressed sometimes toward the one and sometimes toward the other, sometimes to persuade, sometimes to coax some sign of benevolence. The bishop pleaded his case as in another age cases had been pleaded at the forum, and so he looked to Cicero for the techniques of effective discourse. *Orator,* he served up words as offerings to heaven, in the hope of provoking reciprocal outpourings of grace, or, alternatively, words intended to make known on earth what *sapientia* had revealed. Because of his median, intermediary position, the bishop bore a special obligation to contribute to the restoration of harmony between the two worlds, that essential concord which Satan strove ceaselessly to disrupt. With the assistance of the clerks he had ordained and educated, the labors of pruning, of separating wheat from chaff, of pushing back the darkness, occupied him constantly. He enlightened and he admonished—and to do so he called upon a second personage for aid. Like the bishop, this personage was *prelatus,* designated by

15

God because of the virtue in his blood. God had set him over the rest of mankind as their leader. But, in this case, their leader in the domain of the earthly, the material, the carnal: the personage in question was the bishop's leading parishoner, the principal object of his moralizing lectures—the king, or, if not the king, the prince, the man who "by the grace of God" held the *principalis potestas* and who, in the king's place, bore responsibility for that part of the flock that subject to the bishop's tutelage—distinct, that is, from the clergy, or *clerus*—which was known as the *populus,* the people.[3] In the Carolingian tradition, eleventh-century bishops felt obliged to offer kings and princes a mirror in which they might see themselves, a mirror not unlike the polished metal sort then in use, which might reflect the face rather poorly but nonetheless showed up its defects and so helped in correcting them.[4] When episcopal discourse was addressed to the princes of the earth, its purpose was indeed one of correction: it aimed to remind them of their rights, their duties, and of what was not done in the world. It also aimed to incite them to action, to reestablish order—that particular order whose model the bishop found in heaven. It was a social plan. In the Carolingian tradition, the episcopate was by nature the producer of ideology.

Now, both Adalbero and Gerard were Carolingian bishops, the most Carolingian of all. They were Carolingians not only by blood, but also because the ecclesiastical province of Rheims, to which both their dioceses belonged, lay at the heart of *Francia,* the country of the Franks. Remy, archbishop of Rheims, had baptized Clovis. His successors were at this time laying claim to the exclusive right to anoint the king of the western Franks.[5] A century and a half earlier, as the imperial dignity itself was ineluctably slipping away toward the east, toward Aix-la-Chapelle and Rome, archbishop Hincmar of Rheims had garnered the finest fruits of the Carolingian renaissance from Rheims to Compiègne, from Paris to Laon (the "Mont Loon" of the *chansons de geste,* the last retreat of Charles, son of the last Carolingian sovereign, whom Adalbero, archbishop of Rheims, had deprived of his rights, in 987, by designating for royal election the usurper Hugh Capet, and whom our Adalbero, bishop of Laon, had betrayed). Metz occupied no more than a marginal position on the fringes of this mother-province: it was an exposed outpost surveying the Austrasian wilds. But the policy of the other Frankish kings, those of the east, of Germany, of establishing clerks from Lorraine in the bishoprics of Rheims, Cambrai, and Laon, had been designed expressly to regain this outpost, to recover this cultural conservatory. The cathedrals of Cambrai and Laon, as well as that of Rheims, should be looked upon as repositories of Frankish political forms. The memory of these forms remained more alive than elsewhere in their literary storehouses, couched in the Latin of the rhetors. It fell to the bishops of these cities to preserve that memory, to draw from it inspiration

16

for the oratory that constituted their contribution to the proper government of the realm.

The city of Laon fell under the jurisdiction of the western kingdom, Cambrai under that of the kingdom of Lorraine, which had merged with the German realm. The kingdom of the west Franks, i.e., France, and the east Frankish kingdom, i.e., the Empire: two states, separated by the Escaut and the Meuse, whose two sovereigns, cousins, both heirs of Charlemagne, equal in prestige, regarded by writers in the early eleventh century as the twin pillars of Christendom, were called upon to embrace one another in brotherly love and to meet periodically on their common frontier, where they were jointly to attend to the problems facing all the people of God. In 1937, T. Schieffer described Gerard of Cambrai as a German bishop: political passions carried that excellent scholar beyond the limits of the reasonable—Gerard was from Lorraine, not Germany. He spoke Romance, not German. To be sure, he had been in the chapel of the German king, and was loyal to him; in 1015 he labored to convince the count of Namur and the count of Hainaut, his cousins, to recognize the authority of the new duke of Lower Lorraine, his cousin; his principal enemy was the count of Flanders. And the city of Cambrai did belong to the Empire. But to this city was attached the ancient city of Arras, and this belonged to the kingdom of France. So that, as the chronicler Sigebert of Gembloux said, among the *Lotharienses* only Gerard was dependent on the *parrochia francorum*. Thus he was also tied to the king of France, and this, as much as his culture, inclined him toward *Francia*. When the Capetian monarch summoned all the prelates of his realm to his side, Gerard made haste to comply. At Easter in 1018, he was at Laon, in the company of the king, Robert the Pious, and, of course, the bishop, Adalbero. In 1023, he participated in the great assembly at Compiègne, convoked by Robert to reform the Church, that is, the world. As the occupant of two episcopal sees, one of which was royal, Gerard of Cambrai-Arras was a member—though no doubt a less intimate one than Adalbero of Laon—of the circle of bishops who gravitated toward the Capetian king. As "orators" they spelled one another in insuring that the monarch was exposed to an uninterrupted disquisition on morality, or, rather, that he was engaged in a continuous moralizing dialogue.

For the king in the year 1000 had this in common with the bishops: he was sacred. Since the middle of the eighth century, the Frankish king's body, like the bishop's, had been impregnated with holy oil. And therefore his spirit was impregnated with *sapientia*. He was a sage, mysteriously informed of the intentions of Providence, as one of the *oratores*. Adalbero put it clearly to Robert: "The capacity [*facultas*] of the *orator* is given to the king,"[6] reminding him that he must follow the example of the bishops by investigating, by rooting out those among the populace who might deviate from the straight and narrow, meting out reward and punishment as God would do on the Day of Judgment. Yet the position of the royal personage was ambiguous. In addition to the sceptre, the sword, too, was to be found in the king's hand. A considerable portion of his time had to be devoted to arms, and this diverted his attention from the school. If he possessed "wisdom," he did not fully possess culture. It was no doubt customary to educate the heir to the throne in the same manner as future bishops: when he was still only duke of France, Hugh Capet (and this says a great deal about his hopes) had placed his son, Robert, in an episcopal school—the one at Rheims, in fact. The king therefore knew how to read from a Latin book, and could chant his prayers. But he did not know enough to take full advantage of the illumination coming to him from heaven. He had need of assistants to help him decipher the message. This necessary assistance was provided by the other *oratores,* who unlike the king himself were not distracted from meditation upon things sacred by military concerns. Their function was to put into words what the ritual anointment enabled the king to perceive indistinctly. For the bishops had the advantage over the sovereign of being experts in the art of rhetoric. This justified their feeling that with regard to the king they were predominant. Strictly speaking, theirs was a magisterial position. "Rhetoric, based on civic morality, is the source of all civilized life": this paraphrase of a passage of Cicero's *De inventione* was uttered by Gerbert when he was director of the school of Rheims, where Gerard may have heard him lecture. In any case, the intellectuals of the cathedral chapters held that rhetoric was a means of governing, and in the first place of governing what princes did, these personages being regarded as subjects (*subditi*) of the episcopal word. As Adalbero believed and stated with perfect clarity: "all mankind He [God] has made subject to them [the priests] by precept; 'all,' meaning that no prince [*princeps*] is excepted."[7] Adalbero of Laon and Gerard of Cambrai considered themselves the masters (*magistri*) of Robert, the king of France, just as Alcuin had been Charlemagne's master,[8] and Hincmar, Charles the Bald's. They regarded their mission as one of revealing to him the principles behind his worldly actions, and, in particular, the hidden structure of human society, i.e., its tripartite division. The two bishops, cousins by blood, made the same point to the same personage. Were their voices joined in chorus, in unison? The next question to ask is one of timing: when did they speak of the three social functions?

To assign dates to the two utterances which serve as point of departure for this study is not a simple matter: the scribes who committed them to writing failed to include any chronological indications to make our task easier.

Adalbero's words are incorporated into a poem addressed to Robert, of which the manuscript diligently studied by Claude Carozzi is not an autograph; the corrections it contains, however, suggest that the work was carried out under the control of the bishop of Laon, up to the point where it was interrupted, still incomplete, by the death of the prelate—or the king—both of which occurred in 1031. In any case, the author was still at work shortly before that date. What he has to say about Cluny enables us to make the assumption that he conceived his work after the papacy's confirmation of the privileges of that monastic order, i.e., after 1027. Ten twenty-seven to ten thirty-one: a narrow span of years, an exceptionally precise dating for a document of this sort.

Gerard of Cambrai did not himself dictate the sentence with which we are concerned. It is reported in the introduction to a speech he is said to have delivered, in chapter 52 of book III of a work well-known to medievalists, a work celebrated in its time, later revised, many times recopied, and utilized by numerous chroniclers: the *Gesta episcoporum cameracensium*, the *Deeds of the Bishops of Cambrai*.[9] This was one of those anthologies of panegyric biography then being composed in several cathedrals in Latin Christendom to the glory of deceased bishops. The work bears no date, and, as opposed to Adalbero's poem, we do not possess its original draft. It comes down to us reworked, fragmented and rearranged by a continuator. Taking account of E. Van Mingroot's ingenious critical observations,[10] I would like to suggest that the fragment of book III which contains the statement relative to the tripartite division of society belongs to the first draft, that is, that it was written by a canon of the cathedral, someone very close to Gerard, not, as has been believed hitherto, in 1044, but, at the latest, in the first few months of 1025.[11] This revised dating is important: in the first place, it establishes that Gerard exercised very close control over a narrative wholly devoted to the celebration of his merits, that the scribe, in any case, did not distort his thoughts, and, consequently, that it was indeed Gerard who employed the trifunctional theme as support for a definition of the social order. Second, it establishes that this speech was delivered not in 1036, as was believed, but rather in 1024, hence before Adalbero began the composition of his poem.

not much. I have said that there were two sentences: in reality, they amount to but a single utterance. With one voice, Adalbero and Gerard allude to the postulate of social trifunctionality. The only difference between them lies in the tone. Gerard was a young, active man, involved in the persecution of heretics and in debates before assemblies: he spoke, leaving it to others to record what he had said. Whereas, Adalbero, who had been bishop for more than half a century, was a hoary old man, and himself a writer who was meticulous about his labors.

But the canon who composed the *Deeds of the Bishops of Cambrai* was also meticulous. Like his patron, the bishop, like Adalbero, he respectfully obeyed the rules of rhetoric. He wrote with an eye to the *auctores*, the "authorities," careful not to depart from those models of correct composition and logical argumentation inherited from ancient times, from the golden age of Christian Latinity. It should be borne in mind that the trifunctional theme was couched in elegant language set like a jewel in carefully polished works of art warily exhibited to a small circle of experts, offered for the delectation of connoisseurs, friends of the author, his former schoolfellows, his rivals. The writer—whether Adalbero, the anonymous canon of Cambrai, or Gerard, who guided his pen—sought to shine, to surpass his competitors by virtue of the refined literary texture of his work. He knew that it was above all his virtuosity that would draw applause. These poems, these historical narratives were by way of being school exercises, and these intellectuals—even, in spite of his advanced age, the bishop of Laon—were all schoolboys. Writers worked hard to find natural ways to merge a train of allusions with the sophisticated rhythms of their prose and verse— allusions to the books read by every initiate, books whose language filled their memories; the game, the pleasure of the text was to identify these quotations in passing, in their new and more subtle articulation. The statement of the trifunctional principle occurs in a specific place in two of these elaborate compositions. It is worth pointing out once more that the wise course is to leave that statement in context, and to take care not to disturb the surrounding word-sculptures, which set up revealing resonances with it, essential to a correct interpretation. Indeed, only the structure of a system explains why the theme of the three functions should have emerged at this time, in this place.

2

GERARD OF CAMBRAI
AND THE PEACE

The text which records the words of Gerard of Cambrai is manifestly the older of the two. I will therefore begin the analysis of the system with the original version of the *Gesta episcoporum cameracensium,* written in 1024 at the behest of the bishop, then suffering the distress into which the death of his protector, the emperor Henry II, had plunged him. His purpose in having the work written was both to bolster his personal prestige—Gerard is depicted as the exemplary prelate—and to defend the rights of his church, invoking the past as proof of legitimate possession, setting out principles, forging a doctrinal arm to be held in readiness against probable challenges. The work first tells of the activities of the earliest bishops of Cambrai; it then lists the domains of the cathedral and the monasteries of the diocese; finally, in book III, Gerard's performance during the first twelve years of his episcopate is celebrated. This is where the panegyric itself is found, the plea *pro domo,* and in this plea is the brief utterance that interests us. Our first goal, therefore, is to dissect this third book, to lay its architecture bare.

The task is a difficult one because the text was demolished, pulverized, and then rebuilt in 1054, after the hero's death. The revisions that were made further confused the chronology of the incidents recounted, which even in the original form was not sequential. In fact, the original writer had chosen to accentuate his patron's glory by knitting events together in such a way as to give a clearer illustration of the doctrine that inspired Gerard's actions.

The action for which the *Deeds* are the apology involves other characters. Gerard shares the stage with two sovereigns having jurisdictional claims over the dual bishopric of Cambrai-Arras, the emperor and the king of France; he is pitted against his confrères, the cobishops of the province of Rheims, and the *princeps,* his neighbor and competitor, the count of Flanders; and, finally, he confronts one further actor, the "people." Gerard's is clearly the leading role in the splendid theatre he has created as a magnificent showcase for himself. His is the grand oration, in which the truth, that which is just, which heaven decrees, is proclaimed. Unremittingly he does battle with words, for which he ransacks his memory and scours the episcopal library in search of phrases and verses from the Bible or the Fathers. His aim is never to put forward an argument not in conformity with "the decrees of the Gospel, or the apostles, or the canons, or the popes," [1] and he says he takes great pains to amass biblical and patristic references "so as never to suffer the impudent accusation of not purveying a sufficiency of the Gospel's own words." Day in and day out, he speaks of peace.

This was indeed the central theme of the episcopal *Deeds* as a literary genre. It was customary in this sort of composition to depict prelate after prelate endeavoring to secure a public peace, whether as rulers inspiring fear or pastors inspiring love, combining the strength of the king with the complementary qualities of the priesthood, cooperating closely with royal power for the purpose of establishing "justice" on an enduring foundation. [2] Indeed, the intention of the *Gesta episcoporum cameracensium* was to extol the bishop Gerard as a man of "peace." There were three special reasons for this. The first, of a general nature, was that to desire peace was to desire order, to will the good, to conform to God's intentions: was not the perfect city, the heavenly Jerusalem, called *visio pacis,* spectacle of peace? Pacification was mankind's way of making ready for the imminent return to Paradise. A second factor, however, was that in 1024, when, at the prelate's behest, the docile canon of Cambrai sat down to work on this prestigious monument to his glory, peace was the great cause in Christendom: for months Henry II and Robert the Pious had been laboring jointly to restore it, and peace was the sole topic of conversation in the assemblies where all the bishops of Francia, old and young, met in rivalry. Finally, in the name of peace, Gerard was hard at work trying to remove a thorn in his side, trying to dispose of a nasty, palpable, immediate little problem that was causing him no little irritation, preventing him from concentrating his attention on the things of the spirit, distracting him from the messages emanating from the sphere of the invisible: in the name of peace, Gerard hoped to bridle a man who, day in and day out, in his own city and in the shadow of the episcopal palace itself, disputed his power: Walter of Lens, the castellan.

In Cambrai, by imperial concession, the bishop had held the comital powers since 1007. This meant that he exercised all the royal prerogatives: calling to arms, passing judgment, levying royal taxes. But a castle was built in Cambrai. This castle, like the others which dotted the kindgom of France, was the symbol of the supreme temporal authority, of the *postestas,* of the right to repress and to take by force: the very picture of the heavy hand of justice, violent, savage, effective. This castle was garrisoned by a band of plundering warriors, *milites,* knights, whose leader was Walter, warden of the fortress. Like every castellan in this period, he sought to profit from his position. Behind him stood Baldwin, the count of Flanders, whom he supported. This count was naturally the rival of all his neighboring counts, and especially of the count of Cambrai, the bishop Gerard; the city of Arras was in his *regnum;* he already effectively dominated the bishopric of Thérouanne; and he wished to do the same in the bishopric of Arras, then joined to that of Cambrai; above all, he dreamed, with occasional encouragement from the Capetian monarch, of extending his principality beyond the frontier, into Lorraine, i.e., into the region of Cambrai. Walter was one of the pawns he was attempting to position in advance of such a move. His ambitions added venom to the then commonplace conflict within the episcopal city which saw the ecclesiastical power—a power with the capacity to speak and write, hence the source of all that we historians know about this sort of affair—pitted against the secular power, the bishop against the man whom the bishop denounced as a "tyrant" and oppressor of the people, in light of their dispute over seigniorial power. This was a common enough sort of controversy, excruciatingly dull to recount. There is reason to wonder if the *Gesta* were not written largely on account of it. In any case, details of the conflicts' vicissitudes abound in the narrative. The debate had actually begun well before Gerard's arrival on the scene, in the ninth decade of the tenth century, a time when lords of castles everywhere—in the Mâcon region, in Poitou, in Ile-de-France—were beginning to weave around the fortress a lucrative net of trammels, a system for exploiting the peasantry. Immediately after his election, the new bishop encountered this system in all its violence. During his predecessor's last days, Walter, the castellan, had stormed the bishop's house, and later caused a disturbance at his funeral. He would not submit to discipline: the *Gesta* recount how, aided by his henchmen, the knights, he set fire to the outlying districts of the town. Walter the evildoer, the tool of the Devil, is present on virtually every page of book III, in which we never lose sight of two intertwined themes: the theme of tyranny and the theme of peace.

For the main purpose of the encomium is to show how the good bishop, defender of the poor, stands up to wicked aggression. This he does in three ways. His first stratagem was to weaken the count of Flanders, who was stirring up trouble, by offering hospitality to his rebellious son (in those days, most heirs apparent did rebel against their fathers as soon as they outgrew adolescence, out of impatience to exercise unfettered control over the seigniory, in which they were egged on by companions of their own age, equally frustrated and greedy). Second, he tried to arrange specific agreements or treaties with the enemy. Their terms were carefully recorded in the *Gesta,* which could be produced later, if documentary proof were needed, before an assembly of judges. These accords, which dealt with military service and with the parcelling out of the proceeds of justice, were guaranteed, as was then the new fashion, by exchanges of hostages and swearing of personal oaths. The purpose of such pacts was to bind Walter in a web of collective commitments by which his temptation to further seizures might be checked. It was also hoped that he might be constrained by means of a sworn oath: with his hand on the relics, he was obliged to agree to serve Gerard as, according to custom, the "knights of Lorraine" served their lord and their bishop.[3] In other words, Gerard made Walter his vassal—the use of the tie of vassalage as the basis of political relations in the French aristocracy was just then in its infancy. None of these assurances was very secure, and a sudden change of heart was a constant threat, despite the penalties known to be reserved for perjurors in the hereafter. All of this, moreover, was humiliating for the bishop of Cambrai, a great personage, cousin of dukes, relative and favorite of the emperor. But a third course was open to him, the most noble, the most gratifying of all—the ideological. Gerard was sacred. He was imbued with "wisdom." To the quotidian run of events he could oppose sublime theory, to the absurd accidents of the world below he could oppose the immutable regularity of the heavenly order. It was his task to teach, to use the word, to reinstate a structure of powers capable of reducing the disorder of which Walter's intractability, unruliness, and greed were a caricatural example. In one sense, the *Gesta* took the form of a compilation of "evidence" for use in anticipated trials. But their essential purpose was to develop at great length a theory of peace. Within this theoretical discourse we intend next to locate the place of the trifunctional figure precisely.

When the narrative comes to the year 1023, the theme of peace assumes greater proportions than ever. Book III is almost exclusively concerned with the events of that year; in it, the author relates essentially what happened in the few months—crucial for the history of the ideological structure we are trying to apprehend—prior to his commencing work on the manuscript. Owing to the artifices of rhetorical composition, as well as the alterations due to subsequent revisions, other themes interrupt the treatise on the righteous peace, fragmenting it into five separate parts. These are:

1. Gerard appears for the first time in chapter 24: by his admonitions and his proclamations of truth and justice, he dissuades two of his confrères, the bishop of Noyon and Adalbero, his cousin, the bishop of Laon, from settling, a conflict between them by resorting to arms. This is merely a prelude.

2. The first act occupies chapter 27. The scene is set at Compiègne, in the assembly called by Robert the Pious on May 1, 1023. Here we find Gerard's own words, reconstructed for us by the writer: in this speech we catch our first glimpse of the ideological system. The greatest personages of the realm, including Gerard—who is one of them, but not in the full sense, it seems, on

this particular occasion, where he played something of the role of the emperor's proxy—have come to discuss a general reform of Christian society,
and hence to discuss peace. Two of the bishop of Cambrai's co-*episcopi*
suggest a formula, the peace of God, which Gerard condemns, and he then
puts forward a counter-proposal in which we see his general project take
form.

3. Several chapters follow in which the bishop is shown grappling with
apparently different problems, but in reality continuing the same battle,
finding new reasons to vituperate against his confrères, the suffragans of the
province of Rheims, who he says have been led astray from the path of
righteousness by the disorder gradually invading the realm from the west,
while he, the man of Lorraine, has not deviated from the true path. We then
come back, in chapter 37, to the question of peace, in connection with an
event which took place several months after the Compiègne assembly and in
its wake: in August 1023, Henry II and Robert the Pious met on the Meuse
at Ivois, on the frontier between their two kingdoms. "Here were concluded
a final definition [this word is to be understood to mean the sentence which
terminated a debate] of peace and justice and the reconciliation of mutual
friendship. Here, too, with the greatest diligence and thoroughness the peace
of the holy church of God was discussed."[4] *Visio pacis.* It was as though
heaven were about to descend on earth, as though the tide of troubles, the
seas of corruption were suddenly going to ebb: the two sovereign colleagues,
jointly God's lieutenants in this world, had in effect reached agreement for
the purpose of reinstating the framework of law and order envisaged for
the Christian people by the Creator. The canon of Cambrai and the bishop
who inspired him felt that their treatise on the public order ought to feature
at its center this example of a just peace, instituted in accordance with the
divine plan by those sacred personages, the Almighty's proxies by scepter
and sword: the kings.

4. The rest of the narrative speaks of disillusionment. It is an account of
failure, of retreat before the forces of evil, whose offensive was preventing
the dream's coming true. Danger was everywhere on the rise. At the grass
roots, in Cambrai: Walter, the castellan, had gone on a rampage. At the
highest level in Christendom: the emperor had died in July of 1024 (chapter
50). Chapter 51, which I regard as an interpolation of a subsequent writer,
jumps abruptly to the year 1036. In my view, in the original version
Gerard's second speech immediately followed the account of the new tide of
troubles. Like the first speech, it was delivered against the bishops of *Francia*, in opposition to the measures that they had taken shortly before, in
1024.[5] The sentence concerning trifunctionality is the preamble to this
speech, which is the culmination of the description of the perfect social
structure.

5. The last fragment returns to petty contemporary events. But this was

quite natural, in view of the audience the bishop had in mind for his sermon on the just peace. It is true that this sermon was addressed to the whole world, and especially to Robert, the king of France, with whom Gerard— who had not yet recognized Conrad, the new king of Germany—was involved in continual dealings. But it was also, and perhaps primarily, addressed to Walter, the castellan in Cambrai. Walter had actually applauded the proposals made by the bishops of *Francia,* which would have forbidden taking justice into one's own hands and recovering plundered booty by force of arms: how would his rival, the bishop, have been able to resist him thereafter, how could he have sent his knights to do battle with him? In the institutions of peace then being established at Beauvais and elsewhere, Walter saw hope of impunity, an open breach in the line of defense of the Church's temporal interests. In that same year, 1024, he saw an opportunity to complete the task of building the small independent principality around his castle that was his dream. He forged ahead, flanked by two allies: the "people," whom he won to his cause by publicly denouncing the bishop Gerard as an obstacle to peace; and the count of Flanders, the *princeps,* who suggested that a general meeting be convoked to proclaim the new peace, as was being done in the dioceses of the region. Gerard gave way before this offensive, perhaps under pressure from the young abbots of Saint-Vaast and Saint-Bertin, who interceded between him and the count. The assembly gathered on the marches of the county of Flanders, between the cities of Arras and Cambrai, near Douai, in a meadow, as was customary, around reliquaries, holy remains that had been brought to the spot from miles around, to be piled there in a palpable accumulation of sacred mystery. A huge throng gathered: *Maxima turba.* Gerard came. He spoke. He attacked Walter, depicting him as prowling about like the devil tempting Saint Peter, whereas he, the bishop, truly wished to arrange for peace, genuine peace, a peace that would not have required yielding on any point he regarded as essential. Only what was authorized by the *lex,* the canons so familiar to him, and the Gospel, would have been instituted under the terms of peace as he conceived it. In the end it was the prelate who proclaimed the peace settlement. The text has been preserved in the library of Douai, folio 91 of manuscript 856: the "peace of God, commonly known as 'truce'" prohibited attack and plunder from Wednesday night until Monday morning, and during the periods of abstinence and purification preceding the three major Christian holidays, Easter, Christmas, and Pentecost. During these periods no man residing in or passing through the diocese would be allowed to use a weapon, except for the king, when he led his army or his cavalcade. Anyone knowingly violating the prohibition would be subject to ecclesiastical sanctions imposed by the bishop, to excommunication, to seven or thirty years confinement in the *ordo* of penitents, isolated from the world, excluded, disarmed, compelled to sexual abstinence. This edifice of precepts and threats was constructed for the purpose of impeding the display of violence in a disintegrating society, but at the same time it walled off a domain within which repressive action was legitimate when carried out, as authorized, by the king, and the king alone. The anathema against heretics crowned the whole structure, which was indeed built according to God's plan; it was erected by his servant, the bishop, imbued with wisdom by anointment, and defended by his auxiliaries, the priests, who had explicit instructions to pray (*orare*) on Sundays and holidays for all who observed the peace, and to damn all who violated it. The peace of Douai, which I believe can be assigned the date 1024, was thus an affair of the *oratores* and the king. The text of a quite similar episcopal letter appears in manuscript 67 of the library of Laon. It was sent by Adalbero, who followed his cousin Gerard down this path.

Stripped of the anecdotal veneer which obscures and at times interrupts the unity of the exposition, this, then, is the reconstruction of the theory set out by the *Gesta* in justification of the bishop of Cambrai's tortuous policy toward Walter, the castellan; to excuse his compromise of principle; to pardon his ultimate unwilling assent to the movement for the peace of God; and, finally, to explain the specific measures he had just taken in issuing his letter, sacrificing what he had to in order to save what was essential: a theory of order, power, and society. The allusion to social trifunctionality occurs in one of the fragments of this imaginary speech, of which it would be idle to ask when, and in what terms, Gerard might have delivered it. To grasp the whole of the ideal system, of which this speech sets forth only a part, we have to examine yet another sermon, another message from the same speaker, inseparable from the first. This statement of doctrine does not occur in the text we have of the *Gesta*. It is likely, however, that it was prepared by the same writer, the canon who was Gerard's secretary. We know its subject from manuscript 582 of the Dijon library. Again we are dealing with a revised version. In the form in which we know it, then, this second discourse is no less imaginary than the one represented in the *Gesta*. We are, however, certain that it relates what Gerard actually said, and this time we know quite well when and where: in the cathedral of Notre Dame at Arras, in January, 1025, before a handful of heretics whom the bishop had come to judge.[6]

The ideological system thus set forth, therefore, comes down to us as a disjointed composition in three complementary segments, the sermons of Compiègne, Douai, and Arras. All three will require close analysis if we hope to understand how and why, in 1023–25, Gerard of Cambrai decided it would be a good idea to demonstrate to the world that "mankind, since the beginning, has been divided into three parts."

The first indications of the system's lineaments are to be found in Gerard's speech of May 1, 1023, in answer to Garin, bishop of Beauvais, and Beraud, bishop of Soissons.[7] "Because of the king's feebleness [*imbecillitas*]" and the virulence of sin, because, in the view of these two bishops, the "state" (*status regni*) was shaken, the rights of all in doubt, and justice of whatever kind nullified, they proposed, for the good of the commonwealth, to apply in "France," i.e., north of Sens and Auxerre, prescriptions that had been laid down a short while earlier by the bishops of Burgundy. Together, they suggested "that they themselves and all men be constrained by oath to keep the peace and preserve justice." The other bishops of "upper Gaul" concurred. Other sources tell us that in the following year in his own diocese, Garin, at least, administered a collective oath whose text reproduced virtually word for word the one used by the Burgundian prelates in 1016 at the council of Verdun-sur-le-Doubs, in which Robert, the king, and Beraud of Soissons participated.[8]

Gerard refused to go along and stated his reasons why. In the first place, he feared committing a sin. In his opinion, the advice was pernicious: to compel everyone to swear under penalty of anathema would expose all to the perils of perjury. How very gravely the oath, that sacramental act, that challenge hurled at God, was regarded at the time must be borne in mind. It was so terrible that personages already imbued with the sacred—bishops and kings—were forbidden to swear. Frightful punishments threatened anyone who might inadvertently violate his oath. And whoever risked taking an oath, thinking himself strong enough never to break his word, was thereby committing the sin of pride. Beneath the one fear of sacrilege was hidden another, of conspiracy. This was an old fear, one that had been felt by the Carolingians: Charlemagne had stipulated that oaths were never to be sworn, except in three circumstances: to seal a bond between a man and his king, or a man and his lord, or else in a court of law, if a man needed to swear to clear himself or a friend of an accusation. In his wisdom, Gerard showed himself to be eminently respectful of Carolingian tradition on this point. The oath of vassalage he had required of the castellan of Cambrai fell under one of the three legitimate categories. He shared the attitude of the many ecclesiastics, like Abbo of Fleury and Burchard of Worms, who were then busying themselves with the task of collecting ancient judgments, working toward a code of law, and who were as fearful as Gerard of conspiracy, of a resurgence of the old pagan associations that had frightened Charlemagne's advisers, now that men of the people in northern French cities had taken it into their heads to join together, precisely in order to restore peace, in collective oaths sworn among equals.

Gerard had another reason for not wishing to follow his colleagues: their proposal, far from restoring stability, would have shaken the "*status*," not merely of the "kingdom," but of the "holy church," i.e., of all Christendom.

Indeed, the care of this "state" had, he said, been providentially placed in the hands of "two twinned persons," associated as were body and soul, as were the two natures in Christ: the sacerdotal person and the royal person. "It is given to the one to pray [*orare*], to the other to fight [*pugnare*]." Here we encounter the two familiar words: those who pray, those who fight—two of the three functions. In conjunction. Gerard goes on to say: "It is the task of kings to repress sedition by their *virtus*" (that energy with which their blood was fraught, that strength with which they were endowed, the quality, according to Georges Dumézil, specific to the second function), to put an end to wars, to encourage peaceful commerce. The bishops (who are the source of priesthood) are assigned the two forms of action subsumed in the verb *orare*: to admonish kings "so that they may fight manfully for the salvation of the fatherland"; to pray "so that they may vanquish." The role of the *oratores* was to support the king's military action by means of the word. It was not—contrary to the claims put forward by the bishops of Beauvais and Soissons—to engage directly in the prosecution of war and peace.

Here, then, in this preliminary enunciation of the system, we already find the functions present as elements of the state structure. As yet there are only two of them. Text and context do at least give us a clear notion of what sorts of men were legitimately entitled to exercise these two functions. When Gerard of Cambrai speaks of *oratores* and *pugnatores,* he has in mind neither all clergymen nor all warriors. He is thinking of bishops and kings.

To grasp the system in its entirety, I think it best to proceed immediately to the Arras sermon. By far the fullest version, it was revised and expanded on Gerard's instructions to become a veritable summa of orthodox doctrine. In Artois, a sect had formed and proposed a *justicia,* a rule of life, which by itself, without recourse to the sacraments, was supposed to be capable of guiding a man to salvation. The bishop of Cambrai-Arras was apprised of this development. Between Christmas and Epiphany of 1025, during a customary *statio* in his second see, he ordered an investigation, an inquisition. Its task was to uncover the heresies. One Thursday night, without enlisting the secular assistance of the *princeps,* the count of Flanders (whose help he was careful not to seek), Gerard had the members of the sect seized—at any rate, such of them as could be caught. Their "master" had fled; a few followers remained; they were held in prison for three days. During this time, the bishop ordered that a fast be observed by all the clergy and monks of the diocese—but only by the servants of God, not all the faithful: to Gerard, the idea that everyone should fast was repugnant, as was the idea that everyone should swear oaths. The purpose of this fast was to purify. It was to help the prelate in his mission of discovering the truth, so that he might better perceive the content of the Catholic dogma. The third day was

29

a Sunday, day of light—the narrative is full of symbols: the heretics were imprisoned on a Thursday night, the day Jesus was betrayed by Judas; the truth was to shine forth on Sunday morning like Christ's resurrection—the great spectacle was staged in the cathedral, in view of the populace. Symbols of the true faith—the crucifix, the Gospels—had been carefully arranged. The bishop sat in the center, cloaked in all his finery; around him, standing, were the archdeacons, responsible for discipline, and, in front of them, the two distinct segments of Christian society, the clergy and the people. A psalm was sung, imploring the Lord's coming. Then began what was called a consistory: the abbots and clerks, according to the rank of their ordination, sat alongside the bishop. The accused, who were brought in at this point, were presented to the populace by the bishop, who conducted their interrogation. Their testimony was heard. What instruction had they received? The heresiarch, an Italian, had preached to them on the Gospels and the Epistles of the Apostles; he relied on only one portion of the Bible, the New Testament. What doctrine did they profess? They regarded baptism, penance, the eucharist, all the sacraments as useless, "nullifying [thereby the work of] the Church"; they condemned marriage; they refused to worship saints, except for apostles and martyrs. A discussion followed: to the bishop, who remonstrated with them that everything they repudiated was to be found in the New Testament, and hence that their doctrine was in contradiction to the law, they answered that in any case there was no contradiction between the law and their rule of life. A very good response: these people were not on their knees, they did not shun controversy; they were capable of clearly setting forth the rule they meant to follow: to flee the world, to stifle carnal desire, to live by manual labor, to forgive offenses, and to love one another within the sect. Baptism, they repeated, was unnecessary for anyone who observed such a rule; for anyone who did not observe it, baptism was not sufficient. Indeed, there was nothing sacred in baptism: it was administered by men whose lives were not beyond reproach to children not accountable for their actions who, as adults, would sin. After this exchange, the bishop delivered his speech.

In the *libellus,* or "brief," in which his theme is developed, buttressed by references to the Bible and the fathers, in an assured and dogmatic form which came to be widely known (there is no doubt that Adalbero, bishop of Laon, was familiar with this text when he began writing his poem), Gerard is careful to avoid engaging with those he regards as heretics on the terrain of their self-imposed rule, or, as they called it, *"justicia."* For far from challenging the teaching of the Gospels, they were actually putting that teaching into practice. The sect's aim was to present itself as a perfect society. In what respect did it differ from the monastic communities, those fervent congregations isolated from worldly taint, whose orthodoxy no one would have dreamed of contesting? Gerard alludes only once to the morality of the heretics, at the conclusion of his speech: he reminds them that works are not sufficient, that grace, too, is necessary—grace, that gift from God, distributed through the medium of an institution, the Church. Here, in fact, we see the purpose of the speech: to prove that the sacraments are indispensable.

Heresy—radical, disruptive, appearing shortly after the year 1000 as one sign, perhaps the most convincing sign, of that tumultuous vitality that impelled Western civilization forward in its sudden advance—did not consist in criticism of priests, or denunciations of their impurity. It lay rather in the wish to forego their services, in the desire to deny the clergy's usefulness. Why should certain men, setting themselves apart from the rest, claim custody of the extraordinary privilege of administering the sacred? How was one to justify the exercise of such a monopoly by a small group which thereby gained the power to bend the rest of society under its yoke? This was the question, the revolutionary question, raised by heresy. Gerard set himself the task of answering it. It was a fact, said the bishop, that within human society there existed an inviolable boundary marking off a particular category of men, an "order" (ordo), whose members alone were designated to perform certain acts for the benefit of all. This frontier delineated a rigorously exclusive domain, that of the priesthood. "A man of the world cannot validly assume the authority [magisterium] of the priesthood, whose office [officium] he did not hold, whose discipline is unfamiliar to him, and who cannot teach what he has not learned." [9] This meant that the "master" to whom the members of the Arras sect had lent their ears was a false master. This segregation, this monopolizing of a liturgical office, a rule of life, and a body of knowledge derived from a mysterious, quasi-magical act: anointment. [10] The ordo was instituted by such a "sign" of sacredness (this is precisely the meaning of the word sacramentum as used by Gerard). The bishops "ordained" the clergy by anointing the hands of the priests—their consortes, who shared their condition—thus rendering those hands capable of conducting rites of sacrifice on their own. The inexplicable power of the chrism, transmitted from one hand to others, established an ineluctable hierarchy within the sacerdotal order. This body was itself ordered. It was led by the episcopacy. Just as the mind ruled the body, so the bishops ruled the Church. [11]

The meaning of "the Church" was defined in the penultimate article, the fifteenth, of the speech, which immediately precedes the brief condemnation of the sect and is the culmination of the argument, capping the whole polemic. The publicizers of Gerard's work entitled this fundamental chapter "On the Orders of the Government of the Church," [12] rightly emphasizing the key term, ordo. Order, in fact, is really the only topic treated here— order, i.e., precisely the ideological system that I am attempting to reconstruct.

Previously, in his treatment of marriage, Gerard had spoken of order, of the necessity for a distinction of order (*discretio ordinis*) among men, among adult males of the human species (*viri*). His remarks were addressed to heretics who condemned marriage with the intention of proscribing it generally—but he was equally attacking those clergymen, quite numerous in those early years of the eleventh century, whose intention was the opposite, viz., to permit marriage generally, and in particular to allow clergymen to marry. These clerks questioned the justification for forcing them to dismiss their wives, maintaining that men were not angels, that continence was a gift of grace, and that to impose it by fiat was to ask too much. The bishop of Cambrai replied that they were mistaken, that in truth certain men were if not wholly then at least partly angels; "the rule of life they follow divides [the Latin verb he uses is *dividere*] them from the people," he said, adding that, "in particular, they are exempt [this idea is noteworthy because it is directly relevant to that formal notion, the trifunctional figure] from the servile tasks of this world." The men distinguished in this way from the rest of mankind, classified as members of a particular order, forbidden to marry because marriage was clearly polluting, and because they no longer belonged entirely to the world of flesh—these men are clearly the priests. In this portion of the speech, however, the idea is expressed only in a preliminary form. A more coherent exposition of the theory is to be found in the peroration:

1. Gerard at first speaks of order in the singular: the "order of the administration of the Church" is consistent with the "divine ordination." It is therefore a structure, a timeless armature, a projection of the essence of God's thought.

2. The "holy church," our mother, the house of God, Jerusalem "on high" (*superna*) is a part of heaven as well as earth, a part of the invisible as well as the visible. The *ecclesia,* therefore, is governed, and actually instituted, by an order embodied in a two-level edifice. The layout of the lower level (this world here below) reproduces, but with imperfections, that of the upper level. The overall order regulates communication between the two levels, and in particular governs that upward impulse which even now has carried certain inhabitants of this world into the city above, normally populated by angels. "A part of mankind reigns already, sharing the company of the angels; another portion still wanders on earth [en route, progressing like the Hebrews toward the Promised Land] amidst the sound of sighs—aspiring [to rise also]." [13] This assertion is basic. It establishes that no insuperable partition separates the two cities; that in the city above there is a kingdom; that a tension—which, a hundred years later, the sculptor of the tympanum of Autun cathedral was to signify by means of an inordinate elongation of the bodies of the resurrected—impelled men to raise themselves to this kingdom's height; and that some had successfully arrived there.

32

The song of grace's action in Revelation 5:9–10, which all the high clergy knew by heart, made it clear that the latter group was composed of priests.

3. The following assertion is no less fundamental: on earth as in heaven, the creatures are arrayed "in distinct orders" under the authority of a sovereign, who sits enthroned in the city on high—Christ.[14] He exerts his power in two ways. First, as a priest: in the tabernacle of heaven, he continually celebrates the rite of sacrifice, interceding for us, praying, supplicating; seated at the right hand of the Father, in the glory of the paternal majesty, Christ, at the summit of the hierarchy, assumes the sacerdotal function. At the same time he assumes the royal function, as "King of Kings." It is by his example and by delegation of his authority that the kings of the earth reign, and that those responsible for administering the "law" distinguish what is just in the world below. From heaven above, Christ is the source of justice, hence of peace. As Prince, as model of the prince, he administers the two provinces, celestial and terrestrial, of a single principality. As warrior captain, as model of the warrior captain, he leads the "distinct orders" (distinguished from one another as were the various corps of troops in liturgical ceremonies, which were then veritable battles) of a "militia," spiritual and temporal. As Judge, as model of the judge, he presides over the supreme court, the *curia*. At the time, however, this Latin word also denoted the noble household: Christ was seen as a judge; he was also seen as a father, a foster-father—distributing to each according to his needs. At the pinnacle, the summit of the thousand-layered pyramid, a single person reigned. Only the son of God performed both the functions that in Gerard's first speech, the one delivered at Compiègne, were shown divided on earth between "two twinned persons": *orare*, to sacrifice and to speak; *pugnare*, to fight, to avenge. Moreover, we may, if we wish, take the view that these two functions were joined, implicitly, by a third: *decernere*, to distribute, to share out, to feed. To carry out his functions—one and triune like the essence of the Christian God, fundament and epitome of all possible functions— Christ had need of lieutenants: in heaven, he was assisted by the superb "order" of angels; on earth, by the "calling," the "profession" (*ministerium*) of men.

4. Another key element of the system is that human society is led by the "ministers" (*ministri*) of the Lord—meaning the specialized agents of his power. The unique function of the king of the heavens is shared out, allocated, divided in half (here there is no question of a third office) between them. Each portion is separately governed by one of the "twinned persons," the *oratores* and the *pugnatores*, i.e., the bishops and kings, the direct representatives of Jesus. On earth, these are the two sources of all power to pray or to fight, power which flows from above, by degrees, through the "orders" (here the term is plural) which God the Father has "laid down" and distinguished from one another.

5. Order, degree, echelon, hierarchy: the terrestrial order is in effect homologous to the celestial order. There is coordination between the two cities (in truth, the two were but one, and would, with the arrival of the impending end of time, wholly dissolve into one another—this was why it was important to remain in readiness, to assist in the transition, to hasten the dissolution, by reducing the discord that inevitably seeped into the lower level of the cosmos, the level of change, of corruption). At this point in the complex interweave of assertions that constitute the ideological system he is setting forth, Gerard explicitly invokes two authorities in support of his plea for the restoration of earthly order. He makes reference to two "Fathers," two bishops, two *oratores*. The first of these is Dionysius the Areopagite, then thought to have been the first bishop of Paris, the martyr whose remains lay in the monastery at Saint-Denis, as well as the disciple of St. Paul and author of two books, *On the Angelic Hierarchy* [or *Principate*] and *On the Ecclesiastical Hierarchy*.[15] Gerard merely mentions his name. Did he have direct knowledge of his works? Was the original manuscript available in the cathedral library? Could he have cited passages from it? At any rate, he does cite at length from the other author, his principal source: Gregory the Great, bishop of Rome.

There are two citations. The first[16]—not surprisingly—is none other than the passage used by Loyseau in support of his treatise on hierarchy and discipline. I have already given an attempt at a translation of this passage in the introductory pages of this book. It will be worthwhile to have another look at this statement on inequality and the necessity to obey, since it is here introduced by Gerard of Cambrai into his complex ideological machinery as one of its central components. "Providence has taken measures to establish various degrees and distinct orders [orders, grades or ranks—the military of course, is the clearest present-day instance of a formal conception of this kind] so that, if the lesser [the minor] show deference [reverence] to the greater [or rather, to the better], and if the better bestow love upon [or cherish] the minor, unity in concord may be established, as well as unification [structure] of diversity, and so that each function [*officium*] may be administered with rectitude [this clause does not appear in Loyseau's citation: it is essential, however, for this is how the notion of function is introduced into the system]. The community [or: the whole of creation] could not subsist if the total order of diversity did not preserve it." This is the principle: the order of the entire world is based on diversity, on the hierarchical disposition of ranks, on the complementarity of functions. The harmony of God's creation results from a hierarchized exchange of respectful submission and condescending affection. What proves "that creation can neither be governed nor live in equality"? (Pope Gregory was addressing bishops who claimed equality among themselves and refused primacy to one of their number; Bishop Gerard is addressing men who refuse to submit to sacerdotal authority.) "The example of the heavenly host teaches it to us [it is enough to raise one's eyes, to look toward the heavens, toward the less impure, the more perfect, to discover the model, the order established by God, the God-given order]; there are angels and there are archangels, which are clearly not equals, but differ from one another in power and order." It must be acknowledged that there exist two ranks, two grades of power, in the army of heaven. At this point in his dissertation, Gerard enlists the support of two passages from the Old Testament, in which some angels are seen to obey others: certain angels lead, issuing commands; others assist, following orders. If things were arranged in this fashion in the society of angels, if even that extremely pure social organization was based on distinctions, then distinctions were even more necessary in human society. Indeed, angels were without sin; men could not be without sin (as we have seen, this was the objection to the heretical theses: that no human being could cleanse himself unaided, without the grace of the sacraments, of the taint of sin). But it was sin that gave rise to inequality.

At this point we encounter the second citation from Gregory the Great.[17] It is taken from the *Regula pastoralis* II:6,[18] where we find reiterated what the master had written in his *Moralia in Job,* that essential work upon which monks meditated in every monastery in the West in the early eleventh century, but to which Gerard preferred the derivative book, one that could be found in every episcopal library, which dealt with the pastoral matters, with the affairs of prelates, the leaders of the clergy. "Although nature creates all men equal [or: although all men are born equal by nature], error [*culpa*] subordinates some to others in accordance with the variable order |*ordo*| of merits [there were ranks in sin, too]; this diversity arising from vice is established by divine judgment so that, since man is not intended to live in equality, one may be ruled by another." Gerard uses these words to demonstrate the providential character of the ecclesiastical hierarchy to the sectarians of Arras, who deny it, as well as to bolster the condemnation he is about to pronounce against them from the height of his throne and his wisdom.

But he has not quite reached that point. He enlarges upon a verse from Paul and a verse from Peter—the two patrons of the Roman Church, the two cornerstones of the monumental edifice of pontifical Catholicism, of which the restoration was, with the beginning of the eleventh century, just getting under way. Peter and Paul speak of power, of the just submission of every human creature to the sovereign and his representatives. Gerard then recalls that God, through Moses, had instituted "diverse orders" in the synagogue—and the conjunction of the two verbs *regere* and *ordinare* in the structure of his sentence calls attention to the linkage—it is the real crux of the matter—between royalty and order. Finally, he applies Gregory the Great's definitions to the ecclesiastical institution. The Church is called the kingdom of the heavens. It must reflect the hierarchized structures of heaven in the distinctions established within its bosom. Its members were not precluded by similarity of office (*honor*) from acquiring an additional measure of dignity (*dignitas*). The distribution of power (*discretio potestatis*) enabled the superiors to organize their inferiors into a body, out of concern lest the latter be led into some lapse through use of their liberty.

It was daybreak in Arras. The bishop had spoken at length, though he no doubt had had less to say than was later recorded in the *"libellus."* He cited Saint Paul one last time: in "new times," as the final day approached, false prophets would multiply. Standing before him, the small group of men who had succumbed to the blandishments of one of these bad shepherds breathed not a word: the official record states that the heretics were convinced. Gerard pronounced the anathema against the perverse doctrine. He confessed the truth—that was his role, and if ever he should be regarded a saint, he would figure among the "confessors." The truth of baptism, of penitence, of "the holy church, mother of all the faithful," and the truth that "no one can gain access to the church in heaven other than through the church on earth." The truth of the eucharist, of the sacrifice at the altar, of marriage. The Latin of the scholars was translated into the dialect of the simple folk so that the heretics might understand. They recanted, confirming their resolution by marking a cross on a piece of parchment. The word had been victorious. It had defended society—the good society, authoritarian, hierarchized, firmly established on the necessary basis of inequality.

We come now to the third fragment of the ideological manifesto. In Gerard's biography in the original version of the *Deeds of the Bishops of Cambrai* (which, as we have seen, was laid out not in chronological but in logical order), this fragment comprises the text of a speech which seems to have been delivered prior to the speech at Arras. It is quite possible, however, that the panegyric to Gerard was completed only after the *"libellus."* The panegyric would then have concluded with the text of this second proclamation, which deals with peace and the social order, thus enabling the *Gesta*'s author to give a complete and coherent exposition of the ideological system that it was the prelate's glory to set forth and defend in 1025. In any case, the Compiègne manifesto, the Arras speech, and this one are interdependent. They illuminate different aspects of the conceptual architecture.

As the story is told in the *Gesta,* the bishop's final speech appears as the continuation and amplification of the one that pitted him against his colleagues in 1023. The attack has become more vehement, because evil had made advances in the meantime, and the danger had grown more acute. By now the bishops of *Francia* wished to lay hold of the royal prerogatives, on the pretext of repairing the *imbecillitas regis*. There is no question but that these prerogatives did rest in the custody of a king who was vacillating, whose throne was tottering, deprived as he was of his sceptre (*baculus*), of that force which, in accordance with the division of functions, constituted his specific virtue; he nevertheless remained the representative of divine power. The order of the world, the orders, the hierarchy had come under attack by proponents of egalitarian views, views curiously similar, to Gerard's way of thinking, to those held by the heretics of Arras. One of the bishops had received a letter from heaven (which was a commonplace occurrence where messages of this sort were concerned)[19] calling for "restoration of peace on earth." The year was 1024, a time of exalted anticipation of the millennium of the Passion—and in this lies the value of such testimony as Raoul Glaber's, of which I shall have something to say shortly, where we find a precise delineation of the links between the millennium and the convulsive upheavals which in reality were the birth-pangs of feudal society. Christ's coming was near. Near, too, was his Kingdom. Purification was called for, so as to attain on earth, if possible, that purity that existed in heaven—whence the letter had come. It claimed to reveal the appropriate system of relations for a mankind in the process of "renewing" itself, of casting off its old ways, of shouting aloud its renunciation of sin. The consequence of the end of sin was the advent of equality, which took three forms. Equality, first of all, in agreements: men should form their associations through a single, uniform bond, the oath. Once again, a conjuration was being proposed, but now it was to be compulsory: whoever refused to swear the oath should be cast out of the community, like a black sheep. There was to be no pardon for these outcasts, no place for their remains among the righteous in the Christian cemeteries. Second, there was to be equality in penitence: fasting for all, and for all in the same way; bread and water on Friday; no meat on Saturday—which was to be enough to purge anyone of any sin, regardless of its nature. Levelling thus also affected redemption from evil-doing. And finally, equality in peace: there should be no more vengeance, no more sallies to recover booty from its pillagers, no more compensation for the victims. It was to be the end of armed conflict—and, once again, Raoul Glaber would clearly establish the correlation between conjuration, fasting, and the suppression of war.

For Gerard, such innovations—what was new or unprecedented was always suspect in the minds of his contemporaries, who thought human history in the grip of the forces of evil and consequently a history of decline—such innovations threatened the equilibrium of the universe. They were negative, demoniacal, like the heresy they resembled. If fasting were to be accepted as sufficient atonement for sin, what would be the good of the sacraments, and what would be the good of priests? Like the miscreants of Arras, the bishops of *Francia* were bent on "nullifying the Church." And when the bishops, like the heretics, renounced punishment for offenses, they were in effect nullifying the royal office as well, since royalty had been instituted on earth to insure justice for all. To the dangers inherent in the ideas of Garin and Beraud, the present proposal added the inevitable risks attendant upon institution of an egalitarian policy. With the aid of a large number of quotations drawn primarily from the New Testament, Gerard meant to prove that inequality was providential, hence necessary.

In the only complete manuscript of the *Gesta* that we possess, in what is known as the Saint-Vaast codex, which reproduces a twelfth-century copy, the bishop's speech is divided into two parts. Thus it completely engulfs the last episode of the interminable and down-to-earth conflict between the bishop and the castellan in Cambrai. This arrangement of the text (which Bethmann, its editor, believes the result of an error in transcription[20]) is in my view that of the original version. I think the author chose to set down his remarks in this order so as to underscore his contention that the maleficent proposals of a misguided episcopate threatened to increase disorder and iniquity in the world by inciting armed usurpers to brazen acts. The peroration seems to me a natural conclusion for the whole history, devoted to the acts of the bishops of Cambrai and primarily to the deeds of the last of them, Gerard, sponsor of a true and just peace.

In effect, this peroration solemnly affirms the unvarying principle underlying the action of the hero of the tale, throughout his unremitting attacks against the various perverse levelling policies which would have profited only the wicked and in his concomitant justification of the disciplinary powers of the episcopacy. This principle was the following. The kingdom of heaven is not meant merely for the perfect of this world. God imposes certain duties upon those whom he expects to be perfect in this world; he does not impose the same duties on others. Here, Gerard is following Gregory the Great closely, Gregory also having asserted that since the two groups had different merits, different requirements would be made of them. There were distinctions between men, an essential inequality which could be compensated only by charity, mercy, and mutual service, service which everyone was obliged to give and entitled to expect from his fellow man. Service was to be exchanged *ad alterutrum*. This reciprocity was the source of peace on earth. Others spoke of heaven. Heaven was exactly the same. There were several abodes in the house of the Lord. It was God's wish that even in Paradise a certain *inequalitas* prevail, reduced to nought only by charity, collective communication in the glory of God, common participation in the ineffable joy of salvation. This is the cornerstone of Gerard's ideology: a generous redistribution of the available wealth within an inevitable framework of inequality.

Those who, on pretext of making ready to enter the heavenly city, wished to smooth over differences, to refuse forgiveness to some, to mete out similar penances to sinners of dissimilar deserts, were consequently blind to the truth, and in error. Gerard fought as God's soldier. In the thick of life's realities, he had no use for this new "peace." In spite of the count of Flanders, in spite of the rumors bruited about by Walter the castellan, in spite of the shouts of the people assembled before the reliquaries, demanding the equality being held out to them, in his peace edict at Douai he refused to countenance the proposals made by his confrères, the bishops of northern France, who brandished before him the letter that had fallen from heaven into their hands. He would not allow conjuration—nor would he allow anyone who might refuse to join in the work of peace to be excluded irrevocably from the Church; for it was impermissible not to forgive. He imposed sanctions, but they were diverse, to be fixed with reference to a code (the proliferating varieties of crime in this new age were to be judged according to the word of the Gospels, the apostles, the canons of the councils, and the decretals of the popes, which stimulated the ardor of those clergymen who, even as Gerard was speaking, were hard at work collecting judgments, assembling a code of law). Penances were to be assigned according to a strict schedule, since every error was to be punished in just measure; to assign guilt and to absolve, *discreetly,* was the proper function of the possessors of wisdom, the bishops. God's clemency was to be implored for all wrongdoers by means of prayer, but prayer which could be offered up only by specialists, the priests. Paralleling this office of prayer, the administration of punishment was to be made the office of another specialist—the role of the *pugnator,* the royal office. Only the king and his companions were to be allowed, in effect, to draw their swords in time of truce. Because vengeance against obstinate criminals, repression of their crimes, was the role the sword of justice was allowed to play—and not merely was this role allowed, it was, like inequality, providential and necessary.

At this point we encounter a long argument, built on a solid foundation of biblical references, intended to prove that a victim's relatives are entitled to exact blood-vengeance, that it is just to recover booty by force, and hence that there are just wars. At the same time, it is shown that only certain men are entitled to wage such wars. War was a function of kings, "reigning in our mother the Church, the bride of God." [21] Kings, who "establish strict laws" [22] and are girt with the sword, are said to be ministers of God. Of course, they still had to heed the bishops whose subjects they were to remain, as well as follow episcopal advice in issuing legitimate edicts; and they must receive their swords from a bishop's hand. It was to be the role of the priest to "gird kings with their swords." The hierarchical division of labor between the priesthood and the monarchy established an equilibrium which the institutions of peace would destroy if, by some misfortune, they were poorly framed.

This last speech echoes the second, the Arras speech. It reasserts with still greater firmness what had been proclaimed at Compiègne in the first speech of the three. Social trifunctionality is alluded to, furthermore, precisely for the purpose of introducing this final speech and giving it greater weight. Before setting down Gerard's own words, his biographer indicates that "he demonstrated that, since the beginning, mankind has been divided into three parts, among men of prayer, farmers, and men of war"; he "gives clear proof that each is the concern of both the others." Thus, in this quite brief sentence, the triangular figure finds expression and a place in the system. The position it occupies in Gerard's text is virtually the same as in Loyseau's. In both cases, this observation or axiom is used to buttress a dissertation on inequality. In the *Gesta,* however, the necessity of sharing tasks and exchanging services is formulated not in conclusion but in exordium to this dissertation. This exchange of services reflects the perfect exchange that takes place in paradise. The *alterutrum* of line 41 of page 485 of the *Monumenta,* which refers to heaven, is echoed by the same word on line 42 of page 486, which refers to earth.

Compensation, reciprocity, charity. Gerard sets out his meaning in detail:[23] if the *oratores* are able to enjoy the "holy leisure" required by their office, this is due to the efforts of the *pugnatores,* who see to their security, as well as to the efforts of the *agricultores,* who see to the needs of their bodies by providing the food that is the fruit of their "labor." Defended by the warriors, the farmers are indebted to the prayers of the priests for God's forgiveness. As for the men of war, they are maintained by the rents paid by the peasants, and by the taxes paid by the merchants; the good offices of the clergy cleanse them of the sins they commit by their use of arms. For no one who wields a weapon can have clean hands. Even just wars are occasions for sin. And the *pugnatores* need the *oratores* not only to oblige heaven to grant them victory but also to aid in their redemption through the liturgy and the sacraments.

At this point, I think it would be useful to retrace our steps, to stress once again how the trifunctional theme is set in its context.

1. Because the debate bore on the validity of the duties ascribed to the various offices, discussion revolved around the three functions, rather than the three orders. The word *ordo,* omnipresent in the Arras speech, is totally absent from this one. Here Gerard speaks of communication, reciprocity, service, and inequality, but never of ranks, grades, or power. His words are concerned not with power but with action. Their object is to elucidate the relationship between *otium* and *labor,* between leisure and toil. The bishop of Cambrai was defining those tasks which, for their proper performance, required a partition, a *divisio,* of mankind. Nothing in the text indicates the existence of a hierarchy among these tasks: throughout the exposition, soldiers figure in the last place, behind farmers. Was this because their "profession" condemned them to a lesser purity than the others, meaning that in the

procession entering the heavenly Jerusalem their position had to be the hindmost? Perhaps the point was rather that a rhetorical link had to be established between this sentence, whose subject was the three functions, and the following one, which dealt with the use of arms.

2. We see the two categories that Gerard had carefully distinguished in his first manifesto against Garin of Beauvais reappear here, side by side: they are the *sacerdotes*—here called *oratores*—and the *pugnatores*. The remainder of the text shows more clearly than did the first speech who the "warriors" were. Beyond any doubt they were the kings. Of course, royalty did not sally forth alone, but with an escort riding beneath its banner. Decision, leadership, responsibility belonged to the king alone, however. Let there be no mistake on this point. The word *pugnator* was not a synonym for *miles*. The *milites*—or knights—are never mentioned in the several fragments in which the ideological system is set forth. They do, however, figure at various points in the events related by the *Gesta*. In the narrative they are always shown in subordinate roles. Even when the author refers to them as "knights of the first rank,"[24] they are always implicated in bonds of vassalage, as dependents of a lord—the castellan or the bishop.[25] Under the pen of Gerard's secretary, the term *miles* connotes inferiority. It also connotes malice. The knights were wicked men who became worse when their masters—also "imbecile"—failed to keep them bridled.[26] Pillage was their only thought, and whenever Church domains came to be held by them in fief—which appears to have been a commonplace occurrence—they lay them waste and devoured their riches.[27] The good bishop was obliged to protect the poor[28] from this violent breed of "pillagers without prowess." Thus to suppose that the bishop of Cambrai used the trifunctional image to justify the knights' role and provide them a place in the social order would be a serious misinterpretation. The truth was quite the opposite: the trifunctional postulate was used against the knights. In the ideological system of which trifunctionality was a basic component, knights were urged to bring their violence under control and to give satisfaction to the victims of their depredations. Punishment was to be meted out to those guilty of plunder and rapine: the knights. Bound to take up arms against them, in fact, were none other than the kings.[29] Upon a scant few men Christ had bestowed the mission of establishing his earthly reign with the sword, which symbolic object had been solemnly conferred upon them by the *oratores*, i.e., the bishops, thus instituting, indeed ordaining, the royal personages and assigning them their legitimate duty. The military function, therefore, was exalted only in the *bellatores:* that is, the kings—or at least the princes (in the very specific sense this title then had). Their first duty, of course, was to protect the bishops and their auxiliaries, the priests, against the unchecked violence of the knights. But the men who carried out the third function were to be protected as well.

3. The word *laborator* is not used in the *Gesta* to designate this latter group. The text speaks instead of peasants, *agricultores*. Actually, this term is incorrect. Somewhat later, in fact, the discussion turns to the services rendered the men of war by the members of this third functional category, who feed the warrior class, and depicts the mechanisms of seigniorial exploitation—this time quite realistically. In this context, the rents extracted from those who work the fields are coupled with the exactions levied by the masters of roads, toll houses, and markets in connection with the movement of goods. The existence of merchants, wagoners, and bargemen had not escaped the author's notice, any more than it escaped notice in the oath of peace that Garin made the warriors in his diocese of Beauvais swear in 1024. Indeed, how could anyone have failed to remark the fleets of boats on the Escaut, yearly increasing in number, or the wine-carts clogging the road between Péronne and Douai? This constantly quickening, ever more profitable traffic was the great novelty of the time. Nevertheless, when a highly cultivated man thought of the laboring classes at the beginning of the eleventh century, it was inevitably the peasantry that came to mind. Does this prove that the trifunctional model, that cliché which, because Gerard made use of it as a major argument in the debate in which he was involved, emerged for the first time from the realm of the inarticulate, actually came into being in time out of memory, before anything had yet risen to waken the West from its rural slumbers?

One final question: why was a third term added? Why three functions rather than two? Before hazarding any hypothetical answers to this question, I think it best to wait until a little more light has been shed on the subject. Here I will limit myself to making two observations. First, trifunctionality at this stage is presented as a primordial structure, a part of the basic framework of creation "since the beginning": it belongs to the time of myth, not to the time of history. Second, it is worth noting that the author of the *Gesta,* always so careful in reconstructing the thesis to separate the intertwined threads of the logic, confines himself, when it comes to the three functions, to making a very brief observation, a dry summary of a few prefatory remarks: the bishop, he says, "gave clear proof." What sort of proof? Did he really need to give proof? Was the notion not so commonplace that merely to have alluded to it would have sufficed? Was it simply because parchment was scarce, and writing difficult, that in dealing with something so obvious the writer was allowed to be brief? In reality, the important point is that the writer meant to take his stand on the essential issue, the central pillar of the system: the principle of inequality. There were many kinds of inequality: inequality of constitution (there were different forms of bodily health), inequality in wrong-doing ("remorse for sin does not torment equally"),[30] inequality on earth as in heaven. This meant that

42

some men necessarily had to assume command, men invested with a power whose unique source was Christ in heaven; it meant that "officers" and "ministers" were needed—the bishops on the one hand, the kings on the other—to exercise leadership jointly, to take command over the mass of men of minor importance, over the inferior, imperfect creatures, who were nevertheless bound to be looked upon as objects of love. The third function, the agricultural, appears only fleetingly. It is mentioned in passing for the sole purpose of justifying the fact that the *oratores* did not do manual labor and that the *pugnatores* received rents, in order to show that this idleness and this exploitation—i.e., the most characteristic expressions of the seigniorial mode of production—were part of the order of things.

3

ADALBERO OF LAON AND THE ROYAL MISSION

The second of our two sentences—"some pray, others fight, still others work"—is the two hundred ninety-sixth line of a poem which numbers four hundred thirty-four lines in all. It thus occurs virtually at the center of an important literary creation, the last, incomplete effort of Adalbero, bishop of Laon. This composition is neither a treatise nor a narrative. It is a jewel, like those which in that age were polished with painstaking, loving care in the treasure-chambers of cathedrals. The many revisions in evidence in Latin manuscript 14192 of the Bibliothèque Nationale bear witness to a quest for formal perfection. This is a work of art whose value, in keeping with the then dominant aesthetic, lay in its subtle interlacing of symbols. Our task is to uncover an ideological system concealed within a text as convoluted and brilliant in its way as Paul Valéry's *La Jeune Parque*. Or his *Charmes*. Indeed, the title of the poem is *Charm,* or *Song [carmen] for King Robert*. It is all too easy to lose one's way in such a thicket of self-reference. We are fortunate in being able to avail ourselves of the guidance provided by Claude Carozzi's magnificent commentary on this text.[1] What we know of Gerard of Cambrai's thought is also of some help. It was prudent to begin with the latter.

This is a political poem, a pamphlet, a satire based on classical models by a master writer. A writer of some renown: Adalbero's talent was the subject of a dithyrambic eulogy by Dudo, canon of Saint-Quentin, who dedicated to him his history of the dukes of Normandy. The poem is the work of a very old man, who looked upon it as his masterpiece, a masterpiece whose final touches he added in the belief that he would once more shine in the eyes of the men of letters at court as well as in the eyes of the king, Robert the Pious. Adalbero's pose is that of a rhetorician, but a rhetorician freed by his advanced years and his awareness of his gifts to engage in one last dialogue with his king.

Among the antithetical images around which the theme is intricately woven, one, the opposition between youth and age, serves as underpinning for the entire dialectical construction. We find it announced in the very first line: the *ordo* in which the clerks of the church of Laon join around their bishop is said to be composed of "flowers" and "fruits," of the young and the old. Adalbero was the oldest of all. He had aged—terribly. The king, with whom he is shown conversing, was also very old. The king, however, was supposed to embody both attributes, youth and age, in his person—these words, we must understand, were not merely reckonings in terms of years. In Adalbero's day these two concepts were also used to distinguish two groups of adult males within the aristocracy, one of which included men who were unmarried, unstable, without fixed abode, while the other consisted of married men, established as heads of a household. Regardless of a man's chronological age, the words young and old came in this way to define two sorts of behavior in life, action, and progress towards salvation. When the poem speaks of the "flower of youth," it is important to see that what is being evoked is that which, in the visible world, arises out of impetuosity, out of the violent instincts in flesh and blood, out of that vigorous temper with which certain bloodlines were more abundantly endowed than others. It was this temper that conferred "nobility" on these lineages, in the sense of beauty and courage—that valor which made itself felt fully in the ardor of combat. It was therefore the youthful aspect of the king's personality that made him the *bellator,* who by brandishing the sword restored order on earth, though at the cost of some temporary unrest. Age, on the other hand, was responsible for what he possessed of "the virtue of the soul," for his knowledge of the immutable order and regular motion of the heavens: *sapientia,* that "true wisdom through which may be known that which is in heaven, sempiternally," [2] with which the *oratores* were imbued through anointment by the "king of kings." [3] The distinction being drawn here is none other than that to which Georges Dumézil has called our attention, between the crude act whose object is shifting, changeable, ambiguous, and the contemplative gaze focused upon the fixities of the supernatural and the lawful. [4]

Partaking of both natures, Robert was destined to carry out both functions. He was *rex* and *sacerdos,* like Christ, to whose position on high the king's in this world corresponded in the symmetrical relationship binding heaven and earth. All other "nobles" were excluded, by reason of their congenitally violent character, from the performance of ecclesiastical rites. [5] Adalbero appears to have been more Carolingian than Gerard. This may be ascribed to his age—he was older, nearer the roots: in his youth, he had lived in the presence of sovereigns who could with greater justice than Robert claim to resemble Charles the Bald; his memory preserved a more majestic image of Frankish royalty. To him the king was a sacred personage, like a bishop, and at the same time the man who each spring rallied the warriors around his person. He thus stood at the point where the visible arm of the cross that underlay the architecture of all creation intersected the invisible arm. Thus he bore responsibility for peace, that projection onto our imperfect world of law, of the order regnant on high. *Rex, lex, pax*—three words whose consonant echo reverberates throughout the work—are the keys to the whole poem, the nails that hold the entire framework together. To carry out his dual role as legislator and pacifier, the king had need of both his natures, wreaking vengeance, administering punishment, imposing discipline—violently if necessary, but also wisely, with the wisdom that obtained from deliberation, so as to insure respect for the institutionalized order. The danger was that in practice he might not succeed in achieving a balance between his contrasting gifts. If "youth" took the upper hand, disorder would ensue. In that event, it was left to age, to the "orator," in his imperturbable serenity, to intervene on the side of wisdom.

Adalbero acknowledged that kings had the *facultas oratoris*,[6] the right to pray, the right to speak. But given the threat of their being overwhelmed by an overabundance of "youth," it was important that they live, as it were, enveloped by the bishops of their realm, that they receive episcopal instruction in the law.[7] For the bishops' mission was to seek the truth, to inquire into things, so as to be able to distinguish good from evil and mete out proper rewards and punishments.[8] Before passing judgment, therefore, the king was bound to deliberate with them, with the "order of the powerful."[9] One should understand that this appellation referred to those to whom Christ had delegated the power to judge, to distinguish the chosen from the damned, as the Savior would do when he returned on Judgment Day. By virtue of the higher of his assigned functions, the king was a bishop among the other bishops; in carrying out his second function, their advice was indispensable: this was the political ideal of the octogenarian prelate. The same idea is reiterated several times; in lines 50–51, we find the assertion that the bishops are "preceptors" whom everyone, including kings, must hold in reverence; in lines 258–59, it is said that all mankind, princes not excepted, is subject to the episcopacy; and in line 390, Robert is apostrophized as "thou, first of the Franks, thou art nevertheless, in the order of kings, subjugated"—subject to the dominion of Christ, to divine law, hence to the Church and consequently to the bishops.

A mentor responsible for erecting a dam against the youthful torrents raging through the king's body, Adalbero spoke. He taught, he offered advice. For all of this his vehicle was none other than this poem, his last public act. In it he made use of two instruments. He used dialectic—just a little. In truth, this was ground onto which he ventured with considerable timidity—admitting that "I am a grammarian, not a dialectician." [10] Gerbert had reinstated the teaching of logic in the school at Rheims in the late tenth century. But prior to that time, in Adalbero's student days, the training of *oratores* was confined almost exclusively to grammar and rhetoric. The latter remained the primary discipline. In the cathedrals of *Francia* in the early eleventh century, metaphysical problems were treated as problems of language. [11] The art of classification, of making distinctions—and particularly of perceiving the institutional order of human society—remained governed by the laws of discourse. These were laws of which Adalbero was a true connoisseur; he put them to use with the consummate skill of an expert. His concern was grammar, the choice of words; rhetoric, however, was his principal weapon, the token of his excellence and of the mastery he meant to exercise over the mind of the sovereign in whose presence God had placed him. To penetrate the significance of the *Carmen,* we must dismantle it, we must allow light to shine through into the dark arcades upon which the words of the poem are hung. This Claude Carozzi has done brilliantly. If he has been far more successful in interpreting the poem than his predecessors, the credit belongs to his keenness in recognizing the key to the work in the marginal notations made on the working manuscript in preparation for the monumental, and never completed, undertaking, and to his ability to identify the "authority" that guided the composition: the commentary on Cicero's *De inventione* by Marius Victorinus, which was then the basis of rhetorical instruction in the episcopal schools.

The poem is divided into four parts, of which three are speeches. The first is addressed to the *imago juventutis* and describes the contemporary disorder; the second is addressed to the wisdom of the king and depicts the exemplary order; the third, finally, sets forth a plan of restoration. Between this and the preceding section is interpolated a discussion of the two natures, supplementing the description of order. This intervening portion seems less skillfully done than the others; venturing into tortuous dialectical argumentation, the thought goes somewhat awry; this, however, is the section that contains a description of the system of good government, in which the enlightened counsel of the bishops is erected into a sort of protective shield around the sovereign.

In such wise the argument is laid out. The postulate of social trifunctionality occurs, and not by chance, in the second speech, where the heavenly and atemporal model of order is described.

This central speech is in fact a duet. The preceding speech was delivered by the bishop alone, and the king is the sole speaker in the final section, a statement of reform policy. But here, where the two natures—youth and old age, sacred and profane—encounter one another, a dialogue is established between the preceptor, the "master," and his royal pupil.

Logically following up the preliminary—and melancholy—discussion of decline, Adalbero urges the king to turn his gaze heavenward, where he will find guidance for carrying out the repairs necessitated by the terrestrial breakdown. He is told to consider "Jerusalem on high"[12]—Gerard of Cambrai used these very words in his sermon to the heretics of Arras, as reported in the brief. If he follows this advice, he will discover that in that abode of perfection, everything is governed by a "distinction of orders, . . . and that the distribution of power makes some subject to others."[13] This is a direct echo of Gerard's speech, which itself recapitulated the words of Gregory the Great. As in Gerard's speech, this appeal to the example of heaven leads to the assertion that inequality is providential, that the power of the king is one of *distinctio,* of *discretio,* and that the sovereign is responsible for maintaining social differences in this world. With the alteration in tone previously alluded to, the bishop of Laon is merely repeating what the bishop of Cambrai had said earlier. The picture is clear: Adalbero, as a grammarian, playing with words in virtuoso fashion, was giving a poetic formulation of a prior logical demonstration of the truth—of a proof given earlier by his confrère, the "confessor."

The king obeys. He lifts his eyes, contemplates the "vision of peace," and then reports what he has glimpsed: he perceives the exclusive authority of the "king of kings" (Gerard again); he understands that there is an interpenetration of the two cities; Robert remarks the perfect cohesion of this monarchy, he comprehends that essential unity in which the various components of its population are dissolved:[15] this monarchy, the king sees quite clearly, is "composed of angelic citizens as well as troops of men, some of whom reign already, while the others aspire."[16] What these two lines express Adalbero has borrowed either directly from the Arras brief or else from the text which served as Gerard's inspiration for the composition of his antiheretical manifesto. In any case, both arguments—the one from Cambrai-Arras, the other from Laon—share the same central idea, the idea of a coordination (analogous to the coordination between youth and old age in the person of the king, the latter dominating the former), of a set of equivalences and an upward force impelling the imperfect world to raise itself towards the perfect one and to incorporate itself therein. But this is all that the king's mind, itself imperfect, caught in the toils of flesh, can discern. Eager to dissipate still further the mists that cloud his vision, Robert next inquires of the "authors" whose teachings he hopes will help lift the veil a bit more. At this point Adalbero turns to citing sources, the same ones cited by Gerard in his treatise. First is Saint Augustine's *City of God.*[17] This reference does not satisfy the king. He asks whether these "heavenly principalities" (the term also appears in the *libellus*) are equal in strength. In what order are they ranked?[18] The answer is to "read Dionysius—his two books—and Gregory." Next, Adalbero—here parting company slightly with Gerard—refers to the *Moralia in Job* and to the *Commentary on Ezechiel*.[19] Thanks to these four works, knowledge—"mystical" knowledge—of heaven is possible. This knowledge is necessary, for it is revelatory of the very principle of social order, making manifest "the distinct order on high, which is the example for that which is established on earth." This is the crux of the matter. The statement occurs, in fact, in line 228, in the exact center of the work.

Adalbero next uses Gregory the Great's own words concerning orders, ranks, and dignities to describe the ecclesiastical hierarchy—although he uses the word *ordo* only in the singular and has to make certain modifications to make Gregory's words fit the rhythm of his poem. The description of the hierarchy that he gives is put into the mouth of the bishop and is based on the books named previously—all of them available in the cathedral library, not far from the study in which Adalbero tirelessly polished and repolished his composition. These were books whose words the old man had long since committed to memory—he was wisdom incarnate. Again we hear reverberations of Gerard of Cambrai's speech. On God's orders Moses ordained ministers in the synagogue; similarly, in the Church, "known as the kingdom of the heavens," under Christ's principate, the bishops are responsible for arranging the orders:[20] it is they who fix, who institute—the censors: like the magistrates of the Roman republic, they control the composition of the *ordo*. The *ecclesia*, however, in which they carry out this ordering function is at once heavenly and terrestrial—a part of heaven, in which it "reigns," and of earth, from which it "aspires" to rise. And because its territory ranges over both sides of the boundary, over two provinces, it must respect two laws. The community of Christians—which death does not tear asunder, which exists in part beyond the veil of appearances—the "house of God," the *res fidei* (in contrast with the *res publica*, whose censors are not bishops) is governed by two complementary laws: a law of unity, divine law; and a law of distribution, human law.

Divine law "does not divide what it shares."[21] Certain men, living men, came under its provisions: even before death, the other world ensnared these men—the priests. Though among them there might be differences of "nature" and "order," of birth or rank, they were nevertheless gathered together in the substantial unity of their "condition." In what did the essence of that condition consist? Purity was the answer: "they shall be pure, exempt from the servile condition." Because priests were free men, and to be worthy of their freedom, they needed to shun corruption and escape the toils of flesh. They alone stood in such need. In setting priests apart by the obligation which was theirs exclusively to respect sexual and dietary restrictions, Adalbero at this point in the text is attacking the heretics who, as Gerard of Cambrai had put it, "indiscreetly" forbade all men to marry; he also inveighs against the letter from heaven, invoked by his colleagues from *Francia* as justification for their desire to impose fasting on all men. Priests, however, had also to beware of another taint, that indelible stain of which men who labored with their hands could not be cleansed. So as to make themselves better overseers of other men, priests were enjoined not to till the soil, not to cook their own food, not to use their fingers for any purpose, even washing, unless it was to cleanse their own bodies and minds.[22] It befit them to lead idle, asexual lives, shunning meat. As quasi-heavenly creatures, they partook of the angelic nature. They were "slaves," serfs (*servi*) of a unique master, God. On this basis was founded their superiority over the rest of mankind, over princes themselves. Equal in condition, all priests spent their days baptizing, sacrificing, speaking, and praying; in such did the "order" consist.[23]

At this point, the king raises a naive question, pretending to be taken in by the utopian scheme proposed by those "illiterates," the heretics. Ought not everyone to be perfect, ought not everyone to obey the law? Would it not be ideal if all men were equal? "Since the house of God is one, should it not be made subject to a single law?"[24]

The bishop's answer is no: "the state [*status*] of the *res fidei* is simple, but in keeping with the dictates of order, it is triple."[25] In this lay the mystery of the world, made in the image of its creator, one in three persons. Because the end of time had not yet come; because mankind had yet to hear the trumpet blast that would summon it to flock to the hereafter; because some men, still prisoners of the flesh, were yet aspirants to, not citizens of, the kingdom; for all these reasons there existed another law, "human law," for those not yet incorporated into the *ordo,* not yet integrated into that excrescence of heaven in the earthly realm that was known as the clergy—for the "people," in short, this other law existed. A law that did not unify, but divided. A law that distinguished two "conditions" among men: "nobles" and "slaves" (or "serfs"). Independence and leisure were granted the former. The latter were obliged to obey. And as punishment they were sentenced to *labor,* which also meant work.

Originally in this place in the two hundred eighty-sixth line of his poem Adalbero had put the word *dolor.* He changed his mind. He had the scribe cross out that first choice and replace it with the word *labor,* which had a double meaning and so seemed preferable to him. He used the word twice subsequently in specifying what constituted the condition of the *servi.*[26] "Condition" rather than "order." The distinction was based on the relationship to power. Some were in command, others obeyed. Human law governed two conditions which reflected the inequality inherent in the structure of the universe. In the "household" that was Christendom, there were necessarily masters and servants, much as there were masters and servants in great aristocratic residences—such as those of bishop, king, or prince—and much as there were exploiters and exploited within the mode of production. Such was the line of demarcation which, as Adalbero saw it, was inscribed in nature itself, in the biology of living creatures. For on earth sin, flesh, and sex had dominion. It was in this sphere that the *lex humana* ruled, this troubled sphere in which the ineluctably sinful transmission of life was of necessity implicated either in the guilty pleasures of procreation or in the punishment represented by the pain of childbearing. An aspect of earthly rather than angelic existence, the two conditions were defined by birth. They were genetic categories. Nobles and serfs constituted two species, two "races." Foremost among the former were the king and the emperor, the two beacons of Christendom. They were sacred personages, of course. But in virtue of their second nature, like all who were not part of the clergy, they could legitimately possess a wife; they were obliged to take her to bed, to impregnate her—and the whole of the nobility was regarded as their kith and kin; every nobleman belonged to the vast progeny of former sovereigns, their ancestors. The entire nobility shared "the blood of kings," as Adalbero, who was a part of it and knew his genealogy by heart, was convinced.

Only later was a function (*officium*) attributed to each condition, and then as a consequence of the reproductively determined distinction, an effect of "race." The blood that flowed in the veins of noblemen—the source of their beauty, their impetuosity, their martial qualities—qualified them to undertake the defense of the church, first of all, and, secondarily, of the "vulgar," great and small (for among the nonnoble, among the populace, there were, as Loyseau was later to maintain, ranks, just as among the nobles some walked, sat, or spoke before others). It was due to their genetic qualities that the nobles were warriors, *bellatores*.[27] The "office" of the serfs, on the other hand, was to do whatever was appropriate to the "servile condition," which included that whole list of tasks described a few lines earlier by Adalbero as forbidden to priests: washing, cooking, working the soil, i.e., producing and preparing food for others. By hard labor. By the sweat of their brow. *Labor, dolor, sudor.* The dialogue between sage and king culminates in the assertion of trifunctionality: "Triple is the house of God which is thought to be one: on Earth, some pray [*orant*], others fight [*pugnant*], still others work [*laborant*]; which three are joined together and may not be torn asunder." Because—and the conclusion is a reiteration of the notion that prefaced Gerard's second speech in the *Deeds of the Bishops of Cambrai*—"on the function of each the works of the others rest, each in turn assisting all."[28] If respect is shown for this law (*lex*), peace (*pax*) will

51

reign. The enforcement of the law, and hence the preservation of order, is the task of the king (*rex*).

As far as the homological relationship between heaven and earth, the principle of inequality, and the institutional order of the ecclesiastical body are concerned, the exposition of the system as given in the *Carmen* relies heavily on Gerard and through him on Gregory the Great. In Adalbero's poem, however, the notion of trifunctionality is much more precisely formulated than in his predecessors. What the author of the *Gesta* summarized in one sentence is here developed at some length. For our purposes, it is enough to single out three points:

1. Like his colleague in Cambrai, the bishop of Laon speaks of three functions, not three orders. In contrast with Gerard and Gregory the Great, he never uses the word *ordo* except in the singular. It occurs fifteen times in the poem. In seven instances it is used abstractly to designate the order of things. In all the remaining cases it is applied to an instituted body, which in every instance is ecclesiastical. On earth, the only "order" was the Church (in the institutional sense of the word). Indeed, by the rite of unction, a segment of mankind—which included the sacred kings, there being an "order of kings" which was an annex, as it were, of the Church—came to participate in the order on high and was brought under the jurisdiction of divine law. Human law, on the other hand, governed the sublunary realm, the sphere of instability and corruption, hence this law instituted mere conditions, not an order.

2. The word *laborator* does not appear here, nor is it to be found in Gerard's speech. Instead of this noun, whose connotation is clearly functional, Adalbero uses *servus,* which implies servitude, subjection. Was not the reason for this that Adalbero, like Gerard, was interested in power, and so only in the first two of the three functions, that of the *bellator* and that of the *orator,* the one subordinate to the other much as the two natures were, much as the body was subordinate to the soul, or youth to old age? In this connection, it is to be noted that the term *orator* was applied only to the king.

3. Furthermore, throughout the dissertation, the "divisions" and "parts" always establish binary oppositions: there are two orders in the universe, the heavenly and the terrestrial; two parts of the *ecclesia,* one in heaven, the other here below; two categories of dissimilarities, those deriving from nature and those deriving from the *ordo;* two laws; the order of clerks is opposed to the people; human law distinguishes between two conditions; the nobles protect church land and nonchurch land, and in the latter case large holdings are distinguished from small. Ternarity always arises from a combination of binarities, as in the mystery of the divine trinity.[29] Not that Christendom is ever, even covertly, identified with the body of Christ. But it

52

was thought of as having the same structure as the divine, being one in three. Disorder, moreover, could stem either from a disunity among the parts or from an effacement of differences.

On disorder Adalbero expatiates at length. Having described it in the first four sections of his work, he returns to it in the final portion, which contains his proposal for reform. Did he look upon heresy as the source of this disorder, as at Arras in 1025? In the *Carmen* we find only one allusion to "error."[30] Nevertheless, the pains taken to justify the existence of a specialized body responsible for the administration of the sacred prove that the mind of the bishop of Laon was not altogether untroubled by anti-ecclesiastical heterodoxy. Did he engage in doctrinal combat with the propagandists for the peace oaths, as Gerard had done in 1024? Lines 37–47, containing a caricatural version of a topsy-turvy world, show a peasant (homely, listless, base, in every respect the contrary of a noble or a king, whose characteristic traits were beauty, vigor, and gallantry) wearing a crown; they show the "guardians of the right," whose mission was to enforce the law, compelled instead to pray; and, finally, we see unfrocked bishops behind the plow, singing the song of Adam and Eve, which is to be regarded as a lament for the bygone equality of the children of God. Indeed, it was inequality that made this picture scandalous: was it not appropriate for prelates to appear magnificently garbed, like Gerard presiding over the synod at Arras, their splendid clothing reflecting the dominant and influential position that God had bestowed on them; was it not fitting that they be exempt from servile occupations; was it not their essential concern to assign each man his proper place according to his merits, locating him within the "distinction of the orders," in the hierarchy that was predicated upon inequality? In this perverse burlesque of society we see clearly which men in normal times carried out the three functions: who normally prayed, who fought, and who worked. For Adalbero as for Gerard, the *oratores* were the bishops, the *bellatores* the princes, and the toiling masses the peasants. The subversion and disorder represented by the exaltation of the serfs, the clericalization of the nobility, and the humiliation of the episcopacy were in Adalbero's mind, as in Gerard's, the results likely to follow if men heeded the proposals of someone like Garin of Beauvais, who had called for establishing peace on the basis of oaths among equals to be sworn at assemblies in the open countryside. The principal target aimed at by the author of the *Carmen* lay elsewhere, however: his primary adversary was Odilo, abbot of Cluny.

Adalbero's goal was to restore bishops to their proper role as advisers of kings. In his day, he claims, this office was no longer filled by priests, who "jointly serve Christ,"[31] nor by scholars whose prolonged studies had brought them knowledge of the mysteries. Who, then, was ministering to the needs of the king? A layman, who had repudiated marriage (although matrimony remained the norm for anyone not belonging to the *ordo* of priests), and who was not in possession of *sapientia,* because he was not a sacred personage, because he had renounced learning.[32] Quite obviously it was the monk who was the target of this passage. Monks were responsible for society's afflictions. Their influence over Robert was pernicious, upsetting the necessary balance between reflection and action in his person. Inherent in his youthful side was an unruly nature which the monkish influence unleashed. And one monk in particular was singled out for censure. He is referred to as a "master" (the word used to designate the heresiarch of Arras whom Gerard had tried in vain to prosecute).

This monk was Odilo. Odilo, that "prince"[33] who was "master of the warlike order of monks,"[34] a *bellator,* whereas his office should have been prayer, who sat enthroned in a sumptuous palace,[35] whereas he ought to have lived in poverty, and who hastened to Rome to beseech the favor of the Pope, when he ought to have begged the favor of God. "King Odilo," the usurper. If *Francia* had been stood on its head, if confusion reigned in questions of function and rank, the fault lay with the Cluniac order, which he headed.

What did Cluny want, in fact? In the first place, it wanted the nobility to share the monastic condition and accept the prohibitions and duties of monks, to live chastely and chant the Psalms[36]—whereas it was the privilege of only one man among all the nobles, the king, to take an active role in the liturgy. Cluny also hoped to militarize prayer. In a burlesque scene Adalbero ridicules this aim. He alleges that he once sent a monk from Laon to gather information in the southern part of the kingdom. By the time he returns to Cluny, this monk has been won over, transformed, by Cluny, and utters the following words: "I am a knight and yet remain a monk."[37] *Miles*—not *bellator* or *pugnator:* we must pay careful attention to the choice of words. Adalbero, the grammarian, the consummate connoisseur of words, is speaking of knights, of those troublesome, brigandly bands that the princes of this world gathered round them as their armed auxiliaries—gangs of "youths" entirely given over to violence, carrying on like hellions. Corrupted by Cluny, the former servant had joined that gang of swashbucklers, had become an Orlando Furioso, a grotesque, willful, slavering cur, whose indecent outfit alone was proof enough that the proprieties of order had been violated.[38] Because in that era social categories were clearly indicated by one's clothing, by the shape of one's footwear, by the cut of one's hair—for it was important to be able to distinguish by glancing at a person's dress between the monk, the penitent, the prince, the peasant, the decent woman and the woman who was not. In the same period, we hear the upholders of order denouncing the new fashions, vituperating against those southern manners of dress that were then being taken up by the dandies of northern France, who shaved their beards, wore their hair short, slit their tunics to show the thigh, affected leather breeches—no laughing matter. They rather inspired horror. For their ways were likely to lead to confusion between a man of war and a priest or woman, and so they were held to be sacrilegious, disruptive of society's sacred order.[39] As disruptive as the views of Cluny, which looked upon the monastic office as a kind of combat and the monk as a variety of soldier. Cluny's efforts to import into lay society the originally liturgical and monastic values of the *militia Dei,* and its desire to make "knights of Christ"[40] of all the *milites,* all the subaltern ranks of soldiery, contributed, moreover, to the abolition of prescribed differences. Thus Cluny's preaching joined with the movement for the peace of God in spreading disruption through society. For that movement, of which Odilo was in fact a sponsor and which led eventually to holy war, ultimately dislodged the supporting walls of the social edifice's several separate compartments. Already in the peace councils meeting in northern France one could see demagogic bishops shedding their rich gowns and issuing calls for equality, declaring the peasant king, and like latter-day Turpins making ready to lead an expeditionary force against the enemies of the faith. Leaving Adalbero to lament the fate of the men who could neither work the land nor fight: what was to become of them?[41]

Now we can understand why in the latter part of the pamphlet the king is said to give his assurance that he will continue to assume personal responsibility for the administration of justice and peace, and himself appoint the representatives who would be charged with protecting the poor. He further pledges to keep noblemen away from churches at night and prevent their spending their days chanting psalms. He instructs them, too, in Adalbero's poem, to make love and sire children, lest the *genus,* the *"virtu"* be lost to the world altogether. In addition, he is said to have called upon the bishops to forsake the *rura,* or peasant affairs, to drop the pretense that they shared the destitution of the people of the countryside; instead he urged them to deck themselves out in the finery appropriate to their rank or position; and, lastly, he bid them confine the monks to their proper sphere and prevent their venturing outside it.[42] The King Robert of the poem would seem to have committed himself to resisting the encroachments of a perverse congregation of monks then pushing its way out of the south as the Saracens had done before them, as well as to undertaking to restore differences where distinctions had been dangerously effaced. Would he be capable of doing so? Adalbero's satire closes with a derisive round of doubtful laughter.

4

THE SYSTEM

This poem is a vast game of words, the resonances and harmonies of which, like the contemporary architecture of the basilicas, were based on precise numerical relationships. Amidst their complexity there is a danger of losing one's way, or, as in Brocéliande, of falling under their spell. The commentary, at any rate, could go on indefinitely. For the argument of the poem moves forward by allusion, reflection, recursion, by allegory, as Adalbero says, or rather by symbolism, the "cipher of a mystery," never to be "explained once for all time, but forever open to new decipherings, just as a musical score is never finally deciphered but always remains available for fresh performance."[1] The interplay of its thousand facets makes the mirror dazzle. Nevertheless, a relatively simple picture emerges from a comparison of the words of the bishop of Laon with those of the bishop of Cambrai. For both Adalbero and Gerard addressed the same subject, that of their office, of the episcopal function in its relation to the royal function. "The king and the bishops appear to serve the serf." In line two hundred ninety-two, at the center of the poem, we find what is perhaps the most accurate formulation of social trifunctionality and learn what place the image occupied in the thought of the *Carmen*'s author. The respective powers of king and bishop over their subjects, the rest of mankind: was this not ostensibly the real problem whose solution Adalbero and Gerard were striving to give? Both bishops were immersed in the problems of the day, whether faced with a challenge from a minor castellan or a great abbot; both were concerned about the stresses and strains apparent in the political edifice. Scions of old Lotharingian stock, a line fertile in great captains and in confessors of the faith, and perched on culture's highest peaks, these two prelates, or "masters"—legitimately so, not usurpers—were rhetors who had read in

Cicero how eloquence might be added to *sapientia;* old men, sages, part of "the order of the powerful" to which anyone who hoped to civilize the earth, chastise men, and bring human society into conformity with the divine example had to belong, they countered their misguided confrères by setting before the king a model of government, the ideology of a civic order. We are now in a position to identify the key elements by which this system was held together.

1. Central was the assumption of a coherence between heaven and earth, two parts of one homogeneous world, built to a single plan and hence reciprocally related, yet based on a principle of inequality inherent in hierarchy, in which the superior serves as model for the inferior. Thus any attempt to reform man's level in that hierarchy presupposed an effort to overcome the weight of the superposed levels. Hence both authors propose taking action by bringing to bear forces which they include among the things in the cosmos exhibiting the greatest tendency to rise, alongside the quick, the subtle, the soul, fire, the sun—on the masculine side; the feminine, the side of shadow, of water, of the moon, does not come into play: women have no office, no function, no "estate."

2. Order is an attribute of the perfect city. This order resembles that of a military organization, and stems from a law, which establishes peace—this explains why the heavenly Jerusalem can be called a vision of peace, a revelation, an example of justice. On earth this signal order was to be distributed by the issuance of commands, by orders conveyed from rank to rank in a disciplined manner. In view of the manner in which order was extended over humankind, one level in the social pyramid, the highest, though part and parcel of the world of imperfection, might legitimately be designated an order, the order *par excellence:* the body of ecclesiastics. It was unique. In the earthly sphere, it was the model for all social organization.[2] The order of kings was, as it were, an annex of this order, since kings were anointed, the role of unction being to bridle the high spirits permeating the king's body and to subordinate the strength imbuing the royal person to the task of upholding order. The king's anointment superimposed a cultural order upon the order established by nature. In this world, of course, dissimilarities stemmed both from nature and from order. But that which instituted the *ordo* was subject to constant threat, because man lived in the sphere of the unclean. "The laws decay and already all semblance of peace is in disarray; man's mores have changed and order has changed."[3] Thus in disarray, man was drifting farther from the heavenly model, which was immutable. To find firm moorings once again, the "various functions" had of necessity to be suitably fulfilled.

3. *Officium* was a key word, one that these master grammarians wielded judiciously. For them—Adalbero was the more explicit of the two—order

on earth was based on "divisions," or "partitions" (*partes:* in 1824, Guizot translated this as "classes"), which determined the distribution of responsibilities. There were two offices, both concerned with leadership: one set its face to heaven, communicating directly with the invisible and laying down rules of conduct; the other looked to earth and was responsible for enforcing those rules. In a social context, the word *ordo* was applicable only to the men who fulfilled these two functions. Hence there existed two, and only two, "orders," the order of the "powerful," i.e., the bishops, and the order of kings. *Rex et pontifices:* the *bellator,* the *oratores.* This initial division of responsibilities could not have been more clear in the minds of Adalbero and Gerard. Without broadening the base of their order, however, the leaders could not have carried out their functions. Delegating the sacerdotal function, the bishops extended an order of which they were the spiritual fathers over their dioceses: Adalbero regarded the clergy of Laon as an order. The kings did likewise in instituting *rectores,* nobles regarded as their progeny. And rightly so, since kings were not asexual. As sires in the flesh, they headed a quite extensive kinship group identified with the nobility, from which the captains indispensable in warfare were recruited. Thus each of the two offices was delegated in a different way. The office of prayer was transmitted by a sacramental rite specific to the order, an immaterial sign which left the relationship with heaven intact and fell under the governance of divine law: whoever received power in this way was thus "ordained." Whereas the office of war, delegated through the blood, was genetically governed, by "nature": there was no warrior order. At the intersection of the two offices stood the royal person, torn, as it were, in two directions.

4. There were two dominant groups: the priests, invested with their function by the bishops; the nobles, descendants of kings. Their subordinate assistants were by no means looked upon as members of these groups; neither monks not elevated to the priesthood nor knights who wielded no power were so privileged; into their hands fell merely the small change associated with the liturgical and military functions. They were no more than agents, the domestic retainers that waited upon those to whom Christ had assigned the duties of prayer and combat.

5. In the eleventh century, the bishops looked upon no sovereign authority other than that of Christ, the king of kings, as the source of the sacerdotal function. The king of France was weak, moreover, and the bishops eyed the signs of his weakness with anxiety, for it permitted a slackening of discipline to spread among the ranks of the armed, with an attendant threat of unruly knights loosed upon the countryside. This precludes our looking upon the various social responsibilities as a sort of projection onto society of royal missions and attributes, as certain of Georges Dumézil's disciples have done. On the other hand, it makes it easier to understand why a third function was added and a third social category defined.

58

6. Indeed, triplicity is one of the elements of the system. Inequality governed the universe: some were in command, others must obey. Hence two conditions existed among men; a man belonged to one or the other by virtue of birth, by "nature": some were born free and others not, some "nobles," others "serfs." So long as a man inhabited the sin-tainted portion of the world he remained in that position to which he had been born. In so far as God's servants (or serfs) lived their lives in keeping with the requirements of the *ordo,* obeyed the injunction of the divine law to live as angels, and shunned impurity, to that extent could they free themselves from that which caused the institution of different conditions. Only among laymen, therefore, was this yawning breach between two groups important. Thus a third category took its place on the nether side of this line, in a subject status: the category of the "vulgar"—called the "people" by Loyseau—with *oratores* and *bellatores* charged to lead it. On this point Adalbero is perfectly clear: he bluntly contrasts men of the second function with "those who serve." For him, subjection was hereditary. From it derived the painful obligation to work. This was the third function: "toil." A sad word, evoking sweat, affliction, poverty—exploitation. Assigned to fulfill this function were those who, by nature, because their blood was not the blood of kings, and because they were not ordained, were compelled to alienate their strength in the service of others. Note that nowhere in these texts do we find the men assigned the third function designated by a word that means "worker." The exploited are, with good reason, referred to either as "peasants" or "slaves." The principle of necessary inequality accounts for the addition of a third function. This explains why the trifunctional schema came either before or after a treatise on submission and on the structure of a society in which the high reigned in perfection and the low grovelled in sin. Triplicity arose out of the conjunction of two kinds of dissimilarity, that instituted by the *ordo*—there were the priests and the others—conjoined with that instituted by *natura*—there were nobles and serfs. The source of disorder was not that nature changed, but that the order was breached. This occurred, for instance, when "rustics" were included in the deliberations of the peace assemblies (or when a man not born into the nobility acceded to the episcopal dignity), when nobles were required to pray, or *oratores* to fight.

7. The last key concept of the system was that of mutuality, of reciprocity within hierarchy; in structural terms, this called forth ternarity.[4] The driving force behind the exchange was charity. But its pattern was determined hierarchically; brotherly love and devotion were exchanged between levels of the hierarchy, whose arrangement was ultimately determining. At the summit, God was the source of grace, who set everything in motion. Charity, which wove the whole fabric together and coordinated all its parts, was, at its very source, condescension.

These, then, are the lineaments of the system in which we find the first expression of the notion of social trifunctionality. It is an expression of proud superiority, the work of men struggling against "novelties," swimming against the tide, battling others who rode its crest. These men were conservatives. In one of them, bitterness and skepticism are evident. Both were striving to avert what they rightly considered a catastrophe. I used to find surprising Robert Fossier's view that the trifunctional theme was behind the times in the early eleventh century.[5] This view turns out to have been correct. But this theme was only one element among many within an enormous structure. Adalbero and Gerard did not invent the theme, but they did build the surrounding edifice. Before we ask why, let us turn first to the question of how that construction proceeded, in the hope of shedding some light on their methods.

PART TWO

GENESIS

Here before us, then, we have a theory of the social order, engraved on parchment in words gradually heaped up in those chambers where men did hard manual labor—religious labor, to be exact—to lay in that immense literary silage in the expectation that later its seeds would be sown the world over (for the author did indeed believe that his manuscript would be read and copied, that its message would reverberate indefinitely—not a vain hope, as our interest in what he had to say after a thousand years testifies). It is a testament to an accomplished literary talent, but more than that it is a prestige-enhancing monument and an instrument of power. Neither Adalbero nor Gerard invented this theory from scratch. Ideological systems are not invented. In some diffuse form they exist, though man may be scarcely aware of their presence. Not unchanging, they are shaped from within by a slow, imperceptible evolution, a process whose effects are made manifest when at long intervals they threaten to bring down the entire edifice, making renovation imperative. Then craftsmen—such as Gerard and Adalbero were between 1025 and 1030—must rearrange the scattered architectural elements. It is as though an old garment has ceased to fit properly because the body beneath has changed with age. The craftsmen are tailors; the work of cutting and patching constitutes their creative contribution. But they do not create the materials they use. These they find ready to hand. Just as the theme of the three functions was not of their own making, neither did they forge any of the system's other elements.

These other elements they plucked from memory. They were men absorbed in interminable discussion. In those meetings, synods, and "councils" in which the two bishops expressed their own opinions and disputed those of others, the text that we read today took shape. What eventually would become a coherent formulation of an ideology was hammered out in the heat of those verbal jousts that, like war, were occasions for the leading figures of the day to shine, to amuse themselves, and to assert their strength in the intervals between military expeditions. Orators and auditors, they spoke and listened far more than they read, and so their memories were practiced, trustworthy, and constantly replenished by practical experience with liturgy, psalmody, and homily, all of which were replete with Latin phrases. This enormous repertoire, the common property of these many noble sons placed by their fathers in cathedral chapters to become bishops, served as a kind of backdrop. Before it paraded, piecemeal, the various elements of the ideological system; at the opportune moment, these would be assembled into some coherent form and projected onto the backdrop screen. Most of these bits and pieces were taken from the Bible, the Vulgate; others came from the Church Fathers, and from the classics of antiquity commented on by the masters of grammar, rhetoric, and dialectics.

63

What memory required to refresh itself could be found in the *armarium*, the storehouse of books attached to every cathedral. Perhaps the richest of all the libraries in Latin Christendom were to be found in the region where Adalbero and Gerard lived, where they had learned their trade, where they debated, preached, inveighed, and dictated to the canons, their secretaries. Today the contents of these libraries are dispersed and for the most part destroyed. Thanks to old catalogues, we know that in the tenth century the Cambrai library contained some sixty-odd volumes (each incorporating several works); by the eleventh century this number had increased to more than one hundred. These were predominantly legal works, collections of canon law compiled in Carolingian times—quite in keeping with Gerard's taste for order, direction, and action. But also represented were Gregory the Great's commentary on Ezekiel, and eight manuscripts of Saint Augustine.[1] The holdings of the Laon library were five times as large:[2] three hundred volumes in the tenth century (at the end of the thirteenth, after prodigious developments in education and publishing, the cathedral chapter of Paris could boast only half as many); a great number of training manuals—among them, Martianus Capella's commentary and a course in liberal arts taught in the ninth century by Martin Scot; all the necessary equipment was here, including what was needed for dialectical labors: there were several copies of Boethius' *De consolatione*. Also represented were works that audaciously explored the mysteries: the manuscripts of John Scotus Erigena, still in Laon today, quite near the spot where Adalbero worked with them. All this constituted a great treasure to adorn the soul, much as the vestments stored in the same chamber were brought forth to adorn the prelates' bodies on the great festival occasions. A treasure inherited from the past: when Gerard took up his post in Cambrai, nine tenths of the library's extant books were already present. In fact, it was during Hincmar's youth that this storehouse of wisdom was stocked, in the halcyon days of the "Carolingian Renaissance," when the literary culture of antiquity was rescued from irreparable loss. Countless words were horded here. Some, like those of the Gospels, were simple, sprouting everywhere, spreading far and wide like a fine seed, while others were weighty with multiple meanings—and instruction was based on the principle of digging into those meanings by way of analogy and metaphor, allowing different interpretations to collide and resonate. In the memories of these experts, words were of course continually shuttling between one discursive formation and another; when such transfers took place, certain words could be seen to shine with an unaccustomed brilliance, dispelling nearby shadows.

Amidst this plenty, Gerard compiled his "clear documentary proof,"[3] pertaining not merely to social trifunctionality but to other matters as well. No utterance of his was not substantially contained in what he had inherited from others. It never occurred to Gerard, nor any more to Adalbero, to hide this fact. On the contrary, both prelates took great pains to see to it that their sources would be recognized. They sought the backing of tradition. We shall therefore be doing no more than what was expected of us if we try now, as others tried a thousand years before us, to make out the sources of their words, moving against time's current down which flowed to King Robert's episcopal advisers the various principles they thought it worthwhile to articulate anew. Establishing the system's genealogy will aid in understanding its structure, and the place within it assigned to the trifunctional figure.[4]

5

HIERARCHY

We are aided in our purpose by Gerard and Adalbero themselves, who name the three "authors," the three pillars: Gregory, Augustine, Dionysius the Areopagite.

In fact, as we have seen, in the earliest, most straightforward enunciation of the system, the Arras speech of 1025, were two citations from Gregory the Great, flanked by two further phrases, one from Saint Paul ("For there is no power but of God"), the other from Saint Peter ("Submit yourselves . . . to the king as supreme, or unto governors, as unto them that are sent by him"). Here is the real bedrock on which the system rests. Ancient objects here found new uses, like the antique columns incorporated in the second abbey church at Cluny or in the baptistry at Aix-en-Provence, like the cameos mounted by the goldsmiths of Conques—and these venerable vestiges of a bygone time, of the golden age, imposed their style on the new creation that claimed to master them but in fact remained wholly in their thrall. Thus the phrases collected by the bishops formed a counterpoint to a doctrine, to the words of a bishop, a "defender of the city," who—in late sixth-century Rome, when everything seemed on the verge of collapse—threw himself body and soul into the task of shoring up the one remaining wall of the edifice, the Church—i.e., an order, a discipline, a hierarchy. His first concern was with the *rectores,* leaders in the ecclesiastical organization, who held places in the great domains and cities. Being a pope who favored austerity, Gregory treated their status simply, without much ado.

The first text incorporated by Gerard into his argument comes from a list of adminsitrative instructions. Addressed to other bishops, these instructions were intended to strengthen the chain of command by inserting an additional link to insure that orders would be transmitted more efficiently. For functions to be carried out (*administratio officiorum*), according to this document, an "order of difference" was required, the order that held sway in the army, as well as in the Benedictine monastery that Gregory had installed in his residence—a monastery that was a strictly regulated community, a copy of a military organization, based on hierarchy and obedience. The other citation is taken from the *Regula Pastoralis,* a treatise on "the art of being a bishop."[1] But, as Gregory himself says, it actually comes from a previous work, the *Moralia in Job.*[2] Adalbero, for his part, refers back to the original source, recommending that King Robert look in the *Moralia* as well as the commentary on Ezekiel.

Now, Gregory the Great's meditation on the Book of Job is concerned not with administration but with morality, a morality suited to the austere circumstances of a monastic brotherhood under the authority of a common father, the abbot. Hence it, too, is concerned with a hierarchical order based on a series of ranks, but in this case a different series, a timeless one: the "order of merits," an essential order. Underlying the principle of authority, this order upheld and justified it. One part of society was worthy to rule over the remainder. Because they were morally of lesser value, "those behind" were subordinated to "those in front" (*prelati*) "who speak" (*predicatores*), "who govern" (*rectores*), who are "powerful" (*potentes*). The latter might well be "poor," empty-handed, objects of derision: in an Italy overrun by barbarism, Gregory daily saw men who had been toppled from their positions and treated ill but who had the qualities of leadership. For one reason: these men were less tainted than others by sin. All hierarchy originated in the unequal distribution of good and evil, of flesh and spirit, of the heavenly and the terrestrial. As men were by nature differently inclined to sin, it was proper for the least culpable to assume responsibility, with care, affection, and firmness, for leadership of the flock. Some years after Gregory, this idea was more bluntly expressed by another bishop, Isidore of Seville. Neither Gerard nor Adalbero made reference to him. It is nonetheless worthwhile to recall his words because they shed a revealing light on what Gregory the Great had in mind and on what the defenders of the royal order borrowed from him in 1025: "Although remission of the original sin is granted to all the faithful by the grace of baptism, the just God has instituted discrimination in human life, making some slaves, others masters, so that the freedom of slaves to do wrong may be checked by the power of those who dominate. For if all were without fear, how could evil be prohibited?"[3] According to this, not merely inequality was necessary, but also repression. No longer are we shown exchange of reverence and brotherly love. Instead we find "slaves," who are afraid, and "masters," whose yoke weighs upon the necks of other men. Membership in one class or the other is dependent upon God's arbitrary choice. Gregory's words are at once less blunt and less frank. When, in the *Moralia,* he contemplates the unequal inroads made by evil, however, he concurs with Isidore, saying that sin is

67

not what in the last analysis leads to subjugation, but is rather a *dispensatio occulta,* a "mysterious distribution."[4] Predestination determines the earthly distribution of coercive power. This links directly with the second author cited, Saint Augustine.

Also a bishop, Augustine had earlier—at a time when Rome's grandeur was still in evidence—spoken of authority and of necessary submission: "For in the Church this *ordo* is established: some precede, others follow . . . , and those who follow imitate the leaders. But those who set the example for those who follow, do they not follow anyone? If they do not, they will go astray. Hence they, too, follow someone, Christ himself."[5] The image is a potent one. It was the model for all medieval processions, for all the ambulatory rites, corteges, and parades that represented a disciplined organization of progress. Bear in mind that these were always led by an invisible chief, Jesus, who invariably marched at the head of the column. In the procession imagined by Saint Augustine, the priests obviously followed just after Christ, ranked according to their dignity. Leading the entire troop were the bishops. Christ immediately preceded them: they strove to imitate him in every detail. By virtue of this proximity to Christ, they ranked first in goodness, they were the most virtuous, and consequently the most powerful. For the system of obligations—obligation to imitate, obligation to guide—that regulated the progress of the procession reflected the hierarchy of merits. And since the issue was one of value, of relative proportion of good and evil, an order of this kind was of course inviolable. To have broken ranks would have been sacrilegious. It was incumbent on every man to keep his place.

"But every man in his own order: Christ the first fruits, afterward they that are Christ's at his coming": from Saint Augustine the thread can be traced back to the apostle Paul,[6] on whose words Tertullian provides the first commentary in a treatise *On the Resurrection of the Flesh:*[7] "the *ordo* spoken of by Paul is that of merits." Indeed, when we follow the echoes of the formulas that have answered one another across the ages and seek in Christianity's earliest writings for the roots of this vision, we find that it embraces all mankind's wanderings from history's dawn to its final day: out of the void every man emerged in his proper place, and in that place every man will rise from his tomb to face the Judge. The image we thus uncover is one based on the major teachings upon which Latin Christendom has never ceased to meditate, on the New Testament, on Augustine, on Gregory. It is the concept of an obedient formation, the image of a phalanx subjecting the subordinate to the discipline of their superiors, the idea of the necessity of closed ranks, of punishment for failure to execute orders. All of this Christendom took for its own, an adoption facilitated by the fact that in the sixth century the first Benedictine monks, convinced that everything was headed for wrack and ruin, that the world was in the final stages of decay, had taken over, the better to withstand the corrosive forces, the organizational structures of the Roman legions. It was natural that Adalbero and Gerard should refer to this idea, to this image, to this concept: they, too, were witnessing the disintegration of the world. It was this that had made them raise their voices in protest. They knew that some centuries prior to their own time order in Gaul had become shaky; that the Carolingians, with the advice of the bishops, had succeeded in reestablishing it; that the latter had depicted the people of God to the sovereign as a military troop, marching in rank, in step; and that their counsel to the king had borrowed the words of Saint Paul, Saint Augustine, and Saint Gregory. As bishop Jonas of Orleans put it: "it is necessary that everyone strive in his own order."[8] Charlemagne had laid it down as law: "Every man shall keep to his own life's purpose and his own profession, *unanimously.*"[9]

6

CONCORD

Unanimiter. The word mitigated, camouflaged the terror in that implacable ordinance. To make discipline bearable, and inequality tolerable, it was prudent to accredit the notion that in Christian society—much as between parents and children, old and young, or as in any community, in monastery and palace alike, in villages as among soldiers—hearts were bound by ties of affection. *Concordia.* A single heart. Hence a single body, whose several parts worked together in cooperation. The metaphor is from Saint Paul (Romans 12:4). We do not find Carolingian writers adopting it readily, perhaps because the repugnance they felt at the sight of the corporeal was too great. Boniface alludes to it only once in a sermon on the orders: "In our body, there is only one soul which is the seat of life; but many parts whose functions differ; in the same way, in the Church there is one faith which ought to work by charity everywhere, but different dignities each having its own function."[1] Here the bond is spiritual. A symbolic equivalent is provided by the warm spirit stemming from the heart: charity, *dilectio.* A century later Walafrid Strabo ventured to speak more plainly: the "house of God," i.e., the Church, the community of the faithful, "is built in unity by the love and charity of each order; in this way the unity of Christ's body is constituted; each member has a function whose fruit is shared by all in common."[2]

Actually, the metaphor shifts from corporeal to domestic and back again. This seems natural enough. Was not the primary cell in this society the *domus,* the *mesnie?* Within this household, it was mutual love, an affectionate interchange, that created cohesiveness, tempered the rigors of duty, made it easier both to obey and to command, and made discipline an act of communion. Charity established harmony in the household, brought it into tune, as it were, in the sense of creating a perfect order out of disparity.

70

Charity brought peace. *Una domus, unum corpus.* The unity of human society (for the reestablishment of which Adalbero's poem is an appeal) was held to derive, as did the health of the body and the prosperity of the household, from reciprocal giving. From the reign of Charles the Bald on, it appears, men in northern France who reflected on social questions tended to allow the image of the family, in which God figured as the father, or, rather, the *senior,* to overlay the processional and military image. It is quite likely that this tendency grew more pronounced during the tenth century, when dynastic structures were being strengthened in the nobility, and the king's army was disintegrating into mutually hostile groups. Familiarity with relations between kin and between young men and old was complemented by analogous experience with vassalage: this also was a bond of the heart joining two persons—or rather a group of warriors and its captain—and sealed by mutual interchange. A few years prior to the Douai speech and to the writing of the *Carmen,* another bishop, Fulbert of Chartres, also a rhetorician and a pupil of the Rheims school, analyzed the content of the vassalic relationship at the behest of the duke of Aquitaine in yet another work composed in accordance with Ciceronian rules of rhetoric.[3] The man who by doing homage became the "young man" (*vassalus*) of a *senior* was in a position similar to that of a son with respect to his father: he had to "serve"; but in return he received payment: his reverence was met with charity, "kindness" was returned for "service." In everything both men were obliged to give equally.[4] *Mutuo in vicem reddere.* Reciprocity was the norm, but within a hierarchical organization. Indeed, the strongest bonds were not between equals. Disparity of rank invigorated the emotional commerce. Difference provoked interchange: the former sustained, stimulated, and quickened the pace of the latter by the complementarity of services rendered. The lord was a sort of father, usually the wiser and wealthier of the two men; and the vassal a sort of son, usually the more vigorous; hence it was normal that the former receive military help, assistance with the second function, from the latter, in compensation for what he provided himself: food, peace, and fiefs, in general seeing to it that the spirited cohort consisting of his men was provided for and kept harmonious.

If, in reconstructing the ideological system, Adalbero and Gerard chose to emphasize the role of reciprocity, was this not because besides being bishops they were also "lords," judges, providers, surrounded by knights who did them homage? Were they not impelled by forces which ever since their childhood had been slowly transforming the highest nobility from which they sprang into a motley assortment of families, companies of vassals, "houses," to conceive of political relations as family relations? We should not be surprised, then, to find that when the words of Augustine and Gregory are revived in 1025, the image of mutual aid, reflecting the essential exchange of benevolence and allegiance between father and sons, between elder and younger brother, between lord and men, between master and servants, is projected onto the Augustinian vision of a procession marching towards salvation, and onto the Gregorian concept of a "concord" or "weave" (*contexture*) unnaturally draped over relations of subjection. The noble household was indeed the abode of disparity, precedence, hierarchy, and diverse offices that were of necessity mutually coordinated. In the ninth century, Dhuoda, that matron-lady of the highest aristocracy, advised her son that when he had reached the age of maturity, he ought to "organize his household on the basis of legitimate ranks for the profit of all,"[5] thereby maintaining a beneficial equilibrium among the various departments, as in the palace of the king. When well-tended, the seigniorial household, united by mutual affection, exemplified the proper order.

7

ORDERS

"Every man in his own order": the word *ordo,* when it was used in the Latin translation of Paul's Epistles, had two meanings. In the Roman Republic, the *ordo* divided adult males into distinct groups to enable them to carry out their roles more effectively:[1] at first to fight (the *ordo* was a close-order troop of infantrymen deployed in battle); and later to administer public affairs (the *ordo* was "a group consisting of men officially inscribed on a list drawn up by certain magistrates"). Originally, then, ordination was an inscription. This legal and public act, this rite—one of the meanings attributed to the word *ordo* by the medieval Church—conferred a status on the individual, not necessarily related to his fortune or his birth. Ordination both brought men together and sorted them out at the same time. *Ordo* therefore came to denote a privileged body, isolated from the remainder of society, invested with particular responsibilities, whose cohesiveness, superiority, and dignity were plainly visible in the rank accorded to it in religious, military, or civic processions.[2] This was the first meaning. The second was abstract. *Ordo* referred to the just and proper organization of the universe, which it was the task of morality, virtue, and power to maintain. Accordingly, Cicero, in his treatise *De Officiis,*[3] spoke of the "order of things"; for him, the "preservation of order"—*modestia*—was the art "of locating in its proper place what one does or says." Rhetoric, politics: to place words—or men—in appropriate *position* relative to one another, and to arrange the *com-position* of the parts in an appropriate whole—which was predetermined: for in ordination of this kind, a prior, immanent, immutable plan existed, and it was advisable to discover this plan by reflection before proceeding, so that it might be followed closely.

In this form the word found its way into the writings of the Latin Fathers, and particularly into the thought of the two masters to whom Adalbero and

73

Gerard looked as their principal sources of inspiration, Gregory and Augustine. The latter writer elaborated on the abstract sense of the word throughout his work, from the *De ordine* ("order is that by which God calls into being all that exists") to the *City of God,* in which order was understood, on the one hand, to mean peace ("a state of peace, the tranquillity of order"[4]), and on the other hand, the path that leads towards God (virtue is referred to as *ordo amoris,* love in accordance with order). From the Augustinian conception derives the entire socio-political ethic of the Carolingian bishops, the notion of an order that "wisdom" can perceive, establishing just relations of authority and submission among men. According to Jonas of Orleans, for instance, "leaders must not believe that their subordinates are inferior to them by the nature of their being; they are inferior by virtue of order" (the opposition *ordo/natura,* as we know, was a fundamental part of Adalbero's system). Order is thus the sacralized basis of oppression.

As for the concrete sense, Tertullian had earlier had occasion to use it, in his statement that the "authority of the Church has instituted the difference between the plebs and the order":[5] like the magistrates of Rome, the Church distinguished a privileged body, the clergy, from the crowd, by means of ordination. This was the only "order"—and so it remained for Adalbero. But since order in the abstract was an arrangement of diversity, *ordo* in its concrete sense was very quickly pluralized, being used to designate each of the several levels of a hierarchy. For men whose practical concern was the correct organization of the Church—this was, of course, the case with Gregory the Great—*ordo* came to be synonymous with *gradus.* The shepherds of the faithful flock believed that there were *several* orders among men—and not merely in the ecclesiastical institution. They deemed it appropriate to order laymen according to dignities and ranks, for merit raised some people above others, gave them precedence in processions, and after the clergy enabled them to set a good example for the rest: these superior beings constituted "orders"—Tertullian, for instance, regarded widows and the monogamous in this way.[6]

Hence for the Carolingian moralists the order of the *ecclesia,* of the Christian community, that army on the march or halted just prior to battle, whose enemy was evil, was seen as the result of combining many different orders. This was stated in no uncertain terms, before Hincmar, before Leo III, before Alcuin, who was inspired by him, and two and a half centuries before Gerard and Adalbero, by Boniface, Anglo-Saxon and Benedictine, hence Gregory the Great's spiritual son on two counts, in the sermon I cited earlier: "In the Church there is one faith which must be set to work everywhere, but several dignities, each having its own function: there is an *order* of commanders and an *order* of subjects, an *order* of the wealthy and an *order* of the poor, an *order* of the old and an *order* of the young [order,

74

intervening to modify nature, thus introduces three factors that influence preeminence, one deriving from power, another from wealth, a third from age], each with its own path to follow, as in the body each part has its own function." Boniface elaborates this argument, but only as concerns one of these orders, that of the leaders. This was the order to which his audience belonged; his task was to describe its organization, in which several functions were combined: "the bishops' duty is to proscribe what is evil, to bring strength to those who weaken, to grant remission to those who wander from the straight and narrow; after this comes the mission of the king, who must be feared among peoples for 'there is no power but of God'; similarly, the powerful and the judges, who are delegated by the king, must be loyal, humble, generous; they must render judgment equitably, and not according to the gifts they receive; must protect widows, orphans, the poor; must serve the bishops, do violence to no one, shun unjust wealth, and give to the needy rather than take from others."

Different orders. The word *ordo* referred not only to each of them individually but also expressed that exercise of authority responsible for distinguishing them from one another and for insuring their general coordination. Hierarchically arranged within each order were various offices or tasks. Already we glimpse a ternarity taking shape. But within the only *ordo* of importance, the one that exercised leadership, there was to be no confusion between bishops and temporal princes, the latter of necessity being subjects of the former; on the dividing line stood the king. Boniface does not say explicitly that he, too, was obliged to show the bishops obedience; he does, however, make so bold as to state unambiguously that the king followed "next" after his episcopal predecessors. Already we see the king flanked by the *oratores* on one side, the *bellatores* on the other. There is a clear line of descent linking the notions advanced in about 750 by this disciple of Gregory the Great, who reformed the Frankish church on a Benedictine and pontifical model, and those later put forward by Gerard and Adalbero. The latter two bishops were more discreet, however, in their use of the term *ordo*. They applied it only to what was sacred in the social order, to the servants of God and to kings, but never to those responsible for the carnal functions in the overall order of things. By way of compensation, they stressed the distribution of offices, and showed no reluctance to speak openly of three functions.

75

8

FUNCTIONS:
TO PRAY AND TO FIGHT

They spoke of three functions, rather than two as their predecessors had done. If Boniface, for instance, used ternarity to describe the foundations on which inequality was based, he nevertheless shared with Gregory the Great a view which looked upon mankind as constituted of two echelons. Those who gave orders were distinguished from those who carried them out; those in the forefront of the column (*pre-positi*), condescended to cherish those who followed along behind or, rather, beneath them (*sub-diti*), who were inspired with a reverence that could readily turn to terror. Anyone whose naive gaze fell upon the spectacle of society discovered its predominant characteristic to be a series of binary oppositions. What did they see? Slaves and masters, old and young, elder and younger brothers, to say nothing of the natural subjection of woman to her "master," man, a subordination deemed so natural that no discussion of inequality bothered to mention it.

During the Carolingian era, one of these dichotomies had attracted the attention of men of high culture who inquired into the order of things—whose direct heirs Adalbero and Gerard were (just as M. de Torquat is, less consciously, Loyseau's heir: these phenomena of filiation and continuity should be borne in mind, as they play a crucial role in the slow evolution of ideological formations, but the various strands are not easily unraveled). Adalbero and Gerard were men of the Church. For them, Christian society was divided in two: "the order" and "the plebs," in Tertullian's phrase; one part, the clergy, was ordained; the other, the people, was not. Instated by divine law and reflecting the deep-seated order that separated heaven from earth and spirit from body, this fundamental structure was in turn split as though by a prism on order of the "prelates," the "rectors," the rulers, who prescribed that the lords spiritual, the bishops, and the lords temporal, who in Boniface's words "came next," be singled out, distinguished from the rest. Ultimately, then, two binary modes of classification were combined, one of them giving precedence to the possessors of power over other men, the other giving precedence to clergy over populace. Two degrees, two functions. At the top of the scale, however, the second distinction disappeared: on high, in the form that heaven took in Gerard of Cambrai's contemplation, Christ, still subject to his father in virtue of the kinship structure, assumed the office of both priest and king.

The separation of the two functions, that of the priest and that of the king, underlay every conception of the socio-political order of which any trace remains, and which, after adoption by the Carolingian prelates, came to obsess Gerard and Adalbero. Historians concerned with these questions today refer to this separation as "Gelasian." Indeed, Pope Gelasius (492–96) had expounded the notion in the presence of the emperor Anastasius: "that which principally governs the world is twofold, the sacred authority of the pontiffs and the royal power."[1] Two "persons," two roles; two fields of action; two orders that were to be distinguished by "modesty"—as Gelasius put it, borrowing from Cicero: *modestia utriusque ordinis.* Two offices, independent though bound by solid ties: emperors had need of bishops for their everlasting salvation; bishops expected emperors to insure peace on earth. They were not equals, however: the words chosen to designate the two powers, *auctoritas* and *potestas,* indicated the hierarchy; it was connected with that orientation of the universe which placed heaven above and earth below, thus establishing the precedence of the priesthood. Thus among the rulers a breach appeared. Since, however, both "authority" and "power" could be delegated, this breach extended throughout the whole of society: nonslave, free adult male citizens thus fell into one of two distinct groups, according as they wielded arms or not: some citizens fought; others, unarmed, participated in other ways in the maintenance of the divine order.

Once everything nonservile in the Roman world had been militarized by the migrations of peoples, the frontier between the two functions came to seem so necessary and at the same time so fragile that when, in the mid-eighth century, the foundations of the Carolingian state were being laid, learned men attempted to fortify it with words. Boniface had the council which in 742 was working to reform the Frankish Church adopt a prohibition "on servants of God in general and for whatever purpose to bear arms, or to fight, or to go in the army and *ost.*"[2] From this date we begin to see the first signs of the shift that led to replacement of the antinomic terms *auctoritas/potestas* and *clerus/populus* by another pair, when speaking of the rulers of society: *oratores, bellatores.* The two words were to be found as correlatives in Cicero.[3] We know what usage Adalbero and Gerard were destined to make of them. As early as 747 we find, if not the two nouns themselves, then at least the corresponding verbs at the heart of Pope

Zachary's political address to Pepin the Short, the counterpart of the one made earlier by Gelasius to the emperor:[4] "to the princes, to the men of the world, and to the warriors [bellatores] falls the task of guarding against the enemy's cunning and of defending the country; to bishops, priests, and servants of God it is given to act by offering salutary counsel and prayer—so that thanks to God, with our praying [orantibus] and their fighting [bellantibus], the country may remain safe."[5] These words were to endure. Charlemagne himself did more than lend his ears to them in the presence of Pope Leo III; he uttered them personally. On that occasion the king's purpose was to reserve the right to conduct earthly affairs to himself alone, and confine the Pope to prayer.

The formula expressed the Carolingian political ideal. That ideal was based on a monarchical principle. On earth—as in heaven—one reigned alone. He occupied the place of Christ, like Christ fulfilling both functions, one actor playing two roles, embodying two characters (personae). Of this the Frankish bishops reminded the emperor, Louis the Pious, in 829, referring explicitly to Pope Gelasius:[6] "The body of the Church is primarily divided between two eminent persons"—because the body of the king is itself so divided, and because this original duality flows through the entire body of the people of God. This was indeed the essential point: bifrons, the sovereign, the sacred ruler, the Lord's anointed, cast his gaze to right and left upon his subordinates, and it was this split vision, and the mandates issued to one side and the other, that determined the division of society, or at least the important portion thereof, the portion of mankind that was not enslaved. In ninth-century Francia the idea commanded respect. Listen to the words of Wala: "The status of the whole Church is undoubtedly administered by these two orders"[7] (828–29). Or listen once more to Walafrid Strabo, who spoke of "each of the orders" whose close-knit texture and mutual love created the unity of the "house of God."[8] Listen to Hincmar of Rheims, who began his description of the royal palace with this concept: two orders, two functions, two categories of services, two hosts. Admonishing the king in 833, as Adalbero would do two centuries after him, Agobard, the bishop of Lyons, whose words may have been the most accurate prefiguration of the Carmen, recommended that a watch be kept "against the troubles of the times, so as to maintain in readiness each of the orders, military as well as ecclesiastic, that is, those who serve in the worldly host and in the sacred ministry, some fighting with the sword, others disputing with the word."[9] Swords, words: weapons, speech. There we have it: "some fight, others pray."

This duality was plainly visible to anyone with eyes to see. In the order of ceremonies, for instance: when ninth-century kings were anointed at Rheims, the lay dignitaries were ranged on their left, the ecclesiastical dignitaries on their right—the better side: Christ sat enthroned at his Father's right hand.[10] Now, as it was the task of the *oratores* to instruct others, to point out to the *bellatores* where good and evil lay, to proscribe certain behavior and establish values on their behalf, they thus helped to clear the way for the coming of a new *ordo* destined to take its place alongside the *ordo* of widows and monogamists, and alongside that of clerks: the order of warriors. The model figure for this social-ethical category was of course the king. For though the king, *principaliter,* fulfilled both functions, he was set apart from the clergy by one of his roles, or persons, by his bellicose character, by the high spirits of his "youth" and the weight of the flesh, which left him with an insurmountable penchant to favor his left side, a predilection for the earth and for war. The sovereign commanded the other cohort, the temporal: this fact was indicated by painters depicting the *ecclesia,* so long as tradition continued to dictate that it be represented by human figures, with their device of ranging some men behind the emperor, others behind the pope.[11] And when Sedulius Scotus created the symbolic effigy of the king in his *Treatise on Rulers,* he showed him peacefully installed in the great hall of the palace, as though he were one of the sublimest beauties of the visible world, comparable with the sun and the sea, solitary, enthroned, immobile, receiving gifts and distributing lavish boons; his duties were justice and generosity. But if he was generous, if he was just, if peace radiated from him, this was because previously he had fought valiantly. His "principal" duty was to wage war, "more necessary to men than repose: peace lulls, war quickens virtue." Zachary assigned this capital mission to the man he held to be the true king of the Franks. In the ninth century it was attributed to all "nobles" by the mirrors of princes.

Attributed, in other words, to men who, though not of the Church, were nevertheless destined to lead others. The two functions were functions of command. Carolingian high culture looked upon the field of power as divided into two distinct zones. Still, there were parts of space not covered by either one. As early as the end of the eighth century, Alcuin made it quite plain—for his learned friends, it went without saying—that not all laymen were warriors, in urging moral reform upon the clergy of Kent so that "the laymen who are your warriors become strong for you, and the people thus embark upon the path of salvation."[12] The clerks, the warriors, the people. Only the *rectores* were divided by the functional dichotomy. The subjects were left over. Implicit in the dualist Gelasian schema was the tripartite notion, that "division among three species" that Loyseau would much later still deem the most perfect. Are all games not three-way, since "every social interaction is by essence triangular and not linear"? Even in a duel there are spectators, and "the role of the onlookers can change from one moment to the next into an active role [this actually occurred at Douai in 1024–25, when Gerard and the count of Flanders debated before a large assembly, and each addressed the "people," trying to entice them to his side], and amongst the countless linked triads that go to make up a society, the active couples and dominant coalitions are constantly shifting."[13] Manipulation of the concept inherited from ninth-century political ethics gave rise to a three-way division of the social sphere: first, there were those in possession of "authority," responsible for waging spiritual warfare; second, possessors of "power," responsible for waging temporal warfare; and third, all those who did not carry the sword, the emblem of power, and yet did not pray, whose only right was to keep silent, and whose only duty was to obey, passive and abject: the "serfs" or "slaves"—*servi*. Was Adalbero saying anything different?

9

TERNARITY

No, Adalbero was saying the same thing. But he explicitly stated that the division was ternary. A tripartition—and not the one in common use by reflective men in the Latin Church ever since late antiquity.

To such men the idea of dividing the faithful of the *ecclesia* into three groups was indeed a familiar one. But they carried out this division not on the basis of actions performed, roles played, offices assumed, or services mutually rendered, but rather on the basis of merit. They used a ternary model to order the procession toward salvation, under the guidance of the best, the purest, the most angel-like of men, who naturally marched at the head of the line. Now this order was radically different from the political order set forth in the Gelasian formula: the criterion involved was not the use made of arms, but the use made of sex. In consequence, this representation differed from the other in that it included women as well as men. A fundamental difference. This did not, however, prevent the two modes of classification from mingling and interfering with each other in the memories of the thinkers and in the treatises they were composing. Over the course of many generations, this interplay gradually but irresistibly drew this morally based, explicitly ternary classification toward the realm of the masculine, the social, and the functional. There can be no doubt that the positing of social trifunctionality in the early eleventh century was facilitated by the fact that this other tripartite figure had long been present, had advanced through the ages, and had at certain stages in its transmission accommodated modifications in the notion of a ternary hierarchy of merits.

At the outset once again we find Gregory the Great and Saint Augustine. They were preceded, however, by Saint Jerome, who—in his treatise *Adversus Jovinianum,* a eulogy of chastity and reproof of marriage—distinguished among three degrees of sexual purity: that of virgins, that of the continent, that of the married couple.[1] Augustine and Gregory enlarged on this theme. Thus Saint Augustine, meditating on the "three just men" of the Old Testament, Noah, Daniel, and Job—who are held up as exemplary by Ezekiel 14:14—classified the members of the Christian community according to three "types": the leaders—whose preeminence was due to their purity; the continent; and faithful couples joined in matrimony.[2] Gregory the Great followed him, making the same point in the *Moralia* I:14.[3] But rather than "types" he speaks of "orders," and, more important, he goes into greater detail. This further detail is crucial. It marks the beginning of the alteration of the model. Who were the leaders? The bishops. The continent? The monks. As for the last group, the "good" married couples—with the implication that bad ones exist—their role was to work in the world. Returning to this idea in a homily,[4] Gregory attempted on the basis of this outline to give shape to the very forms into which, five centuries later, Gerard of Cambrai and Adalbero of Laon would insert the trifunctional figure. He in fact lay stress on two points—hierarchy and unanimity: "Though the excellence of preachers far surpasses that of those who observe continence and silence [Gregory, who was familiar with the subject, looked upon the monks as men who lived in silence: they were not *oratores*], and though the eminence of the continent distinguishes them from married persons, . . . the measure of all three is one, for if there is great diversity in their merits, yet there is no distance in the faith in which they travel."

As early as the dawn of the Carolingian Renaissance this tripartition was taken over by learned men among the Franks. It proved its utility straightway. With its help it proved possible to make room in Frankish society for that utterly distinct, coherent, independent body, that true *ordo*, straitened by a purpose, a rule, a discipline: Benedictine monasticism. It had been born amidst the temptation to seek refuge in continence and silence that had seized the West in the time of Gregory the Great; in Britain it had struck deeper roots than elsewhere; and from Britain, of course, men like Alcuin and Boniface had come in the eighth century to work for the reform of the Frankish Church, to lift it out of its uncultured mire. No doubt given clear formulation during the course of that very effort of reform, amidst the reverberant words of Jerome, Augustine, and Gregory the Great, was the following idea: within the ecclesiastical institution, i.e., the higher of the two orders discussed by Gelasius, a careful distinction should be made between two styles of life, two manners of service. As early as 751, the reform council of Ver had laid it down in its eleventh canon that "some were in the monasteries, in the regular order, others, under the bishop's control, in the order of canons." Two orders. And already no doubt the dream existed, though still inarticulate, of recognizing the rest of mankind, i.e., the laity, those whose blood was spilled in battle, whose brows were damp with the sweat of servile labor, who slept with women and fathered children—the dream of

82

making Jobs of them, "good spouses," of bringing them together within an order.

To that end, two generations later, at the height of the cultural "renaissance," the bishops set about composing "mirrors," treatises on the good life addressed to laymen, expounding their duties, their specific tasks in life. In a poem on hypocrites the bishop Theodulf of Orléans maintained that there were two orders, the clerical and the monastic, in addition to the "plebeian populace"; but these were really three orders, as he recognized, united by a single faith. Jonas of Orléans, moreover, (already) attributed the judicial function to the *ordo laicorum*. Thus the persistent efforts of the Frankish prelates supported by Louis the Pious and Charles the Bald, those rash attempts to pluck society from the savage depths in which it lived, to regiment men to keep them upright, fitted naturally into a tripartite framework. And when tribulations again beset the western world, overrun in the tenth century by violence and rapacity, when righteous monasteries once more seemed the storm-battered isles, the citadels of perfection withstanding evil's onslaughts that they had been two centuries earlier, the ternary, hierarchized configuration of the moral order came more forcefully than ever to the fore. As the year 1000 drew near, that configuration sustained hopes for reformation of every kind. When Burchard, bishop of Worms, attempted to convince his best canons, beset by "contempt for the world," to remain in the clergy, he referred to the three degrees of merit.[5] To appreciate how powerful a hold was exerted in the time of the *Gesta episcoporun cameracensium* and the *Carmen* by this manner of classification—not according to function (prayer, work, combat) but rather according to orders (monks, clerks, laymen)—we would be well advised, I think, to turn our attention now to the words of two men who had just finished speaking when Adalbero and Gerard began: a clerk, Dudo of Saint-Quentin, and a monk, Abbo of Fleury.

DUDO OF SAINT-QUENTIN

Between 1015 and 1026, Dudo wrote his book *On the Customs and Acts of the First Dukes of Normandy*.[6] This was the first rhetorical composition in northern France to recount the history not of the royal house but rather of a princely dynasty. What is generally referred to as feudalism was also the fragmentation of monarchy, which not only brought about the establishment of an independent power in each province, but also in the wake of more profound shifts stripped the sovereign of his monopoly of certain virtues, duties, and cultural attributes, and bestowed them upon local rulers who were not sacred.[7] Dudo was a canon;[8] he hailed from Vermandois, an old Frankish region; his culture came to him from the school at Rheims, a culture founded on the books in the libraries at Laon and Cambrai. His place might have been at court, where his knowledge would have served the king of France, and where he would have sung in the king's chapel and worked for the king's glory; instead he came to Rouen to serve the "duke of the pirates." Even as Robert the Pious was succumbing to his exhausting efforts to restore peace through assemblies such as the one at Compiègne, and Gerard was making arrangements for the writing of the *Gesta* and Adalbero pondered his poem, Dudo was busy writing the book ordered by Richard I, count of the Normans. In the prince's shadow he went about his business, gathering information from relatives, taking meals in the house of his brother, the archbishop, and at length presenting his work to the heir of the princely dignity, Richard II, whose chaplain and notary he had meanwhile become. It was dedicated, however, to Adalbero of Laon. That this homage was no doubt imitative[9] only adds to its significance: the author—and his patron—in this way evinced their concern to tap the roots of high episcopal culture, the culture of *Francia*. With the beginning of the eleventh century the long process of restoring power in the regions the Normans had settled after having laid them waste was coming to an end. To cap this restoration it remained to install a clergy at the summit of an administrative framework whose key element had hitherto been the monasteries. Duke Richard had set himself the task of reviving the Norman cathedrals; for this he stood in need of good assistants and had done his best to recruit them; and so Dudo had been called. Just as the independence of the dynasty of Norman counts was being asserted by its assumption of the ducal title in Neustria,[10] this canon, this expert in princely panegyric was put in charge of the project of erecting a prestigious monument to its glory. Was it accidental that he chose as a model for the prelates of Normandy the bishop Adalbero, the "master" who had aided kings to govern wisely with his rhetorical arts; was it accidental that he began with praise of that rhetorician an account that glorified his patrons by describing their efforts to found a civilization?

This was indeed the idea of the *De moribus,* a work in four parts, each devoted to one of four successive rulers. Hasting, the most distant ancestor, was still a savage through and through; Rollo had taken the first step with baptism; William Longsword, the third ruler in the dynasty, used monks in beginning the restoration of order; in 942, he had some very fine ones brought from Poitou; everywhere he established monasteries and enriched them by his gifts; by these means Christianity and peace were gradually restored in the province, while the duke himself, another William of Orange, made ready to turn his back on the world, to end his days under the cowl. His son Richard carried on in the world and in the fullness of his reign achieved perfection: Dudo goes so far as to draw a parallel between his hero's qualities and the eight beatitudes. What our clerk meant to say was that the Norman chiefs had emerged from the depths of barbarism and had by degrees risen to Christian culture and to the divine grace conveyed therein. At first they had relied on the monks, and later had concluded their civilizing works with the help of the secular church. At the time of Dudo's writing, this was where matters stood: the character of the book describing this evolution and the condition of its author attest to the fact.

In describing the monastic phase in this development, Dudo refers to the traditional model of the three "orders," the three degrees of merit. Duke William is shown arriving for consultations with a sage[11]—which at the time Dudo was writing was just what was being done by another duke, William of Aquitaine, who called upon bishop Fulbert of Chartres to discuss the obligations of vassals. But in mid-tenth-century Normandy it would have been pointless to have looked for a bishop with the qualities necessary to counsel the prince. Hence William's questions are answered by an abbot, Martin of Jumièges. As interlocutor to the man of war, who brandished the sword, whose power was that of brute force, whose wish was to use that power as he ought, but who was unsure where the good lay, Martin's role was that of mentor—the same role Alcuin had played with Charlemagne in that far-off age before the country of the Franks had emerged from this primitive phase, during which models for restoring the state had to be sought in the monasteries. The duke was worried: "The Church is organized in tripartite order [*tripertito ordine*]; men are distinguished by different functions [*dispares . . . officiis*]. Is it possible that there is the same reward for all?" The question concerned salvation: how could one secure an advantageous position in the hereafter? Bear in mind that when Dudo was writing, Christendom was all astir with millenarianism; the end of time, the great judgment were expected. Note, too, that William, though not sacred and in contrast to kings not in possession of the keys of mystical knowledge, was aware of the original tripartition; neither the notion of function nor that of *ordo* was unknown to him; illiterate, he was nonetheless familiar with the views of Augustine and Gregory the Great. Martin answered that "each will be rewarded according to his labor." The judgment is clear: what counted was *labor,* pains taken (Adalbero, as we have seen, hesitated between *labor* and *dolor*). The Christian worked for God, in the sweat of his brow, and retribution would be earned by the ardor with which he did his job.

A good teacher, the abbot of Jumièges gave a brief explanation of what he meant. There is, he went on, no doubt an order, which is tertiary (in this treatise, as in the *Carmen, ordo* is used in the singular, in its abstract sense of ordering); laymen, canons, and monks, working together, bring Christ's *religio* under the plow (the agricultural metaphor is worthy of note); this is to be done in keeping with the following article of faith: "trinity in the persons; one God in substance." Three personages, three roles, a single *substantia:* this passage of the *De moribus* seems to be the only place in the writing of this period where the unity of the three parts of the social body is explicitly related to the mystery of the Trinity—Adalbero's poem did so only by allusion, through terminological harmonies and overtones. Martin next establishes the effect of this oneness: all who render the service required of them will make their way towards heaven at the same rate. Here we see Dudo putting into the mouth of the abbot of Jumièges words used by Gregory the Great in his *Homilies* on Ezekiel. Even though there are three orders (here, *ordo,* used in the plural and in the concrete sense, denotes the three categories of the moral hierarchy), there are two paths. To designate them, Martin—i.e., Dudo, who had perhaps read the books used by John the Scot in the library at Laon—speaks Greek: the first path, the "practical," is of action on the world; it is called canonical, for authority (*ditio*) is given to the canons (Dudo was not a bishop, nor even a simple priest, and the men we see exalted here were of his own condition, his confrères; at the same time the Gelasian theme, the idea that the order of laymen is subordinate to that of clerks, emerges). The other path, the "theoretical," is the more arduous of the two, for it does not belong to this world: it is the path followed by monks.

This discussion of the social order, which an accomplished rhetorician has chosen to include in the portion of his treatise intended to celebrate the monastic condition, is worthy of attention. It sheds light on the open breach that separated the world from those who turned their backs on it, who cut themselves loose from it. On this point, Dudo shows himself faithful to the legacy of Gregory the Great: the breach he discusses is not social, but moral; it relates to life's purposes, to "justices," to self-imposed ways of being, to a choice between Martha and Mary, between the active life and the contemplative. Social questions, questions of functions and offices, had a place only in the realm of the "practical," which was part of the earth, of flesh. In that sphere the division was binary, Gelasian: the *clerus* and the *populus,* the order of canons and that of laymen. Now, this was the domain whose mission it was the count's to administer, responsible as he was for keeping the peace, by means of law and war. Such was his proper function: "defender of the fatherland," he was charged with the role that Pope Zachary, in his letter to Pepin, had assigned to the secular powers. As it happened, William was tempted by the theoretical path. Indeed, this fact accounts for his question: he wished to go beyond what was easy, to pass through the narrow gate; he had been made count in spite of himself; not he, but his father and the great men of the country had wished it. Martin is categorical: he shall keep to his place, where God has put him, in his rank, in his order.

Thus the work Dudo dedicated to Adalbero set forth a ternary system of social classification. But not a trifunctional system. It is clear how the slightly later discussions of Adalbero himself and Gerard of Cambrai would at once continue the *De moribus* and diverge from it. Indeed, in the eulogy of the first Norman princes we find an early statement of the concept of a substantial solidarity uniting disparate elements, and a twin dichotomy which gives rise to a triple division. We also see a comfortable accommodation struck between the binary notions of Pope Gelasius and the ternary of Saint Jerome, Saint Augustine, and Saint Gregory. Nevertheless, Dudo considered only two functions. He looked upon social space as the Carolingian bishops had done: all laymen, including the duke, were morally subordinated to the *ordo canonicus,* to that episcopal clergy that Richard of Normandy had just restored, under whose auspices the canon of Saint-Quentin spoke, wrote, taught, and pursued his career with great success.

ABBO OF FLEURY

Some thirty years earlier, Abbo of Fleury had played in reality the role that Dudo's imagination attributed to Martin of Jumièges. Like Martin, Abbo was a monk, and he, too, expounded the three degrees of perfection to a prince. This particular prince happened to be the king himself, or rather the two associated kings: Hugh Capet, and by this date, Robert, his son.

Born in about 940, Abbo was some twenty years older than Adalbero; like Adalbero he had studied at Rheims, a little Greek, the arts of the *quadrivium* (he wrote a treatise on calculation), and above all rhetoric. Then he entered the great abbey of Fleury-sur-Loire. Two successive events had increased the prestige of this Merovingian institution: first, the acquisition of the relics of Saint Benedict, stolen from the abbey of Monte Cassino—and the venerated saint, father of all the monks in the West, had immediately spread miracles far and wide in Frankish territory; then the accession to the throne of the dukes of France, ancestors of Hugh Capet, whose principal seat was Orléans, near Fleury. In the tenth century, Fleury—also known as Saint-Benoît—was deemed the major repository of Benedictine tradition in the West: the bishops of England went looking there for artisans to undertake the reform of their monasteries. It was also a center of learning of the first importance, where, in addition to novices, a good many secular pupils were trained. Abbo soon took charge of this school. He left for a time to teach at Ramsey, the English monastery that had been renovated by the monks of Fleury. After his return, he devoted tireless efforts to the improvement of Fleury's literary workshop. After the anointment of 987, he dreamed of making the house of which he was now the abbot the great royal monastery, and himself supplanting the abbot of Saint-Denis. Like Alcuin before him, he wanted to offer guidance to the king, and to comment for him on the mysteries.

This ambition obviously brought him into conflict with the bishops of the kingdom of France, and primarily with the bishop of Orléans, who claimed control over all the monasteries in his diocese, including Saint-Benoît-sur-Loire. This conflict had reached an acute stage as early as 991, when Abbo collected legal documents to be shown to the two kings.[12] The canons collected therein were used to lend weight to a sermon on politics, whose purpose was to define the royal office and to delineate its role in the government of the Church—a tract that was, in short, a "mirror of the king." In it we find the idea that the sovereign alone cannot meet the needs of the country; that he requires the assistance of the prelates and the "foremost men of the kingdom." Thus Abbo, like Gelasius and Zachary, is here discussing two orders of service, the order of *oratores* and the order of *bellatores*. Temporal princes should, he adds, seek assistance and advice with utmost "reverence," as their "honor" obliges them. The word "reverence" is taken from Gregory the Great: it implies that the order of lay leaders (and not the clerical leadership) is subordinate to the sovereign. What we are witnessing here, then, is a resurgence of a model of state organization, just prior to the year 1000, that stands in a direct line of descent from Carolingian principles, principles affirmed by the council of Paris in 829 and set forth in the treatise *On the Royal Institution* by Jonas of Orléans. This model placed the king at the head of the "nobles," but under the spiritual guidance of the princes of the Church—among whom Abbo quite plainly imagined himself in the forefront. Now, the dispute between him and the bishops of *Francia* was growing increasingly venomous—coming to blows, in fact, in 993, when monks and clerks fought at Saint-Denis; the abbot of Fleury defended himself by writing the *Apologetic against Arnulf, Bishop of Orléans, to Hugh and Robert, Kings of France.* As the title indicates, this was a plea to the sovereign, sitting in majesty, in his character as judge.[13] In the midst of his harangue, the orator evokes the schema of the three orders. It formed a main pillar of his argument.

With this short, vigorous, biting treatise, to which Jean Batany has provided a highly pertinent commentary,[14] Abbo launched his counter-attack. He was accused of heresy; he turned the accusation back against his enemy. He claimed to be battling against heresy—and, even at that early date, in 993, thirty years before the heretical outbreak at Arras, against the worrisome agitation in the air, against the rising fever of the times. The great danger. Abbo's strategy could not have been simpler, consisting merely in casting as an enemy anyone who spoke against him at the royal court. In his attacks he pointed out the path of righteousness and sought, as Adalbero's poem would do after him, to incite the rulers of the people to action, and to castigate the subversives, those who in various ways were upsetting the order of things, rending the seamless fabric of society.

Who were they? The *Apologeticus* names names. It points an accusatory finger at three errors. The least of them was millenarianism. This is discussed only at the end of the work.[15] Recalling from his youth the memory of a Parisian priest who in the seventh decade of the tenth century announced that the world would end in the year 1000, Abbo maintained that it was impossible for anyone to know either the day or the hour. Thus in its small way his pamphlet was written in praise, as it were, of hope, or rather of the permanent and confident expectancy of the Second Coming, that "adventism" which served to justify monasticism along with the various purificatory practices of which the monastery was the locus. The second error lay in confusing the two orders of service, lay and ecclesiastical, in confounding the two Gelasian functions. It was urgent that an end be put to this confusion, to which some had surrendered themselves in practice. It was urgent that servants of God be forbidden to act in ways unworthy of their estate. Abbo plainly had military activities in mind: some clerks were known to carry weapons; he may also have been thinking of manual labor, which some in the Church, in advance of the heretics of Arras, sanctioned as an act of humility and an instrument of salvation; and finally, Abbo was surely preoccupied with the workings of the flesh, copulation: there were married clerks; they ought not to be part of the clergy.[16] The worst of the errors was the third: the claim that the bishops had power over the monks. Even if a monk became a priest, it was heresy to believe that he was obliged to "serve" as a clerk did. Here we come to the heart of the polemic. The purpose of the treatise was to assert the independence of the monasteries.

At this key point in his argument, the abbot of Fleury introduces a description of the well-ordered Christian society. Mankind, he says, is composed of orders which are also degrees. Identifying order and rank, he placed the accent on hierarchy within the tripartite schema. For there were, of course, three parts to the division. "We know that in the holy and universal Church there are three orders, three ranks, for the faithful of both sexes." Abbo has shrewdly combined two tripartitions. Indeed, he distributes men and women along the degrees of Jerome's scale of moral values: virgins, abstainers, couples—the first outranking the second, and the second the third, by virtue of being less tainted by the sexual act. Given the circumstances in which mankind then found itself, watchful for premonitory signs of the end of the world—the *Apologeticus* explicitly takes note of such concern—this order was of prime importance. Was Christ not about to return, perhaps the very next day, to judge living and dead alike, to sort them out according to just such a pattern? According to the degree of purity in the flesh, the depth of pollution due to that capital sin which obsessed the monks of Fleury as it did all monks? At the same time, men—and only men—were subject to another classification. They were ordered in accordance with their mode of action in public life.

The key move is Abbo's way of superimposing the two schemes. In his own words, "*similarly,* for men [*viri*] there are three ranks or orders, of which the first is of laymen, the second of clerks, the third of monks." The distinction was the same as that which Dudo of Saint-Quentin would some years later put into the mouth of Martin of Jumièges, between the theoretical path and the practical path, with both clergy and laity following the latter, each in its own manner. But in the *Apologetic* we find a bold insistence upon the superiority of the monks, whose eminence is held to exempt them from all episcopal control. On this crucial point Abbo is firm: "the first is good, the second better, the third best." [17] The hierarchy of practical functions subjects adult males to a second hierarchy in addition to that of merits, by which monks are placed above all other men. This claim results from the amalgamation of a moral with a social tripartition, from a shrewd confusion of the ethical with the political. Abbo continues: "The order of clerks stands between laymen and monks: just as much as it is superior to the inferior, by so much is it inferior to the superior." [18] This amounted to a contradiction before the fact of what Dudo would later say: that the three orders advanced toward heaven at one pace. It contradicted Burchard of Worms, in whose judgment one could work toward salvation in the clergy or in the lay estate as well as in a monastery. To perch the monks above the clergy was to invert the schema of Gregory the Great. It was a veritable revolution, which repudiated the whole prior tradition, and in particular the Carolingian theories on the distribution of powers.

Abbo was a wrecker, but even more he was an innovator, and on a crucial point. After the brief discussion of order—of the moral order, it may be said—and before treating the relationships and differences between monks and clerks in detail, the abbot of Fleury slipped in a sentence concerning the order of laymen. "Of the first order of men, that is, laymen, it must be said that some are farmers [*agricolae*], others are fighters [*agonistae*]; the farmers, in the sweat of their brow, work the fields and in other ways labor in the countryside so that the multitudes of the *ecclesia* may eat; as for the fighters, who should content themselves with their military pay, let them not make war within their mother's bosom, and turn their efforts rather to extirpating the enemies of the holy Church of God." With this turn Abbo's argument leads directly to trifunctionality in the form in which it was set forth thirty years later by Adalbero and Gerard. Like the treatises of those two bishops, Abbo's parenthetical remark is concerned not with "rank" or "order" but rather with a distinction of offices, and hence duties. Among men normally married and allowed to indulge in the sexual act, whose progress toward perfection is consequently slowed, a split is instigated by the two activities of work and armed combat—forbidden, as we know, to the men of the two other orders. On one side of the breach are farmers, as in Gerard's view of things, who toil, as in Adalbero's, and whose function is to produce food for the entire society, as both Adalbero and Gerard thought. On the other side are the "heroes."

Like Gerard and Adalbero, Abbo does not use the word *miles*. He may have chosen the rare word *agonista* for the sake of his prose rhythm, or because it was more felicitously consonant with *agricolae*. It should be noted, however, that Saint Augustine had applied it to the soldiers of Christ.

Carl Erdmann[19] deemed this passage a foreshadowing, as it were, of the notion of crusade. Indeed, Abbo does sanctify the warrior function, the *militia* (which term belonged to the vocabulary that would be taken up by chivalry), insofar as he defines it, far more clearly that Adalbero and Gerard, as having an external goal. *Expugnare* (but even as early as Pope Zachary, the role of the prince was to resist the incursions of Christ's "external" enemies). He sanctifies it also insofar as he uses the words of the Gospel to assign two clear and precise duties to the men who perform this function— something he does not do in dealing with the peasantry. First, they were to content themselves with the soldier's pay. Clearly, this meant that they were to refrain from pillage and rapine—did Abbo have in mind the collection of seigniorial taxes, exactions by which the newly secured peace was paid for? It was in the time of the *Apologeticus* that these taxes began to weigh upon the peasantry, and on the inhabitants of episcopal and monastic domains in particular, thereby moving the Church to come to the defense of the "poor." Second, it was their duty not to maul one another, to renounce intestine warfare. Precisely these two precepts would later be promulgated by the peace of God. Already they were being solemnly proclaimed by the first peace councils assembled in southern Gaul around reliquaries and in the midst of prostrate multitudes. The formulation of the concept of military function given by Abbo of Fleury foreshadows not that of Adalbero and Gerard but rather that of their adversaries, Garin of Beauvais, Beraud of Soissons, and other proponents of the new rules of peace.

This helps to make clear how two deviations from orthodoxy were intimately connected from the beginning. One of these was the heterodox view that was to meet with Adalbero's denunciation: this was reflected in the monks' efforts to twist Gelasius' binary model to their own advantage, to set themselves up at the pinnacle of the hierarchy, in another city, as it were, in the dominant position and ostensibly free of the tutelage of either bishop or king. The other deviation was the one that Gerard was to denounce: the political organization being put together in the assemblies of the peace of God. Beneath all of this, though, we discern a steady accentuation of the distinction between the prince's military companions, the horsemen, and the peasants, a rift deepened by the emergence of this political organization, and at the same time by the implementation of the new form of worker exploitation, the banal seigniory. Still, the fact that in Abbo's mind various modes of classification overlapped did not lead to his formulating a tripartite model. The game involved not three players, but four.

It is nonetheless clear that thirty years before the *Song for King Robert* and the *Deeds of the Bishops of Cambrai* the groundwork for the emergence of the trifunctional figure was laid by the way in which the abbot of Fleury combined the various classificatory schemes in the interest of his monastery, and by the way the traditional ternarity of orders of merit was refracted onto another ternarity based on action. Is it correct to think that Gerard and Adalbero were content merely to take Abbo's schema and eliminate one of the four parties by relegating monks to the clerical order, i.e., under their own, the bishops', control? Were matters that simple? One thing is certain: already in the decade preceding the year 1000 there was a feeling in northern France that the political order was disintegrating. What were the movements that presaged the outbreak of heresy in the third decade of the eleventh century if not, among other things, symptoms of such a dissolution? The metaphors that Church intellectuals in this region had been using for generations in their imaginings of social order, in representing God's will as to the distribution of power among men, and in composing the moralizing sermons intended for the ears of the sovereign, had already ceased to be fully satisfactory. They felt these metaphors needed not to be discarded but rather brought back into line with reality, prudently, by means of judicious taps. Believing themselves appointed to guide the powerful of this world, if not to wield power directly, the "prelates" manipulated the old formulas so as to restore their usefulness for justifying the ways in which authority was exercised, which were undergoing imperceptible change. This sort of repair work cleared the way for the use of the trifunctional postulate, a form which may perhaps have been a prevalent obsession of the common mentality but which continued to be excluded from scholarly musings on society. Other shifts, long since underway in the rhetoric of power, also prepared the way for the implementation of this commonplace.

The Powerful and the Poor

When the historian Nithard spoke in the mid-ninth century of Saxon society, he said it was divided into "three orders," the "nobles," the "free men," and the "slaves."[20] This tripartition owed nothing to patristic tradition. It was profane, purely juridical. It of course concerned not three functions, but three statuses: this was a curious particularity of an exotic legal system that Nithard wished to make known to cultivated men in the Carolingian palace. Note, though, that this skillful writer, less inflenced than the bishops of his time by sacred authors and particularly concerned to see that the language used at court was transposed into good Latin, denoted by the word *ordo* each one of the three hierarchically arranged categories that Saxon judges and military chiefs used for classifying adult males. Observe also that the social attributes, *nobilis* and *servus*, were the same as the ones later used by Adalbero, and were situated at either extremity of the hierarchical scale—but was there not already a tendency for social evolution to close the gap between the two by compressing the intervening level? Yet I do not believe that this fleeting allusion should distract us. More worthy of notice are the expressions and images used by the "orators" in discussing not society but the monarch.

Indeed, these orators show a penchant for distinguishing among three kinds of virtues in the man chosen by God to keep good order in the visible world. As has been mentioned, the natural application of the tripartition brought to light by Georges Dumézil was in the praise of heroes and princes. Hence it is not surprising that we find in moralizing panegyrics to the Frankish kings certain early indications of the trifunctional schema's latent presence. In the ninth and tenth centuries, moreover, reflective men were convinced that there was an organic relationship, analogous to the relationship between body and soul, or head and limbs, between the person, or rather the standing, of the sovereign and the whole of the community which it was his mission to protect and to guide towards salvation. As Alcuin[21] put it, "the goodness of the king makes for the prosperity of all the people, for the victory of the armies, and for the health of the plebs." Conversely, if it happened that the prince was corrupt, in his body through illness, or in his soul through sin, everyone was persuaded that the whole state would in that case go awry. This led to the position that only a healthy, judicious, and—insofar as a king could be—pure man could validly occupy the throne. If the king contracted leprosy, or even the grippe, if he had two wives at once or committed a passing act of adultery, rot at once gained a foothold in the kingdom and began its undoing. In such a case it might be best to kill the prince. In any event, the inevitable consequence of this belief was that the monarchical ethic was projected first onto the royal "house," or, as Hincmar put it, onto the "order of the palace," and then, beyond that, onto the whole of society. If this led to the formulation of a clear conception of this morality in terms of functions, and these were three in number, then there was every likelihood that trifunctionality would promptly acquire a social aspect.

In the minds of the intellectuals who reflected on the practical use of royal power at the height of the Carolingian Renaissance, this natural coherence between the sovereign and the vast family of which he was the putative father and whose health and virtue he thereby insured came to be more conscious. To them it seemed that if the king was to exercise his magistracy, supervise the successful fulfillment of the various social functions, and play his own role, the epitome of all the others, then he stood in need of his people, much as God stood in need of the king. The relationship was the same, necessary and hierarchical. Organic, consonant with the order that governed the visible and invisible universe, the association of the people and the king was necessary if the state was to stand. This idea was expressed by the sovereign himself in 823–25 in the preamble to an *Admonition to All the Orders of the Realm*.[22] Louis the Pious assumed the pose of an orator, appropriate to his sacred status, and like a bishop resorted to oratory to proclaim the stability of the *ordo*. He began by stating that it was incumbent upon him to assure "the defense, exaltation, and honor" of the holy Church of God and of those who served it, and to secure "peace and justice in the generality of his people." This "office" (*ministerium*) was in its "totality" (*summa*) assumed by the king. However, the "people"—meaning all free men—participated in it. "Divine authority and the ordering of men distribute this office among them in the following manner: . . . let it be known to all," said the emperor to his subjects, "that each of you has a share in our office in the place and in the order that he occupies [*unusquisque . . . in suo ordine,* in which we see logical use being made of the words of Scripture, from the Epistle of Saint Paul, describing the providential organization of a procession in which mankind follows Christ toward eternal life and light]. My duty is to be your guide; yours is to be our aides." *Admonitor:* the king gave guidance. Indead, he was doing just that in uttering this admonition within his palace walls in the hope that its echoes would reverberate even to the borders of the territory that he ruled, i.e., to the ends of the civilized world. *Adjutores:* the subject's duty was to assist, with mind and hand. But every man was to lend his assistance in accordance with the function assigned him by the social order. For while all the functions were reduced to one in the ministry of the sovereign, the one God's one lieutenant on earth, they were parceled out in separate lots among the remainder of mankind. The logic of the moral argument bids one look upon this distribution as being similar to that of the several virtues which the king, the guide, was called upon to exemplify. And these no doubt already tended to be classified into three categories.

Inherent in the structures of the royal ethic, tripartition was accentuated in the sermons of the moralists, who exhorted the sovereign to show particular charity to certain of his subjects, namely, the weakest of them. Subjects were divided into two groups by the principle of inequality first formulated by Gregory the Great, and later by Boniface: the rulers and the ruled. The other principle, the Gelasian, distinguished between two subgroups within the former, depending on whether a man was "militant" in the service of God or in the world, whether he had been delegated spiritual "authority" or temporal "power." Invested with a portion of the royal *potestas,* the lay rulers, the *potentes,* the "powerful," played an indispensable role. It was thanks to them that the king could exercise his brute force. As a result, there was a risk that these auxiliaries would become dangerous, that they would use that force and that brutality abusively. For they had not been anointed. They lacked the "wisdom" that would have been capable of mitigating their violence. The constant threat was that they would be carried away and use the power with which they were invested for doing ill. For this reason, the rhetors, the men who pieced together the Carolingian code of ethics, kept an eye on these natural agents of disorder. The "mirrors of princes," the "institutes of the laity" that were written especially for them attempted to inculcate the notion that by "nature" all men are equal, and that they, being as formidable as their master the king, ought to show themselves as just and temperate. Above all, the moralists made it the sovereign's major obligation to keep this group under strict surveillance. Indeed, the primary aim of the royal precepts recorded in the capitularies was to hold the powerful in check and to protect the meek from their inevitable oppression.

Among the meek some were particularly vulnerable. The king was urged to defend them as he defended the clergy. The Bible, whose words saturated the memories of the prelates of the day, clearly indicated which laymen merited special royal protection: in the first place, widows and orphans— the segment of the populace temporarily deprived of the protection of a head of family; and second, the "poor." Clergy, potentates, paupers: tripartition. As early as the beginning of the seventh century, Isidore of Seville, in a three-volume treatise on civic morality, had chosen first to lay out the duties of bishops, then those of princes, and finally to treat the "oppressors of the poor"—not addressing the poor directly, as he had addressed the others, but rather speaking to their superiors, the poor being regarded neither as active participants nor as having any particular obligations, but rather as passive, as perfect victims, which made it advisable to throw over them a protective mantle of interdictions. Thus with the intersection of two dividing lines, one separating the clergy from the people, the other the strong from the weak, a tripartite schema had long since been taking shape, a schema which in a very clear way foreshadows the one that Adalbero and Gerard would incorporate into their system. There were three categories, two of which were dominant, bishops and princes: *oratores, bellatores.* Under them, the poor. The *oratores* kept an eye out to see that the powerful were effectively controlled by the king. There was general awareness that this control was beginning to slacken in the French kingdom as early as the mid-ninth century, especially at Rheims, where around Hincmar, the archbishop, political thought was probing more deeply than it had earlier. By this time the *oratores* from the height of their magistracy could distinguish only a dialectical opposition, expressed in the Latin of the Vulgate by two antagonistic terms: *potentes/pauperes.*

The poor? In the social vocabulary, the meaning of the word was not economic. Nor was it legal: at issue here were not the slaves, the *servi,* who were not part of the "people," who fell outside the sphere of royal action, belonging as they did within a different order, a domestic, private order, and falling like women under the jurisdiction of another power, another morality. The poor were adult males of free condition who could not defend themselves. As a group, the poor were the unarmed portion of the "people."

Inerme vulgus. This expression is to be found in texts that Gerard and Adalbero might have read or heard read. To track down these texts is to blaze a new trail, to survey a new foundation for the edifice incorporating the first known formulations of social trifunctionality. The expression appears as early as 826 in the poem dedicated to Louis the Pious by Ermold the Black. This Aquitainian clerk naturally referred to the traditional schema, familiar to all churchmen: there were the clergy, the people, and the order of monks;[23] more perspicaciously, however, he contrasted the "fighters," the "heroes," the *agonistae* (as we have seen, this word recurs a century and a half later under the pen of Abbo of Fleury) with the "unarmed people."[24] Ermold was aware that the deepest breach among laymen belonging to political society was determined by the criterion of bearing arms, by having weapons or not having them. Indeed, this was the primary distinction in this period of European history. Whether the question was one of wealth, power, or legal status, every value system tended to refer to the military. This reference came to stand out with greater clarity at the turn of the tenth century, when that semblance of order and peace whose establishment had exhausted the Carolingian sovereigns collapsed, and as the pace of evolution in techniques of warfare accelerated in the face of new waves of invasions. At stake was the survival of the Christian people. Henceforth it was to depend on the castle and the cavalry, those two pillars of the structures that we call feudal.

This is the point at which we find two allusions to the *imbelles* among the few extant texts. The first is in the *Miracles of Saint Bertin*[25] in a passage devoted to the celebration of a victory won by the residents of Saint-Omer over the vikings in May 891. Boldly venturing beyond the walls, the warriors repulsed the attack. They brought back a booty which was divided into three parts: the participants in the battle shared one of them according as they were "more noble" or "more humble," i.e., depending upon the quality of their equipment: already the horsemen were set apart from the others; the second portion was heaped around sanctuary altars; the third went to men of prayer and to the poor. This was an unusual distribution: the fruits of battle were not customarily turned over to those who had not taken part in the fighting. To justify such an apportionment, the author's idea was to show that in reality the war was a holy one, waged jointly by the whole Christian community. Some of its members had used weapons in playing their role in the action, namely, the warriors, or *bellatores*. It should be noted that here this term was not applied merely to the princes, the custodians of lay power; its meaning had broadened; vulgarized, it came to include everyone who faced the enemy, even the lowliest, who had set out on foot armed with a club or a sling; similarly, the "orators" included all members of the clergy. But for our purposes the essential point is the introduction of a third actor, the *imbelle vulgus* "that wailed to heaven its lament." And not without effect. For when it is asked which "order" was responsible for the success, the answer is that quite plainly "in this uneasy battle, the men of prayer and the unarmed, importuning the ears of God

96

with continual and obstinate prayer, impelled him to grant his clemency." As the battle reached its height, the victory came from God. His hand was forced by the warriors' strong arms and the priests' tenacious supplications. As a rule this was the way things worked. This was what took place at Bouvines. But here at Saint-Omer in the late ninth century a third "order" (the text of the *Miracles* attests to the appearance of a radically new view of the social organization) intervened: not the order of monks, but the order of the poor, an order of layman unable to participate in battle, associated with the specialists in prayer, and just as useful in securing victory as they or the military, hence entitled to a portion of the spoils thereof.

Notice is again taken of the unarmed segment of the "people" in a work more recent by several years, the *Life of Gerald,* written about 920 by Odo, the abbot of Cluny. The subject of this biography was a figure from whose tomb in the monastery of Aurillac many miracles emanated, though he was neither a monk nor a bishop nor a king. From this sepulchre, as from the reliquaries of the greatest saints, a remarkable power flowed forth. This offered proof that a layman could remain within his "order" and yet achieve spiritual perfection. In point of fact, Gerald, like his contemporary, Duke William of Normandy, whose history Dudo invented, had wanted to enter the monastery; but out of respect for the divine purpose which had invested him with a temporal power, he had resisted this temptation and kept to his appointed office, just as Duke William had done. It is noteworthy that for this he here receives the praise of a monk, rather than a canon such as Dudo was. Of course the abbot Odo was a long way from equating the condition of the layman with that of the monk. His whole life and all his works attest to the fact. For him, to enter into the monastery was to undergo a new baptism;[26] the perfection of monks rivalled that of angels.[27] And yet—and this was what accounted both for the grandeur of the text and for its novelty (so disturbing that Gerald's biography was soon revised, and every trace of the praise it had bestowed on essentially lay virtues removed)—neither vestments nor obedience was sufficient to set apart the true servants of God, who were distinguished by the dispositions of their hearts. Hence it was as eminently praiseworthy to pursue the purpose of "religion," i.e., to renounce the world,[28] in secular habit,[29] as it was ignominious to remain attached to the world in monastic habit.

Cluny's longterm effort to monasticize the laity from within, which would lead a hundred years later to its denunciation by Adalbero, quietly got under way at this date. To monasticize, at any rate, that portion of the laity worthy of, capable of, achieving sanctity thanks to the original *virtus* they possessed—meaning the well-born, the gentlemen of good stock: the nobility. Indeed, Gerald's biography may be viewed as a manual of correct conduct aimed at the powerful. Odo does not demand of them a renunciation equal to that of the monk. But he does ask them to shun three occasions of sin: lovemaking (Gerald renounces marriage), money-handling (Gerald gives his deniers away to the poor, generously redistributing the guilty profits of seigniorial exploitation), and arms-wielding, which for Odo is essential. For though he is obsessed by the dangers of lasciviousness and greed, he seems still more to abhor violence, because it engenders pride. Having come to central France from Neustria in the early tenth century, he had come upon the first signs of the breakdown of order that would result in the world's gradually being delivered into the hands of unfettered men of war. In his mind, what would become the moral code of the peace of God took shape. Repeatedly, Odo says that he has chosen voluntarily to lay down the sword placed in his hands by birth. He extols *patientia,* nonviolence, which he says he would like to see at the summit of the Benedictine hierarchy of virtues, in place of humility. Like Saint Augustine, he contrasts the Cains, the proud, the rich, with the multitudes of Abels who succumb to their torments.[30] In his eyes the horsemen are predatory wolves, and on occasion the invisible powers miraculously unhorse them and cast them to the ground before they can carry out their pillage. Unlike the author of the *Miracles of Saint Bertin,* he does not regard all warriors as being of a kind. Like the later institutions of the peace of God, he saves his utmost contempt and reprobation for the squadrons of horse, over which the prince exercised scant control; thanks to advances in weaponry and tactics, these were growing daily more dangerous and less vulnerable before his very eyes, and were beginning to make their own law. For him—as for Hincmar before him—the evil rested with the cavalry, the knights. And if his hero, Gerald, decides to remain in his order, it is to attempt to subdue the fury of these armored squadrons, which should also, he says, be the duty of kings. Gerald lets loose his war-cry and rallies his knights, but his purpose is to wage the good fight—not a war of aggression but one of defense (during which his horsemen do not even raise their swords but keep them pointed at the ground, in spite of which God gives them the victory). A war was just only if it was defensive. Who was to be protected? The "poor," the "unarmed people." "It is legitimate," proclaimed Odo of Cluny,[31] "for a layman in the order of warriors [*ordo pugnatorum*] to carry the sword to defend the people without arms."[31]

With these words the abbot Odo not only anticipated Gerard and Adalbero by a century but went much farther than they eventually would. For neither Abbo nor Gerard ever claimed that the men of war constituted an order. Odo did. He graced this functional social category with the title *ordo* because he was convinced that it must be forced to respect a particular moral code. He looked upon this code as not different from the royal one. Where royal action involved the wielding of weapons, the duties and interdictions to which the king was subject also applied to the *pugnatores.* Kings had long been exhorted to brandish the sword on behalf of the poor. With this concept of social ethics, an order of fighting men found a place established for it alongside the order of kings and that of orators. By contrast, however, it is clear (for proof one has only to read the remainder of the *Vita*) that all other laymen, all adult males of free condition who did not (and were not entitled to) bear arms were limited to a passive role, bleating lambs in need of protection from predators. They did not constitute an order—because they were not actors, but objects of solicitude. Because they had no specific duties. Because they fulfilled no function.

Now, seventy years later, Abbo, unlike the authors of the *Life of Gerald* and the *Miracles of Saint Bertin*, did not set the poor, the people without arms, the segment of the populace excluded from political activity, over against the warriors. He reserved this position instead for men charged with an office, a positive, arduous, gratifying office. Men whose function was to secure a supply of food by working the earth in the sweat of their brow—the peasants. Something had changed in the interim. It had become apparent that the estate of the poor could contribute to the social equilibrium, not merely as at Saint-Omer with the *basso continuo* its lamentations provided for the priestly chanting, but through palpable and productive activity. By the end of the tenth century, some were beginning to think that what defined the third category of adult males was no longer submissiveness or weakness, no longer a passive attitude or a negation, but rather a useful activity. When in his *Apologetic* Abbo of Fleury made this idea his own, it may have been new to northern France. But it had been set down in writing a century earlier on the other side of the Channel, in England. I have deliberately confined this study to a tiny province on the European continent. Nevertheless, the time has now come when we must take a glance at what was happening in England.

THE ENGLISH

We need first of all to examine the page of an Anglo-Saxon translation of Boethius' *On the Consolation of Philosophy* of which the king, Alfred the Great (871–899), claimed to be the author.[32]

Abutting Cornwall and Wales, the tiny kingdom of Wessex was then resisting as best it could the Danish incursion.[33] To that end its sovereign was attempting to stiffen its cultural backbone. He wanted his household stocked with books, but books that could be read, not books in Latin: books filled with words in daily use in the king's country. With a team of assistants, one of whose most active members was a monk who had come from Saint-Bertin,[34] he set to work on the translation of Bede's history of the nation, of a treatise *Against the Pagans* by Paulus Orosius—of a kind to fire a man's ardor to do battle with the vikings—and, finally, of the three principal "authors" of late antiquity, venerated by medieval Christian culture: Augustine, Gregory the Great, Boethius.

Book 2, chapter 17, of the *De consolatione* treats the question of the nature and value of temporal power.[35] Boethius imagines a dialogue with "reason." He has gotten as far as convincing his interlocutor that he is without ambition, that his only concern is to administer as well as possible the domain entrusted to him. He asks for the necessary tools and materials. At this particular point in the dialogue, the translators deemed it worthwhile to interpolate a brief commentary: no man, they say, can practice a craft or be crafty, nor can he govern a state, without tools and material to work with. Hence the king should "have a well-populated land; he must have men of prayer, men of war, men of labor [*sceol habban gebedmen and fyrdmen and weorcmen*]"—these are the tools *(tolan)*; as for material *(ondweorc)*, "he must have for these tools, for these three pillars of the community [*geferscipum biwiste*]" land, enough to secure an adequate supply of arms, food, clothing; "otherwise he cannot keep these tools, and without these tools, he cannot do any of the things he is responsible for doing." But to practice his craft, to govern his kingdom well, he needs one more thing, wisdom. Because, of course, matter must be dominated by spirit.

At the time that Alfred and his friends were writing the trifunctional theme into the margins of Boethius' text, God was subjecting Wessex to cruel tribulations. To extirpate this mortal danger, the sovereign had to call on all his powers. Both armed force and law would be needed. In his entourage a bitter meditation on sovereignty was being pursued—and numerous commentaries analogous to the one just cited were produced with regard to other texts, such as Gregory the Great's *Regula Pastoralis*. I think it worthy of note that as was to be the case again in France one hundred and twenty-five years later, reflective men should have employed an image of society in which the subjects of the realm were seen as performing three functions just when the throne seemed tottering on the verge of collapse, and that they should have done so in order to consolidate the monarchy's power. Nor is it less worthy of note that the theme entered written culture at a much earlier date in the Anglo-Saxon kingdom. In my view, this has to do with the fact that in England this form of culture was much less tightly bound within an ecclesiastical straitjacket. Britain could boast of a large group of men who, though not clergy, were nonetheless literate, and "wise" *(witan)*. Hence there was an independent, profane way of conceiving the world and translating it into speech, an independent manner of composing and interpreting vernacular treatises on the mechanisms of power and the relations between the sovereign and his people. In the state Alfred ruled, these relations were far more intimate than in the west Frankish kingdom, because Wessex was more primitive, less emancipated from the grip of tribal structures, and above all not so far-flung. Moreover, good political communications were maintained from one end of Wessex to the other by a coherent system of taxation and military requisitions and, even more important, by a system of interconnected assemblies in which free men met for discussion. So it is also quite remarkable that, in spite of all this, the interpolated paragraph in the translation of Boethius is not a concrete analysis of the social reality. It is an abstract thesis. A theory. Indeed, quite plainly, when King Alfred refers in succession to men of prayer, men of war, and men of labor, he is not enumerating distinct classes or clear categories into which free men were classified in accordance with their exclusive roles: historians have convinced us that most free men in England at the turn of the tenth century sometimes fought and sometimes did manual labor. The tripartite figure is a notion; it is revealed to us "in an intellectual climate of political theorizing."[36]

Yet this form did not emerge from the void, any more than those of Adalbero and Gerard did. Nothing was invented by Alfred and his assistants. They certainly heard echoes of ancient musings, those of the Carolingian bishops in particular. In this period the English Channel was less than ever an obstacle. Thousands of pilgrims crossed it to reach Rome by way of Boulogne, Cambrai, Laon, Rheims. As they traversed these less savage lands, they watched, they listened, they admired. And when they returned home, they told what they had seen. Taken by so many clerks, so many men of culture, who went forth into the world and returned home to tell of what lay beyond, this grand tour claims our attention. The upheaval that impelled men to travel must be borne in mind, lest we lose sight of the freight of theories and formulas they no doubt carried with them toward the rhetorical workshops in which the bishops of Laon and Cambrai mused on power in the early years of the eleventh century. Equally, though, since our interest now is to climb our way back up the genealogical tree, the spectacle of these countless travelers should remind us of the cargo that might earlier have been carried in the opposite direction, toward England. In the time of Alfred, who married his daughter to the count of Flanders and was surrounded by Flemish and Artesian monks, Anglo-Saxon chronicles were based on Frankish models. When, for instance, Asser wrote the king's biography, he showed him being educated in the way Charlemagne was said to have been. Discussions of the principles of good government in Alfred's court were certainly not less influenced by the moral literature composed two generations earlier for the edification of the sovereigns of *Francia*. The political theory elaborated in Wessex was based on the same maxims that would later inspire Adalbero and Gerard. Beyond a shadow of a doubt, indigenous forms of thought and expression profited from continental contributions during the period that preceded the *gesta* and the *Carmen* by a hundred and twenty-five years, when that vernacular sentence was being hammered out in which we find three linked nouns, denoting three distinct functions, carried out by men who together constituted the supports, the "pillars of the community," of the *respublica*, men the king used as tools for

101

action—but for action on earthly matters, in the domain of the temporal. Hence it is impossible to decide whether the tripartite figure was imported from the Empire, borrowed from some gloss on Boethius elaborated in the schools of Rheims or Compiègne and unknown to us, or alternatively whether it should be looked upon as one of the original forms of a conceptual system of the islands's own making, as a reflection glancing off "mirrors of the prince" fashioned in still Celtic Britain—since the Asser I mentioned was Welsh, and since Ireland, if not Wales (as Georges Dumézil has shown[37]) was wont to conceive of power in terms of triads. All that we can be certain of is this: in the course of the complex process of acculturation then under way in the tiny Anglo-Saxon kingdom, a schema probably familiar to the people of the British isles and very likely equally familiar in Rheims and Saint-Bertin, was used, precisely because of its simplicity and familiarity, to clarify the meaning of the passage from Boethius that Alfred was taxing his wits to translate and make available to those "sages," the literate laymen.

The important point is that on the English side of the Channel, the figure carved out a place for itself among the implements of learned thought. We find it being used by two Church writers, Aelfric and Wulfstan, a century after Alfred—i.e., at the time Abbo of Fleury was writing, Adalbero was holding forth in the Capetian assemblies, and Gerard was beginning his studies. This was also a time when bonds were growing tighter between highly cultivated men on either side of the Channel: the Benedictine monasteries in England's episcopal sees had recently been reformed by righteous monks called in from Flanders and the Loire valley, and by Abbo, who for a few years taught at Ramsey what he had learned—as Adalbero's predecessor—at Rheims; most English bishops, moreover, had been trained as monks.[38] And finally this was a time when people sensed that evil and disorder were on the rise in Anglo-Saxon and Frankish kingdoms alike, and anxious intellectuals were working desperately to locate the source of the troubles so that they could quell the disturbance and restore peace.

Social trifunctionality found expression in Aelfric's work on three occasions. Monk as well as priest, he took an active part in efforts for moral reform and cultural revival. He aspired to be another Alcuin. As an educator, in particular as an educator of sons of princes admitted into monasteries before learning Latin, he hoped through the children to reach their fathers, the rulers of states. Hence he worked on translations of the standard authors, compiled a glossary of three thousand words, and attempted to adapt Priscian's grammatical methods to the English language, for which he made use of the old translations done under the auspices of Alfred the Great.[39] The trifunctional theme thereby found its way into his work.

It made its first appearance in about 995—the time of the *Apologeticus*—in a brief explanatory dissertation appended to a sermon on the Maccabees.[40] The title—in Latin—raises a question: "*oratores, labora-*

tores, bellatores, who are they?" The answer—in Saxon: "in this world there are three *endebyrdnysse* [three social categories, three 'classes' in the translation of M. Dubois], *laboratores, oratores, bellatores* [once again in Latin]." Then comes the definition: "the *laboratores* are those who by their labor provide our means of subsistence, the *oratores,* those who intercede for us with God, the *bellatores,* those who protect our cities and defend our soil against the invading army. In truth, the peasant [here the Saxon word is used] must work to feed us, the soldier must do battle with our enemies, and the servant of God pray for us and do spiritual battle with the invisible enemies." This is followed by a comparison of the moral qualities, not of all three categories (nothing is said about the workers: they were included only for the sake of the form, or rather *by virtue of* the form, the habit of mind that naturally and unconsciously introduced the triad into the discussion), but merely of the warriors and men of prayer. This comparison established a hierarchy, identical with Abbo of Fleury's. The monks (for Aelfric the *oratores* were really the monks) waged their war against demons, so that theirs was a more valiant struggle than the warriors', who fought with earthly enemies that anyone could see. Hence "it would be truly cause for distress were monks to leave the service of the Lord for the battles of this world that in no way concern them." Aelfric is here using the commonplace notion of trifunctionality to resolve a real problem: the renewed Danish attacks had created a militant climate in which more than ever Anglo-Saxon churchmen were being pressed to take up arms and join in the resistance. With the inroads made by monastic reform, however, the indecency of their participation in battle had been made abundantly clear. Monks had withdrawn from the world; they ought not to spill blood. Among these young converts, however, there were no doubt many impetuous sons of military families, ardent for sacrifice. Groups of them ritually accompanied the companies of armed men to intone blessings prior to the attack and to beseech heaven for the victory; some surely would not long have resisted the temptation to pick up the sword or javelin fallen from the hands of a relative wounded or dead on the field of battle, to throw themselves into the breach. "Why would the monk who submits to the Benedictine rule and renounces the things of this world," Aelfric went on, "go back to earthly weapons, why would he abandon the battle against the invisible enemies, and why would he displease his creator? Not since the Savior's passion has any servant of God cared to besmirch his hands by participating in battle." A question of ecclesiastical discipline, of interpreting the rule of Saint Benedict. Not theories but quite practical matters were at issue here: in 1016 the abbot of Ramsey was killed in the battle of Ashingdon. Events of this kind explain the resurgence of the postulate, and make clear why men were impelled to say that society consisted of three categories that cooperated and exchanged services among themselves. Three rather than two.

103

Why three? The problems of the day made it imperative to emphasize just one cleavage, the one that fell between the churchmen and the rest. Another text written at the same time for the same reasons and concerned with the same questions did precisely that, adhering strictly to the Gelasian distinction: "there is division between the secular power and the spiritual power. It behooves righteous seculars to defend the Church and fight [*propugnatores*] for Christ's flock; it befits spirituals to be intercessors for all God's people. The soldier of Christ shall not use human weapons."[41] Thus Aelfric's position was singular. He spoke of a third function, of agriculture, of supplying food. This had been done before not only by Alfred the king, but also by Abbo. Was Abbo not his source? Interestingly, Aelfric used Latin to designate the occupants of these three offices: in the commentary on Boethius that originated in Alfred's court, he could have found three Saxon nouns. No less interesting, however, is the fact that of these three Latin nouns, one was not used by Abbo, Adalbero, or Gerard. Only Aelfric spoke of *laboratores*. Did he take his inspiration from an authority that Abbo himself discovered during his stay in Ramsey, which he then took back with him to Fleury as a souvenir of his journey?

In a letter (1003–5) to archbishop Wulfstan, Aelfric returned to the same subject. Again he considered the question of bearing arms, in this case not by monks but by clerks. The danger was graver, since the men who served God without having taken leave of this world marched off to slaughter Danes in defiance of synodal prohibitions with far greater alacrity than did the monks. As he was addressing a prelate, Aelfric used Latin. This induced him to add a considerable codicil to his remarks (and once again, he was the only man of his time to say what he did: Abbo did not apply the word *ordo* to the professional soldiers, much less to the peasants); in it, he maintained that there "exist three orders in the Church of God: the order of workers [or peasants] who produce food for us, that of warriors who defend our fatherland, that of *oratores*—these are the clerks, the monks, and the bishops [a new triad: clearly this is a habit of speech]—who pray for all." For the latter to wield the sword affronted decency. Unless they curbed their desire to brandish weapons, they should be labeled apostates.

Trifunctionality was mentioned a third time in Aelfric's work in 1005–6, and was couched in the Saxon tongue, since his interlocutor was a lay prince, the ealdorman Sigeweard.[42] Matters were going from bad to worse. Mankind had entered its sixth age, the age of turmoil. It was up to rulers like Sigeweard to restore justice, to set the world on its feet again. In the same key as Adalbero, Aelfric next evoked the task, the toil (*gewinne*—but the Saxon word's coloration is not at all pejorative) assigned to each man: "when there is too much wickedness in mankind, the counselors must through wise deliberation seek to know which of the legs [*stelenna*] of the throne [the royal seat: *cinestoles*] has been broken and repair it at once.

The throne rests on three legs [*stelum*], *laboratores, bellatores, oratores.*" Latin, once again. Once again three categories, but in a different position, located now relative not to the moral order but rather to the power of the king. Thus in a treatise whose deliberate intention was to stimulate a layman to think about politics, an image recurs identical with the one earlier proposed by King Alfred, namely, the image of a threefold support, a tripod. "*Laboratores:* they are the ones who secure for us the means of subsistence. Ploughmen and husbandmen [note that by *laboratores* Aelfric meant all the peasants, and not merely the leading ones, the ones who owned a team and a tilling implement] are devoted exclusively to that task. *Oratores:* they are the ones who intercede for us with God and who foster the Christian spirit in the Christian people, who serve God through spiritual labor, to which they devote themselves exclusively for the benefit of all. *Bellatores:* they are the ones who guard our strongholds and also our land, engaging in armed combat with any enemy who might invade it." Aelfric goes on with the words of Saint Paul: "The warrior does not carry the sword without reason; he is God's minister." Note that the verse Aelfric is paraphrasing is the same one invoked by Gerard of Cambrai to justify the repression carried out by those he refers to as *bellatores:* a similarity. But there is also a difference, a very interesting one: the Saxon word is *knight;* like Abbo, but unlike Gerard and Adalbero, Aelfric does not assign the warrior function to princes alone; he bestows it, if not on all soldiers, at least on any who are provided with an efficient harness, whose equipment is the equal of those men who on the continent were just then coming to be known as *chevaliers.* "On these three legs stands the throne. If one is broken, then immediately the other legs suffer injury." The source of the trouble lay in a confusion of offices. Some clerks were taking part in battle. Some horsemen were using their swords to strike *sine causa,* unjustly. Admonishing the leader of one of these armed bands, a delegated military representative of the royal power, Aelfric again employed the figure he had used twice before. But this time he refrained from giving any indications of hierarchy—the balance of the tripod clearly requiring the legs to be of similar size and equal strength—and deemed all three estates, including the *oratores,* subject to the king's authority, thereby restoring that figure to the form it had originally in Alfred's commentary.

Wulfstan conceived the ternary configuration in exactly this way. Unlike Aelfric, he was neither a monk nor an abbot. Like Adalbero and Gerard, he was a bishop, first of London (996–1002), then of Worcester (1002–16) and concurrently archbishop of York. Political leadership was his business. He had formalized the code of King Ethelred, and later that of King Cnut, applying his expertise as *orator* to the promulgation of *lex* by *rex.* His position was identical to that of the Carolingian bishops. The legislative structure that he was in the process of building up bore a fraternal resemblance to the legal code set forth in the capitularies of the Frankish monarchy at its height: one God, one faith, one king, guarantor of peace and justice, assisted by bishops and secular officers. Just a few years prior to the writing of the *Carmen* and the *Gesta* he expounded the theory underlying this practical program of government in a work copied in numerous manuscripts, entitled *Institutes of Polity Civil and Ecclesiastical* by its editor.[43] This was in fact a treatise on political morality, a reflection on the respective duties of the various groups within society and on the responsibilities borne by those whose task was to guide the people in the path of righteousness. Like Gerard and Adalbero, Wulfstan spoke with the intention of correcting those who strayed from the straight and narrow. His message was not addressed to the king alone. He spoke to the people in a language that they could understand. He did so, again like Adalbero and Gerard, no doubt primarily to exalt the episcopal function, to which he devotes four times as many words as to all the others combined. But obviously he dealt with the "royal throne":[44] "every legitimate royal throne," he says, "stands on three columns [*stapelum*—the metaphor is related to Aelfric's, yet more monumental], *oratores, laboratores, bellatores*."

The bishop thus also used Latin words to denote the three functional categories, given in the same order as in Gerard of Cambrai, but he immediately translated them into the vulgar tongue, repeating two of the three terms used earlier by Alfred, *gebedmen* and *weorcmen*. Like Aelfric, he maintained that if one of its legs buckled, the throne would totter, and that if one of them gave way it would collapse; on the other hand, he asserted that the people were happy when the three supports were lent strength "by the wise laws of God and the just laws of the world [*sapientia, justicia* were the two regulative virtues and, according to Adalbero, the two laws that formed the backbone of the social order]." Order reigned when the monarch, with the vigorous support of his people, showed himself capable of enforcing respect for the divine will. More clearly perhaps, and with greater stress on the mutuality of services, Wulfstan was stating what Aelfric had earlier called to Sigeweard's attention. Yet what the bishop was laying down was not quite identical to what Aelfric had affirmed: the words are similar, but in a new context their coloration is different. In the *Institutes* the triangular figure is subsumed within a broad theory of good government. As in Gerard of Cambrai's speech, it is included (virtually without commentary, without emphasis, which the author feels unwarranted, referring to the idea as to something self-evident, generally accepted) in a discussion of what Abbo called the *ministerium regis*, preceding the detailing of the tasks assigned bishops, dukes, intendants of royal domains, priests—i.e., the two parallel and hierarchical corps that helped the monarch to fulfill his office, one in the spiritual domain, the other in the temporal. Note carefully that only the leaders' duties and tasks are analyzed. Nothing further is said of the toiling masses. Once again their appearance was a fleeting one. They disappear at once into the shadows. But again note carefully that like Gerard of Cambrai and Adalbero of Laon, Wulfstan, before laying down the framework of the organization, before assigning each powerful figure his respective place, and before designating their several roles, felt the need to expound the homology between the earthly kingdom and the heavenly one, to discuss the mysterious correspondences of which it never occurred to either Aelfric or King Alfred to say a word. And the statements of the bishop Wulfstan and of the two bishops of *Francia* are connected most closely on this particular point.

What are we to think of this connection? Wulfstan wrote some years in advance of his confrères in Cambrai and Laon. Had they caught some echo of his words? Had they looked to him for inspiration? Had English oratory somehow altered the course of the river of words, formulas, remembrances of phrases read and heard, that constantly flowed through their minds? Will it ever be possible to say with certainty? The known facts permit us to say no more than this: in the time of one generation, between 995 and 1025, between the writing of the *Apologeticus* and the synod of Arras, new structures, feudal structures, were coming to light on both sides of the Channel, in an area embracing Fleury, Winchester, York, Saint-Bertin, Saint-Quentin, Cambrai, and Laon; within this region an ever tighter network of relations bound the whole of the high aristocracy together, prelates and warrior captains alike; during this period of a single generation two learned men, their minds formed on what had been taught at Rheims since the time of Hincmar, had taken up a theme. This theme was already in existence, present in everyday thought, in common turns of phrase. They turned it into "something literary."[45]

The figure was commonplace, so much so that neither writer thought to comment on it, to explain his particular rhetorical use of it. Emerged from time out of memory, it had no relation whatever with the realities of the contemporary social configuration, with the pragmatic or juridical classifications applied to the populace, or, in particular, with the taxonomic system employed in the legal code then being formalized by Wulfstan himself. It stood as far removed from reality as, for instance, the late twentieth-century ideological dichotomy that lends credence to the existence of an autonomous "popular" culture. Thus eddying and whirling in the depths of chaotic currents of linguistic and mental habit, a form was conveyed through time. It rose to the surface: there were three ways to "militate," to do service for the Christian people, hence three socio-functional groups united by mutual exchange. This ternarity had nothing in common with the one laid down by ecclesiastical morality; but it could forge links with it, the new could overlay the old. Minor adjustments sufficed to bring the two figures into line: combining the clerks and the monks, splitting the body of

107

laymen in two. But it was just as easy to couple the new ternarity with the Gelasian dichotomy, at the cost of making two additions: first, by accentuating the hierarchy that was uppermost in minds obsessed with censuring the carnal, the sexual, with all that Adalbero implied in uttering the word "blood"; and second, by allowing the two "ministries" to be joined by a third vocation, meritorious by virtue of the fact that it provided nourishment and was arduous. Trifunctionality, that formal notion, was invoked in debates over Church discipline: who had the right to wield arms? What was the proper use of physical force? All these debates revolved around a problem raised by the increasing disintegration of the decrepit political framework, the problem of violence, i.e., of peace, of justice, of law, of *ordo*. Those who feared the effects of a weakening of royal power that became more visible with each passing day clung to this commonplace notion. They made it the preamble for a plan of reform, of restoration of the ancient order of things.

Clearly, the schema was more bluntly formulated by the English, and by Aelfric in particular. Perhaps it was he who originated the triad of Latin nouns ending in the suffix *ator*. Only he referred to the three functional categories as orders. What did this firmness and simplicity owe to the insular cultural milieu? The formula did, of course, occur in the vernacular—and yet we have seen what care Aelfric took to Latinize the terms of the classification. Was this to wrest them from the grip of barbarism? To raise them to the level of the liturgies? To make them sacred? Or was it because he had read them in this form? The formula was also applied, of course, to describe the relationship of the people to the monarchy, to show how, if the king wished to practice his "craft" with "craft," he ought to use the various aptitudes of his subjects to his advantage. This inevitably calls to mind certain triadic complexes with deep roots in traditional Celtic political imaginings. Will it eventually be possible to press the genealogical investigation further along these lines? Such, at any rate, is not the purpose of this book.

Equally clearly, Gerard of Cambrai and Adalbero of Laon seem backward by comparison with the English contemporaries: they set forth the same ideas, but less bluntly; they refrain from discussing order. Less abstract, however, they refer to the countryside and to the seigniory in connection with the third function. Yet they resist the temptation to indulge verbal resonances and avoid using the word *laborator*. Opposite *oratores* and *bellatores,* they place the *agricolae,* the *servi;* opposite priests and warriors, they place peasants, serfs.

If they were influenced by words recently and probably still contemporaneously uttered in England, did these words not work their effects indirectly, by awakening echoes of still other words—Carolingian words? Indeed, we find a rough outline of the trifunctional figure in a commentary on the Book of Revelation due to Haymo, a monk at Saint-Germain of Auxerre in the first half of the ninth century. Haymo's concern was not to reform society, nor even to describe it, as the "mirrors" then did in order to remind princes, laymen, of the duties of their estate. Instead, his efforts were directed at dispelling the obscurities in a sacred text, one of the most fascinating, most mysterious of all. In the fourteenth verse of chapter three of Revelation the word "Laodiceans" may be found, along with its Latin translation, *tribus amabilis domino*. What did this mean? Which "three" could it have referred to? Haymo did his utmost to answer these questions.[46] These, he wrote, were three "orders" established among the Jewish as well as the Roman people: *senatores, milites, agricolae*. From his reading of the classical historians, he had learned that in Rome there were two *ordines* that ruled over the common people, the senate and the equestrian order; and because in his own time he was witness to a complete ruralization of the cities, he dared not refer to the third group as "citizens"; instead he wrote "peasants." He went on to say that these three orders had become three "modes of life" in the Church (here taking care not to use the word *ordo*, which would have entailed making distinctions of quite another kind), three ways of being: the ways of priest, warrior, and farmer. Thus half a century before King Alfred, a highly cultivated scholar working on the Burgundian fringe of the Frankish world had set forth the principle of the people's trifunctionality in a work that met with great success. He mentioned it in passing, without emphasis. Now, the manuscript of Haymo's commentary was to be found on the bookshelves at Laon. Of this we are certain, because the masters of the school of Laon, in composing their own gloss on the Book of Revelation in the early twelfth century, copied out fragments of it.[47] During Adalbero's lifetime, moreover, men meditated more fervently then ever on Saint John's text. If one is determined to insist strenuously that Adalbero and Gerard would have required an erudite reference before laying down the postulate of the three social functions, would it not be simpler to look for one in Carolingian rather than English libraries?

For the obvious reason that Haymo's work was to be found among the volumes they had at hand. More than that, Haymo was the first person, so far as we know, to have inscribed side by side on a piece of parchment the three nouns that express social trifunctionality: *sacerdotes, milites, agricolae*.

Finally, between what the two Frankish bishops said in about 1025, and what Haymo of Auxerre and the English had said earlier, there is another dissimilarity, an important one. Only the former pair incorporated the trifunctional figure in an ideological system of a scope and majesty that Wulfstan's system was far from attaining. They explicitly linked the three social functions with the exemplary structures of the heavenly Jerusalem.

10

THE HEAVENLY EXAMPLE

That the vision of the two Frankish bishops was grandiose cannot be repeated often enough. What was only of peripheral interest in Wulfstan (and even that much surely borrowed from Carolingian thought) became the central rib-work in the theoretical cathedral that Adalbero and Gerard were building. The mission of royalty; the place of the bishops—intercessors, prophets, orators; order; the relationship among the three areas of human activity; all these derived from a primordial structure, a structure that established an isonomy between the visible and the invisible, between the Capetian kingdom and the heavenly city. Like Cicero in *Scipio's Dream*—well known to Adalbero and Gerard from their reading of Macrobius—our two authors intended to link the political order with the order of the stars.

Once again, however, they were treading an old and well-traveled path, following in the footsteps of a long line of predecessors. Earlier, Alcuin (and who knows what Alcuin may have brought with him of the British Isles' own culture) had thought to attach the earthly monarchy more firmly to the divine by laying down the principle of the identity of the two cities. Like Alcuin, Adalbero and Gerard dreamed of the beyond while meditating over the very same texts that had preoccupied their predecessors: Gregory the Great—commenting on Ezekiel, the visionary, invoking the "example" of the heavenly host; and above all, Augustine, who had pressed much farther, not merely seeking a model in heaven, but imagining the interpenetration of this world and the other. The population of the city of God, he wrote, consists for the most part of angels; nevertheless "a part of the community . . . is an assembly formed of mortal men destined to be united with the immortal angels"—a colonization of the Kingdom by mankind: for Augustine, moreover, there was no justification for the procreative act other than that it secured for migrations of this kind a steady supply of man-power. To think in this way was to maintain that the veil of appearances was permeable, that the frontier dividing the carnal from the spiritual was easily crossed: Adalbero adopted this idea when he showed mankind partially engaged in the eternal. Indeed, Augustine's discussion related not only to the dead but also to the living: "this part of the community is now wandering on earth [in pilgrimage, on the road, in migration, as men of the year 1000 were wont to be, always on the move, heading for battle, the fair, the pioneer fronts of land-clearing, or adventure] under the condition of change, or else at rest, in the persons of those who have passed from this life, in the secret resting places of the souls of the departed." We may admire his discretion as to the topography of these invisible regions. Still, and it is this that sets them clearly apart from Alcuin and all the English writers, Adalbero and Gerard did not draw solely on Gregory and Augustine. Their inspiration came principally from Dionysius the Areopagite.

In the Acts of the Apostles, 17:34, it is reported that in Athens Saint Paul converted this Dionysius, to whom he gave instruction. Legitimately, one might imagine Paul expounding to his disciple what he had seen in the third heaven. Hence it was possible to regard Dionysius, recipient of this amazing revelation, as a connoisseur of the other world. So it happened that in the late fifth century, a Greek, assuming the authority and the pseudonym of Dionysius the Areopagite, had written two books: *On the Celestial Hierarchy* and *On the Ecclesiastical Hierarchy*. Now, in the minds of Adalbero and Gerard—and everyone else—this Dionysius was identified with the Dionysius of Montmartre, the confessor of the faith, the martyr whose sepulchre was attended by the monks of Saint-Denis [the French form of Saint Dionysius—Trans.] and who, like the two prelates, had been a bishop. He was the special protector of the kingdom of France: all Gaul had benefitted from this "splendid light of the divine word." This fact was recalled in the preamble of a grant of privilege accorded the abbey of Saint-Denis in 1008 by the king, none other than Robert the Pious.[1] There we read that Dionysius had reserved his greatest boons for the kings of the Franks. "Those among them who gave their services to Christ's martyr, who concerned themselves with his cult, were exalted in glory and royal power, while those who scorned him lost the kingdom and their lives"—which words served to justify the usurpation of the throne by the Capetians, whose ancestors, the counts of Paris, the dukes of France, had always venerated Dionysius: even before the dynastic change in 987, they had chosen the abbey of Saint-Denis as their burial place.

Whoever evoked Dionysius in the time of Gerard and Adalbero was returning deliberately to the Frankish roots, was going back to Clovis and his descendants, was claiming as *Francia*'s birthright a heritage, a continuous cultural tradition, and was relegating the German kingdom—along with

Brittany and the isles—to the periphery, proclaiming the primacy of the Capetians. To appreciate what value was attached to the relics of Saint Dionysius, that treasure stored in the Ile-de-France, recall that the Germans dreamed of seizing these remains and carrying them off for new burial in their own lands. In 1049, during the reconstruction of the choir of Saint-Emmeram at Ratisbon—Ratisbon being the principal city of the Salian emperors and Saint-Emmeram their monastery—an ancient tomb was discovered, and the story began to circulate that it was the saint's, that King Arnulf had placed his bones there on his return from a victorious campaign in the lands of the western Franks. A legend. As the eleventh century began, the fact was that to invoke the writings attributed to Dionysius was also to place the accent on the slow shift of the centers of sacred culture away from Rheims and towards Fleury on the Loire and Saint-Denis in France.

The body of the pseudo-Dionysius the Areopagite was held by "France"; it rested near Paris. His books were also kept in "France." The Byzantine emperor had offered a set to Louis the Pious, which gesture had been deemed a legitimate restitution. The two books "on the angelic principate and the ecclesiastical principate"—as Gerard of Cambrai referred to them, Latinizing "hierarchy" as *principatus*—had first been translated into Latin by Hilduin, abbot of Saint-Denis and arch-chaplain of the emperor; later, at the behest of Charles the Bald, himself abbot of Saint-Denis since 867, a much better translation had been prepared by John Scotus, known as the Irishman, who headed the palace school, knew Greek, and provided the work with a commentary. The episcopal library in Laon held a manuscript of this translation at the beginning of the eighteenth century; the catalogue calls the codex "very old," which means prior to the eleventh century. Thus it was available to Adalbero.[2] This document had exerted a prodigious influence in Charles the Bald's entourage. An image of paradise thereby came to be rooted in scholarly imaginations, an image that painters worked to represent figuratively (as in folio 5v° of a *Sacramentary* that was illustrated in about 870, probably at Saint-Denis).[3] It helped focus attention on angels, which came to occupy a larger place in pious observances, and assisted Saint Michael in gradually displacing the Savior from the upper chapels to the top level of the porches. It established a peaceful and orderly setting in which eschatological dreams might unfold. For more than a century such dreams were purged of dramatic gestures and histrionic outbursts. Thanks to knowledge of the works of Dionysius, the Heavenly Jerusalem could truly seem a "vision of peace," a model of that order that kings were being pressed to maintain on earth. In any case, I am certain that the exalted aspects of the system set forth in 1025 by the bishops of Cambrai and Laon derived directly from these two books: to the precepts of Gregory the Great, very Latin, ascetic, deliberately dry, they added the lyricism that was lacking; they increased the amplitude of the Augustinian themes still further. These pages were endlessly read and reread in northern France. From them stems the originality of what was indeed the "French" concept of political action in the central Middle Ages.[4]

"Whoever says hierarchy means thereby an order that is perfectly holy."[5] The thought of the pseudo-Dionysius transferred the notion of order—in the two-fold sense of *taxis* and *ordo*—into the realm of the sacred. It divinized the Gregorian principle of authority and inequality.[6] Above all, it made the invisible, inviolable law discussed by Saint Augustine—which prescribed keeping to one's place, remaining in ranks—into a vitalizing law, the law that governed the incessant expansion and contraction, the continual ebb and flow by which the light emanating from the One God descended to awaken into existence creatures from top to bottom of the chain of being, calling them to gather on high in the unity of the divine. Indeed, "the aim of hierarchy is, so far as possible, assimilation and union in God."[7] This law was not unlike charity, not without resemblance to the will of the creator. For it was God's wish that intelligent beings "be arrayed in sanctity and overseen in order."[8] If—and here lay the evil, the worm in the fruit, the rot—this movement should fall into disorder,[9] men, obedient to God's intentions, should then work with all their hearts to restore calm and regularity to the cycle. The Dionysian notion of hierarchy thus required continual reformation of that which was constantly undergoing deformation.

More, it ordered men to cooperate in spreading the truth. Since "hierarchy, sacred order, is a science and a force in action which impels beings to resemble the divine insofar as they are able, and which, by divine illuminations, raises them up, insofar as their strength permits, to the imitation of God,"[10] the system's imperatives implied that "those who are more advanced carry out the purification of the others." Furthermore, it was through this "force in action," which was also knowledge, that the two worlds, invisible and visible, were able to communicate, just as between the two books of the *Hierarchies,* that of heaven and that of the *ecclesia,* communication took place and a hierarchical relationship was established. With clear signs God revealed the imperatives of the immaterial order to mankind. He thus awakened, attracted to himself "the passive part of our soul, which lifts itself toward the most divine realities by correctly combining allegorical symbols in figurative representations."[11] Suger, in rebuilding Saint-Denis, was to have this text inscribed virtually word for word in the stone of the edifice as a manifesto of his aesthetic intention. Coordination between the societies of heaven and those of the perceptible world was established by the analogical relationship between their structures. God "also institutes us in hierarchy so that we may participate in the liturgy of the heavenly hierarchies through the resemblance of their holy and quasi-divine ministry."[12]

Now, the mysterious dynamic of order and knowledge unfolded in a triune configuration. "The division of every hierarchy is ternary[13] [hence tripartition was indeed 'the most perfect,' as Loyseau was later to say: it was sacred], as follows: the most divine signs; the divine beings who know these signs and are the initiators; those, finally, whom they righteously initiate." Thus we understand why those pure intelligences, the angels, were arrayed in heaven in interlocking triads, which were neither Ireland's nor Georges Dumézil's. "The word of God attributes nine revelatory names to the angels according to their hierarchy: the master who initiated me divided them into three ternary groups." In immediate contact with God were the Seraphim, the Cherubim, and the Thrones, "constituting a single hierarchical triad and truly the highest . . .; to enable lesser natures to rival themselves, they raise them up, imitating the supreme goodness and communicating thereby the splendor visited upon themselves. In turn, these natures of secondary rank [another triad: the Dominations, the Virtues, the Powers] transmit to the next lesser grade this splendor, and at each degree the superior distributes to the lesser a portion of the gift of divine light."[14] Through this third angelic triad (comprising Principates, Archangels, and Angels), illumination, "revelatory for human hierarchies," finally came to cover the earth.[15] In the lowest rank of the "celestial hierarchies" stood the angels; in the highest rank of the "ecclesiastical hierarchies," the bishops: from the former to the latter the message was transmitted.

The immaterial order was in effect projected onto our world by the incarnate form of God, Christ. God made flesh, sharing the human condition, speaking to his disciples, Jesus established the unity of the two hierarchies. He epitomized them in his person. At the point of suture, he ruled both realms. Hence the inferior hierarchy was not part of eternity. It had come into being on a certain day, in historical time, with Jesus, and through a sacrament, an initiating sign, baptism: so said Gerard of Cambrai to the heretics of Arras, who were not in agreement with this view, in attempting to convince them that baptism was sacred. Consequently, this hierarchy could well be called ecclesiastical. In the Church established by Christ, all order on earth resided; from and by the Church, the divine law was conveyed to all mankind: did Adalbero's view differ from this? Because human society was imperfect, however, it contained only two triads. First was the initiatory triad consisting of those capable of enticing others toward perfection. It dispensed the three sacraments: baptism, to purify; the eucharist, to illuminate; confirmation, to mark the accomplishment of the mission. It was organized on three echelons, three degrees of power: the "ministers" (ordinary clerks), who purified, baptized; the priests, who brought illumination, who distributed the body of Christ; and, finally, the bishops, "learned in all holy knowledge"—"in them all the imperatives of the human hierarchy are fulfilled and completed."[16] Symmetrically, on a lower level, we find the "perfectibles": first, those awaiting purification, catechumens, energumens, and penitents; followed by the faithful populace, led by the priests, who bid them join in the feast of the eucharist; and, finally, the monks, purer than other men, but without a leadership role in the Church, their place being with the people at the gates of the sanctuary, subject to the authority of the bishops.

This was the order of things. No sooner had it been laid bare by John the Scot's improved translation, the Dionysian vision at once fascinated the Carolingian intelligentsia: in the *Manual* she wrote for her son's use, Dhuoda meditated on the "nine orders of angels"; a capitulary of Charles the Bald referred to the bishops as the "Thrones of God."[17] In the early eleventh century this vision hung about the loftiest summits of learning in *Francia* and Neustria: painters continued to transfer it to the pages of liturgical books;[18] when Fulk Nerra, the count of Anjou, founded the monastery of Beaulieu-les-Loches in 1007, he dedicated it to the Trinity and at the same time to the "celestial armies over which God reigns, namely, the Cherubim and Seraphim"; patronage was thus bestowed upon those powers that Dionysius had shown assembled at the Almighty's side, watchful, ready to descend upon the enemy, like the counts, heads of terrestrial armies, who in this world were to be found together with the bishops flanking the person of the sovereign.[19]

Clearly, such a conception of order had all that was needed to satisfy Gerard and Adalbero. It placed the monasteries under the authority of the bishops; it held that the latter received their wisdom directly from heaven; it made them guides in all political action; it set them above human law, along with the whole ecclesiastical institution of which they were the rectors, in that "middle-ground in which mankind progressively shed its involvement in space and time."[20] Indeed, "the ecclesiastical hierarchy is throughout both celestial and legal. By virtue of its intermediary character, it participates in both extreme hierarchies. With one it shares intellectual contemplation, with the other, the variety of perceptible symbols by which it raises itself in righteousness towards the divine."[21] Dionysius was quite plainly the source in which Gerard and Adalbero discovered the plan of their wonderful edifice, and, more than that, reason for suggesting that ternarity shaped all just human relations. Hierarchized, which meant sacred, these relations also established the necessary inequality; they were regular relations of affection and reverence, of ceaseless interchange from top to bottom of the endless chain through which the love that moved the sun and the other stars flowed mysteriously from on high and at the same time ascended from below back toward its source.

The triangle lay at the heart of the work of the pseudo-Dionysius, but the functions did not. For this work was, as Adalbero said, "mystical": it paid no heed to society's material aspects; it neglected that which was governed by human law. To propose an earthly ternarity symmetric with the invisible triads, duly emphasizing the effects of the *lex humana,* describing the unequal relationships of which every kingdom, every seigniory, provided examples—was this not to finish what Dionysius had begun? Now we see the usefulness of the introduction into the system of the commonplace, hackneyed idea, the schema discussed by the scholars of Great Britain, the trilogy of *oratores, bellatores,* and the rest. This image had the advantage of being ternary, of lending itself to analogies, and especially of being related to another ternarity not to be found in the work of Dionysius himself, but rather in the *De divisione naturae* of his commentator, Erigena, the Irishman. In this work, John the Scot established an analogy between the structures of the Trinity and those of "nature." In the latter, he distinguished in turn the body, to which the *essentia,* i.e., the production of material goods was subordinate; the soul, "whose portion is virtue," i.e., the source of military valor (in the eleventh century, one praised the good warrior by calling him *animosus*); and, finally, the *intellectus,* which, using *sapientia,* intervened through *operatio,* i.e., control of all action through inspiration. *Operatio, oratio:* the two words echo each other; in dreams the difference between them was easily blurred. And thus within the bosom of the created world, barely veiled, perceptible, it was possible to distinguish three functions, in perfect correspondence with the three divisions of nature, wth the three corps of the angelic armies: the three functional categories of human society.

We have already paid a visit to the workshop near the cathedral to which the Frankish bishops of the year 1000 turned in order that they might more justly judge, more equitably mete out penance, and more effectively instruct their flock, at the head of which stood the king. There they also composed sermons, dissertations which the king, seated opposite the bishop, on the other throne, was the first to hear, and whose echoes were meant to reverberate throughout the populace, thanks to the organic coherence uniting the person of the sovereign with the humblest guests in his household, i.e., his kingdom, and thereby to disseminate a morality from one echelon to the next, from the head on down to the remotest extremities of the realm. In this workshop we found both "tools" and "handwork," as Alfred the Great might have put it: for tools there were the weapons of speech, rhetoric, but even at this early date also dialectic; along with a complex range of materials sorted in memory and in books, an enormous stockpile of words. Here Adalbero and Gerard worked, taking up one piece, casting another aside to replace it with something better. While making few modifications, they nonetheless rearranged the parts, ordered them in a new way.

These two "prelates" began with three concepts. The concept of authority—i.e., of inequality—tempered by charity; the concept of order—

116

but sacralized, for the society of which they were dreaming was not a "society of orders": in their eyes there was only one genuine order, the clergy; and, finally, the concept of functions—their own, those assigned to the others—defining themselves, along with the order that they headed, by opposition to other offices deemed inferior to their own. They scrapped the old binary system of Gelasius. They took it apart in their workshop. The system as such was no longer usable. Their meditations upon Dionysius' hierarchies had brought home the need for a new design; from England, perhaps, had come the idea that two pillars were not sufficient to insure stability, that three were required; practical experience, the battle that they had to wage each day against the castellans, the people, against their confrères in the councils, against the monks, the pope, against everyone, had taught them that in the theater of political action, every scene was played by three actors. Building on the ternary, they set two other actors facing the clerk. Not the monk and the layman: this would have been tantamount to recognizing the independence of the monastic institution, if not its superiority. Thus they repudiated the old ecclesiastical model of the three "orders." Grown ripe was the idea that the unequal distribution of power, the growing specialization of the military profession, and the effects of the mechanisms then taking hold in the seigniories had traced a dividing line through the laity, a cleavage unknown to the pseudo-Dionysius. This experience resulted in their formulating the trifunctional postulate.

But in so doing they made the image hierarchical, superimposing on it the ranking derived from the three orders of merit established by Jerome, Augustine, and Gregory the Great, and from the three angelic orders established by Dionysius. Taking up the widely accepted idea that a consecrator of the host ought not to fight, nor a master take part in servile labor, they abolished the theoretical equality among the three parties involved in the mutual exchange of services. While each of the functions was indispensable to the other two, this did not mean that all were equally noble: on this point the bishops were utterly convinced. They also severed whatever connections may have existed between the trifunctional figure and the royal person. In this they were aided by Dionysius. They did not look upon the three functions as upholding the throne or as reflecting the king's virtues and obligations in the social body. For them, trifunctionality reproduced the heavenly order on earth. Consequently, contrary to what some have maintained, they in fact did regard the triad of functions as including all human conditions, with each of the categories ranged behind a leader, a head, as was appropriate for any "order," one or another of the three figures of perfection—the good priest, the good soldier, and the good peasant—the figures that still preoccupied M. de Torquat as recently as twenty years ago. This configuration stemmed from the (Dionysian) intersection of the two axes of cleavage, one imposed by divine law, the other by human law.

At the intersection of the two jurisdictions, we find not the sovereign but now, instead, the bishop. Inspired directly, without intermediaries, by the spirit (Adalbero and Gerard saw themselves in Saint Gregory as he was depicted by illuminators in northern France on the pages of the *Moralia in Job,* seated on a royal throne and visited by the dove), the bishop, books in hand (those of Augustine and Gregory, and the two books of Dionysius), revealed heaven, i.e., the angelic triparition, to the sovereign. He addressed the king, making a pretense of defending the monarchy. In fact, the point of episcopal argumentation was to domesticate it. The king was no longer the arbiter, but the executant—the advocate, to use the Carolingian term, the secular arm, the instrument of a power that God bestowed directly on the prelates of the Church.

The ideological system of Adalbero and Gerard was Carolingian. It was the last expression of the Carolingian conception of royalty, by which we mean that of Hincmar, of the bishops of Charles the Bald. The conception not of Aix but of Rheims, Compiègne, Paris, of John the Scot's translation of Dionysius. Thus we understand why even in its innermost recesses this system seems so peaceable, why the *Carmen* never looks upon the upheavals it discusses as a warning sign of the impending end of time. Calmly and imperturbably, it looks into the beyond and finds order, peace, and hope. Insofar as the system was "mystical," however, it lent itself to the purposes of the bishops who were promoting the peace of God, even though this was ostensibly one of its targets. Like them, it sought to strip the sovereign of responsibility for *pax* and *lex,* for order. Frightened to find themselves challenged by competitors, who rose from their midst and under the protection of their immunities, in their cities, on the crest of that great wave that brought forth feudalism fully formed, these count-bishops—who felt they needed a strong king and a hierarchy to stiffen their resistance—no longer deemed the monarch the linchpin of society. They would have liked to have seen the king, sacred like themselves, enthroned among the other *oratores,* episcopalized. And had the monarch managed to free himself from that entourage of bishops who held him in leading strings, it would only have been to fall amongst the *nobiles,* the *bellatores,* to descend a rung on the scale of social values. Hence it is incorrect to maintain that it was the progress of monarchy that led to the emergence of the trifunctional figure from the realm of the inarticulate between 1025 and 1030 in its earliest known formulation. As had earlier been the case in England in the time of Alfred the Great, of Aelfric, and the bishop Wulfstan, so now it was rather the danger, the crisis in which royalty seemed to be foundering that saw this theme pressed into service.

A crisis. Ideological formations reveal themselves to the historian in periods of tumultuous change. In such grave times, the custodians of the word speak incessantly. The time has now come for us to step outside the cathedral workshop. Then perhaps we may be able to gain a better under-standing of why tools and material were put to the uses we have seen as we followed the meanderings of memory and the hazards of action.

PART THREE

CIRCUMSTANCES

Fruit of the late autumn of the Carolingian Renaissance, the ideological system, the superb, complex ideological edifice built by Gerard and Adalbero was also one of the flowers—on a par with the abbey church of Tournus and the porch-towers of Saint-Benoît-sur-Loire or Saint-Germain-des Prés—that blossomed with the rising sap which even as the prelates were holding forth was stimulating general material growth throughout western Europe. Let us not confine our attention exclusively to these texts. Let us not lose sight of the overwhelming vitality of the productive forces, or of the continuing progress in agriculture, whose pace was accelerating, owing no doubt to a change in climate, a variation which, though minor, was enough to increase crop yields. Nor should we neglect the demographic upsurge which followed the elimination of the last vestiges of slavery from the seigniories, whose lately too rigid framework was smashed by the last of the invasions in northern France. The cultural artifact whose origins and pattern I have attempted to describe first looms into view at the dawn of a vigorous phase of very rapid progress. Forged by men who, as bishops, felt obliged to work tirelessly for the elimination of the festering corruption, indefatigably promulgating the inaccessible truths revealed to them by virtue of anointment, this artifact was an instrument of reform. It was a weapon, specially tempered and honed to attack the malady in one quite specific point. As far as we can tell, with our imperfect historians' eyes, groping in the mist-enshrouded past, scrutinizing traces that have been almost entirely effaced, this weapon seems to have been brandished between 1025 and 1030. Why these particular years? Most important, why was the theme of the three social functions, that latent form, until that time held in reserve, as it were, in the nebulous recesses of a *mentalité*, then made one of the cutting edges of that instrument of restoration, the sword of justice? To be clear about it, the reason why the bishops of Cambrai and Laon began to dictate to scribes words earlier uttered in pomp before tribunals, in debate, and in the ceremonies associated with power, was that for some time they had been aware of an increase in the virulence of the evil infections that were always active in this world below. The texts we have been studying were born in the midst of a political crisis of the day; the time has now come to examine this crisis carefully. These texts were also rejoinders to antagonistic propositions; they challenged the words of false prophets, whose numbers, as we know, were on the rise at a rapid rate with the first glimmerings of the end of time. Attention should also be devoted to the projects for social reform that aroused the opposition of Gerard and Adalbero, since these formed the negative, in a sense, upon which the trifunctional image, together with its enveloping system, was superimposed. Finally, that this system should have been formulated when and as it was owed largely to powerful currents stirring the depths of the social formation, currents that had been plainly visible for some time and that had to be taken into consideration, requiring modifications in the models earlier generations had used in conceiving society. Hence we shall also need to gather additional evidence so that we may observe as closely as possible the widespread unrest that ideological oratory attempted to bring under control.

11

THE POLITICAL CRISIS

A crisis of royalty. *Imbecillitas regis:* the king has no further support. The metaphor used by the writer of the *Gesta episcoporum cameracensium* harks back to the one used a short while earlier by Aelfric, and to the one used a century before by Alfred the Great. This collapse of the monarchy was crucial: the "speculators," people who held up the mirror (*speculum*) of virtues, now turned it to face not toward the sovereign but rather toward society. The pragmatic virtues came unstuck from the royal person, and the functions of wisdom, armed force, and generous productivity thereby came to be located within the social body. The crisis, moreover, was one that came on quite suddenly.

In the summer of 1023, nothing in the Frankish people seemed changed: at Ivois on the Meuse, on the frontier which since the treaty of Verdun separated the western kingdom from Lotharingia, the two sovereigns, King Henry of Germany and King Robert of France, held discussions amid the most precious jewels from their coffers after exchanging sumptuous gifts as tokens of friendship and demonstrations of their respective magnificence; their talks bore on peace, justice, and the protection of the Holy Church. Louis the Pious had treated the same subjects two centuries earlier. But in fact all this was a facade. Behind it things had already come apart at the seams. A year later, the disintegration became apparent. In Lorraine (that former kingdom, now joined to Germany, in which Cambrai and its bishops were located) when Henry died, Duke Frederick, Gerard's (and Adalbero's) cousin, rejected the man named by the Germans to succeed the sovereign. King Robert tried to take advantage of this situation to march into and seize Austrasia, or at any rate Romance-speaking Austrasia, the country around Metz, and land of Gerard and Adalbero. In 1025 he gathered his troops; meanwhile, the most powerful of the princes of western France, Odo, count of Blois and Troyes, made ready to invade the kingdom of Burgundy. It was at this moment that Gerard set forth the postulate of social trifunctionality. At Compiègne in 1023 he had been with King Robert, taking part along with the other bishops in the preparations for the meeting at Ivois and for the broad pacification effort that that encounter was to have inaugurated. Now, left helpless by the death of Henry, his patron, he was very likely dreaming of renewed independence for Lorraine; he sent gifts to Robert, perhaps to stop him, in any case to initiate talks. Actually, the troubles abated fairly quickly in the Lotharingian portion of Frankish territory. Before the end of 1025, the dukes, and Gerard with them, had gone to Aix-la-Chapelle to offer their allegiance. The old order was restored.

Meanwhile, however, in the western kingdom, where innovation had proved more disruptive—this being the region then in the van of European growth—the structures of the state, long undermined, finally gave way. When Adalbero referred in his poem to the "youth" of King Robert, he was being ironic: Robert was old, decrepit. His throne was tottering. We know this from other evidence, from direct, not rhetorical, testimony, bluntly provided by the acts of the royal chancellery.[1] The pompous reminiscences that embellish their preambles do not conceal all that was going to wrack and ruin. In the first place Robert the Pious was concerned about his succession: less than forty years earlier, his father had become king of France by what many considered to be a usurpation, which had not been forgotten. Hugh Capet had attempted to found a dynasty by associating his eldest son to the throne. Robert had followed his example by having his first-born son, Hugh, anointed. In 1027, however, Hugh died. This was not too serious a blow: the king had other sons, and on Pentecost of that same year, holy oil was poured over the body of Henry, the second eldest.

More serious, indeed irreparable, was the dwindling, the shrinking away of the monarch's authority. The entire southern portion of the kingdom had found it could manage without a sovereign; a few years earlier, the count of Barcelona, alarmed by the Moslem advance, had called the king of Orleans and Paris to the rescue; to whom now in the region south of Angers or the Solonge would it have occurred to follow suit? The south of France was for a century and a half to be a country without a king, a country of princes, independent in their own "kingdom," as they put it. In 1029, Adhémar of Chabannes praised one of them, Duke William, "the Great," of Aquitaine: though the duke was not anointed, Adhémar recognized in him that eminently royal virtue, *sapientia*. It is true that by way of compensation Robert had just asserted his power in the duchy of Burgundy, part of the Burgundian nation and one of those *regna* placed under the authority of the king of western France by the Carolingian partitions. Duke Henry had died without an heir more than twenty years earlier. He was Robert's uncle, and the king wished to claim the legacy. In the end he overcame the resistance. In 1017 he succeeded not in making himself duke but in placing one of his sons at the head of the duchy. Since that time he had multiplied his direct, thorough, and effective interventions in Burgundy, which little by little was becoming Capetian. But it was a dependency, a foreign territory. For Robert the important thing was his own "kingdom," the *Francia* of which his grand-father had been duke, the land of the Franks, north of the Loire, west of Sens and Lorraine. This province was no longer under his control. Principalities had grown up in Flanders and throughout the region in which the Norman pirates had settled. On that front, all was lost. The rest was threatening to slip from his grasp as well. Most importantly, how was the count of Angers, the most intractable of all the enemies, to be held in check, with both Blois and Champagne under his control?

It might be supposed that Robert still reigned over *Francia* like a Carolin-gian, periodically gathering around his person, for the important Christian holidays, the powerful leaders of that vast territory. Such he had done on the occasion of Pentecost in the year 1008, when virtually all the bishops had come to the abbey of Chelles, as they had been wont to do in the time of Charles the Bald: the archbishop of Rheims, the archbishop of Tours, seven of the thirteen bishops from the province of Rheims, and, among them, Adalbero. At Compiègne in 1023 we witness a similar influx; the count of Flanders and the duke of Normandy had come, together with an even greater number of prelates of the Church, including Gerard, the bishop of Cambrai, to deliberate over *pax* and *lex*. The latter were words that had rung in Charlemagne's own ears. But this was the end. By examining closely the subscriptions on the diplomas drawn up in the king's name, J.-F. Lemarignier has been able to date the change precisely in 1028: it was brewing even as Adalbero was at work on his poem. The assemblies in which the king heard the advice of his counselors prior to passing judgment all at once take on a new aspect. No longer, or only exceptionally, do we find bishops or counts among the participants; around the sovereign we now see only men of lesser quality, lords of castles and even mere knights. That most venerable public assembly, which for generations had served to bind together the king and the generality of the populace in western Frank-ish lands, suddenly has the appearance of a family council. Henceforth the king was to seem like one more head of household among many, conversing in private with his relatives, his provosts, his comrades of hunt and battle, and using his table companions as witnesses to the acts of his chancellery. At the same time, the language of these acts shed the theatrical embellishment inherited from the grandeur of Carolingian days: the royal diploma itself lost the solemnity that had distinguished it from private charters. Ten twenty-four; ten twenty-eight; ten thirty-one: the coincidence in chronology between the weakening of the monarchy and the enunciation of social trifunctionality is striking.

If the bishops of *Francia* no longer troubled themselves to grace the royal court with their presence, this was because they no longer saw any advantage in doing so. It had become patently obvious that the Capetian monarch no longer had the strength to protect the interests of the high Church effectively. There was no one to whom the bishops could appeal. They would have to fend for themselves. For some time already, their colleagues in the southern part of the kingdom had been doing just that. What was to prevent their following suit, what was to prevent them from taking the king's place and, since they, too, were sacred, assuming responsibility for defending the earthly order? Openly. Or, at the very least, covertly. Before the rising tide of dangers—and for the prelates, the most pressing peril was that of standing out alone against the nearby lay powers, against the dukes, the counts, the castellans—a welter of new projects emerged. A fertile, heated polemic raged in the tiny world of highly cultivated men, of men convinced that they were directly inspired by heaven, who continued to meet together, if not in the sovereign's presence, at any rate in discussions held elsewhere, each of them enamored of the sound of his own voice and spurred on by it to contradict everyone else. Coteries and clans formed, the clerks finding themselves confronted with steadily increasing numbers of ever more arrogant monks, for the structure of the Church was changing as well—another sign of the general turmoil of the times. In the confusion of proposals and counter-proposals, the fervor of ideological invention took a sudden bold turn. Amid this chaos, the system of Gerard and Adalbero was hammered out. Knitted together to form a single body were the three themes of necessary inequality, of isonomy between the society of humans and the society of angels, and, finally, of the three functions. From the heat of controversy, this system emerged in opposition to others, which were denounced as ruses of the devil that would help spread the disorder. The model containing the trifunctional postulate was advanced to counter three antagonistic models, also intended as remedies for the weakness of the Capetian throne, models that took that weakness into account and gambled on it: the heretical model, the model of the peace of God, and the monastic model.

12

THE COMPETING SYSTEMS

The three proposals fought against by Adalbero and Gerard arose out of widespread movements born in the south. The true dimensions of the confrontation cannot be grasped unless note is taken of the contrast between, on the one hand, the Frankish, Carolingian heritage with its vestiges in Ottonian and Capetian lands, along with the cultural renaissance from which the views of the bishops of Cambrai and Laon derived directly, and, on the other hand, another latinity, a latinity not revived by erudition. For this latter latinity had never died out in provinces where what Rome had planted with deep roots had not lost its vital force, regions in which the Franks had remained intruders, an occupying force, incapable of overcoming national traditions—whether Lombard, Gothic, Provençal, Aquitainian, or Burgundian: an area of civilization whose creative power medievalists long fascinated by the legend of Charlemagne are beginning to perceive. Its vitality was no doubt fostered by material prosperity. Less favored than the northern French countryside by the climatic changes, these regions continued to enjoy advantages built up over a long period of time. Bordering on Islamic territory and the Byzantine Empire, they stood in their neighbors' debt for a good deal of stimulation. This was an area whose resources reveal their quality and fertility as soon as one looks at the field of religion: was it not here that three of the pillars of medieval Christianity struck their roots: the Benedictine style in monasticism, the affirmation of the primacy of the Roman pontiff, and finally, the call for holy war? Now, on the threshold of the second millennium, we find these countries threatening *Francia* with a kind of cultural colonization. That which emanated from the south was able to penetrate the north all the more easily owing to the quickening of traffic along the old trade routes, particularly those which passed through western Frankish and Burgundian lands to join England to Italy; owing also to the

129

orientation of Capetian policy, in furtherance of which the king advanced on Sens and Auxerre, on Saint-Bénigne of Dijon—whose abbot was William of Volpiano, an Italian—and on Cluny. The Frankish bishops Adalbero and Gerard witnessed the disruptive current's slow infiltration. In the *Carmen* Adalbero intended an allusion to this rising tide in the south when he evoked, sarcastically, a new Saracen invasion, an absurdity, a scandal. I see the trifunctional schema and its whole encompassing system as a defensive barrier, a wall raised around the sanctuary, a part of a strategic withdrawal to within the Carolingian breakwater, a reaction of self-defense whose effects included, in particular, a stimulus to reread the author held to be the greatest ever to have written on Frankish soil, Saint Denis, Dionysius the Areopagite.

HERESY

Of the three waves, the most worrisome was heresy. It represented a radical challenge to the established order, in the face of which, setting their quarrels aside, Adalbero, Gerard, and the other bishops stood fast. The outbreak was sudden: 1022, Orléans; 1024, Arras; slightly later in Champagne. All of northern France seems to have been infected at the same time as Aquitaine by germs which everywhere were said to have come from Italy. This was both true and false. False, certainly because the pestilence was breeding locally and ready to surge forth from these domestic sources. True because as the shreds of information in our possession attest, the disease was highly virulent in 1028 in one trans-Alpine locale, Monteforte in the region of Asti, on that trade route mentioned above, the main line of communication between the northwestern and southeastern extremities of Latin Christendom.

Of heresy we know nothing other than what has come to us through those who persecuted and vanquished it, in acts of condemnation and refutation, or by way of chroniclers like Raoul Glaber or Adhémar of Chabannes, who reported hearsay, blackening and dramatizing as they went. These sources, more than most, must be subjected to scrupulous criticism.[1] Monteforte offers the most perspicuous case, the only one in which the heresiarch's own words are audible to us.[2] But the details of the Arras affair are not too obscure, and this, along with the Orléans case, touches most closely on our inquiry. From the incomplete, gap-ridden record, a few impressions emerge. The clearest of them is of the movement's uniformity. Everywhere, it seems, the adherents to the heretical doctrine came from the same social milieus. Not, as their enemies repeated time and again to discredit them, from the dregs of the populace. More than just "rustics" joined the sects. Apparently, moreover, very little recruiting was done in the far reaches of the coun-

130

tryside, most members coming rather from the new quarters of the growing cities. It is beyond question that the leaders were clerks, and frequently clerks of the best sort. Heresy cropped up at Orléans in the royal chapel, i.e., in a center of learning as avid of novelty as Rheims, Laon, or Cambrai; it spread to the most enlightened cathedral chapters, to the best-purified monasteries. The infection attacked the highest levels of the Frankish state's ideological apparatus. Its agents were scholars. To be convinced of this, it is enough to hear the rejoinder made to the archbishop of Milan by the "master" of the heretics of Monteforte: he was aware of the most subtle doctrinal controversies of the day; he had meditated, perhaps, over the most arduous system of thought, that of John Scotus. But it is no less clear that "illiterates" were also affected and converted: at Arras, the act of refutation had to be translated into the vulgar tongue so that they might understand it. Bear in mind, however, that among laymen, the powerful understood Latin no better than the poor. At Monteforte, the documents explicitly acknowledge the presence of high-ranking figures among the sectarians. These were not adventurers, but simply Christians no longer satisfied by the Church's traditional teaching, awaiting a different message. Among them—this is equally certain and caused a scandal—were women, a group ordinarily neglected by the ecclesiastical institution.

Heresy dreamed of a different soceity. Not a disorderly one, to be sure—what society could endure without order? But rather a differently ordered society, based on another conception of the truth, another conception of the relations between the flesh and the spirit, the visible and the invisible. At Arras, at Monteforte, one's doctrine and the kind of life one led were declared to be inextricably bound up together. Like Adalbero and Gerard, the heretics found in the word of God, elucidated by wisdom, the source for the perfect social order they wished to establish. But they had the presumption to forego the services of the bishops in interpreting that word. They denied that communication with the sacred must necessarily be established through acts and formulas—through rites. The protest was anti-ritual in principle. Its proponents maintained that grace and the holy spirit instilled themselves without mediation in minds and hearts. Hence that the eucharist, baptism, absolution were useless. And anointment as well. Consequently, moreover, the heretics denied that the bishops in any way monopolized *sapientia*. This denial of the virtues of anointment made it possible for another accusation to be leveled against them: they were said to be endangering the authority of the monarchy, undermining the foundations of the political state. Heresy contested the elements of magic that encumbered religious practices. The sectarians of Arras refused to worship Christianity's petty gods, refused to prostrate themselves before the little boxes encrusted with gold and gems from which miracles were said to emanate.

They did respect martyrs—for they had a taste for suffering, for that radical and tragic purification of which acceptance of death might be the instrument. This accounts for their acceptance of Saint Dionysius: he had been decapitated. Still, they did not venerate the magician in him, much less the prelate. They had no use for the "confessor" saints. They rebelled against the spread, in the same period, of the cult of bishop-saints and saintly kings; they derided the innumerable inventions and translations of relics, which were being found everywhere in the major digs occasioned by the reconstruction of churches around the year 1000. The outbreak of heresy signifies that like everything else at this time and in this part of the world, Christianity was freeing itself from savagery.

Thus it comes as no surprise that we find these men and women—convinced that they were in constant, immediate contact with the spirit—professing the most radical contempt for the flesh. Blood and sex were repugnant to them. They abstained from eating meat. They were shocked by the wounds in the crucifixion, by the sacrifice in the mass, by the bread that became flesh, the wine that became blood. They wanted no part of marriage. And not merely because it was their intention to remain chaste, but because they condemned procreation, dreaming of a humanity that would reproduce itself without copulation, as bees were thought to do. Contemptuous of all the corporeal envelope of the created, these spiritual beings wished, quite naturally, to pay no heed to any distinctions in human society, least of all to that distinction embodied in the flesh, separating the two sexes. Receiving women as full-fledged members of their community, they eliminated the primordial social barrier. This was not done with impunity: to abolish the difference between masculine and feminine was to justify the worst calumnies and was, I think, principally responsible for the sect's failure. The heretics filled in another yawning abyss: rejecting the privileges of the sacerdotal "calling," they confounded *clerus* and *populus;* they invited all Christians to fast and to pray in the same way. Since, moreover, they urged that offenses be pardoned and that vengeance and punishment be curtailed, they were in effect proclaiming the uselessness of the specialists in repression and the use of brute force: the military. Finally, in the sect everyone worked with his hands, no one expected to be fed by others, no one toiled in the service of a master: the line of demarcation between the workers and the others, the lords, judges, protectors, and avengers, was eroded. The wish to see this barrier—nearly as high as the wall between the sexes—leveled was utopian, in any case audacious: it had been raised up by the mode of production. Heresy proposed equality, total equality. It is not difficult to understand how it could easily have recruited followers among the oppressed, the victims of injustice, wives persecuted by their husbands, sons and daughters persecuted by their fathers, journeymen persecuted by their employers, students persecuted by their masters, not to mention clerks by their bishops—men and women hoping for liberation in fraternal friendship, in "charity." At all levels of society, in houses rich and poor. Heresy "rejected outright the imaginary structure of society [*l'imaginaire social*] . . . by opposing to it the reality of an essential equality among men."[3]

The equality of a paradise regained. It is precisely this hope that accounts for the rejection of sexuality. Adam's sin had made copulation necessary, had set the human apart from the angelic. When human beings reached the point of living in total chastity, when, as John the Scot said, "sex which signifies that which is inferior" had been taken from man, then the earth would once again be joined to heaven.[4] This was what heresy was: a project for a new society, but a mutant one, a society in the process of breaking all its chains, making ready to escape from this world, that foul prison. Everywhere in the third decade of the eleventh century sects formed and hatched conspiracies to flee, to lose themselves in the bedazzlements of the imaginary. Anxious to hasten the end of the world, eager to rush headlong into the hereafter, by whatever means. Notably by abolishing differences. With the exception of those spiritual distinctions that were connected with merit: the sectarians recognized leaders, guides—the "perfect." Perfect, imperfect: the imperatives ordering the heretical utopia hark back to the ones laid down by Dionysius. They are reminiscent too of monastic priorities, monasticism having a similar purpose, claiming to attain a higher degree of perfection through an heroic ascesis, through contempt for the world. How are we to distinguish between the monks—who were chaste, who purified themselves through fasting, who humbled themselves through manual labor, who, though not priests, devoted their days to perpetual prayer, who strove indefatigably to become angels—and the exponents of heresy? Was heresy anything other than a fanatical desire at last to cast off the moorings, to bring all Christians within the embrace of a kind of monasticism? What was heresy but the hope of an immense monastery that would suddenly turn into paradise, with the end of the species, the end of procreation, the end of "human beings"?

In the meantime, this chimera presented the established order with a challenge of a quite visible kind. It defied the dominant ideology. The proponents of that ideology dug in their heels. It was no accident that the system put forward by Gerard and Adalbero first appeared in the form of a stern reproach to the Arras heretics, as an answer to men and women whose purity and fidelity to the teachings of the Gospel were manifest. But how were they to be answered? Robert, the king, his hand forced at Orléans, had ultimately had to have these respectable but headstrong people dragged off to the stake; the only alternative was to try to force them to accept the three propositions that formed the backbone of the system: that heaven is not the Garden of Eden before the fall, and that if it did in fact extend to earth, this was in the institutional form described by Augustine, Gregory, and the Areopagite; that the divine purpose is not equality, that everything in creation is hierarchized, the society of angels in particular; and, finally, that among angels and men alike, hierarchy is based on a ternary pattern. On this point, in the presence of the heretics, it would have been maladroit to have attempted to uphold the dogma by invoking the ecclesiastical triad of orders of perfection: *virgines, continentes, conjugati.* Reviling marriage, preaching continence, and dreaming of castration, the heretics themselves employed this image. In order to rebuke heresy, the bishops had to integrate sexuality with the earthly order. Consequently, they had to assert the existence of two distinctions: first, between the feminine and the masculine; second, between those men already coupled with the paradisiacal—God's servants, already under the jurisdiction of divine law, in virtue of which they were free, or rather exempt, from both servile labor and the taint of sex—and laymen, who were obliged to procreate, to copulate, and hence to accept the constraints of matrimony. The bishops were obliged to proscribe marriage for clerks but to extol its values for the lay population; they had to create the sexual morality that was to take root in western Christendom and remain firmly implanted for a millennium. Finally, proclaiming the necessary subjection of those who obey to those who, weapons in hand, guide and punish them, the bishops spoke of a ternary of offices, of functions: some pray, others fight, still others work. This ternarity corresponded to the structures of heaven and to the nature of the kingly calling, the king being charged by Christ with the task of maintaining order, i.e., peace.

According to the text of the Arras "brief," this answer was accepted by the heretics. Their defeat was inevitable. Aspiring as they did to undergo purgatory tribulations, perhaps they wished for it. Be that as it may, the values they attacked were all too thoroughly anchored in the very thing that inspired their aversion, matter. With all the functional categories of carnal society in league against them, they were muzzled, or when necessary destroyed by fire and by the sword. Virtually no mention of them is made in any document that has come down to us from after 1030. Does this mean that Gerard and Adalbero were the organizers of this victory? In truth, the genuine society, that which did not vanish into the thin air of unreality but was firmly anchored in bedrock, the society based on the domination of woman by man, of peasant by lord—that society had no need of their treatises to defend itself.

The Peace of God

The second of the three antagonistic proposals, which called for the establishment of the peace of God, corresponded closely to concrete social relations. This accounted for its strength. It, too, came from the south.[5] The plan had been elaborated in 989–90 at Charroux in Poitou and at Narbonne; it was put forward in 994 at Limoges, at Le Puy, and at Anse near Lyons. Its aim: to defend the temporal rights of the churches, in a region where the greed of the powerful was no longer held in check by the sovereign, where the men of war were beginning to bleed the "unarmed people" white, and to bleed them even within the confines of the ecclesiastical domains.

The peace of God was a palliative. It was a substitute for the peace of the king. Nothing more. It changed nothing in the framework of peace, in the manner in which control was exercised, or in the justice rendered: the organizational forms remained Carolingian. The new peace was promulgated in assemblies of free men similar to the general courts of the ninth century, assemblies which met outside the cities, outside the walls, in the open country, in the meadows. The only difference was this: the place formerly occupied by the king was now taken by that which on earth most nearly approached the divine, the holy remains, piled high for the occasion in reliquaries withdrawn from every crypt in the province. Around this heap of relics imbued with a mysterious, protective, terrifying power, the participants divided into three groups—a quite visible ternarity. This arrangement derived from the intersecting axes of cleavage inherited from Frankish tradition. The sharpest split separated the rulers, the "powerful," from the "people," the "poor." But we glimpse certain changes. First, a nuance of contempt: the "people" little by little became the "plebs" (Raoul Glaber). Second, status began to be more precisely described: the popular masses were seen as composed of "farmers" (Charroux), "peasants" (Le Puy), "villagers" (Anse). The latter two terms were borrowed from the vocabulary of the seigniory, an institution which was establishing itself little by little. In effect, as the ways of exercising power changed, the division between the "poor" and the others took on a new meaning: on one side were those from whom one took, on the other, those who did the taking. Among the latter, as was customary, "two orders of princes" (Raoul Glaber) were distinguished, the "ecclesiastical order" (Limoges) and the "nobles" (Le Puy, Narbonne)—i.e., the *oratores* and the *bellatores*. Now, however, the confrontation between them was more direct, involving as it did a dispute over power and its profits. As for the measures taken, they originated in the law of interdiction which the king had previously been responsible for enforcing and which henceforth God would impose without intermediaries: the interdiction protected the immunity of the sanctuaries against violation; prohibited attacks on the men of the *clerus;* and proscribed pillage of the property of the poor, confiscation of their livestock, and appropriation of their physical labor (Le Puy). We detect the first still indistinct glimmerings of a new idea: that what the "powerful" rob from the "poor" is first and foremost their labor. To guard against the threatened alienation of what was theirs, the poor were enjoined to take refuge under the cloak of divine, i.e., ecclesiastical, protection, as the shield until recently held over them by the earthly sovereign lay smashed to bits and could no longer afford them cover.

These prescriptions instituted an ethics of temporal power, that is, a code governing the use of weapons. *Arma secularia:* the sharpest line of demarcation henceforth separated the men who wielded the instruments of war, coercion, and pillage, on the one hand, from all the unarmed, the "villagers" and the clergy, on the other. At the center, then, of this whirlwind of reform projects and proposals from which we have seen the trifunctional theme emerge—in France, as in Aelfric's England—lies an apparent problem, the problem of the legitimacy of military action. The edicts of the peace assemblies are explicit about this: adult males (no one else is involved), regardless of their status, their "order," cease to be protected by the interdictions once the sword is girded on: clerks quit the peace of God if they take up arms; conversely, warriors who, out of a spirit of penitence, decide to lay down their weapons come under its provisions and remain under them so long as, stripped of their military accoutrements, they remain inoffensive and vulnerable.

The distinction between armed men and others became sharper as the movement for the new peace spread. During the decades centering on the year 1000 men gradually grew accustomed to the idea that the important frontier dividing laymen ran not between "princes" and the "vulgar," but—as Abbo and Aelfric also believed—between "farmers" (since virtually all noncombatants shared this status) and "heroes." Apart from national rulers, men who boasted of "military sublimity" (Anse), this term applied to all young men equipped by these rulers to assist in combat, to all horsemen, to knights. These subordinates, these henchmen, unreasoning and brutal, whom neither divine election nor blood destined to rule over the populace, whose actions were unchecked by an ethic of leadership, apparently bore primary responsibility for the depredations, injustices, and abuses of seigniorial power—in a word, for all disorder and evil. Denounced as "maleficent" by the assembly of Le Puy, alarmed to see them "on the rise amidst the people," these troublesome underlings were the target of the efforts made jointly by "prelates" lay and ecclesiastical in the councils of peace to set up a system of checks. This purpose emerged more clearly during the second phase of expansion of the new institutions of peace, which began in about 1015, nearly a decade before Gerard and Adalbero rose to speak. The idea was to bridle the knights by means of collective oaths. The system of prohibitions did not change. But to enforce respect for them, "all who are horsemen and bear secular arms" were compelled to swear, as at Verdun-sur-le-Doubs in 1016.[6]

All horsemen. The effect of this practice of administering oaths was crucial. It united in a single body all sword-bearing men, thereafter isolated from the mass of the people as only princes had been previously, owing to the commitments they had made and the moral code they had laid down for themselves, a code adapted to the particular way in which they lived and acted within society and to the particular sins that dogged their steps. A word was needed to designate the members of this quite clearly delineated social category. Rather than the Latin word *miles,* a familiar term was preferred, *cabalarius,* a word borrowed from the speeches delivered in the assemblies by laymen, from the phrases in the vulgar tongue by which one pledged one' faith. Owing to habits of speech, people came to speak of these men, governed by a specific ethic, as they spoke of an order. The vocabulary of texts concerned with these regulations remains prudent, still hesitant on this point. Nevertheless, it was already taken for granted that all knights assumed an office in society, a positive office, which imposed on them not only prohibitions but also duties. According to the *Life of Gerald of Aurillac,* this office was that of the *pugnator,* i.e., that which fell under the military aspect of the royal ministry.

Now, it was precisely in the form of an oath required of all horsemen that the movement for the peace of God penetrated northern France. It proceeded up the Rhône valley and across Burgundy. The southeastward shift of the seat of Capetian power was directly responsible for its advance into Frankish territory. In 1016 Robert the Pious had been present at Verdun-sur-le-Doubs. He had been conducting his cavalcade through the duchy. The meeting took place in the county of Chalon, ruled by his friend the bishop of Auxerre. The king took the opportunity to show himself among the archbishops and abbots at the border between his kingdom and the kingdom of Burgundy, at one of those frontiers between two great political entities where it was customary for such councils to gather around "relics of the saints brought from diverse regions."[7] At Héry in the diocese of Auxerre, again in Burgundy, Robert himself organized a council of this kind in the year 1024. In the same year, two French bishops, Garin of Beauvais and Béraud of Soissons, followed his example; they used the text of the oath sworn at Verdun as the basis for the one they administered to the knights of their dioceses, revising it only slightly but nevertheless making room within its provisions for the king, guarantor of order. In the environs of Orléans and Paris, in the province still held by the Capetian monarch, his declining power was no different from that of a prince, from that of the duke of Aquitaine, for instance. Thus it was quite natural that the system elaborated in Burgundy and to the south of the Loire should have been extended to northern France.

This system was soon to find its theoretical justification in the sermons of Adhémar of Chabannes.[8] It was the role of the bishops, he maintained, to protect the poor and the clergy against the forces of disruption; to defend these two groups, as Saint Martial had done before them, to institute the peace of Christ, i.e., the earthly reflection of the celestial—that was their mission; to accomplish it, they ought to rely, he said, on the might of the secular princes; the princes should be made auxiliaries of episcopal authority, responsible for carrying out the orders of the bishops. A system of this kind relied heavily on the Gelasian tradition. It was different from the system upheld by Gerard of Cambrai only in that it was more realistic: it harbored a clear awareness of the collapse of the monarchy. As at Limoges and Chalon, the bishops of Beauvais and Soissons counseled the king to secure peace through the establishment of obligatory oaths. Was this not to revert to practices instituted by Charlemagne, who had required his subjects to swear to respect order and to refrain from taking violent action against the poor? The only difference was that the oath ceased to be required of all free men: henceforth it was to be obligatory only for those men among the "people" who continued to engage in military action, hence who remained truly free: the horsemen. The rest of the *vulgus* had become truly "poor"; they had gone and got themselves mixed up with the descendants of slaves to form an inert, passive mob, the "plebs," dominated, crushed by the new seigniory and so totally deprived of liberty that it would have been inconceivable for such people to have continued to pledge their faith by sworn oath. Thus it used to be possible to maintain that the peace oaths put forward in 1024 by the bishops of *Francia* with the king's consent were mere adaptations of the old Carolingian public oaths to the new configuration of social relations. If that was the case, however, why was Gerard's attack on the peace-men so vehement, and why did he bring up the argument of social trifunctionality? Why did he try to bring peace to his diocese (and his example was followed by Adalbero) by other means, by episcopal mandate, instituting the truce of God, which formula he may have invented, setting limits on its scope and guaranteeing it by means of ecclesiastical sanctions, without putting a stop to the activities of a repressive system of public justice?

Gerard acted as he did first of all because he feared an alliance between powerful laymen and an advanced element of the populace, that petty aristocracy of wealth whose rise was attracting notice in the cities of northern France. Such an alliance would have posed a direct threat to the prerogatives of the bishop-counts in their cities. And such an alliance was actually being forged: the masters of urban castles, hoping to consolidate their judicial and police powers, were making overtures to the most enterprising subjects of the episcopal seigniories, who dreamed of freedom and were themselves beginning to come together through collective oaths of unity. But Gerard's primary motive lay in what he saw, clearly, with his own eyes: that deflection of the purpose of the peace movement that took place in the third decade of the eleventh century, turning it in the direction of what both Gerard and Adalbero could only regard as heresy: the assertion of the existence of another order, another society. A society of penitence. The information provided by Raoul Glaber is correct: as the millenium of the Passion approached, the yearning for the peace of God found its place within the context of a more general striving for purification; in this context it was associated with compulsory fasting and repression of incest, polygamy, and fornication. Recall that just before setting down the speech of Gerard's to which the trifunctional theme serves as preamble, the author of the *Deeds of the Bishops of Cambrai* alludes to a letter fallen from heaven, calling upon the common of the faithful to respect certain ritual prohibitions. In this missive, the two challenges to orthodoxy which made the movement subversive found expression. Imposing on all men the obligation to swear oaths, to fast, to forgive offenses, the movement abolished social differences—even going so far as to abolish the essential difference, the one between the sexes, by devoting attention to women, to *"vilaines"* (the protection of whom had earlier been of concern to the council of Le Puy), to "noble matrons," afforded special protection by the oaths of Verdun and Beauvais; men who had sworn an oath in common tended to unite (as was soon to happen also in the cities with the communal oaths, which derived directly from the peace oaths) in aggressive egalitarian fraternities, bearing a curious resemblance to heretical sects. The other error, one that the heretics had not yet been guilty of committing, was that of making such a conjuration obligatory by threatening any recalcitrants with assault or with being left unburied. This second heterodoxy was the result of the peace-men's paradoxical but irresistible penchant for violent action, and the principal danger (as Adalbero and Gerard saw quite clearly) was precisely that if distinctions, orders, classes were denied, potent popular demands might be set loose. The bishops who went "stark naked, wailing the lament of our first parents" to the people, hands on their hearts and insults on their tongues against the rich and against those who upheld order—were they not demagogues, who roused hopes that the seigniorial mode of production might be destroyed? Did not these turncoats pretend to take the part of the exploited in what might be called—why not?—the class struggle?

The Cluniac Order

A third influence, like the two others of southern origin, was the rise of monasticism. Monasticism of a certain kind, obviously. At Cambrai and Laon there were long-established communities of monks living under the rule of Saint Benedict. Gerard, a friend of Richard, the abbot of Saint-Vannes, and Adalbero, who had lived for several years during his youth in the abbey of Gorze, were far from being hostile to monasticism. They saw in it an ally, a collaborator, as long as it remained within the compass of episcopal authority, as long as not all the monks aspired to the priesthood but remained for the most part content to assemble in a brotherhood of penitents at the cathedral door, in the subordinate, abject position assigned them in Dionysian theology. But before their eyes a new spirit in monasticism was on the rise, an arrogant, conquering spirit. Thirty years earlier Abbo of Fleury had been its spokesman; now it was embodied in Cluny, in the Cluniac congregation, the *ordo cluniacensis,* whose influence and ambitions were beginning to attract attention in northern France. They were still Benedictines, but interpreted the rule after their own fashion and entertained dreams of a quite different sort.

The monks of Cluny dreamed of a society guided toward the good by truly pure men, by men wholly free of corruption—a society guided by the "perfect." By themselves. No longer were monks to be looked upon, as Dionysian theology looked upon them, as open to further perfection. On the contrary, Cluny saw them as perfecting other men. This they could do because of all mankind none stood nearer to heaven than they, who constituted that portion of humanity that still wandered on earth and yet had already entered into the society of angels, of which Saint Augustine had spoken. The Cluniac monasteries were meant to be colonies of the immaterial on earth, bridgeheads of the heavenly kingdom. To that end these monks subordinated the work of the intelligence to what they looked upon as the *opus Dei,* the "enterprise for God," *par excellence:* the practice of the liturgy. The monks' main role was to chant the Lord's praise in unison. They thus identified themselves with the chorus of angels. By amplifying their prayers in this way, they were able still further to whittle away the distance between the visible and the invisible. Cluny wanted its basilicas to be the anterooms of paradise. Thus the breach between Cluny's monks and the clergy grew to be as large as that between clergy and laymen. This much Abbo had already maintained to be true. Frequenting haunts said to stand even closer than did the cathedrals to the angelic abode, the Cluniacs deemed themselves superior to bishops and refused to submit to their control. They claimed exemption from all episcopal jurisdiction.

By the time Gerard and Adalbero came to hold forth, the battle over monastic exemption in the kingdom of France had long since been joined. It had been raging, in fact, some thirty-five years, first waged by Abbo of Fleury, and by the papacy with which Cluny was allied. By 1024 the struggle had grown more bitter than ever. After talks with the emperor, Henry II, Pope Benedict VIII decided to extend the privilege of exemption accorded to the abbey of Cluny since 998 to all the priories of the congregation, wherever they might be located. Now it happens that they were everywhere. The abbot of Cluny at that point found himself the head of an immense conglomerate of monasteries; new subsidiaries were constantly being swallowed up by merger. It was truly a kingdom. An invasion. When a rural monastery became a Cluniac priory, an enclave was thereby created in that

140

diocese, a place thereafter impervious to episcopal intervention. The accelerating expansion of the *ordo cluniacensis* thus led to a widespread collapse of episcopal authority, provoking a breakup of regional powers precisely analogous to the disintegration of the power of the counts brought about by the growing independence of the castellans. The two phenomena were precisely contemporaneous. The extension of the feudalizing process to the echelon of the castellans and the spread of monastic exemptions are two faces of the significant modification of coercive structures that took place in France during the third decade of the eleventh century.

The new monasticism's outlook worried traditional bishops all the more because of the close ties which grew up between the reformed monasteries and the powers that had worked themselves free of royal control. In attempting to assert their independence, feudal lords relied on their own monasteries. What Saint-Denis near Paris and Fleury near Orléans were for the Capetians, Saint-Bertin represented for the count of Flanders, Saint-Aubin for the count of Angers, Jumièges, Fécamp, Montivilliers for the duke of Normandy, Saint-Martial for the counts of Angoulême: necropolises in which new dynasties could strike roots, sites of liturgical celebration, centers of literary production to turn out panegyrics bestowing upon the person of the prince virtues that had once been monopolized by the king. Temporal potentates, petty and great alike, had a clear sense of what they stood to gain by protecting, enriching, and purifying private monasteries of their own: what other institution could better have filled the role of gracing them with the qualities they lacked for want of anointment—the charismas, the mysterious links with transcendental forces that were in those days indispensable to anyone who would be obeyed? Here was a way for them to gain a more secure grip on the attributes of sovereignty. Moreover, it was a way to maintain control over the Church in their province. In northern France, the idea had survived that episcopal sees were subject to royal patronage. Interference in their affairs was to be undertaken only with the utmost prudence. It was easier to found monasteries, easier still to reform existing ones by bringing in good monks—Cluniacs—and immediately claiming an exemption. Thanks to the competition for secular power, the monks were able to pursue a profitable strategy, using their protectors, the princes, to wrest privileges from the bishops, turning to the king whenever the patron proved burdensome. Turning to the king, or else (and, in the south of the kingdom, first) to God himself. Gathered round the "humiliated" crucifix, cast to the ground and covered with thorns, the monks raised a cry to him who was nailed there with arms extended and waited for the wrath of heaven to descend upon their enemy. Or else they worked for the peace of God. On behalf of the latter movement, and in connection with quite material concerns, the abbots of Brioude, Limoges, Saint-Victor in Marseilles, and Cluny had shown themselves ardent propagandists.

141

This political infighting had profound repercussions on the religious life of the lay aristocracy. Indeed, its aim was in a sense to make monks of the *bellatores,* where this word should be understood, as Adalbero and Gerard understood it, to mean the princes. The collusion of the princes and the abbots in the idological sphere is one aspect of feudalization. Indeed, this complicity hastened the principalities' achievement of autonomy by opposing to the image of the sacred king surrounded by bishops the image of another alliance, different yet nonetheless advantageous to order, peace, and the populace. If the prince, who had not been anointed, submitted to monkish abstinence and participated alongside the monks in their most important observances, would he not thereby acquire a modicum of that spiritual valor that according to some was not the least bit inferior to *sapientia,* to the sanctity previously limited to martyrs, bishops, and kings? In support of this hypothesis we have a text, a fundamental document, of which I had occasion to speak earlier: the biography of Gerald of Aurillac. Gerald was a prince. He had become a saint not merely because, like a king, he had protected churches and upheld the peace, but above all because, like a monk, he had chanted the Psalms and lived in humility, obedience, and chastity. Who depicted him in such wise? The abbot of Cluny. And after him the monks of Cluny, who revised the manuscript so as to speak exclusively of monastic virtues. How many princes were there on the routes of pilgrimage in the early eleventh century, unarmed, garbed in white, escorted by monks and chanting psalms, preparing themselves to follow in the footsteps of Saint Gerald?

The result of this education of the laity initiated by the reformed monks was therefore confusion of the *ordines.* The monastic order's claims of independence from mandatory episcopal control were scandalous not only for this outcome, but also because they represented a proposal for a new social structure. Consider Adalbero's mocking description of the world turned upside-down: it harbors princes who refuse to make love, who shun the eating of meat, who leave their beds at night to chant rather than sleep. Like monks. Or like heretics. In so doing, moreover, they were in effect usurping a royal privilege, since only one layman, the king, had the right to comport himself as an *orator.* It was precisely this challenge to the privilege of anointment, the privilege of kings and bishops alike, that aroused the opposition of Gerard—and, more directly, of Adalbero. Thus the postulate of social trifunctionality was also leveled at the monks, and specifically at monks fallen under Cluny's spell. It was dredged up at the moment of reformed monasticism's triumph.

This triumph was general. Therein lay the cause of the most besetting concern: the king of France himself had been vanquished by it. Unbeknownst to himself, the king was becoming merely the prince of the

Ile-de-France. More and more he was behaving as other princes behaved, and as his father had done in the years before his seizure of the crown. Already in 993 Robert had turned his attention to the reform of Saint-Denis. He fancied himself accomplishing this task as king. In the diploma he granted the abbey in 1008 his tone was such that he might have been deemed the successor of the good Carolingians—reestablishing continuity with Charles the Bald, accusing the last kings of the former dynasty of having neglected the martyr and of having allowed "secular pomp" to infiltrate the monastery. He spoke as sovereign—as he had done in 1006 in confirming the privileges of the monastery of Fécamp, which was not part of his *regnum*. Particularly, and here the bishops were entirely in agreement with him, with regard to protecting the monks from the encroachments of the lay powers: around Saint-Denis Robert laid down a protected zone, an area of heightened immunity. In point of fact, he was careful to avoid any mention of exemption (which he had just confirmed outside his own territory, at Fécamp). Nevertheless, he had entrusted the internal reform of Saint-Denis to the finest representatives of the monastic institution, the abbots of Cluny, first Maieul and after him Odilo.

Why Cluny, which was so remote? Once again note must be taken of the Capetian policy's southern tilt. It was directed outside Frankish lands, toward Burgundy. Robert had earlier attended his uncle Henry, the duke, when Paray-le-Monial was ceded to Cluny in 999. But the alliance with the Cluniacs was forged when the king actually took the duchy in hand. In 1025, the abbot, Odilo, supported his action against the count of Sens; the following year, during Robert's stay in Rome, we find the pope hurling anathema against the violators of Cluny's privileges. The complicity is clear. Ten years later it was still more so. Saint-Bénigne of Dijon placed itself under Capetian protection; the monarch took Cluny under his special care; William of Volpiano, Odilo's friend, was called upon to reform Saint-Germain-des-Prés. During the months that Adalbero was hard at work polishing his satirical poem, it is clear that the aging king of France, striding boldly towards his death, had succumbed to the blandishments of reformed monasticism. He had become the bleating lamb whose memory the monk Helgaud of Fleury would celebrate as that of a saint, a saintly monk, suffering under the frock in the throes of death, with his last breaths softly humming the Psalms. Downtrodden, but exalted in prayer, he had lost that vehemence due to his youthful part, and with it had gone his power over events. When Adalbero uses the trifunctional figure, he is venting his wrath against "King Odilo," the usurper, against the new realm, the new structures in which an abbot had supplanted the bishops in the principal role. Once again let us praise the old prelate's lucidity. He was clearly aware of the fact that to carry through the reform of the Church (which had proceeded with astonishing speed and had affected not only the ecclesiastical institution but the whole of society), Rome and Cluny, the pope and the exempt monasteries, had joined forces against the king and the bishops.

Adalbero's discourse, like Gerard's, was therefore reactionary. It should be noted, moreover, that the polemic in which it figures kept well above the problems—let us call them political problems—connected with the organization of earthly society. Like the quest for the peace of God and the worries of the heretics, Cluny's efforts were inspired by an expectation of the end of time. Abbo of Fleury had mentioned the premonitory signs of millenarianism when he wrote the *Apologeticus*. Thirty years thereafter the distress had reached a more acute stage. In his *Histories,* the Cluniac monk Raoul Glaber is right to relate, retrospectively, to the millennium of Christ's death the unfolding chronology of peace assemblies, heretical outbreaks, successes in monastic reform—as well as the monumental renovations that led to the building of new churches everywhere and helped throw a "white robe" of purificatory rites over the body of Christendom. The three positions attacked by the bishops of Cambrai and Laon drew largely upon visions of a dramatic eschatology. The "terrors of the year 1000," or in any case the conviction that Christ's return was imminent, must be counted among the reasons why repentance was preached in one key rather than another. There was an urgency about making preparations for the passage over, about cleansing oneself of the stain of sin, foresaking the pleasures of love, the joys of combat, the power bestowed by money, and about pushing back the boundaries of that area known as "land without evil." Evil seemed to infect the society whose structures were crumbling. All the present turmoils presaged the coming of the Antichrist. Hence the carnal world had to be rejected *in toto,* as it was impossible to "belong simultaneously to the imperfect earth and to the land without evil": they were opposed, like order and counter-order.[9] One could only stand back, flee—but to do so was to draw nearer those provinces "where social relations were disappearing,"[10] along with those "distinctions" invoked by Gerard, following in the footsteps of Gregory.

The heretical sects, the conjurations of equals born of the peace movements, and the reformed monasteries were so many refuges, cloisters free from sin. Places where the only power allowed was that exercised by the most perfect, who led men in brotherhood towards a better world. Starting points on a great journey, wherein all were busy making ready for the crossing of the Red Sea, whether with foot-washing as among the heretics or by making processions across the abbey lands and their surroundings in imitation of the Exodus. As for the knights, forbidden to attack Christians, they took to the road in earnest, the long road to Santiago, Rome, or Jerusalem. One of the most visible signs of the new times in the third decade

144

of the eleventh century—Raoul Glaber was struck by it—was no doubt the sudden swelling of the "order" of penitents. This was an *ordo* long since set apart, classified by Church moralists, in which all attributes of sex and power were abolished. Its members could be recognized by their ceaseless wanderings, their fasting, their abandonment of arms, and their continence. Heretics, pilgrims of the Holy Land (and among them, to Raoul Glaber's amazement, increasing numbers of women, rich and poor), and, finally, monks: a great migration, an escape. And with it went the sentiment of setting out on the path of righteousness, contempt for those who did not follow, and a desire to carry them off in spite of themselves. This general upheaval brought to light another ternary division in mankind, wherein above the adepts of purification stood the tiny elite of *majores,* the "perfect," the leaders of the migration; here, moreover, black was strongly opposed to white, pure to impure, those who departed for the land without evil to the "wicked" who stayed behind.

Still, not everyone was carried away by this current. Many managed to keep their feet on the ground, many whose desire to escape this life was less ardent than their desire to order it, who believed that this world was never without evil—nor without good. Whose judgment, therefore, was that the undeniable incursions of disorder were being abetted by the very people who preached equality, in the belief that time had run its course, who confused the garden of Eden with the heavenly Jerusalem, by those proud, mad people who dared to claim that they were free of sin and fancied themselves escaping the human condition, people who wanted to go too far, too fast, and who were forcing the hand of God. People who were perverting the simple and with ease stirring up malcontents against the king, against the bishops, against those who had providentially been placed in command. Among those who then spoke and whose voices are audible today were some who were wont to repeat time and again that "time is not yet over; thou shalt not tempt the Lord thy God; no man can say the day nor the hour. . . . " Of this Gerard and Adalbero were convinced. The collapse of the world did not frighten them. They, too, expected; they, too, hoped for the passage into the hereafter, but in peace, for they knew, as the Carolingian bishops had known, that it would be done in an orderly manner. Therefore, even though they, like the others, intended to clear the way for the ultimate transformation, they wanted to do so in a different way. They were convinced that mankind, then caught up in the whirlpool of history, in the imperfections of the visible universe, must neither emulate the angels nor succumb to fantasy, but ought rather to arrange itself in proper order, to form up in ranks, so as to be able to pass through the gates of the true life without panic, without a scuffle. There is no reason to think that the two bishops were more concerned with the earth, with society, with politics than their opponents. The hope of deliverance obsessed them no less, and their gaze rested on heaven's perfections. But these they found to be monarchical, hierarchical. Hence they put up a bitter resistance against concepts which, having made their way up from the south in so many incongruous forms, were more than just open heresy (for in that case things would have been far simpler, the stake would ultimately have sufficed), concepts which, like their own, invoked the support of venerable Benedictine and Roman traditions and the authority of Gregory the Great. In the face of an incursion they deemed subversive, Adalbero and Gerard held fast to that which, in the time of Charles Martel, had saved Latin Christendom from another peril risen out of the same quarter, the Saracen invasion. They took their stand on the national soil, with the Frankish nation, the chosen people, taking their place behind those Parisian kings, Clovis and Charles the Bald, and behind their exalted protector, Dionysius. In opposition to those who wished for fusion, or confusion, for merging "order" and "condition," or submerging "order" in "condition," as voices were merged in monastic plainsong, they, musicians and polyphonists, proposed something different—like their condisciple and master, Gerbert of Rheims, who in a bygone day had tried to distinguish between tones, semitones, and quarter-tones on the monochord. They pressed for logical distinction, for "discretion" of differences. Between man and woman, ruler and subject, old and young. And so they were led by their argument to point out still another logical difference: between men who pray, men who fight, and, finally, men who cultivate the earth.

Their rhetoric answered the rhetoric of others. To be persuasive it had not merely to be more finely chiselled, more faithful to the teaching of the Bible and the Fathers. It had also to accommodate itself to precisely those aspects of concrete social relations which were undergoing change, thereby necessitating renovations in ideological discourse. Did the system incorporating the trifunctional figure make it possible to arrive at a more adequate conception of the first tentative manifestations of feudalism? Before venturing an answer to this question, we need to acquire a new perspective on what was really changing, on what was being set in place: the revelation of feudalism. A revolution.

13

THE FEUDAL REVOLUTION

Another "source," as we historians like to say, becomes available to us in ever greater abundance with the turn of the millennium, it, too, revived by the general progress in all things: surely not more was being written, but rather what was recorded was better preserved than before. I am speaking of deeds drawn up as warrants for rights, of charters, of notices in which accounts of agreements, judgments, or transfers of power were set down. Unlike others we have seen, these texts do not tell of fantasies, projects, utopias. To decipher these documents is to quit the realm of the imaginary, the realm of hopes and special pleading—the abode of a supposed tripartition in conformity with the divine will—to explore the terrain of what I shall refrain from calling the "real" (since mental representations have no less reality), but rather of the tangible aspects of existence. It is to lift the ideological veil, to observe what was going on in village, castle, and family. Documents such as these constitute the raw material of a retrospective sociography—and, together with what is laboriously being unearthed through archeological research into material culture, this is the only material accessible to us regarding a France still in its infancy.

Regarding everyday experience, the picture yielded by this kind of document is a less distorted one. I say less distorted, for these texts do not altogether escape being shaped by the pressures of the dominant ideology, if only by the constraints of literary style. Through them certain words are transmitted to us, the words of the *Gesta,* of the *Carmen,* Latin words: for in those days nothing but Latin was set down on parchment. The scribes who drew up charters therefore had to be translators, had to find equivalents for the words uttered in assemblies great or small in which rights were conferred and disputes adjudicated. The skill of these writers varied. Some contented themselves with giving hasty travesties of vernacular terms;

others, more pedantic, contrived to ransack the poets for pompous language capable of reproducing common speech. All were prisoners of formalism, obliged to fit their innovations into the Procrustean bed of traditional formulas. Hence there were two kinds of style. On the one hand, that of *sapientia,* of ideological utterance, more nearly resembling the language of the sacred texts. And on the other hand, the style of archival documents, which tended to reflect the spoken language. But frequently both styles were employed by the same men. The author who wrote the *Deeds of the Bishops of Cambrai* and recorded the proceedings of the Arras synod was certainly called upon to draft charters. For both purposes he would have used the same vocabulary, but in two different keys, in which identical words would not necessarily have had identical meanings. The connotations of the words *miles* or *servus* in Adalbero's poem did not necessarily coincide with their connotations in a charter of donation prepared in the scriptorium of Laon. No doubt such terminological traffic tended to unify and simplify the semantic field. Still, for these intellectuals Latin words remained polysemic. Slight nuances altered the meaning of a word depending on whether it happened to echo Biblical verse or legal debate. The ensuing scatter of meanings means that we too must use *discretio,* to distinguish differences carefully.

Stockpiled not on the shelves of the book-cabinet but in the coffers where the parchment warrants were kept, these words also served to classify men, for practical rather than theoretical purposes. For these documents had been drawn up to be read eventually before judicial assemblies, or, if need be, to refresh the memory of witnesses brought before the judges. Writers of charters and notices therefore deemed it useful and at times indispensable to specify the social positions of the parties to a contract, of their near relations, of the witnesses brought forward in their behalf, of the personage who delivered the judgemnt, and of the men present when agreement was reached—men brought together for that specific purpose, to witness the formulas and observe the acts by which the understanding was established. All this multitude had to be assigned appropriate places on a scale of power, a scale that would be recognized by whatever judicial bodies might someday have occasion to examine the document in question.

This classification might take several forms. One was to list the participants in hierarchical order, observing the accepted order of precedence, that of the common ritual processions, which on public ceremonial occasions paraded a visible representation of the imagined social ordering before the eyes of all. Another was to characterize a particular individual by an emblematic title indicative of his status. By observing these rankings and identifying such characterizations, we can reconstruct the system of social taxonomy. Bear in mind, however, that once again we are dealing with an institutionalized image, with the idea of social relations that had been formed within a certain milieu, consisting of scribes, lawyers, and so on. The force of these particular distinctions depended on the extent to which they could be deemed immutable, much as the law was supposed to be. Immutable, and respectable, respected for remaining faithful to time-honored usage. Consequently, the modes of classification that we find in texts of this kind are naturally conservative, and are fraught with residual forms. Far less supple than literary style or the language of ideological manifesto, these legalistic pronouncements prolonged the life of antiquated formalisms. Their rigidity rendered them insensitive to what was changing in the social body and kept change hidden for long periods. But in the end, because such documents were employed in practical affairs, they had to yield to modifications in social relations. At certain times these changes were so disruptive and so sharp that the customary formulas—like the customary ideological configurations—proved unusable. At such moments other words had to be found. Invention turned to boldness when the judiciary or the small group of scribes were themselves affected by the transformation, when, for instance, the documents came to be drawn up not by professionals but by amateurs. Now, as it happens, this was just what was taking place in the time of Adalbero and Gerard. In every sphere in which historians have looked closely at these phenomena, they have found a breakdown in French social vocabulary in the second decade of the eleventh century. During this period the assemblies in which the law was promulgated changed in character; where they had been public, they became private, domestic; the written language therefore had to register a new outlook. At Verdun-sur-le-Doubs in 1016, as we have seen, the clerks responsible for writing down the terms of the peace oaths were anxious to set down exactly what they had heard: to designate the knights, they preferred *caballarius* to *miles*.

"Feudal" society is revealed to us by the renovation of this vocabulary. With the obsolete formulas at last abandoned, the threadbare curtain that since Carolingian times had hung in front of social reality is torn away, disclosing the interplay of forces that had long been active but had hitherto developed in the private sphere, outside the legal domain—which explains why we used to know nothing about them. This disclosure came as a revelation not only to the historian, who may now date the feudal revolution from this moment, but also for contemporaries, who were obliged to admit that things were definitely not what they had been. A stupefying discovery. The sudden turn in the formularies made men aware of a disorder that needed to be exorcised as quickly as possible, with support from heavy ideological weaponry. To forge these ideological weapons it was necessary to incorporate the new elements that had suddenly been introduced into the hieratic literary formalisms, thereby gaining official sanction—that whole panoply of words long since applied to the constitution of a dowry, the allocation of a bequest, the acceptance of a judgment, or the conclusion of a peace, words which hitherto had been judged unworthy of being written down but which henceforth no one hesitated to transcribe, latinized, onto pieces of parchment.

Revelation? What, then, is "feudal society"? Clearly, Marc Bloch's admirable work must be read and reread. Still, the fact is that this book stimulated so much fruitful research that most of its suggestions, now nearly forty years old, stand in need of correction. Thus it is no longer possible, for example, to maintain that what we call feudalism emerged fully formed from the region between the Loire and the Rhine. The south, too, was a fertile area. A south which begins in Burgundy, in Poitou. Certain recent studies compel us to reconsider the far-reaching significance of a change that affected the whole area once subject to Carolingian domination.

The sudden changes we see in the nature of power and in the way it was conceived stem from transformations of the mode of production. These proceeded extremely slowly, almost imperceptibly. Begun some century and a half to two centuries earlier, they gradually destroyed a system of relations based on war and slavery. Formerly, each spring, the Frankish kings had led their people into battle and pillage; every autumn, the captives and the booty carried back from these seasonal escapades were shared out among the military chiefs and the guardians of the sanctuaries; it was through their good offices, moreover, that the people partook of the spoils. Military activity, predatory and primordial, established the five degrees of the social hierarchy. At the top, the king; next, his subordinates, the "premiers" (*primores*), who gathered the soldiers from a single province under their banner; below them, the cavalry, spearheads of the offensive, made up of the warriors *par excellence* (*milites*), distinguished by an emblem, the sword and its cross-belt, from the *populus,* or mass of free men; bearing less noble arms, the latter took part in the expeditions and shared the spoils, but less directly and less fully, taking turns in rotation, unless the enemy got the upper hand in battle and threatened the home territory, in which case all were mobilized; at the bottom of the scale, finally, were the slaves (*servi*), totally excluded from military activity. This organization of the body social, or strictly speaking, of the body public, asserted itself most strongly when the contingents gathered at the outset of the campaign, and was maintained throughout its duration. During the off season, when combat ceased, the formal organization was periodically revived in judicial assemblies: there the army formed up once again, convoked and commanded as before by royal delegates, but now concerned with peaceful works, arms set aside and words taken up in their stead, thereby converting the military organization into an instrument of internal pacification. Turning to local tasks, however, the army divided into smaller groups. Ensconced in their own territory far from the sovereign, the powerful figures in each region came to feel that they had free rein. That element of their authority that in summertime under the king's control was public in wintertime grew more ambiguous, being adulterated with other practices of a private, familial nature, confounded with another order of obedience. From top to bottom of the hierarchy, from the royal palace down to the humblest village dwelling, this other relationship, shielded from royal intervention, subjected to the head of household's utter dominion all his kin by blood, by marriage, or by rites of adoption—everyone he "fed," as it were, his servants, dependents, and slaves. The real arena of power was no longer the army but now the great domain, the vast congeries of fields and meadows, which, though extensively worked, was only of secondary importance as a productive source, since the relatively small population still drew the major portion of its subsistence from uncultivated areas, and since the shares of booty, the profits of depredations outside the domain, were adequate to the needs of luxury, festivals, upkeep of the dead, and service to God and the patron saints.

Now, in the course of the ninth century, the Carolingian empire having expanded enormously, and the areas tempting for rapine thus having receded to considerable distances, the tribes led by the Franks ceased to be conquerors. Political ideology adapted itself to this new reality. Eventually, the sovereign came to be thought of as the *rex pacificus,* and the state that he governed as a "vision of peace." In a complete turnabout, this state was not long in becoming the object of attack from without. From that moment commenced an obscure movement that turned the whole military system—i.e., the predilection to seize property by force, to engage in depredations (*praeda*)—inward upon itself. At the height of this phenomenon, we find Christian horsemen, as always, formed up under the banner of a chief, ready for pillage, sword in hand; but now they no longer rode off to join forces with the king in one great army; instead, they sallied forth from a thousand lairs, from those castles dotting the countryside that had been built to ward off the invading foe. At first they did battle against the enemy, defending the homeland. But when in the tenth century the intervals between the waves of invasion grew longer, instead of laying down their arms they continued their rapine. Only the prey was different. What they still took now and then from the pagans they began to demand in the interim from the "plebs," from the "unarmed people." After the year 1000, in the Frankish kingdom, the populace became the sole object of their pillaging, which went on with still greater impunity than before in view of the king's inability henceforth to check their violence and rapacity. In the time of the *Gesta* and the *Carmen,* the most serious political and social problem was that posed by this turning inward—an open sore, a calamity which manifested itself in two forms: first, the castles—castles of all sorts, the one in Cambrai, the ones that Robert forbade to be built near Cluny, the ones that were at that time going up in increasing numbers everywhere, as archeology has shown wherever the investigation has been judiciously pressed, in Provence just as much as Normandy; second, the destructive hordes of warriors camped in these fortresses, supposedly to protect the surrounding region against "wicked men," but in truth occupying the land, picking it bare. Small independent garrisons, these troops were absolutely uncontrolled. This was the political aspect of the problem: power had disintegrated; it could only be effectively exercised within the boundaries of the castellany; this explains why the names of castellans and their associated knights replaced those of counts and bishops at the bottom of royal diplomas after 1028. Men of war living on the land, bleeding it white, forcing the peasants, free or not, to produce ever greater quantities, in order to obtain from their labor the pleasures of life never renounced by the professional soldiers, in order to satisfy the aristocratic taste for luxury and waste, which could no longer find its fill in foreign razzias: this was the economic aspect.

Such was the change that finally, in the early eleventh century, the vocabulary used by the writers of charters and notices had to reflect. From that time the title *dominus* (formerly applied only to God, the king, and bishops, but during the tenth century bestowed on counts as well) was used to characterize any of the hundreds of marauder captains ensconced in castle fortresses. For they had become the real lords of war and peace. The laymen referred to as *domini* in the cartularies were the *bellatores* treated of in ideological manifestos: men in control of the military aspect of temporal power, of *potestas*. This divine, this royal attribute was seized by the castellans. In the charters, moreover, the Latin word *potestas* was now used quite straightforwardly to denote the organism that supplanted the great domain in establishing the fundamental framework of the relations of production: the seigniory. A territory; at its center, the fortress, guaranteeing the security of the lands; all who lived within its confines and who, normally unarmed, did not participate directly in its defense, were subjugated to the master of the tower, to his "ban," to his coercive powers, defenseless before his demands, exploited on the pretext of paying for the peace that he secured. The "peasants," the "villagers" settled therein, as well as the "aubains," or foreigners passing through, paid him such of the old royal taxes as had survived, and acquitted themselves of the fines with which they were deluged for the least offenses, and the tolls; teams of forced-laborers were pressed into service when stockades and moats were in need of repair; protected, judged, punished, they periodically yielded up something quite like a ransom, those myriad exactions that certain documents refer to, euphorically, as "gifts," ostensibly the fruits of their gratitude. These seizures were known as "customs." In the vicinity of castles he still held, the king himself levied them; Robert the Pious in 1008 turned over what customs he collected from the peasants on abbey lands to the monks of Saint-Denis. What emerges from documents of the kind we are now examining as characteristic of the period immediately following the year 1000 is, as some would put it, a new "mode of production." It is better not to call it feudal—the fief plays no part here—but rather seigniorial. Indeed, it was based on the seigniory, the *potestas*, the right of confiscation within a zone of military occupation, rather than, as before, on the network of tenant obligations or on the slaves of a great domain. Am I wrong to speak of revolution? Its pace was quite slow, of course. What is more, we can observe only the end result of the process, when the system of exploitation that was its central element at last breaks its silence and its cover and assumes a guise of regularity, of legitimacy. With the beginning of the eleventh century, what penetrated into the realm of customs, i.e., into law—for which reason we are able to observe it—was nothing other than the whole range of extortions that the populace had had to bear whenever its rulers were not on campaign, a burden of oppression which the Carolingian sovereigns had unsuccessfully endeavored for centuries to lighten: the oppression of the "paupers" by the "potentates." In times past kings had been able to limit this oppression by making lavish gifts to the *primores* from the spoils of what they jointly confiscated outside the confines of the realm. By the eleventh century, however, the king had nothing more to give. He was obliged to allow the "lords" to take. He himself took where he could. This was the meaning of the *imbecillitas regis*.

The consequences of the all-powerful transformation of the relations of production were immense. From the warriors' greed ensued intensification of rural labor, cultivation of formerly virgin lands, improvements in agricultural technique—more extensive planting of oats, for instance, to provide feed for the cavalry's horses. Nothing precludes our believing that the new lords, whether consciously or not, encouraged the growth of the population, because in their eyes the most profitable form of capital was henceforth not land but the laborer. All these changes, furthermore, broke down the barriers that in the early Middle Ages had prevented the public power from interfering in affairs within the family redoubt, in the "manses," the households: the castellan and his squadron of horse took no notice of these obstacles; their aim was to exploit, in the same way as they exploited other villagers, people belonging to the "families" of other men, slaves, servants, protégés, clients.

All of this affected the social structure in three ways. First, within the peasantry that which distinguished landowners from tenants, freedom from slavery, was gradually eroded. Subject to identical levies, far heavier than the services formerly rendered, all the villagers, the *"vilains,"* were lumped together. In this sphere the old divisions were blurred. By contrast, the differences between laymen and clergy came to be more sharply defined— with the clergy waging an intense struggle to accredit the notion that their function, like that of the specialists in warfare, exempted them from all exactions, from the customs. Most important of all the consequences was the third: a fundamental social dividing line was henceforth drawn according to a new criterion, the bearing of arms. Thereby distinguished from the "people" were not merely the "potentates," the "sires," the *bellatores,* who still numbered only a handful, but also the whole troop of their "ministers," the helmed lieutenants of their power: the horsemen, the knights.

These warriors, who garrisoned the castle in rotation and all rallied to its defense in time of danger, comprised a kind of military domestic staff of the *dominus.* His subordinates, they were bound to him by ties of vassalage—it was also in the third decade of the eleventh century that feudo-vassalic institutions in northern France were finally organized into a system, with the fief, however, never playing more than a peripheral part in what is generally known as feudalism. Faithful servants, the youngest were devoted to the oldest, the *senior,* as in every household. These vassal-knights must be seen as the agents of seigniorial exploitation. Their valor aided the sire in gaining the upper hand over his neighbors, his competitors, helped him extend the reach of his taxation as far as possible, and lent him assistance in establishing his authority over Church domains as their generously remunerated guardian. Throughout this aggressive phase, which reached its height between 1020 and 1030, these squads of horse played a crucial role in the rivalry for the profits of the new power, a rivalry which, as we have seen, by pitting the castellan in Cambrai against the bishop, was directly responsible for Gerard's speech on peace and order. But it was also the knights who, not without difficulty, inspired fear whereby the peasantry was compelled to bend to the yoke, to assume the new function of toil, of productive labor, assigned it by the potentates.

Writing about Catalonia, Pierre Bonnassie[1] has described this "conditioning" of the peasants in abundant and accurate detail. He has shown what the actual role of the "cavalcades" was: periodically, the castellan would lead his squad of horse on patrol throughout the petty principality, the "district"—yet another word that bespeaks coercion—around the fortress in a terrifying show of force whose aim was to rekindle that "fear" among the rustics that according to Isidore of Seville was actually salutary because it kept the subjects from sinning. The villagers were thereby impelled to pay up their taxes without raising too much of a fuss. The knights were oppression incarnate. Of the thoughts of the peasants, we are condemned to ignorance. But the ecclesiastics, who, though individually exempt, saw their domains subjected to the exactions of the lay lords, rivaled one another in denouncing the knights as henchmen of the devil, guilty of "rapine" and "depredation," as the "customs" and all else that went to fatten the masters of the ban appeared in the eyes of the clergy.

These masters of the ban did not exploit their comrades in arms. On the

154

contrary, they shared with them the fruits of exploitation. To insure that their "friends" not abandon them, as they themselves had abandoned first the king and then the princes, the *domini* had to be generous, had to give. Their authority was measured by their generosity. Largesse was the primary and indispensable virtue of the ruler. What the knights had forced the peasants to yield up served to arm them, to clothe them, to regale them, filling the cornucopia of that feast without surcease that every *dominus* was obliged to lay on. Like their lord, the knights enjoyed the right to take lodging and food for themselves and their horses in the hovels of the peasants, which they visited in rotation, living a day or two in each. They claimed their share of the gifts that the subjects, marching in single file, carried up to the castle gates at Christmas, Easter, and Saint Martin's Day. Taking with one hand, receiving with the other, the knights were the real hub of the seigniorial economy, the driving wheel of the system of exploitation.

Where did these agents come from? Of this we have no clear picture. How many of them were domestic servants chosen for their courage, for their expert horsemanship? How many were soldiers of fortune emerged from obscurity? Primarily, it seems, the group was made up the wealthiest landowners in the territory protected by the fortress, men sufficiently well off to equip themselves adequately, sufficiently at leisure to undertake the necessary training—the heirs, quite simply, of the *milites* of the Frankish army, of the horsemen girded with the cross-belt who, as early as Hincmar's day, constituted the active membership of that host. Twenty or thirty times more numerous than the "sires," than the "great," than the "rich men" whose vassals, or associates, they were, whom they served, with the expectation of receiving benefits in return, the knights and their masters together made up the dominant class within the laity. At the same time, however, the knights were kept beneath the lords of their fief, subordinated. Thus the aristocracy consisted of two strata—and it was this structure that the charter writers wished to convey through their use of new words. Other terms therefore came into use in the formularies alongside those such as *domini, proceres,* and *principes* which designated the chiefs. The scribes groped their way, settling for a time on *nobilis* (the term was too vague), or *caballarius* (too close to the vulgar term). They avoided, in any case, the use of *bellator* and *pugnator*. Finally, one title came to the fore, as early as the late tenth century in the Mâconnais, perhaps a few years later north of the Loire; in any event the term was thoroughly established by 1025 in *Francia* and Lotharingia: the word *miles*.[2] This was at once given a highly pejorative connotation by the ecclesiastics who employed it. *Militia, malicia:* the knights who had brusquely elbowed their way to center-stage of the political scene, who were the apparent agents of the change that had to be accepted as irremediable and devastating—were they not the advance guard of the armies of evil?

In fact, the institutions of the peace of God were forged as weapons to be used against the knights by the prelates and the princes, by the good *bellatores,* friends of the purest monks, whose dream it was to replace the faltering king as upholders of the *ordo.* In its first phase, until around 1020, the ideology of the peace of God was resolutely anticavalry, antichivalric. To quell the disturbances, this ideology envisaged confining one of the two layers of the lay aristocracy, the lower, broader one, within a system of moral constraints to be overseen jointly by the "prelates," spiritual and temporal, working hand in hand. But this ideology was in no sense anti-seigniorial. For the heads of the Church were themselves *domini.* They possessed fortresses; these castles were manned by *milites,* who did homage to the bishops and abbots and pledged their fidelity, with that oath of the "Lotharingian horsemen" that Gerard of Cambrai attempted to force his rival to swear in order to put an end to the castellan's encroachments. Using these warriors as agents, the ecclesiastical lords levied on a territory's villagers exactions which despite their claims to the contrary were no less burdensome than the exactions of laymen. *Oratores* and *bellatores* were "potentates." Within the network of social relations they occupied an identical position. At the outset, they were accomplices. But in the course of the competition for power and its profits, which intensified as the king showed himself increasingly incapable of maintaining the balance between the rivals, the alliance broke down. In northern France this breakdown became manifest during the third decade of the century. To maintain the right to exploit their own subjects, the great ecclesiastical lords went to war against the field marshals, using the weapons they knew better than anyone how to wield. With the word they waged war according to their own peculiar strategy on the social battlefield.

To their adversaries they presented a united front. Even the causes of divison among themselves, particularly the monastic exemption, were ultimately forgotten. Once again they pressed Gelasius' hoary theses into service, loudly advertised the superiority of the spiritual, and invoked the privileges promised by the kings to all the servants of God. The bitterness of the conflict enforced unity. Thus after 1015, the provisions of the peace of God, which for a quarter of a century had concerned only the clergy, began treating monks and clerks on an equal footing. So, too, do we find not a few priests striving for monastic purity, and growing numbers of monks anxious to enter the priesthood. Against the "tyrants" who threatened the earthly patrimony of God and his saints, the sacerdotal and monastic orders struggled together for the Church's freedoms, just as they mustered their forces against the challenge of heresy with both groups repudiating the flesh and participating in the eucharistic sacrifice in equal measure.

This led them to consign all sword-wielding laymen indiscriminately to the side of evil, to shut their eyes to the differences between the knights and the lords they served, between *milites* and *bellatores*. This want of discrimination comes to the attention of us historians on the occasion of its first formal enunciation before the council of Limoges in 1031, where the wrath of God was called down "upon all knights, upon their arms and upon their horses," the same curse being invoked against "princes of the knightly order" who would not oblige their warriors to respect the peace. But already in 1025, the canon of Cambrai, writing on behalf of the bishop, betrays the same outlook in referring to the castellan Walter and his friend the count of Flanders as *raptores,* deeming them guilty of the sin peculiar to knighthood, namely, rapine.

To say that the "princes" and their myrmidons sinned indistinctly was to assign them the same duties, to impose on them the same moral rules, hence to extend to all the *milites* the obligations that previously applied only to the *bellatores.* It was to preach to the knights that they ought to accept the same responsibilities as princes, first to protect the poor, and second to take part in the liturgy. And it was to hold out Gerald, the count of Aurillac, as an example for all to follow. During the same period, moreover, the Church was just beginning to dream of slowly diverting the violence of the men of arms away from the Christian people and into holy war, of sending them off to Santiago of Compostela or Jerusalem to fight; rekindling the memory of Charlemagne, the Church dreamed of the halcyon days when pillage afflicted not peasants but pagans; it envisaged turning armed marauders into heroes of the righteous cause, soldiers of evil into knights of Christ. Not only was this a way of reducing the danger naturally inherent in the knightly order, but also a way of assigning that order a place within a system of values, a way of legitimating its privileges and justifying the position it occupied in the seigniorial relations of production.

Thus the dispute over the profits of the seigniory ultimately accentuated the division of the dominant class into two bodies: on one side, the clerks and the monks, exempt, because they prayed, in their person and in their property from the taxes collected by the temporal powers; on the other side, the lords and the knights, who, because they waged the good fight, were entitled to collect those taxes. These benefits the former owed to their purity, the latter to their valor. Hence the matter was one of morality: inevitably these two bodies were seen as two orders in the ethical sense of the term. But a rivalry of the most intense sort pitted them against each other. This accounts for the intervention of a third participant in the contest. The strategy adopted by the lords spiritual forced them to back this third party, to win it over to their side, to lend it their support, and to rely on its support in return: this third participant was, of course, the peasant populace. Clerks and monks claimed to be fighting for its "freedom," i.e., its exemption from seigniorial obligations. Under their own dominion, they claimed, the peasantry was better off; in fact, owing to its stricter management, ecclesiastical seigniory may have seemed more exacting. The passive populace—passive, yet called upon to accept a role in the global system, to assume specific obligations, to take its place in the system of values. The value specific to the populace, to which was attributed a saving grace on a par with valor and purity, was the pain of the flesh, the suffering due to labor. *Dolor—labor.* Just as the function of the pure was to pray for their fellows, and that of the valiant to risk their lives in defense of all, so the function of those whose value consisted in their weariness was to win the bread of other men in the sweat of their brow. This toil they offered in exchange for the salvation of their souls and the security of their bodies. Justifying themselves, but in the same stroke justifying the seigniorial mode of production as well.

How were the ongoing transformations at this level of the social edifice reflected in the vocabulary of the charters and notices? Ultimately, this vocabulary adapted to the changes, which adaptation took place under ecclesiastical control. The clergy sought words to designate, in lists of witnesses in particular, men who were not like themselves men of the Church, nor knights, men among whom the distinction between servitude and freedom was vanishing. *Pauper* was not really appropriate: it suggested too great a degree of passivity. Hesitant, the scribes sometimes chose *agricola,* since labor in the fields was in those days responsible for all growth, or else *villanus:* this was the term the lords used to denote those whose strength they exploited. Most favored was *rusticus.* The word *laborator* was not adopted. No doubt a thorough search would turn up occasional instances of its use in charters from central France, between Limousin and Dauphiné. On its first appearance in the Mâcon cathedral cartulary in an edict drawn up in 928, a hundred years before the composition of Adalbero's poem, it attached to the best-equipped among the peasants. But by the time Adalbero came to write, the term was still extremely rare, and to me it seems quite noteworthy that in this same Mâcon cartulary and during this very period (1031–60), in a formula quite similar to the tenth-century one and to characterize the very same social group, the "best peasants," the owners of plow-gear, the scribe avoided using this particular word. In the early eleventh century, as the new relations of production were taking hold, the term *laborator* apparently did not strike the men responsible for drawing up edicts and transcribing them into compendiums as a suitable one for defining the subjects of the seigniory, the producers, the exploited and protected element of the population.

The men who were confecting treatises on the ideal society—in some instances the same men—show no greater inclination to employ the word, despite the evident attraction of its consonance with *orator* and *bellator.* Of course, the very considerations that in view of the new configuration of

158

power relations were laying the groundwork for incorporating the trifunctional theme in a project for a new society impelled these men to apply to the
populace terms having functional connotations. Already in the late tenth
century Abbo of Fleury had ceased to be satisfied with the negative expression *imbelles* and *inerme vulgus,* which his predecessors had used; he had
preferred *agricola.* This was the word employed by Gerard of Cambrai's
secretary. He and Adalbero did use, if not *laborator,* at least the noun *labor*
and the verb *laborare.* Was it true that in their minds these two terms
implied improvement, expansion of cultivation, an eminently productive
activity whose yield was just then being increased by advances in agricultural technique stimulated by seigniorial requirements? Did they mean to
exalt, alongside the positive role of the *oratores* and the *bellatores,* that of a
peasant elite, manning the outposts of economic progress? I do not think so.
And I am not sure that at the time these words carried such a meaning in
charters drafted in northern France. That they are included in the various
ideological models put forward by ecclesiastics reflects, to my mind, the
perception of the essential, initial phenomenon, the structural change, the
process of seigniorialization, that bound to labor any layman who was not a
man of arms, and forced him to intensify his toil. "Those who labor" are not
yet the "ploughmen" of modern times, better equipped than the "day-
laborers," hence in a better position to make the Garden of Eden bloom.
They are rather those who, like Adam after the Fall, are condemned to sweat
in forced labor, condemned to the "servile condition."

The incontestable growth of the rural economy accentuated the contrast
between leisure and labor in this period; it made men aware—in a major
upheaval in mental attitudes—of the part that production played in the
social organism, of the role of that surplus product of peasant labor that fed
the specialists in both kinds of combat, spiritual and temporal, a surplus
consumed by the soldiers of both armies. That which in the time of Hincmar
was merely passivity in the "poor" became, in the time of Adalbero and
Gerard, in the "villager" and "peasant," an object of seigniorial levy, a
profitable and necessary activity. Hence a function, complementary to the
two Gelasian functions. But the establishment of new relations of domination had shifted the locus of the food-producing function in social space.
Previously, the obligation to toil in order to feed a master had been relegated
outside the sphere of the "people": it fell upon slaves. After the year 1000,
with the increased weight of the power of the ban, this burden came to be
borne by all "rustics." Toil was the common fate of all men who were
neither warriors nor priests. Some peasants might well claim to be free; they
were nevertheless like the others subjected to the new seigniory. *Servi*—in
the end, this was the word Adalbero chose to denote the agents of the third
function.

That *labor* and its derivatives referred much less to the fecundity of manual work than to its pain, its humiliating pain, is proved by Adalbero's correction of the manuscript of his poem, where he substituted *dolor* for *labor*. Further proof is provided by Abbo in the *Apologeticus,* where *laborare* is rejected in favor of *insudare,* a word evocative of the sweat of Adam, i.e., of the original sin, that foundation on which inequality, hence social order, rested, buttressed by the penitential spirit. Indeed, according to the rule of Saint Benedict (but just as much in heretical doctrine) to work meant voluntarily to renounce liberty and nobility, to lower oneself to earth, to the condition of the slave, to humiliate oneself. Adalbero's inclusion in the *Carmen* of a *planctus,* a lament over the condition of the workers, was surely not intended to be merely another criticism of the monks for exploiting the *servi;*[3] did the bishops not exploit them? His point was to emphasize this humiliation. For every ideological model that is put together to serve the needs of the dominant class aims to induce the oppressed to venerate the ways of life from which they are excluded and to despise those that are imposed on them.[4] Furthermore, in the timelessness of a system of values that sublimated the tangible relations that existed within society, humility bestowed a redemptive value on labor. The body's pain redeemed its sins. The peasants were supposed to accept the notion that if they put their hearts into their work, they would have a greater chance than other men of being saved. Over their weary bodies, therefore, Adalbero shed some sanctimonious tears.

Thus in the representational system imagined by the bishops of *Francia,* trifunctionality, in conjunction with the principle of necessary inequality, served in the name of "charity," in the name of reciprocity of services, to justify seigniorial exploitation. Agricultural production had to increase so that the warriors and priests might live comfortably on its surpluses. Physical forces had to be sent into the field to accomplish this end. This additional effort was sanctified. Not all men were expected to take part therein, but only those who were exempt from prayer and combat. In the third decade of the eleventh century the need to stress this division of roles asserted itself with even greater urgency than before, as the heresiarchs were suggesting that everyone in this world be put to work. Their minds were fixed exclusively on heaven; but among those who heeded their words were many, no doubt, who were thinking of earth; heresy, calling for equality, therefore fostered resistance to oppression; it rallied the victims of the feudal revolution. It was the lords, who profited from that revolution, who spoke of the three functions; their words were addressed to the peasants: "Work, take pains, and you shall enter into the Kingdom." If the Church's only concern had been with competition from the temporal powers and with the troubles caused by the knights, to have proclaimed the Gelasian doctrine of binarity would have sufficed. As things were, the ternary figure was far more suita-

ble, because it expressed at once the antagonisms existing within the dominant class and the structural complicity of its two antagonistic opponents,
ecclesiastic and lay. It was of assistance in maintaining the populace in a
submissive state. Was this not the primary intention of those who first
employed it in argument? At the time the trifunctional postulate was set
forth in a clear statement, was the class struggle not intensifying, was the
peasantry not balking at the increasing burden of "customs"? And in the
forefront of the struggle, did one not find the wealthier element of the
populace, whose status was diminished by the rise of the new seigniory?
Was there not a new animus perceptible in the clamor for "freedom," i.e.,
exemption? Were the lords spiritual momentarily tempted to use these protests against their rivals? How many peasants, not fortunate enough to be
classed among the knights, but nevertheless unwilling to be lumped together
with slaves, in those days loudly sang the "song of our common ancestors"?
What is the significance of the outbreak of heresy? What is the significance
of the peace assemblies, to which the chronicles tell us multitudes thronged?
To what extent was the movement for the peace of God a protest movement? Did prelates, abbots, and princes not find that here and there their
hands were forced, that oaths sworn on the spur of the moment against
noble marauders compelled them to act? The available texts disguise the
rebellious tensions. They do not altogether conceal them. What is known of
the revolt of the peasants of Normandy at the very end of the tenth century,
other than that it was put down brutally? Conceivably, of all the dangers
manifestly on the rise in northern France at the time Gerard and Adalbero
were holding forth, that which stemmed from popular uprisings, whether
overt or not, may have been deemed the most serious. Hence it was important that a niche be carved out in models of the ideal society for the third
partner—risen to a formidable position in cities undergoing rapid expansion, such as Cambrai, Laon, Douai—important that an appropriate place
be found for the people, under the authority of the heads of the Church,
under the power of the masters of castles. Obedience and resignation were
desired of the populace. The merits attaching to willing acceptance of the
laborer's lot were held up for popular admiration. In the world of the dead
the people were promised redemption, which indulgence would soon be
promised to the crusades. An attempt was made to convince them that there
was in fact a mutual exchange of services, that they were themselves served,
that the "great," the "nobles" sacrificed themselves for the populace, in
virtue of which their privileges were rendered legitimate.

Without any doubt, the four ideological models that confronted one another
in 1025 all took into account the upheavals in social relations disclosed by
charters and reports. One of them, the heretical model, did so to deny that
upheaval by fleeing to a place far from reality. In league against this view,

161

the three others took heed of the changes to erect above the new social configuration an order in conformity with God's intentions. All three used the trifunctional theme, but they did not locate the boundaries between the social categories in precisely the same way. But more important than the dividing lines were the points of convergence, i.e., the functions. In all three antiheretical proposals these were the same. And in all three the fundamental division set that which was ordered (*ordonné*) apart from that which was subordinate (*subordonné*), namely, the "plebs," third member of the triad. This frontier was traced by the seigniorial mode of production, just then achieving its ineluctable completion. The three formulas declared it to be in conformity with God's will. On this point they were in agreement. They were also in agreement about proclaiming the natural alliance between the people and the Church. The only question on which Adalbero and Gerard differed with the proponents of the peace of God and of reformed monasticism involved the proper strategy for defending the interests of the ecclesiastical lords.

On the continent, men of culture apparently did attempt to adapt the figures of ideology to the manifest changes in the social structure from as early as the end of the tenth century. This labor of ideological realignment was begun in the countries first deprived of royal tutelage, in the southern part of the French kingdom and in those particularly fertile border provinces, Burgundy and the Loire area, at the same time in both the peace assemblies and the monasteries battling for exemption. In these contexts a system of values based on the reciprocity of the three functions was forged. In the decades following the year 1000 this system made its way into *Francia*. The monarchy was not thereby repudiated, but rather obviated, whereas Adalbero and Gerard deemed the monarchy necessary. In the name of Carolingian tradition, of Frankish tradition, they reacted. In the still malleable terms of the argument set forth by the Rome-backed monks and their episcopal confrères, who were attempting to set up institutions similar to those of the Burgundian peace movement, they discovered the outlines of the trifunctional proposition. More resolute than their forerunners, they adapted it to their own purposes. Gerard enunciated his proposition with respect to the populace, whose dreams of freedom had been inflamed, perhaps at Douai, by the propaganda of the peace-men, and to a castellan who was using the popular clamor to usurp the bishop's powers. Adalbero stated his with reference first to Abbo of Fleury, and then to King Robert, who was being "Clunyized." Thus both bishops had seized one of the enemy's weapons; honing it (theirs was the first clear statement of the principle of social trifunctionality), they then turned it back against the adversary in the form of a counter-argument. This perhaps accounts for the fact that the couplet concerning the three functions gives the impression of being a patch

162

crudely sewn in as a preamble to Gerard's speech, and as a conclusion to the positive portion of Adalbero's pamphlet. What this tirade formulated was a postulate, an axiomatic fact; it furnished a supplement to the main argument.

A supplement that served a conservative enterprise—conservative of the old Carolingian order. A reactionary enterprise, reacting against the movements that were completing the reduction of that order to ruins. In summary, let me stress once again the obstinate conservatism of the two prelates. Both men based their ideas on outmoded social relations, primarily slavery. This survived only in linguistic habits whose obsolescence was increasingly pronounced. Astonishingly archaic, Adalbero's thought was based on a classificatory schema that had been inadequate since the eighth century and that refused to acknowledge the existence of intermediaries of any sort between the *servi* and the *nobiles*. Both Adalbero and Gerard, moreover, attributed to the king of western France a power that had long since ceased to be his. At the time they were writing, how could anyone have believed the king capable of punishing nobles if they committed crimes, how could anyone have thought the king alone responsible for the protection of widows and orphans, how could anyone have imagined that he had the means to instate good *rectores,* hence to dismiss unworthy princes, and to control the organization of the peace? How could anyone have looked upon the temporal power exercised by the "great" as a delegation of the power of the king? Underlying the whole *Carmen ad Robertum regem* is an idea that is nothing short of folly, the idea of an earthly sovereign who, like the heavenly "king of kings" whose lieutenant he was, possessed the capacity to distinguish (*discreta potestas*),[5] which gave him the right to establish priorities, to marshal processions in accordance with the correct order, and to work for stability by silencing the false prophets, by forbidding them to modify the *ordo* whether by force or else, insidiously, as the Cluniacs were doing, by "changing customs." The idea of an earthly sovereign capable of enforcing the strictest imaginable law of interdiction, that would have confined every man to his own condition and restored anyone who might escape to his proper place. Folly, because if the French kings had ever enjoyed such power, it had eluded them for at least two centuries. In the manner, finally, of their ambition to counter the rise of monasticism and knighthood, the theses of Adalbero and Gerard again were conservative, reactionary. Indeed, it was against the knights and the monks that Gerard and Adalbero first rose up, denouncing them both, as Claude Carozzi has ably shown, as heretics, as agents of disorder, as troublemakers. As "youths" challenging the power of the old and "wise," of the "lords," youths who stood in urgent need of discipline, a discipline to be achieved by making the monks subjects of the bishops, and the knights of the princes—confining them within a context of domestic obedience wherein they would be obliged to show their elders the respect due them from the adolescent members of any well-ordered household. The *Carmen* is the anti-Roland: it takes the part of Ganelon.

For Adalbero's tripartition was in fact based on a simple distinction, on the division that existed within every family (then the basic context of social relations, the family's image dominated all modes of thought, obstinately superimposing itself on every representation of power, whether that of God, the king, the bishop, the abbot "father," the lord of the castle over his vassals, or the village squire over his tenants): the division of adult males into two age groups. One of these, the high-spirited one, was charged like Varuna with the function of displaying strength, while the other, like Mitra, was self-possessed, just, temperate, prayerful. Thus power was dichotomized on the basis of age, in virtue of which each individual was assigned his proper place in that other procession, biological and genetic, wherein the successive generations were made to follow one after the other in orderly sequence in households, in dynasties, in an ineluctable order whereby the liberal exchange of affection and respectful devotion that was the key to the Gregorian system of necessary inequality was instituted between fathers and sons—and metaphorically between lords, *seigneurs* (*seniores:* the old), and vassals (*vassali:* young men); on this dichotomy Gerard and Adalbero based their theses. They were bishops, sacred personages. Hence they were sages and therefore ranged among the elders. Serene, as befitted old men, they could not accept the idea that the end of time, the subsumption of history by eternity, could take place in tumultuous conditions. Profoundly cultivated, classically minded men, more sensitive to Augustine's words than to those of the Apocalypse, they condemned, from the height of their throne, the excesses of youth—not only the disorders, but also their secondary effects, which were proving disruptive and smacked of rebellion: change, taste for those novelties that everywhere seem incessantly to blossom whenever springtime descends upon the world.

The final avatar of Carolingian thought, still their model of society had nothing of a nostalgic dream about it. No fools, they were well aware that in Capetian territory the monarchy they called upon in desperation to uphold the new order was no more than a brave facade, behind which real power had crumbled to dust. It was no accident that the reform proposals pronounced with assurance by Gerard, who hailed from Lorraine, bordering on less advanced Austrasia wherein Carolingian institutions still stood fast, were expressed in Laon in the form of a disillusioned satire. Was it possible that the two bishops failed to appreciate the strength of millenarianism, of the penitential upsurge? They were persuaded to fight a rearguard action. They felt that victory was smiling upon their enemies, the reformist monks, the proponents of the peace of God. Can we doubt that to bestow the cachet of sacredness upon associations sprung up of their own accord among squadrons of knights and urban merchants was to respond to the aspirations of the middle stratum of *milites* and *cives,* knights and bourgeois, who made up the more enterprising and robust element of the population of northern France at the time? Can we doubt that it was to follow the channel cut by the social structure itself as it evolved through time? Because the ideology of the peace of God, like that of Cluniac monasticism, "merely put into place what society at every level was already saying about itself,"[6] it was most likely to succeed in domesticating the knights, demystifying heretical preaching, and keeping up the hopes of the impoverished, whom the aging aristocrat Adalbero in his candor bluntly relegated to a position lower down on the scale, nearer the category of slaves.

Even though the system built up by Adalbero and Gerard was reactionary and attacked the most vital elements in the social formation as it then existed—knighthood, reformed monasticism, and the exuberance of urban life—whereby it was doomed to failure, it did nevertheless cleave closely in a certain sense to the deep-seated movements that carried "feudalism" along with them into the broad light of day. This was a consequence of its terrestrial, incarnate aspect. Imbued with civic humanism and with the highest culture, the system rejected the illusions of otherworldliness, of flight into the timeless beyond. Indeed, Gerard, before the heretics at Arras, and Adalbero, before a Robert grown altogether too pious, both asserted the value of the carnal. Obsession with sin, with the sin inherent in sex and blood, formed the rib-work of the three competing ideological models. Indeed, in the early eleventh century the major objective of the ecclesiastical reformers was to rid the Church of clerks who were overly fond of women and of warfare.[7] But the enemies of Gerard and Adalbero envisaged going further still, broadening the demand for purification to all of society. Gerard and Adalbero refused to chase this chimera. Invoking discretion, in the sense the word then had of a concern for making distinctions, and backed by the principal of functional division, these bishops, these pastors kept their feet firmly planted on solid ground. If, invoking Dionysius, they situated the order of *oratores* in the portion of the universe under celestial dominion, thereby imposing upon all the servants of God the obligation to equal the "perfect" among the heretics in purity, they refused to force other men to emasculate themselves or to lay down their weapons. Among the laity, they said, it might as well be admitted that the flesh weighed more heavily, necessarily so, as this portion of mankind came under the head of the *genus.* Its function was to engender, to perpetuate the species through reproduction and to insure the continuance of the incarnation, until that unpredictable day when the trumpets would sound; clearly, this was in accordance with God's intention, since he had decided to make himself incarnate.

Man did not procreate without sin. Sin was the source of inequality; the carnal mechanisms of generation created the "genera," according to which laymen were hereditarily assigned to one of several social conditions. At the lowest level of a hierarchical scale inherent in the genetic code the "servile condition" mentioned in the *Carmen* was located, this being the condition which according to the Dionysian theory of illuminations stood at the farthest remove from the spiritual, verging on bestiality. Bent low to the ground, the servile were compelled to toil over the earth, to cook, to wash, to wrest food from the soil and prepare it for the table. Whereas the "nobles," whose *genus* shared the blood of kings, whereby they enjoyed the benefits of a higher degree of illumination, might accede to sanctity, and had both the duty to protect the poor and the right to exploit them. Class division and seigniorial oppression were thus justified by a natural inequality residing in impurity. Nevertheless, the deep-seated impurity of the laborers, who sweated and stank and coupled like animals, might be redeemed through physical pain, just as the warrior, who made love less crudely and who killed not hogs but men, might, by making a gift of his life to the good cause, redeem the less repugnant faults with which his soul was tainted. One fact was certain: this world could dispense with neither armed men nor toiling men. This was the order God had wanted. And so it was the order that existed.

As used by Adalbero and Gerard, then, the trifunctional model anticipated the waning of monasticism and contempt for the flesh, as well as the discovery, which came as the fruit of clear-sighted reflection upon creation and matter stimulated by the continuing economic advance, of the positive values of manual labor. It anticipated the second phase of Church reform, which culminated in a restoration of the episcopacy. And finally, it anticipated the renaissance of the monarchical state. A bright future lay in store for it. Nevertheless, at the time it was set forth by the bishop of Cambrai and the bishop of Laon, it was rightly looked upon as backwards. Thus for a considerable period it was not accepted.

PART FOUR

ECLIPSE

14

THE AGE OF THE MONKS

Adalbero and Gerard preached in the desert. We must yield to the evidence: during the hundred and fifty years subsequent to the drafting of the *Carmen* and the *Gesta*, there is no sign that any man of high culture in northern France adopted the phrase set forth in unison by the two bishops to buttress their proposed model of a perfect society. This is not due to a scarcity of evidence as to the manner in which thoughtful men conceived the world; the abundance of such evidence, on the contrary, continued to grow. But a search of the available writings would prove fruitless, for they contain no explicit statement like the one made by the two prelates, claiming that the social order was based on the complementarity of three functions, assigned respectively to the heads of the Church, the commanders of warriors, and the subjugated peasantry.

Someone will object, "But look here, what about this passage that we find in two twelfth-century manuscripts? True enough, it doesn't come from France, but it is from Lorraine, the country of Adalbero and Gerard. Was it not composed in the same period as the *Carmen* and the *Gesta?* Is its point not the same? Does it not represent a third, contemporaneous statement of the principle of social trifunctionality?" It behooves us to take a closer look.

The passage occurs in the life of a saint, a "passion," that of a martyred king, a Merovingian: Dagobert II or III.[1] His tomb at Stenay, on the Lotharingian side of the Meuse, not far from the old Roman road leading to Rheims, Laon, and Cambrai, was once an object of worship. Stenay was formerly a royal domain. In 872 Charles the Bald had had transported there the remains of his predecessor, assassinated two centuries earlier in the nearby forest of Woëvre, and had established a chapter of canons on the site to watch over the relics. Subsequently, the domain and the chapel passed into the patrimony of the dukes of Lower Lorraine, relatives of Gerard and Adalbero. The canons' vigilance waned; they may have fallen into dissolute ways. In 1069, Duke Godfrey the Bearded, judging them unworthy of their mission, replaced them with proper monks. In those days such substitutions were common: they evinced the triumph of monasticism. The relics, the sanctuary, and the land constituted a priory dependent on the abbey of Gorze. This burial place and the cult surrounding it were the subject of the *Vita Dagoberti,* of which we know neither when nor by what hand it was written. It puts on Merovingian airs, but was in fact the work of a skillful *pasticheur* who found, in a well-stocked library such as the one at Gorze may have been, works of the pseudo-Fredegar and Paul the Deacon and borrowed occasional phrases from them, around which he built his tale, which was deemed only the more fascinating for seeming to have emerged from the depths of the ages. In point of fact, it was as recent as yesterday. No earlier, certainly, than the eleventh century. Whether the early part of that century or not, I am uncertain. I am inclined to think not, and to concur instead with R. Folz, F. Graus, and K. H. Krüger in assuming that the biography was written after the monks had replaced the canons at Stenay and in the course of their efforts to restore the devotion attaching to the chapel, hence subsequent to 1069, some forty to sixty years, perhaps, after the proclamations of Gerard and Adalbero.[2] But in that case, would it not be even more significant if, after two generations, a Lotharingian writer had repeated the words of the two bishops so faithfully? Did he in fact repeat them? Listen to what he says.

"The sacerdotal order [*ordo*] at the prescribed hours sang hymns to the all-powerful God, and dedicated itself even more devotedly to the service of its king; just as the peasant order [*agricolarum ordo*] tilled its fields in joyfulness, and blessed him who kept the peace in their region and surfeited them with an abundance of grain; the noble youths, as well, who, following ancient custom, disported themselves from time to time in play with hounds and hawks, but even so continued their tireless distribution of alms to the poor, their succour for the unfortunate, their aid to widows and orphans, giving clothes to those who went bare, shelter to worthy visitors and travelers, comfort to the ill, and burial to the dead. To those who act in this way, the practice of hunting, it must be believed, can do no harm." Later, he continues: "Instituted prince over his people by the King of the Universe, [Dagobert] is ardently to be venerated by all the secular powers [*secularis potestas*]. . . . The sacerdotal dignity [*sacerdotalis dignitas*] shall render him all honor, because in heaven he is to be found conjoined unto that dignity of which it is said 'thou art a priest forever after the order of Melchizedek,' and, with the angels, the priestly order sings for him. He shall in addition be escorted by the farmers, whose labor is honorable, since they are in his debt and owe to the excellence of his deserts the abundant harvests they take from the earth: may even the lowly toiler in the vineyard not fail to devote his each and every thought to the honor of this saint, who stands beside and assists him in his joyful labor."[3]

This second, triumphal scene was repeated each year on Saint Dagobert's Day. The prince approached; he came to walk among the blessed, to make his entry once again into the city, accompanied in procession by the exultant populace in its entirety. As befitted such an occasion, the parade was subject to strict regulation. It was in fact a manifesto on good government, treating the order which it was the prince's mission to uphold and God's wish to see implemented. Accordingly, the procession represented society in its perfect orderly form. Tripartite: in certain respects the image closely resembled the one in Adalbero's and Gerard's dreams. Yet there were differences, appreciable ones. In the first place because the secular society here paraded before our eyes in no way embraced a proposal for its reform. Its purpose was neither to instate nor to reinstate an order. It was no part of the *Vita*'s intention to strengthen either state or throne. Its hero happens to be a king, but a king who is primarily a saint and who performs miracles. The hagiography's aim was to enlarge the cult devoted to a certain reliquary, to arouse and sustain religious ardor. It shows a pilgrimage taking place on the twenty-third of December, the day of the ceremony. To indicate how this was organized, the various categories of possible visitors—and donors— were passed in review. One after another, they were invited to appear.

The call was addressed primarily to workers on the land, a circumstance which is not without its element of surprise. No pity is wasted on their "toil"; on the contrary, it is called "joyous," and far from abasing them, it is said to do them honor. This proclamation—of which no similar example from this cultural area is known to me—flatters the peasantry. It goes so far as to declare the peasants an "order." On the other hand, it is silent as to any services that this *ordo agricultorum* might render to the other social categories. Not the slightest concern to justify seigniorial exploitation is shown by the author. Not a word is said about confiscations to which the fruits of agricultural labor might be subject. Farmers and vine-growers were urged to serve Saint Dagobert so that they might see their vines and their wheat stalks heavy with fruit. He was their *adjutor,* less by virtue of the peace he secured during his lifetime than by the mysterious gift that enabled him after his death to spread the blessings of fertility throughout the realm. The miracle shall not be forgotten by the villagers. Dagobert cured not scrofula but barren fields: returning from his anointment, while on his way from Rheims to Austrasia, he passed through the region of Stenay, and the peasants asked him to sow the seed with is own hands; that year the harvest was a splendid one.[4] The sovereign's relics were therefore a reservoir of

171

fertility, and his feast day, at the solstice, was an agrarian festival. If the third function, that of providing food for the table, is treated here, it is the martyred saint who fulfills it.

Turning to the subject of the nobility, and more precisely to noble youths, the manuscript treats virtually nothing other than the hunt. Hunting was in fact a very old adolescent ritual in the Frankish aristocracy. In the *Life of Saint Trond,* the *Deeds of Dagobert I,* and in Merovingian texts similar to those whose patched-together bits and pieces form the web of the narrative that concerns us, the king's sons are invariably shown prior to the age of puberty chasing game in the forest as custom would have them do; they were escorted by huntsmen, young men of their own age.[5] To arouse the interest of noble adolescents and entice them to make gifts, it was not a bad idea to take Saint Dagobert, himself a hunter and like Saint Eustache murdered while on the chase, and fit him out as a sylvan rather than a rustic divinity, as a purveyor of wondrous quarry. It was also wise at the same time to exonerate the young by maintaining that hunting was not forbidden to the well-born, provided they did not devote their time exclusively to it and redeemed the offense by doing good works. But where is mention made of the nobles' military function? No *miles* here, no *bellator.* This was not, moreover, merely because hagiography normally avoided mentioning war. The writer of this little advertising brochure shows no interest in the functions, military any more than agricultural. The "secular power" is not set apart by its weaponry; nothing is said of the services it might render the other segments of society, other than by way of its generosity in giving alms.

Nor does the *orator* appear. In his stead, we find the priests, subjects of the king, obliged to "serve" him. Far from echoing the exhortations of Adalbero, Gerard, and the Gelasians, the *Vita Dagoberti* contradicts them on this point, by placing the clergy in strict subservience to the royal power. Finally, it is implied that priests are inferior to monks. Nothing is said of the latter. Supposing that the text was composed in the *scriptorium* of Gorze, it is easy to explain this omission. Monks were now in possession of the relics; to exploit this capital, they gave a horn-blast to call in the pilgrims; thus the appeal went out to chanting priests, toiling peasants, and hunting noblemen, to men who had not quit the world and were free to come and go as they pleased. But not to other monks. What would have been the point of tempting them? Monks could not leave their cloister. Had they come to Stenay on December 23 with the others, they would have sinned against the rule.

To sum up: the tripartite figure, as I said earlier, must not be isolated from its context, from the system within which it was articulated. The *Vita Dagoberti* illustrates the danger in doing so. Within it we do find a ternary system of classification employed. The notion of function, however, has become quite peripheral. As for the concept of a social harmony based on the exchange of services among three functional categories, this would seem to have been forgotten altogether. Finally, in the *Vita* the tripartite schema does not apply to all of society. Outside its framework a place is reserved for the monks, so that the social organization is in fact quadripartite. Thus the two sentences I have cited are quite close—closer, certainly, than any others that have come down to us—to the words uttered in about 1030 by Gerard and Adalbero. But they are far from saying the same thing. Virtually identical words are used to support an ideological system which in my view was clearly not derivative of the one put together by the two bishops. Even in the land of their ancestors they had not been heeded.

Perhaps the problem was that they had not raised their voices loudly enough? It is true that Adalbero died leaving his poem incomplete and unpublished: the only manuscript is a rough draft. But its author was a public figure, a man of importance, admired, and it is difficult to believe that the light that he did his utmost to shed on the strife he saw obtruding upon society was allowed to remain hidden beneath a bushel basket. Gerard, for his part, shouted with all his might: amidst the general concern provoked by the outbreak of heresy, the dogmatic treatise occasioned by the Arras synod was, beyond any doubt, widely distributed. So, too, was the text of the *Gesta episcoporum cameracensium* that for decades was enlarged upon, revised, copied. Laon and Cambrai were not remote places. They were rapidly growing cities situated on a very heavily traveled route, and what was said within their precincts was likely to spread far and wide. We have devoted a good deal of attention to our first problem: why was the trifunctional postulate wrested from the grasp of the inarticulate in about 1025? That it should immediately thereafter have disappeared from view, that it should once again have slipped beneath the surface of discourse into the depths of the unsaid, leaving behind no trace but for a few soon-to-vanish ripples, raises a question no less troubling.

To me, only one explanation seems satisfactory: the sudden precipitous decline of the Capetian monarchy after the death of Robert the Pious in 1031 dragged the episcopal institution down with it. The bishop of Laon and the bishop of Cambrai had not been mistaken: their power and the sovereign's were inextricably intertwined. They collapsed together. With the king no longer firmly in control of the episcopal elections, there sprang up around the episcopal sees a web of intrigue, a traffic in influence, a corruption in the selection of prelates known by the name of simony, that to Raoul Glaber was one sign, together with epidemics and famines, of the general disorder in the universe brought on by the approach of the millennium. The corrupt recruitment practices diminished the independence and lessened the human qualities of the episcopal body. Whatever remained thereof was being squandered in the chaotic struggles over seigniorial prerogative. In the

173

fourth and fifth decades of the eleventh century, the great archbishops of the Gauls, at Bourges, Vienne, Lyons, Arles, Besançon, had become temporal princes, leading squadrons of vassals on horseback into battle against their lay rivals—dubious battles, fought inch by inch, day in and day out, at times in the shadow of the cathedral itself. The best of the clergy became entangled in mundane dynastic politics.

The monks immediately profited from this decline. The diversion toward the reformed monasteries of lay ardor and the flood of alms that went with it rose to its crest. After 1030, the monastic invasion that Adalbero had called upon his colleagues to combat pressed forward, overwhelming the structures of the Church for a century to come. And with the Church high culture, too, succumbed; in particular, none of those monuments of social discourse magnificent enough for their image to have persisted a thousand years were left standing. Clerks still declaimed, no doubt. But we can barely make out their voices; the monks drown them out. Virtually all the extant texts from a century-long period between 1030 and 1120 originated in the monasteries, and such images of social organization as we have the means to reconstruct are for the most part of monastic making. The ideological system built around the trifunctional theme served the interest of the bishops. For us it has disappeared from view. Had it necessarily vanished altogether from consciousness? Or had it merely withdrawn from the quite limited field under the historian's surveillance, owing solely to a redeployment of the sources? Were matters this simple?

The eclipse was a lasting one: for a century and a half we hear nothing further of the idea that mankind is divided among those who pray, those who fight, and those who toil, where these three functional categories are united by a mutual exchange of services. But this prolonged period of latency consisted of two phases. Only in the first of them, which concluded in about 1120, were all the expressions of ideological sentiment of which traces remain subject to the strict control of the monks. Let us first confine our inquiry to this monastic period.

It went on for quite some time. The world continued to change. The rate of agricultural growth held its own and even increased, and we glimpse signs that gradually money was coming into virtually universal use. These deep-seated changes had not yet, however, entirely destroyed the last vestiges of the old relations of production in the social formation. Thus until about 1110, charters, notices, and inventories relating to the great domains of northern France continue to distinguish free peasants from the apparently unfree, and exhibit a system of rents and *corvées* stemming directly from types of exploitation prevalent during the Carolingian era. The growth rate seems nevertheless to have been high enough to calm—and this was its most clear-cut consequence—the popular restiveness provoked by the establishment of the new seigniorial regime. The monk Raoul Glaber saw things aright: the troubles, the spasmodic episodes that had agitated the universe in the decades following the year 1000 had abated. A new alliance had been struck between God and his faithful. Again there was peace on earth, and prosperity. Raoul dates the calming of the troubles from 1033, the millennium of the Passion. But he wrote in mid-century. The most recent research into the history of feudalism confirms that it was at that point that the major conflicts pitting lords against both their rivals for power and their subjects, whose exploitation was being intensified, came to an end virtually everywhere. Long-lived disputes were terminated by conciliatory agreements which established the boundaries of castellanies and sub-infeudations. The princes of the Church were obliged to acknowledge that since they were themselves precluded by Gelasian theory from spilling blood, hence from meting out punishment and defending themselves, it was necessary to allow "powerful" laymen to take repressive measures against crimes committed in their own seigniories, necessary to allow them to cut off hands, pluck out eyes, hang, burn; also imperative was that these "advocates" and "wardens" be paid for services rendered by granting them the right to appropriate a portion of the seigniorial taxes. This was also the time when the cleavage in the middle stratum of society took on its conclusive form, distinguishing the horsemen, who were free of restraints, from the "rustics," who bore the full weight of the power of the ban. *Milites, rustici:* henceforth the scribes saw to it that these two groups were set apart when the names of witnesses and signatories were inscribed at the bottom of a parchment. This social boundary was the one that had been laid down by the institutions of the peace. The type of peace rejected by Gerard of Cambrai had thus won out, and with it came the mode of classification likewise rejected by Gerard and Adalbero. After some hard jolts, "feudalism" was finally taking hold. Concomitantly, power was coming to be organized along new lines. The two prelates had supported the preservation of the old form of organization in the name of their own conception of trifunctionality. In the new system the functions were not allocated in precisely the same way as in the old.

The same period witnessed the confirmation of Cluny's triumph—another defeat for Adalbero. The congregation conquered northern France. In 1079, in Paris itself, in the heart of Capetian territory, it annexed the abbey of Saint-Martin-des-Champs. It captivated the young knights and trained them as fighting angels, ready to go into battle with as fiery a spirit as the monks, their brothers, against the common enemy, the devil—who, according to one of the abbot Odilo's biographers, burst into tears in the face of Cluny's victories. And such nobles as the *ordo cluniacensis* did not catch in its toils while young succumbed to its blandishments *in extremis,* at the moment of their death: the taste for taking the habit of Saint Benedict on their deathbed was quite generally acquired. Offering its children as "oblates," allowing its dying men to be converted *in articulo mortis,* the lay aristocracy in this period thronged eagerly to Cluny. But Cluny was not eager to receive adult princes and knights. What was there in the cloister to occupy the "lay brothers with beards," boisterous men, too old to learn to chant or submit to the sophisticated etiquette of liturgical ceremonial? Prudently, like their predecessor Saint Odo in his remarks on Gerald of Aurillac, the eleventh-century abbots preached that every man should remain "in his order." The nobility they expected to secure peace for the congregation's countless houses, to provide young recruits in whose veins flowed that good blood that saints were made of, and finally, of course, to give alms, donations of considerable portions of their seigniories. But the nobility was to remain in the world, where it was needed. Cluny had, moreover, another way of keeping the nobility in line, based on the solidification of family structures, on the growing importance of ancestors and their burial places in the aristocracy's evolving self-image. In its propaganda, Cluny made use of the emerging idea of a purgatory from which lost souls could be rescued, of the belief that knights who had died in sin could still be aided by the living, and that no one was in a better position to help them than the monks, who could bury their remains close by the cloister, mention their names in the obsequies, and serve ritual dinners on the anniversary of a benefactor's death when the community gathered to share with the defunct some out-of-the-ordinary dishes. The Cluniac order made intercession its most important function. It aspired to be an instrument of resurrection, a gateway to heaven. Accordingly, within the walls of its basilicas it laid on a splendid feast. That feast, those obsequies were the secret of its success. While the new society, caught in the trammels of the peace institutions, shored up its foundations, it seems that Cluny, ruling over the empire of the dead and projecting a clear reflection of the heavenly Jerusalem on earth, also succeeded in disarming heresy.

Historians of religious heterodoxy have identified the period between 1040 and 1120—i.e., the very period of monasticism's triumph—as a "slack season" for heresy. I should like to call attention to the close coincidence with the demise of the monarchy in France. How firmly was heresy in fact put down? When, in 1049 at Rheims, Pope Leo IX prescribed a profession of faith, insisting on belief in the necessity of a Church, baptism, remission of sins, and resurrection in the flesh, was his purpose not to stamp out movements of protest very similar to those that Gerard of Cambrai had fought against at Arras? There are traces of an outbreak in Toulouse in 1056. And if heretics did in fact become harder to find, perhaps we ought to conclude that a good many of them fled to join the hermits in the free world of the forests, as earlier the sectarians of Arras had attempted to do. In the period in question many laymen hungry for perfection turned to making charcoal to live, and the virgin reaches of western and northern France came to be populated with small communities of the fervent. Not much was known of them, and they were perforce suspect. Indeed, they did at times turn to an eccentric eschatology for illumination—one thinks of Eon de l'Etoile, surrounded by angels and archangels, in the forest of Brocéliande. Be that as it may, there can be no doubt that Cluny, through its insistence on purity, was able to take up the gauntlet thrown down by heresy. And through its liturgies, shimmering images of paradise, together with the pomp it was shrewd enough to introduce into the cult of the dead, it was able to withstand the assaults of those who were calling for an immediate storming of the barricades of the beyond.

Thus, with the popular masses apparently held in check, while the "customs" took on a patina of age which made them seem more legitimate, and the rhythms of production accelerated, leading to an increase in wealth from which the peasantry somehow profited sufficiently to have quelled its restiveness within the space of two generations, the second half of the eleventh century seems to have been the period when the tangible disposition of social relations came to resemble more closely than ever the model put forward by the proponents of the peace of God and the monks. Of the four ideological propositions that had confronted one another amid such high passions in 1025 or thereabouts, two had been defeated: the heretical one, of course, but also that of Adalbero and Gerard. The real victory had gone in the end to the monks, the proponents of the new peace finding their views subordinated, as it were, to those of the monasteries.

The trifunctional figure was by no means absent from monastic thinking, whether at Fleury or Cluny. But it, too, occupied a subordinate position. In monastic thought it was applied only to the society that existed in the world from which the monks had withdrawn. This figure had been wielded against them as an instrument for subjecting the monasteries to the domination of the bishops. Once their success had been achieved, the monks deemed an overt revival of the trifunctional figure superfluous. Success itself laid the groundwork for different dreams, or rather for the burgeoning of the same dream. What I have undertaken here is to write a history of fantasies. In this history of the realm of the imaginary, the onslaught of Cluniac ideology in the second quarter of the eleventh century opens a period of bewilderment. With the confidence that came with victory, the monks, in possession of the enormous power stemming from a monopoly of the highest forms of culture, laid the groundwork for a new society that was to be organized wholly on the example of the monastic community, in which the corporeal was to draw its breath, as it were, from the other world. Toward that end they divided mankind into two classes. One group consisted of the "perfect," the Cluniac monks, or monks reformed by Cluny. Clerks were admitted into their company, but in a strictly subsidiary role, whether that of the bishops, called upon from time to time to consecrate the holy chrism, or that of the hired curates, assigned the task of ministering to the parishes under the jurisdiction of the priories of the order: in a complete inversion of Adalbero's system, the clergy passed under the tutelage of the monks, the *continentes* became subjects of the *virgines*. In the second class were placed the "perfectibles." Between the two stood a wall, but a wall with a gate in it, which gate was held slightly ajar: this was the "conversion," the second baptism offered laymen, particularly the greatest of them, as they approached death and the end of their earthly wanderings to await, in the "mysterious region" spoken of by Augustine, the moment when they might repopulate the heavenly city.

Standing before this gateway, it befitted laymen to organize themselves in ranks according to their condition. Better than any treatise, the layout of the houses of the Cluniac order testifies to this vision of the social world. The community of brothers occupied the zone of perfection, which was surrounded by an enclosure, a rampart, as it were, against the ravages of evil. On certain days a scant passage was unblocked through this cloister wall to admit for a brief period those ordinarily kept outside, so that they might contemplate the feast from afar, so that its splendor might move them to abandon all they possessed in order to join in the celebration. Upon entering, the guests were lodged in separate quarters. One was reserved for the nobles, who were treated therein like monks, royally, served white bread; their horses were fed oats—indeed, these horses were the mark of distinction that indicated which men were to be shown to the first-class accommodations: those who rode, who were horsemen, knights. The other guest-quarters were reserved for the "poor," who came afoot and were entitled only to black bread, the pittance appropriate to laborers such as they. Thus there were two classes, *milites* and *rustici*, both of them necessary, as the monastery had not yet wholly severed its earthly moorings, and remained a part of this world.

Its inhabitants aspired to be angels. Servile labor would have degraded them. Only with their fingertips did they contact material tasks, towards which they made little more than symbolic gestures. Thus they stood in need of laborers to keep the cellar, the stables, and the refectory stocked, and to produce the goods whose sale provided money to buy fabrics, incense, spices—whatever was needed to embellish the existence of the brilliantly befrocked squadron of monks, who could not conceive of their office in a setting less sumptuous. The relations of production that developed within the confines of the seigniory enabled the monks to accomplish their assigned task. The seigniory yielded profits, and thereby made possible comfort and leisure that they believed further lessened their attachment to the flesh. Horsemen were also necessary. For the earth remained vulnerable to evil-doers, infested as it was with pillagers who, if no precautions were taken

178

against them, would destroy the peace; and peace, too, was indispensable if the monastery was to be made the theater for the pageant of paradise on earth. Even more important, there were still many miscreants in the world; either they must be compelled by war to embrace the true faith, or destroyed. Hence the monks of Cluny had need of "those who work" and "those who fight." And even though they acquired the sacerdotal dignity themselves, one by one, the Cluniacs needed priests as well, on whom they could unload the cares and the tedium of pastoral work. On the other hand, they could get on quite well without the king. A king would only have been a burden. With one foot already in heaven, they were provided for, amply, by the king of kings.

Thus virtually all that is accessible to us of what was being thought about society in northern France between 1030 and 1120 comes from the "perfect," from men conscious of having climbed halfway to salvation and striving to complete the ascent, men who observed from a distance, from the remoteness of their confinement, the world from which they had detached themselves, standing apart from it and devoid of any real concern to modify its structures. Precisely this indifference distinguishes them from Adalbero and Gerard, this lack of interest in action in the world—is it not the same indifference we find in the *Life of Saint Dagobert,* whose unknown author was no doubt also a monk? The function of the monks was not to work toward perfecting the structures of corporeal society. Had they allowed themselves to take too great an interest in the world, they would have chanced breaking their vow of isolation, would have chanced turning back to gaze upon the enthralling splendors whose image they contrived to recreate within the shelter of the monastery walls, whereupon they would have run the risk of being captivated by things ephemeral, by the unrest they had decided to flee. In their eyes the only change that mattered was conversion, transition, a clean break, and the only mission they felt obliged to undertake with regard to their fellow man was that of assisting others to take the step, to join their company, in life or in death. Unlike the cathedral, the monastery was not an instrument of social reform. Like the bands of penitents trooping along the highways, like the huts of hermits ensconced in the forest depths or the underground conventicles of heretics, the monastery embraced a different form of soceity. The monastic kingdom was not of this world. To enter into it, one had to be born again, enticed not by the rhetoric of oratory or the dialectic of rational proof but by an impulse of the heart and a pricking-up of the ears at the warning blast of Judgment's trumpets. Seen from this territory apart, from this emancipated ground, the world below seemed in hopeless disarray. Night and day the monks prayed for remission of its sins. If they were tempted to descend again to earth to restore order to mankind, they were persuaded by the rule that their efforts would have been in vain, and, what is more, forbidden to try. Hence it was not the vocation of the monastery to engender reformist schemes such as social ideologies by their very nature are.

Monastic writers did, however, consider their social surroundings (this was already true in Abbo of Fleury's tenth century). They described their environment. Not merely because some of them in spite of everything continued to harbor a taste for what was going on outside the cloister walls, but above all because they considered themselves the privileged interpreters of the mysterious and assigned themselves the role of closely scrutinizing the world's unrest in order to uncover therein what they deemed divine omens. Among the cultural activities that went hand in hand with liturgical celebration in the monasteries of this period, one of the most important was history, as exegesis of everyday occurrences.[6] Especially "instant" history. The chroniclers had no choice but to find out for themselves what was going on, and the job they were doing exonerated them of any possible charge that they were thereby displaying an indecent curiosity for the vanities of this world. This world—how did they see it?

15

FLEURY

I shall first examine two texts, both composed at Fleury-sur-Loire, where in the vicinity of the Capetian throne the tradition of political and topical reflection inaugurated by Abbo continued to flourish. Both these texts are actually treatises on power, i.e., on peace, one concerned with the peace of the king, the other with the peace of God. They are the immediate successors of the pronouncements of Gerard, Adalbero, and Dudo, the canon of Saint-Quentin. In them we detect reverberations of the controversies of the twenties, but attenuated by the passage of a decade of two. By this time the trifunctional schema had been coopted by the victorious ideology and made to uphold another system, a monasticized model of the feudal order.

HELGAUD

The first text of the two is an *Epitome of the Life of Robert the Pious*.[1] It was written, no doubt in 1033, by Helgaud. He was one of the *seniores* of the monastic community (into which was carried over and institutionalized the basic division of secular society between the old and the young). Helgaud had been "offered" as a child in the time of Abbo. During the troubles of the early part of the century, he had not taken Abbo's side, which had brought him closer to Adalbero and Gerard. The work is a eulogy of the Capetian king. But its purpose was to show how the king was captivated by monasticism: all the virtues it celebrates can be traced to Robert's steadily growing resolve to take up a place among the monks. Like Adalbero, Helgaud distinguishes two "persons" in the figure of his hero, one facing heaven, the other, earth, one praying, the other fighting. But of the latter "youthful" component, engaged in military action in the world of flesh, Helgaud deliberately elects to say nothing: "as for the rest, that is, the battles in the world, the enemies he vanquished, the fiefs he acquired by his

181

physical force [*virtus*] and cleverness [*ingenium*], we shall leave the telling of all this to the historians."[2] Indeed, the author was writing not a *historia* but a *vita*, such as were customarily written about saints. In this literary genre discretion with regard to participation in warfare was no doubt imperative. Still, Odo, the abbot of Cluny, had depicted Gerald of Aurillac mounted on horseback with sword in hand. Helgaud shrank from imitating him: weapons sullied whoever wielded them; the din of battle ought not to reverberate in the retreat of the perfect.

He claimed to speak "in the name of the monks, the clerks, the widows, the orphans, and all Christ's poor."[3] In other words, in the name of all who were grouped together in one body in the peace assemblies in opposition to the wicked, to the warriors; in the name of all whom the peace protected and kings safeguarded in keeping with the order of things, who looked to the sacred king as their father. Our "father": the word recurs incessantly in the account of Robert's funeral rites. When Helgaud was writing, the king had been dead two years. What was left of the royal power? Clearly, only God remained to maintain the structures of peace intact. As best he could, therefore, Helgaud identified the sovereign, that earthly father, with the Father who was in heaven. But the best he could do was to transfer or translate the monarch towards the spiritual realm. As Helgaud puts it, already during his lifetime Robert numbered among the saints; forever involved with what was left of them on earth, their bones, their relics, he thought of nothing else, always anxious to add to the beauty of the churches built over their tombs, to bejewel the reliquaries that held their remains. In the translation ceremonies, which were quite frequent in an era when moving holy corpses from crypt to crypt was a popular pastime, he always carried the reliquaries on his own august shoulders, and he was constantly setting out on journeys to pay personal visits to the saints. He became such an intimate member of their company that in the end he, too, performed miracles. Was this shift of the monarchical toward the miraculous—this was the period during which the myth of the miraculous replenishment of the oil in the holy flask used for anointing the kings spread throughout *Francia*—was this shift not a way of dismissing the sovereign by relegating what remained of his prestige to the sphere of the unreal? In any case, there was no doubt that from the moment he drew his last breath, Robert had ascended to heaven to take his place as one of its "jewels"; a sort of fief awaited him in those heights, with which he was immediately invested by the Lord. After having spent his life trudging back and forth between the visible and the invisible, at last he joined his comrades, the saints.[4] In recounting Robert's life Helgaud's aim was to portray an example of such a migration, of that ultimate ascension of which the monasteries aspired to be the predestined site.

For the king the transition was easy because over a period of time his resolve to live as a monk, as one of the perfect, had strengthened. After withdrawing from the vanities of the world, he had grown ever more humble (*humilissimus*) and little by little freed himself from the grip of that capital sin, pride, the sin of the *bellatores*. Previously, at a time when he had not yet lost interest in the men of this world, he had been wont to gaze upon the poor, hordes of whom used to invade his palace, stealing from it, making off with whatever could be taken, thereby unwittingly contributing to their sovereign's salvation, for pilferage by the destitute had stripped his body of its vain covering of carnal riches, leaving it bare. Robert was pleased by this. Once purified by the paupers, he had turned himself over to the to the Church, setting up his throne, as Helgaud tells us, between the two "orders."[5]

Which two? *Oratores, bellatores?* No: because by then the process of purification had cut his ties to the military. The two orders referred to here were the *ordo ecclesiasticus,* which held fast to him, attracted by his virtues, while he himself held fast with all his might to the other *ordo,* the monastic. In his ascent, the king came to roost in the interstice that set apart two echelons in society's hierarchically ordered segment. The hierarchy was Abbo's: the monks, having achieved a greater degree of perfection, dominated the clergy, still imperfect. The king fell in between. Not, as Adalbero had seen him, midway between the spiritual and the temporal, between the bishops and the princes. Nor, as in Gelasian theory, was he relegated to the laity. His virtues had raised him to the midst of the *ordo*—i.e., within the portion of mankind engulfed by the swelling of the heavenly order—and put him in position to rise still higher. Already he had surmounted the echelon of the bishops, his colleagues in anointment. Why? Because he had been clever enough to turn half-Benedictine. Through penitence, in atonement for the sin of bigamy that he, like King David, had committed. As Claude Carozzi has shown,[6] this misdeed is alluded to precisely at the midpoint of the biography. For Helgaud, the transgression of the interdiction represents the turning point where Robert's life was providentially shunted toward the good, toward the spiritual. The sin had triggered the conversion process, the turnabout. From that moment the king had begun to free himself. First, he had broken his shackles with that essential act of the penitent, pilgrimage. During the Lent prior to his death, he had taken to the road, leading his household from reliquary to reliquary, pausing to pray over the tomb of those great saints that abounded in the southern part of his kingdom, albeit unbeknownst to the king. Among them was Gerald of Aurillac, whom the author of the *Vita,* quite alert to the social vocabulary used by the charter writers, characterizes as a "most valiant knight" (*miles fortissimus*).[7] Had any other saint led his exemplary life without renouncing warfare? On Palm Sunday the procession reached Bourges; on Easter it entered Orleans. Then, during the final twenty-one days of his life, Robert, who could no longer move, devoted himself body and soul to the monastic routine, attempting to emulate Saint Benedict himself, and in the end died like the great saint, chanting the Psalms.

A "reading" written to be read out to the monks during meals in the monastery's refectory, Helgaud's *Life of Robert* was a treatise whose substructures did in fact incorporate, unformulated, the notion of social tripartition: there were the warriors, discussion of whom was avoided; there were the poor; there was the "order" of the clergy: this was the ternary plan according to which worldly society was constructed. But Helgaud, silent as to the manner in which the military function was to be fulfilled, has no more to say about the other two functions. The clerks are mere supernumeraries whose role is uncertain; the poor, parasites, or else faceless bit-players in a ritual of charity. The monk's intention was to magnify a king in the process of freeing himself from the three functions whose arena was secular society, so that he might enter into the other portion of the visible world, the righteous portion, the gateway to heaven. In Helgaud's mind men were actually divided into four categories, on four levels. Forty years earlier Abbo had seen mankind ordered in the same manner, with the three secular categories subordinated to the "monastic order," which incorporated the dead and claimed as its own the sacred shards scattered about in tombs and reliquaries, with its arms outstretched to the angels. In such wise did monastic writing in the first half of the eleventh century contrive to hold the trifunctional model at some remove.

This was apparently still more true of another *lectio*, another edifying biography, written at the same time in Saint-Maur-des-Fossés, a monastery in the same royal province, that had been reformed by Cluniacs. I will have just a brief word to say about it. Its hero, Bouchard the Venerable, was a mere count of Paris. Nevertheless, apart from the miracle and that assumption thanks to which Robert the Pious was able to experience the joys of Paradise from the moment he expired, Bouchard is assigned the same place by the author of the *Vita* as Helgaud granted the king. Like Robert, the count also dies a Benedictine. He is praised for having provided special protection for churches and for the "unarmed",[8] whereby he substituted himself (this is what feudalism was) for the sovereign in demise, thus associating himself with the good princes who promised in the peace of God assemblies to be especially vigilant with regard to priests and paupers. *Defensor ecclesiarum, largitor eleemosynarum*: "defender of churches, distributor of alms," he used his power and his wealth in the only two ways that were legitimate. Behind his coffin, a cohort similar to the one seen at Robert's funeral accompanied toward the grave and toward resurrection the "very pious supporter [*sublevator*] of monks, clerks, widows, and virgins who serve God in the monasteries." Monks, clerks, nuns: another hierarchized triad, but in this case strictly ecclesiastic. True, warriors are missing from this procession, but so are the poor. "Each in his order," following the deceased to glory, came first the monks, then the priests, and finally even women—women not possessed by any man, who accepted only one master, Christ. Eyes have here been averted altogether from the flesh. This was less true with Helgaud. We now come to the second text mentioned at the beginning of this chapter, in which it was not true at all; its author was Andrew, also a monk, in the monastery of Fleury.

Andrew

Andrew wrote about a decade after Helgaud. He was responsible for book 5 of the *Miracles of Saint Benedict*.[9] Although a hagiographer, he did not refuse the historian's role. On the contrary, to him the telling of the miracles worked by that most powerful personage whose relics lay in repose at Fleury seemed to provide a propitious occasion for recounting the curious local happenings, rumors of which came constantly to his ears. Andrew makes no mention of the king, who was slowly drawing away from Orleans and whose prerogatives were being swallowed up by those of the princes. But he does discuss the social order, which he saw according to his own lights. The judgments he made were influenced directly by lingering memories of the old struggle for monastic exemption, by the monk's strong resentment of the bishops. This prejudice prevents him from making explicit reference to the trifunctional postulate. In certain habits of speech and thought, however, we find signs of its presence, and a particularly good light is shed on trifunctionality's place in his thinking by his account[10] of an event that took place three or four years prior to the date of his writing, in 1038—we know of it only through Andrew's own work, apart from a very curt reference, of uncertain date, in the fragments of a chronicle drafted in the monastery of Déols.[11]

The affair erupted at Bourges—i.e., outside "France," in Aquitaine. In that province, in the third decade of the eleventh century, Duke William the Great himself, following the example of King Robert, had organized the peace of God, diocese by diocese. He died in 1030. Undermined by feudalism to the same degree as the royal power in France, the ducal power collapsed, and from then on the enterprise of pacification in the province was led, as in Burgundy and *Francia*, by bishops. "Our peace," as Jourdain, bishop of Limoges, put it clearly in 1031, before calling down curses upon both wicked princes and knights. In the same year, the peace of Limoges was extended to the diocese of Bourges by the newly elected archbishop, Aymon—a scion of the lords of Bourbon, castellans not even graced with the title of count, who had nonetheless been able to gain control over the metropolitan see: such was the pass to which feudal disintegration had come. Seven years later, the time had come to revive the sacred ritual which it was hoped would check the belligerence of the warriors. Aymon therefore called for a provincial council to meet at Bourges. But he wished to go even further. To "restore" the trammels, to tighten the mesh of the net, he chose to adopt the Burgundian collective oaths condemned by Gerard of Cambrai. He saw to it that a *compactum,* a conjuration, was agreed upon.[12]

At the same time he was responsible for two innovations. In contrast to the oaths sworn on reliquaries at Verdun-sur-le-Doubs, and later at Beauvais and Soissons, not only horsemen but all males of more than fifteen years of age were required to swear this oath in the name of the law (*lex*). Thus the "people" themselves were included in the league, as well as the clergy: touching the reliquary of Saint Stephen with his hand, the bishop was the first to utter the vow. Furthermore, the obligation incurred was not merely negative—I will not attack, I will not plunder this or that; like the obligation of vassals, it had a positive aspect as well, in that it engaged its adherents to prepare for combat. One had to swear to do battle against the instigators of disorder, against anyone who might disrupt or besmirch the peace, "violators" and "corruptors." Setting aside all ties of kinship or friendship, abolishing all differences in condition or function, those who took the oath "with one heart" were obliged to make after "trespassers upon the property of the Church, those who incite pillage, oppressors of monks, nuns, and clerks, and those who prosecute the war [*impugnatores*] against our holy mother the Church." On this point Andrew's classification is plainly reminiscent of that of Helgaud and the other monastic writers: being confined to a fixed location, monks and nuns were singled out as the only categories not required to take the oath; in effect, they had taken a vow insuring their stability. Set apart, they formed a small, hermetic society. But in the "world," the theater of unrest, posturing, and instability, the contemptible stage of corruption and violence, men were divided into three groups.

First, there were the men referred to in the text as knights. *Milites, equites:*[13] Andrew hesitated to choose between the two words; he even spoke of the "equestrian order" (this is the first time that we find the word *ordo* applied to horsemen in northern France), but it should be borne in mind that Andrew prided himself on being a good writer and that he had read Livy. Of great significance, in any case, is the meaning he gives in passing to the word *militia*.[14] He used the term not merely as did all his contemporaries, to distinguish a social category invested with a military function, but already, well before anyone else, to evoke a moral quality: stout-heartedness. Describing the rout of the knights, he says that "they lost heart, because they forgot knighthood." In his eyes, knighthood was an affair of the heart, of courage. If he ran like a scared rabbit, the knight thereby showed himself false to the obligations of his order.

In the other laymen, the foot soldiers in the engagement,[15] Andrew saw a seething mass. It was from a very great height that he looked down upon them. He had not himself emerged from their midst: his father—he prides himself on the fact—was rich and generous, hence noble, and could feed as many as two hundred of the poor in time of famine. Like Bouchard the Venerable, he was a *largitor eleemosynarum,* who with generosity and almsgiving, by opening his granary and distributing his gifts, took upon himself the third function of the kings of old, that of provider. Monastic society, it must be observed, recruited its membership almost exclusively from the nobility. It was one of nobility's roles, one aspect of its "generosity," to see to the carnal aspect of monastic society's reproduction. A scornful aristocrat, the monk Andrew thus refers a little later to the foot soldiers merely as plebeian. No doubt he was deliberately varying his choice of words, always in keeping with the fine classical style of the school, but under his pen this particular word takes on a plainly pejorative tone. Regarding the "populace," Andrew provides further details: it was composed of peasants, consisting entirely of *agrestes,* "countryfolk," which was the term applied to the populace by the ordinances of the peace of God; it was "humble"—in this instance the word is taken from the Psalms; most important, it was of necessity unarmed, *multitudo inermis vulgi.*[16]

Finally, as a monk certain of his superior status, hence condescending, Andrew deemed the members of the third group, the clerks,[17] mere subalterns, "ministers" (*ministri*).[18] In every seigniory this word was then in current use to designate the intendants, stewards, and game wardens. The clerks were thus depicted as ministers of the divine, as underling administrators of the provinces of the sacred.

Hence there was tripartition. Not that of Adalbero and Gerard but rather that of the councils of the sworn peace. Nevertheless, as the event unfolded the situation resembled that which obtained in those same peace councils and again in 1031 at Limoges, in that there were in reality two parties engaged in a Manichaean confrontation. On one side, evil: the horsemen; on the other, good: the people, organized by the clergy, mobilized, parish by parish, behind the banners of the saints, brought forth from the sanctuaries for the occasion and flaunted like gonfalons, emblems of the avenging arm of justice—the army of the poor. At first this was an army without arms, strong thanks solely to its righteousness and God's aid. It succeeded in forcing the princes to enter into the "pact." All the princes save one—the lord of Déols. Then the redoubtable battalions of peace set about destroying castles, i.e., the symbols of oppression, the foundations of seigniorial exploitation, the lairs to which the packs of knights repaired to squander the fruits of their marauding expeditions in pleasure. This initial campaign Andrew deemed good. For him, the army of the poor remained—as the metaphors he attaches thereto attest—the God of Israel's instrument for cutting the haughty down to size.

Good—and yet, owing to its very success, embarrassing. How was it comprehensible that "the multitude of unarmed people could, like armed troops, strike fear among the warriors and frighten them so much that, forgetting their knighthood, they had fled, abandoning their castles, before the platoons of humble countryfolk, as before those of the most powerful of kings"?[20] This was surely a prodigy. An astonishing event. And to some extent a scandal for anyone whose passionate devotion to order was only heightened by membership in the dominant class. Had the customary organization of things not been disrupted? It is quite apparent that by the time Andrew composed his rhetorical piece, he was already convinced that this was so. By then he knew the sequel, the right restoration of the natural order that followed soon after. Indeed, success had proved intoxicating. The prelate himself, the archbishop, was the first to experience this effect. Swollen with pride by the victory of the "humble," he himself had become "haughty" and had fallen victim to "greed." Not that this was surprising to a monk: bishops remained in the world, contaminated, swayed by a predilection to resort to arms, and by a taste for money and even women; outside the perfect city of the monastery, the wheat was still mixed with the chaff—i.e., with deniers. As Andrew put it, some men had taken to selling peace, that gift from God. (What did he mean? Were they organizing collections and levying taxes to subsidize a continuation of the campaign, as was subsequently to be done in Languedoc in the second half of the' twelfth century? Or did the victorious archbishop himself supplant the masters of the deserted castles, arrogating their rights, collecting in their place the taxes required of the protected peasants?) From that moment events had suddenly changed course: good became evil, white turned to black. Continuing the offensive, but now beyond all reasonable limits, the archbishop laid siege to a fortress which its defenders refused to surrender. Taking refuge therein were not only knights but also ordinary folk (as we see, not all the villagers had taken the side of the proponents of peace: the safeguard promised by the lay lords was thus deemed neither ridiculous nor outrageous in price). To take the castle, Aymon employed the customary tactic of setting it ablaze. An apocalyptic scene ensued: Andrew speaks of fourteen hundred victims; he describes the horror, the pregnant women and children burned alive. The massacre of the innocents. One fact is clear: the extraordinary victory turned the "wretched"[21] into an infuriated mob of the sort that was said to be a precursor of the coming of the anti-Christ. They had failed. For them, it was the beginning of the end.

For God from that moment abandoned them. By grace he gave warning of his intentions, however, leaving them one last chance to make amends. With the troops of the archbishop now face to face with those of the last rebel, the lord of Déols, God issued still more warning signs. A field battle was about to begin, the final test: appeal was made to the Almighty to deliver his judgment, to indicate which of the two camps he held to be in the right by giving it the victory. Then God hurled his thunderbolt, which fell between the two armies. Blinded, albeit by pride, the partisans of the peace refused to understand the message. They had provoked God's wrath. They would be defeated. Another miracle? A surprise. Why had the Lord on that day favored the most wicked of lords, the one behind whose banner all manner of wrongdoers had rallied, the one who obstinately refused to accept the peace settlements? Why this apparent injustice?

As Andrew tells it, God had as it were placed the lord of Déols in reserve, as the arm of his vengeance.[22] He had used the nobleman as a kind of bait, a decoy, to see how far the "poor" might take their arrogance. For (and here is the aspect of Andrew's thought that is important to us) it was not God's wish to see the advent of a new social organization in which functional distinctions would be blurred. He had earlier been suspicious of conjuration, owing to its coercive, aggressive aspect: because it involved a denial of differences, there was a risk—was there not?—that eventually the balanced structure founded on a just distribution of offices would be undermined. Adalbero and Gerard had foreseen this eventuality in their struggle against the propagandists for the peace movement. The terms of the sacramental oath and the way in which it was taken had already extended the military function to populace and clergy. While the monks, for their part, might remain safe from temptation, was there not a danger that the clerks would fall victim to chivalric pride and greed and be captivated by a dream of equality? This dream, furthermore, to the extent that it came true, would not carry mankind back to paradise, since nothing could reverse the course of history, but would rather lure it into evil, into disorder and that confounding of social roles that already had been responsible for one dumbfounding and unprecedented occurrence: the flight of warriors before peasants.

The scandal had been laid bare in the course of the battle waged in spite of heaven's warnings, and with the revelation came the inexorable consequences of God's wrath. The two armies faced each other across the Cher river. The archbishop's forces counted fewer knights among their number. In the ranks of the soldiers of peace were a few horsemen, but the bulk of the cavalry had rallied behind the prince, the last hope of the feudal resistance. A stratagem then occurred to someone. It was grotesque, loathesome: Andrew was not a mocker like Adalbero. He was revolted. Such vile imitations, such travesties, disgusted him. A few men of the people tried to pass themselves off as knights. They had taken the first available mount. Usurping the place in the saddle reserved for the military function's legitimate representatives, they thought to gain unauthorized access to the "equestrian order." Perched on the backs of asses, these madmen sallied forth in a grotesque cavalcade. This proved imprudent, as their blood was unsuited to the mission, lacking the genetic "virtue" that gave the knight his valor. Within seconds their ridiculous assault was turned into a rout. Panic-stricken, the terrified "knights" plunged into the river. Some of the firebrands were swallowed up by the waters. The rest, mad with fear, slaughtered one another. The men congenitally destined to battle were spared even the necessity of spilling blood with their own hands. With this rout, this annihilation, God delivered the verdict he had been forced to render. First to be punished because they stood first in guilt were the clerks. The archbishop eluded death but was wounded; the next day a great many priests were found, skewered in bunches on the shafts of the sacred banners; they had made the mistake of misusing these banners as standards in carnal battle. Enraged, God condemned the heterodox inversion of terrestrial social functions, in which serfs had brazenly attempted to dominate lords, and curates instituted as shepherds had turned into wolves.

Primarily, then, Andrew of Fleury's object lesson was addressed to the clergy. Andrew renewed the admonition issued by Adalbero and before him by Abbo and Aelfric: the servants of God ought not to bear arms. Going further still, Andrew maintained that popular participation in combat was wicked. He advocated mistrust of the demagogic bishops who in seeking their own glory had misrepresented the prescriptions of the peace of God and who recently had gone so far as to arm the poor, thereby opening the gates to subversion. Defending society, he shared the attitude of Gerard of Cambrai. Following Gerard, he set himself up as trifunctionality's defender.

Let me make my view clear, however, lest there be some misunderstanding: Andrew saw society as divided not into three parts, but rather four, just as Abbo did. If he held that secular society was necessarily tripartite, this was on condition that a distinct category, the monks, be recognized as superior. Now, in order to achieve perfection, the monastic institution needed the support of the seigniorial institution. Reformed monasticism in the eleventh century attached its roots firmly to the new seigniory. To the monks "feudal" society seemed an excellent one: "let nothing change," they said to the lords temporal, "but only let us keep watch together and put down ruthlessly anyone who, in peace or war, might raise egalitarian expectations among the subjugated populace." Subjugated, protected, looked after: evoking his father's charity, Andrew saw in a limited redistribution of seigniory's profits the justification for exploitation of the workers. Order rested on the sympathetic affection of the masters and on the respect owed them in return by the plebs. The mission of the clerks and the knights was to uphold that order by whatever means, spiritual or temporal, had been conferred on them, whereby certain men, enjoying the comfort of the monasteries, would then be able to advance toward salvation, carrying the others along behind, or rather underneath, them. To the king, Andrew of Fleury paid no heed; he bore a grudge against the bishops; but he was even more resolutely set against the common people. This, as one can sense in the text, left him rather well-disposed toward the lord of Déols. There is no doubt that he supported Étienne, the lord whose castle, the refuge of children and paupers, was destroyed by fire. In any case, he was in agreement with Helgaud on one fundamental point: society should remain organized as it was until all mankind had been absorbed, in proper order, into that hereafter of which the abbeys were prefigurations. Neither Andrew nor Helgaud was laying down a social plan. They regarded mankind as divided into four categories by decree of providence. They themselves belonged to one of them; to the other three were assigned, according to suitable criteria, those upon whom they looked down from the lofty heights to which their merits had destined them. These others they hoped their liturgy would save, having every intention of making use of their respective functions in the tranquil pursuit of their own ascension.

16

CLUNY

RAOUL GLABER

To the monks integrated into the Cluniac congregation, quadripartition appeared no less evident. Let us enter next into their world. We must first cross the border from *Francia* into Burgundy, where Raoul Glaber was putting the finishing touches on the five books of his *Histories* prior to 1048, thus just shortly after the writing of book 5 of the *Miracles of Saint Benedict*. He exhibits as much curiosity for the things of this world as Andrew of Fleury, perhaps even more. Everything alive and stirring outside the cloister attracted him. Rather than stick to one place, he took advantage of every opportunity to travel. He knew how to look and listen. He was an excellent observer—to my mind the best we have—of a world in which the old order, from top to bottom, was tottering dangerously. To be candid, his reputation is bad; besides his overripe Latin, positivist history has held against him his tendency to distort the "truth." Quite recently, R. H. Bautier has rightly shown how he manipulated the information he had received concerning the Orléans heresy. Of course he distorted. That is precisely what interests me in his case. He is worth looking at because he gathered rumors from various sources and combined them into a powerful portrait of the whole. What is more, that portrait was the one then current at Cluny. Indeed, the *Histories* were dedicated to Odilo, "King Odilo," which alone is sufficient to make clear the distance, and I would even go so far as to say the antagonism, between Raoul and Adalbero.

On occasion Raoul Glaber traveled outside Burgundy. Most of his days, however, were passed between Auxerre, Saint-Bénigne, and Cluny. This region, his homeland, found itself at the time without a native king or duke. Of the king and the emperor, Raoul was not unaware. He bowed quite low before them, but from a distance, standing equally aloof from both. None of the controversies concerning the monarchy, Carolingian tradition, or Frankish tradition concerned him. To matters of that sort he was indifferent. This indifference emerges quite clearly in his work: he has not a word to say of the century of Charlemagne, the great century, the ninth. He begins his story afterwards, without reminiscence. With him we enter into another province of memory, a province innocent of the recollection of Hincmar and of the teachings of the Rheims school. The rejection of the Carolingian cultural legacy is even more significant in this case because the text in question is in fact a *historia*. Not a national history—the Burgundian nation, dismembered, no longer existed—but a general history: the history of the entire world. Despite the taste he exhibits for crypts, sarcophagi, and epitaphs, Raoul's discussion was not limited to saints. He had no need of a pretext, such as pretending to write of miracles. His design, as he freely admitted, was to relate all that he knew of the latest happenings, of those "novelties" that showered down in prodigious torrents as the millennium approached, of "novelties" that would burgeon by dint of Jesus' power until the last hour of the last day. These phenomena were never without some relationship to Christ. For that very reason, Raoul Glaber set himself the task of subjecting them to scrutiny. He meant to expound each event, to disclose its several meanings. Anxious and hesitant, he went about his mission. One might justifiably call mystical, in the Dionysian sense of the term, his analogical commentary on events, which established correspondences between ephemeral occurrences in time and atemporal structures.

This explains why his treatment of the world of events was preceded by a lengthy meditation on divine quaternity. This fundamental order reflected the correlation between the four Gospels, the four virtues, and the four rivers of paradise, on the one hand, and the four cardinal points, the four elements of which matter was constituted, and the four periods of human history, on the other. With the work's opening passages a quadripartite pattern was laid down. This presupposition was based, according to its author, on the teachings of the 'Greek Fathers." Which of them did he have in mind? Certainly not Dionysius: the quadrangle had here supplanted the triads. All of man's historical adventure has been inscribed within a square figure, the square circumscribing the monastery and symbolically representing the armature of the visible world. Nevertheless, since, as Saint Jerome argued, "all earthly things tend to rise heavenwards, where their corners are rounded off to conform to the circle, the most beautiful of all figures," the four corners of history would ultimately be embedded in the stable, circular, more perfect forms of creation, so that their destiny was to mold themselves eventually to those forms and vanish in the eternal. The *Histories'* constant concern to ferret out the symptoms of this gradual process of accommodating the ephemeral to the eternal makes it quite an irritating work for anyone who approaches it in search of petty factual detail.

By contrast, it is fascinating to the historian of ideologies or dreams. Fascinating in the first place by virtue of the conception of time it manifests. Precise indications of dates are few. What mattered to Raoul Glaber was the direction of time's flow. Sometimes the stream seems to meander; now and again historical time might abruptly change its course. But it never turned back on itself like the time of the liturgies. In a more or less straight line it made for its goal. Thus people who imagined that every year at Easter the Savior came to empty hell and lead his people into heaven were falling into a trap set by the devil. On a certain day the Judge would reappear. That day would be the culmination of a linear series of events, each one a prefiguration of the final hour; these Raoul Glaber invested with a value, either beneficial or noxious, interpreting them all as mysterious messages. Raoul rode the tide. Lately this tide had been troubled by violent eddies. Somewhat prior to 1033, after the thousand years of the fourth age had elapsed, a knot of anxiety had formed. Then subsequently, when God had grown calm and the stars had ceased their celestial war, this knot had come unraveled. By the time Raoul came to write, order had been restored. History was unfolding in a climate of diminished unrest. No fifth age was coming, however. Quadripartition was necessary.

Until the end of time, men would gather in two abodes: on earth, and in that secret place where the dead were still living. In the meantime, however, they were visited by angels and devils. These emissaries arrived from two further regions: heaven and hell. Thus the four parts of space were like adjoining chambers. Raoul was fully as convinced as Gerard and Adalbero that between what one saw of the universe and what lay beyond the reach of the senses, only to be divined, there existed a correspondence. But he looked upon this correspondence not as something merely static, in the nature of exemplarity or isonomy, but rather as historical, in the true sense of the word: at certain times and in certain places beings passed from one realm into another. To such passages he was keenly attentive, and well-placed to observe them in the favorable vantage afforded by his Cluniac monastery, situated as it was at the point of tangency of the four spheres, angelic and terrestrial, demoniac and ghostly. Relations among the living interested him less than the denizens of the invisible realms whose sighing swarms one sensed; less than those weird fleeing forms that loomed in the twilight near tombs and reliquaries; less than those cavalcades that galloped across the stormy heavens; and less than those huge white shapes that paraded, often in silence but sometimes uttering intelligible sounds, as harbingers. Demons. Ghosts. To tell them apart was not easy, nor was it a simple matter to distinguish them from saints or angels. Within this nebulous society there was one very sharp division: between the good and the bad. This division was projected, moreover, onto human society, which was also divided between good and evil, and into which malevolent forces were constantly forcing their way. Indeed, mankind ran the risk of being wholly engulfed by these forces, once such germs of corruption as Jewish communities and heretical sects, not yet completely purged in spite of burnings and massacres, again began to ferment. As much as the world of the dead, the world of the living, too, had been scourged, unsettled, tormented, as Raoul Glaber saw it. Infected with sin, it was beset with inequalities.

Several echelons of subjection and coercion were contained therein, but always to one side or the other of a fundamental breach. This breach was not the one laid down by the seigniorial institution: scant mention is made by Glaber of either "lords" or "serfs." The distinction he notes instead is the same one observed by Augustine and Gregory the Great, between subjects and rulers, between the "vulgar," or the passive, stupid, rustic "multitude" that was ridiculed and despised, and the "nobles," who set the example, led, gave orders, called the pace, and were the actors on history's stage. Among these rulers was the king. Raoul, too, admired Robert the Pious; he extolled his "wisdom," the instrument capable of quelling disorder; but Robert wins his praise primarily for having followed the advice of Odilo, of William of Volpiano, of Cluny. Ranked on an equal footing with Robert were other princes, like the dukes of Normandy, just as powerful, redoubtable, and generous as the Capetian, and like him governing their states much as good fathers ruled over their families. Also on an equal footing with the king, ranked not above military captains but alongside them, Raoul placed the bishops, the "eyes of the Catholic faith." Were they to suffer blindness (which occurred frequently: Raoul Glaber is no more tender toward the episcopate than Andrew of Fleury), pride, greed, and lust would afflict the populace, and chaos would again reign on earth. Indeed, this was the way evil infiltrated society, from above, through the infirmity of "rectors" and "princes," the heads of dioceses and feudal principalities, those great households, families that suffered immediate contamination should their patrons commit a sin.

Thus underlying human society, huddled in one of the four abodes, was a binary structure. In fact, however, Raoul's way of looking at things really combined two dichotomies, even though he was hardly aware of it. One of these, the one just discussed, he did not define explicitly, for it was patently obvious. To the other he applied the word *ordo* in its social sense. Just as there are two sexes, he says, so there are two orders,[1] themselves hierarchized. Which two? The "order of clerks" and the "order of laymen."[2] It was important to distinguish quite sharply between them—thus Raoul condemned modern manners in dress and in wearing hair and beard, which were conducive to confusion between warriors and priests, if not women. To these two orders a third was added: the order of monks. But was this latter order a part of the same world?

In fact, the monasteries were home to society of a special sort, isolated because its purpose was to withdraw from the world and because it had achieved a high degree of perfection, yet organized like worldly society so as to present a model for it, so as to entice it towards the monastery. To achieve this end, monastic society envisaged assuming all three functions itself, autonomously. The first of these was the sacerdotal. This function the monastery had fully captured. At Cluny the monks did not merely chant the Psalms. They spelled one another in celebrating "mass without interruption, bringing to this office such dignity, piety, and reverence that they seemed more like angels than men."[3] By performing the sacrificial rites associated with the first function, for which the highest *ordo* in the secular hierarchy bore responsibility, the monks succeeded in raising themselves to the heights of angelic perfection. But what they placed on the altar with their own hand as an offering was also food, food distributed by the monks, whereby they sustained the suffering souls, comforting them, restoring them to peace and life. The monks also aspired to be providers, and not merely of food for the spirit: they opened their granaries and distributed the seigniory's excess yield among the poor. Finally, monastic society took over the military function. It is not only that symbolic warfare waged night and day on the liturgical battlefield by monks organized in squads, chanting in unison against the forces of evil, that I have in mind. In a more palpable sense, monks participated in holy war. Cluny's influence in Spain was widespread. Raoul Glaber was apprised of events taking place beyond the Pyrenees, in the region where Christians and infidels clashed. He was aware that in the offensive of Almancour, "the want of troops forced the monks themselves to take up arms."[4] He sought to justify what might seem a relapse into the carnal world. The monks did what they did, he says, "out of love and fraternal charity, far more than out of a pretentious desire for glory." The proof: heaven had not punished them. Some monks had died in combat while carrying out the royal mission, the mission of the *bellatores;* they had reappeared one morning at dawn in the church of the monastery at La-Réome-en-Tardenois; a bishop marched at their head—a former monk, as were all the leading prelates at the time Raoul wrote; all wore white. The sign was clear: they had gone to the good place, they were saved. Some of them spoke a few words, saying that their visit would be brief, that many more would follow, and that they had been called by God to share the fate of the blessed. Thus the priest-monk was committing no sin if he joined in battle with the men of war. Here, then, we see Raoul Glaber defending what Abbo and Aelfric had condemned a few decades earlier, and what Andrew of Fleury was condemning still. Was he so sure of himself? Had he not elsewhere depicted Saint Martin straining to wrest from the devil's claws several canons of Tours, who, "serving in military costume, had had their throats cut in battle"?[5] Of course, these were canons, less pure than monks, and the war in which they died was probably not a holy war. In any case, the *Histories* do describe three social functions, all borne by the monastic community, just as the king had formerly been responsible for all three; they are herein wrested from the material sphere, sublimated, and little by little caught up in the current of a history of salvation for which Cluny's monasticism laid the groundwork, whereby they proceeded from stage to stage along the path leading back to the original unity.

Within that inferior, abject, perfectible society that was of this world, Raoul observed an analogous tendency. He saw a gradual reunification of what he, like Adalbero, called the "conditions" taking place therein in accordance with divine intentions.[6] Within each household the whole gamut of these conditions was to be found, under the authority of a "prince," whose position was analogous to that of the abbot in a Cluniac monastery, or to that of God in heaven. Indeed, because he deemed this reversion to homogeneity esential, Glaber rarely used such social adjectives as *miles, servus,* or *rusticus,* even though they occur frequently in charters from the period preserved at Cluny. Even though men of this world were divided into two groups according to their condition, being either among those who obeyed or among those who commanded, it was nevertheless true that when tribulations came, when God punished his people with Saint Anthony's fire or with famine, or even more clearly during the untroubled interludes, when mankind again took hope and set out afresh in search of the good, only one body, one unanimous congregation, then existed. Nowhere were distinctions of sex, order, or condition so seemingly effaced as in the councils for the peace of God and in the pilgrimage to Jerusalem. There the tide of sin ebbed before spiritual exaltation and purificatory practices such as fasting and abstinence, and society returned to a condition of equality—the equality of paradise—based on the equality of the monastery, wherein paradise was reflected on earth. What had been a sharp cleavage between masters and subjects, between powerful and poor, became a fringe of fine distinctions wherein passage from degree to degree was imperceptible, until ultimately differences of rank were effaced altogether. To express this range of gradations, Raoul Glaber used two comparative terms, the "best" (or the "greatest"), and the "least"; between the two extremes he intercalated a scale of the "middling," thereby establishing a ternary figure.[7] He even went so far as to stand this on its head: in front of the procession, *primitus,* just behind the monks but ahead of all the others, he placed the "lower plebs." The poor, who constitute a kind of order, are shown preceding the proud.[8] What was the occasion for his inverting the image this way? As it happens, Raoul was here discussing a departure, mankind's departure. Bestirring itself, as penitents were bound to do to erase their sins, as Robert the Pious had done in the months prior to his death, and as Saint Augustine had described the elect, "wandering" on earth, humanity was making ready for the journey. Made over by the calamities of the millennium and reconciled

197

with its God, mankind was with one mind beginning its migration toward salvation, setting out on a pilgrimage whose destination was the Promised Land, the tomb of Christ. Even as Christ's soldiers, victorious over the unbelievers on the Spanish front, were dedicating to Cluny treasure seized on the field of battle, gold and silver with which the abbey church might be made still more dazzling, still more an image of the heavenly Jerusalem, even then mankind had begun its march towards Jerusalem on earth. Glaber's whole story moves back and forth between two poles: Jerusalem and Cluny. After 1033, human history enters upon a tense period of eschatological expectancy. The history of that time is a history of escape. The *ordo cluniacensis* had weighed anchor and taken to the high seas, leading the way. Men and women, rich and poor, clerks and laymen, everyone, without distinctions as to condition, prepared to make the crossing. Delivered from the terrors of the year 1000, a new society was brewing, a society that Raoul Glaber foresaw in his mind and fervently wished to see in the flesh: crusading society.

The Crusade and its Aftermath

The words that Pope Urban II uttered in 1095 at the council of Clermont, whereby he started Christendom on the great adventure, have not come down to us. Geoffrey of Vendôme reports that he ordered laymen "to become pilgrims on the road to Jerusalem," that he forbade "monks to make the same pilgrimage," and that he told clerks who wished to take to the road to ask permission of their bishops.[9] Laymen, monks, clerks: the organizers of the expeditions were thus said to have paid heed to the old ecclesial tripartition, that of Dudo of Saint-Quentin. If, however, Fulcher of Chartres[10] is to be believed, the pontiff's speech, whose intended audience included laymen of all ranks, "rich and poor, knights and villagers," recognized another cleavage, one established by the seigniorial system of exploitation, which split the laity into two classes. But according to Baudry of Bourgueil,[11] whose testimony is probably the most reliable, the pope is supposed to have made reference only to the oldest of the classificatory systems, the prefeudal Gelasian system, saying of laymen merely that bishops and priests will have them for *pugnatores;* they will have priests for *oratores.*

There should be nothing surprising in Urban's ostensible use of this primitive Gelasian description: formerly head prior of Cluny, he was by this time bishop of Rome, Gelasius' successor; already there were signs of the upheaval in the Church that would restore the clerks to the first rank. The purpose of what is known as the Gregorian reform being to free the spiritual completely from the grip of the temporal, a part of its effort went to distinguishing more clearly than ever between two groups of God's people. There was consequently a reversion to binarity, to the two orders, *clerus* and *populus,* the clergy and the *ordo laicorum.* In this second body, distinctions were no longer of consequence: bear in mind that the sermon of 1095 was first of all a proclamation of the peace of God whereby that peace was extended to all Christendom, so that any of Christ's faithful who had reached fighting age might participate in the holy war. In fact, Urban, bishop of Rome, laid down the same prescription as Aymon, archbishop of Bourges, namely, that the peace oath be taken by all men over twelve years of age, who were to hold themselves in readiness to take part in righteous warfare if called upon to do so by their pastor.[12] Unanimity was demanded of the laity, the same singleness of purpose that Glaber had dreamt of—unanimity in temporal action, in the conviction that the end of the world was imminent, as well an unanimity in penitential practices and in indulgences, the remission of punishment promised to all equally, regardless of whether or not they were knights, and without distinction, all bearing the designation *bellatores* because they were about to face adversity, about to march forward in singing columns toward death and resurrection.

Those who have spoken of the armies of the crusade have been anxious to have us believe that disparities of condition among laymen were reduced, as it were, to nought. To make the attenuation of differences visible, they have described the pageantry of the adventure's high points, staged so as to reveal in gesture and pantomime the reduction of disparity they wished to bring to light. Before the besieged city of Jerusalem, for example, on July 8, 1099, a procession marched about the walls in the hope that like the walls of Jericho they would fall of their own accord; this procession consisted of two distinct groups, once again the *clerus* and *populus.* But the "populace" comprised only penitents: the knights, barefoot, without arms, stripped of the emblems of their estate, were no longer distinguished from the rest. Subsequently, moreover, during a ceremony of forgiveness at the Mount of Olives, the participants promised never to wrong one another, much as men had earlier vowed in the peace assemblies, the heretical fraternities, and in conjurations of equals like the ones opposed by Gerard and Adalbero. In preparation for the attack, according to the chroniclers, the knights worked with their hands, bathing the earth in which they dug with their sweat, like peasants. And yet they remained knights: tales of the crusades never go so far as to confound those on horseback with those on foot. Rather they suggest that the distinction was bound to lose its meaning when the pilgrims reached the Promised Land. Going farther still, they envisaged an inversion of the hierarchy, much like the one of which Raoul Glaber had caught a glimpse. At Antioch, with anxiety at a fever pitch and crusaders breaking ranks in disarray, Saint Andrew hoped to rekindle their ardor. He decided to reveal the place where the Holy Lance was hidden, to urge the crusaders to seize it for use as a spur to prod the offensive forward. Now, he chose not to show himself to Adhémar, the bishop in charge of the expeditionary force, but rather to a peasant, a "rustic," a "humble" fellow, to whom he said, "you, the poor, have the advantage in merit and grace over those who used to precede you and who shall follow after you, just as gold has the advantage over silver."[13] Here, then, we see the first become last, or, rather, we witness the apparent coming true of the dream of a soceity without orders, without distinct functions. The dream that had enchanted the heretical conventicles before going up in smoke at the stake, the dream that once more took shape in the discussions of the peace of God, and that Cluny had reworked, amplified. In the Crusade it flourished.

It was a dream. Crusading society showed no greater purity, no greater unanimity, than any other. On the contrary, in the overseas adventure the fissure between the two lay conditions deepened, since the values of knighthood were enhanced in armed combat. From the outset, the crusade, in organizing itself, had expelled the poor from its ranks: they were indeed the first to set out for the Holy Land, but in unruly, vulnerable groups, of which soon nothing remained. The knights waited, banding together under their banners, standing aloof. In due time they took to the road. It was then, during the course of the journey, in the ideological mirage of unity among "Christ's knights," that we see a reinforcement of the structure of precepts, conventions, and prejudices within which the difference between those whom Adalbero and Gerard used to call the *bellatores,* meaning the princes, and the mere *milites* steadily diminished. The real result of the barons' expedition, a continuation of the assemblies of peace, was to increase the cohesiveness of the lay aristocracy around an ideology of noble service, and to set that aristocracy more clearly apart from the vulgar. Missing were the kings. Never were the structures of "feudalism," by which we mean a social organization based on the seigniory and its profits and constraints, more openly revealed. The poor never constituted more than an advance guard, contemptible victims to be offered up in sacrifice; as at the court of Robert the Pious they were mere straw men, or else figureheads like those adorning the portals of Cluny; equality and fraternity between lords and louts was visible nowhere but in the dumb show of penitential ritual. Let us add that the lesson of reality and the ensuing disillusionment were not long in coming. The poor marched off to extermination; invulnerable, the knights vanquished, but in what respect did their efforts differ from the various other marauding expeditions then being dispatched to Andalusia and Sicily by the Christian West, which had for so long had to put up with them itself? The princes fought over the spoils; the knights carried off what they could; in their wake followed hordes of women, and Pisan and Genoese mariners trafficked in everything imaginable at each port of call. Fornication, pride, and greed besmirched the army that arrived bathed in blood at Christ's tomb, much as they tainted every other army. No doubt the best of the crusaders marched forward in ecstasy toward the end of the world. But the end did not come. Now, the myth of a perfect society, in which all class distinctions would be abolished, required its coming, and required that history reach its end in July 1099. This was the myth of paradise regained. On earth, in the realm of the temporal, to restore mankind to its primordial condition of equality was an impossibility. This had been well said by Adalbero and Gerard. The utopia whose first stones had been laid by Glaber and which men thought they saw coming to fruition in the first stirrings of the great pilgrimage could not survive the return of the crusaders. Now the crusaders, at least such of them as wore armor, for the most part returned home before having reached their destination. During the retreat their eyes were opened, even as they witnessed the foundation of those absurd artifacts of the temporal world, the Latin states of the Orient, which had hardly come into being when they were destroyed by their contradictions and their rivalries. Subsequently, other men set out, but with diminished enthusiasm. From the beginning of the twelfth century the journey to the Holy Land became a habit, an institution that went hand in hand with an expectation of profit.

Now it happens that this was the time that Cluny's social ideology came to be expressed in its most resolute—and arrogant—forms. These are to be found in the biographies of the abbot Hugh, works commissioned in about 1120 for use in his canonization, but also to be read and reread in all the priories in order to heighten the monks' veneration of their deceased father and to encourage them to emulate his virtues. They constitute a manifesto, a monument erected to the glory of the congregation at a time when, beset with criticism from all quarters, particularly from the Cistercians, it was beginning to be reshaped from within by a strong internal protest movement. From these works we learn how Saint Hugh's successor, the abbot Pons, and the older inmates of the monastery had come to picture society. Between this picture and the one formed some two generations earlier by Raoul Glaber, the resemblance is strong. Yet the features of the more recent version have a noticeably harder edge.

The *ordo cluniacensis,* an order, *the* order *par excellence,* was enthroned far from unrest and corruption at the center of the terrestrial world. Intermediary between that portion of humanity still caught in the toils of the material world and the heavenly abodes, the place it occupied was the one reserved for the episcopal body in the system of Dionysius the Areopagite (Dionysius, like everything else, had fallen into Cluny's hands: he had entered its service, troubling himself to appear in person, in one of *Francia*'s priories, to give notice that haste was of the essence if the monks there wished to visit Saint Hugh alive).[14] Surmounting the visible hierarchies, the Cluniac congregation embraced an ever-growing population, in two parts: in keeping with Augustine's conception, some continued their pilgrimage in

201

the world, while others had already crossed the divide. For the order was in the first place the army of the dead. The dead, whose number had been counted, whose census had been taken, whose names appeared in the books that laid down the rules for the funeral liturgies, and who therefore constituted an *ordo,* in the primary meaning attributed to this term in Rome. Commensals of the monks, the dead were closely tied to the monastery by dint of the commemorative meal that the community shared with each of them, after chanting prayers for their souls. In Cluny and its hundreds of affiliates in the early twelfth century we see an immense refectory for the dead, that invisible throng in whose midst walked the greatest princes of the earth and the ancestors of every noble house, grateful and confident, subsumed by the monastery. Though far less numerous, the other, living portion of the *ordo cluniacensis* was nevertheless vast beyond counting: in the abbey of Cluny alone were four hundred monks; how many thousands were there in all Christendom? And all of them convinced that they lived in the hiatus between the human and the angelic. To stand as a visible sign of this median position was the intended purpose of the great church whose construction Hugh had undertaken in 1088. Built with booty from the holy war waged by the kings of Castile, consecrated in 1095 by Urban II on his way to Clermont, the abbey church just reaching completion in the time of the *Vitae* was indeed a "vision of peace," Jerusalem. And this Jerusalem was as solid as a rock, protected against all evil, far more capable than the other Jerusalem, the one in Palestine, of securing passage from the sphere of the transitory to that of the eternal. With the rising tide of disillusionment swirling all about, this church stood as a condemnation of the crusade, with its heterodoxies and excesses. All its forms expressed its function: the sculptures on the facade, depicting Christ's ascension; the interminable nave, guiding the progress of those who "aspired" to rejoin "those who reigned," punctuating the stages along a path of progress similar to the crusaders', thereby rendering the crusade futile; beyond the crossing of the transept this immense avenue culminated in what one of the biographers called the "promenade of the angels," the new choir, the *tabernaculum,* modeled on the one in heaven wherein Jesus, king and priest, sat enthroned; a hemicycle of columns, on whose capitals were placed together symbols of the notes of plainsong and the ways of knowledge, as Saint Hugh had ordered: in the highest heaven—in the center of the sanctuary, in Christ's place, the abbot's place—was this not where the source of all wisdom was found, surrounded by the chorus of seraphim?

For this supersociety of dead men and monks was ordered like the heaven of Dionysius, hierarchically. Monks and ghosts alike were fettered by a chain of command that converged in a single point. Like heaven, the congregation was a monarchy. One father, one abbot. Obeyed by all the monks, his angels, he appeared in the guise of an archangel. Already, fifty years earlier, a *Vita* had said of Odilo that "you would have taken him, not for a duke or a prince, but for the archangel of the monks," which was more than a metaphor; ever since the beginning of the eleventh century the abbot of Cluny had claimed identity with the archangel Michael, the weigher of souls, worshipped in high chapels and on mountain peaks: Adalbero was well aware of this; mockingly, he attributed to Odilo the title *princeps militiae,* which belonged to Saint Michael. A hundred years later, no one denied the abbot of Cluny this preeminent position. On his deathbed, Saint Hugh was said to "resemble a divine angel, not merely by dint of his striking posture, but also by the radiance of his visage"[15] This raised him well above the kings of the earth. He also dominated the bishops. He wore dalmatic and mitre, the insignia of prelacy conferred on him by the bishops of Rome, resigned to the fact that the eminent personage who had served as arbiter at Canossa in the dispute between the pope and the emperor should be deemed their master, Saint Peter's true successor. Hugh engaged in a direct dialogue with Christ: the latter had been seen by one of the biographers standing at the abbot's side on great occasions, inspiring him. The "great church" was truly a triumphal monument, celebrating a power which was not merely spiritual. Indeed, the Cluniac order, that luxuriant forest whose leafy canopy scraped heaven's floor, struck its roots deep into the material base of the structures of command, and the archangelic creature who ruled over it claimed also to reign over this world. At the portal of the basilica, near the guest quarters where passing popes and kings were treated so magnificently, a palace was built. Sumptuous stables stood alongside it, for when the abbot traveled to one of the dependent abbeys or priories he went, like the Savior in the miniatures of the *Beatus,* accompanied by a not inconsiderable prancing cavalry. He was the prince of peace, the peace of God. Sovereigns, dukes, and bishops, he was convinced, were no less his servants than those "advocates" and "wardens" employed in the Church's manors as menial overseers. Had not the great-grandson of Robert the Pious, Louis VI of France, agreed to accept such a role in 1119? Assuming responsibility for the order's safety, he became its seneschal, as it were, agent in charge of its defense. Helmeted, sword in hand, he rode out on his mission, while inaccessible in the heights the archabbot sat enthroned, majestic and immobile, assuming the very posture in which the sculptors of the Moissac tympanum had depicted the Eternal One.

There he remained, carrying out the function of the king of kings, disparaging the haughty. All the *Vitae* portray Saint Hugh as an enemy of "tyrants," a redresser of wrongs, who used his miraculous powers to topple over-greedy castellans who squeezed the peasantry unconscionably. He also punished grasping knights, as kings ought to have done. For—and herein lies the novelty—by the early twelfth century, when on the pretext of glorifying its defunct abbot the Cluniac order was loudly proclaiming its political options, it no longer supported knighthood, but rather challenged it. Saint Hugh was represented as an exorcist, expelling demons from an assembly of knights,[16] and his successor, Pons, was depicted exhorting young nobles not to be deluded by knighthood's claims to preeminence. Even as the ideology of the crusade was tending to unite princes and knights in a single body, Cluny rose up against laymen who profited from the exploitation of the seigniory and pretended to take the side of the poor. And pretense is indeed the word I mean to use. For if the monks, all of whom were recruited from the dominant class, were truly poor in spirit, they lived as lords, fed, clothed, and housed like the children of kings. Once penetrate to the bottom of their thought and aristocratic prejudices as blunt as Andrew of Fleury's are much in evidence. Like King Robert in an earlier time, they liked to live amid the poor, to make solemn distribution of alms, and to put on a great show of playing the provider's role that they also felt to be incumbent upon them. In reality, however, did they not despise the rustic populace, abandoning the cure of its soul to that clerical proletariat which already was grumbling and soon would rise against them, incited by the bishops? With the aid of those petty village despots, their provosts, did the monks of Cluny not make quite thorough work of exploiting their peasant subjects? It was the seigniorial system at its most rational, if not most productive, that enabled them to approach the celestial glories. With a clear conscience, justified by the ideology of the Dionysian hierarchies.

In fact, by 1125 or so Cluny could rely on only one ally—the bourgeoisie, the social group that had come into being and gathered strength under the impetus of the growing productive forces within the feudal order. This was an alliance which would last: half a century later, the inhabitants of the town would fall victim to a massacre while defending the monks. Ever since the leading monks had decided to build a magnificent replica of the heavenly Jerusalem, and had begun hiring quarrymen, masons, carpenters, and haulers by the hundreds, whereupon it became necessary to open the economy of the great house to commercial transactions and money, the village at the abbey gate had grown steadily in size and wealth. Its inhabitants (called "bourgeois" in what was perhaps the first use of the word in a social sense in the West, at the end of the tenth century in the Cluny cartulary) received privileges from the abbot Hugh; they were protected against exactions by neighboring lords who rightfully claimed them as serfs; they provisioned the community, worked for it, and accepted its pay. These bourgeois were the last supporters of the abbot Pons, then under attack by a coalition of bishops, knights from the surrounding castles, country curates, and their peasant flock. With the abbot they suffered excommunication. And they accompanied him when he went to Rome to defend his cause.

Between the concrete relations maintained by Cluny at its apogee with the ambient social formation and the image of society that it fashioned as an instrument of its temporal interests and a salve for its conscience, there are obvious correspondences. In its imperial and hierarchical aspects, this image derived from the model of Adalbero and Gerard. The opposition between the powerful and the poor was inherited from Carolingian ideology as conveyed by the ideology of the peace of God. On the other hand, Cluny downplayed anything that might have been harmful to its interests, such as the *clerus/populus* dualism raised against it by jealous bishops. The history that I am recounting, the history of a social fantasy, is made up of such imperceptible displacements, partial superimpositions, and imperfect condensations. It is also made up of lapses of memory, whether conscious or not: the monks of Cluny did not emphasize functional tripartition, because the only social category on which Cluny in its latter days could rely performed a function, the commercial function, which held only a rather insignificant place in the ideological system associated with the peace of God, and which had no place at all in the ideological system of Gerard and Adalbero.

17

NEW TIMES

Resolutely, Cluny had forged its alliance with what was most modern in the world, with money, with trade, with the city. But money, trade, and the city carried within them the germs of Cluny's condemnation. Disenchantment with the crusade and the bankruptcy of theatrical eschatology went hand in hand with an aggravation of the contradictions between the predilection for disincarnation and the taste for power and riches, between Benedictine humility and the will to power over the world; and above all, the contradictions between monks and clerks grew worse. In 1120 or so, a century after trifunctionality was set forth at Cambrai and Laon, the evolutionary process that we have been tracing reached a major turning point. Like the Capetian monarchy in the previous century, Cluny was tottering. In itself this was an event of considerable significance: it meant that a certain conception of the perfect society was passing into obsolescence. But it was also the clearest indication of a change in the ecclesiastical institution. This change had direct repercussions on the ideological systems accessible to our scrutiny. For however autonomous the history of these systems may be, it is influenced by the backlash stemming from changes affecting certain men, one of whose functions is to advance exemplary images of society. Now it happens to be the case that during the period in question, all such men belonged to the Church.

The crisis that shook the Cluniac order in the first quarter of the twelfth century was provoked by the breakdown of a very old alliance. This had been attacked by Adalbero: it was the complicity between the papacy and monasticism's leading elements. This link had been forged at the time of Cluny's founding, when the new monastery had welcomed Saint Peter and Saint Paul, the patron saints of the Roman Church, as its own patrons. The pope had long lent Cluny his support against the bishops of Carolingian tradition, in part because of this alliance, but also because the Cluniac congregation set an example in the necessary virtues for all the servants of God. This example was one that was actually followed. During the eleventh century there was a proliferation of small groups of clergymen whose dream was to eliminate sin's corruption from the priestly estate. But these fervent communities did not adopt the monastic ideal as such. Their outlook underwent an adaptation sufficient to alter its intention completely. A new wish supplanted the desire of individual purification nourished by meditation on the *Moralia in Job,* and the desire to convert a few "perfect" exemplars, to induct them one at a time into that outpost of paradise that Cluny prided itself on being, to record the names of certain of the living and certain of the dead in the book of life—these desires gave way to a new aim, to reform the whole body of the faithful from within. The pope understood that leadership of this reform fell naturally to him. He carried the effort first into the very theater in which Cluny had made its conquests, in southern Gaul, where the task was facilitated by the absence of kings. The reform was fitted into the context of the related concerns of the peace of God and holy war. Its first task was to purify the entire secular Church. In southern France cloisters of genuinely ordained canons grew up beside cathedral churches. These canons adopted a communal way of life, and refused to bear arms or keep women. In spite of the resistance to the work of the reforming prelates and the accusations of heresy leveled against them, these cathedral churches came to rival any of Cluny's monasteries in purity, and once this was achieved, Pope Gregory VII carried the battle northwards, nearer royal territories. There the struggle became even more bitter. In the end the clergy emerged victorious over the princes, and at one stroke over the monks as well. Not Hugh, the abbot of Cluny, but the pope preached the first crusade, and by 1095 the greatest voice in northern France was not that of a monk but rather a bishop, Yves of Chartres, who divulged the path of righteousness, berated kings, and exhorted laymen to put the Gospel's teachings into practice. This he did in the conviction that man ought to leave the angels alone, that God expected to be served on earth and to see his word spread among his people. On earthly society the monks had been wont to turn their backs, unconcerned to see it changed. The clergy did want changes, and wanted to compel human society to conform to God's wishes. After a century's delay, this amounted to adoption of the program put forward by Adalbero and Gerard. Like them, the bishops of northern France intended to establish control over the monasteries and so resumed the fight against exemption with an attack on Cluny and its privileges at the council of Rheims in 1119, in the presence of the pope. The bishops were sure of themselves because they now had the assistance of new groups, organized as solidly as the monastic communities yet still involved with the world; these groups were specially trained for the sacerdotal ministry, which office they themselves filled in the countryside, rather than leave this task to subordinates as did the monks. Similar to the cathedral chapters, these groups of canons proliferated everywhere. In the early twelfth century, princely foundations of monasteries declined, the princes choosing to establish collegiate churches in the vicinity of their castles instead. These were of greater usefulness than the monasteries, capable not merely of calling down grace upon the master, his family, the tombs of his ancestors, and all his subjects by means of righteous prayer, but also fit to lend a hand in the business of justice and the counting of deniers. Three hundred years earlier the Carolingian church had shifted its seat from the monasteries to the cathedrals and the prince's chapel, and now, in a comparable movement, we see the Church once more electing to build on the foundation of the priesthood. The bishop of Rome, the organizer of the reform, chose personally to take the sword from Saint Peter's hands. And accordingly to take it away from the abbot of Cluny. Between 1120 and 1125 Cluny was abandoned to the attacks of the episcopacy by Calixtus II, the first pope for half a century not to have come out of a monastery, the former archbishop of Vienne, cousin of kings and emperors, and successor of those venturesome prelates who had led cavalry charges on behalf of the peace of God. Rome no longer had need of monks.

In order to wage war, not as it was waged in the cloisters and basilicas of the monks, against shades, against the intangible legions of the Prince of Darkness, but rather in the light of day, hand to hand, against quite palpable adversaries whose blows struck home, the reformers had honed their weapons. To the arms of liturgy they preferred the arms of law. The monasticized Church of early Christianity had paid scant attention to juridical texts. As it became clericalized in the eleventh century, the Church placed these texts at the center of its reflections. From them it drew a model of social order—quite a simple model, befitting a time when the conflict was at its height. This conflict was a Manichaean struggle, a duel. Hence the Gelasian figure—*uterque ordo,* "two orders"—came once more to the fore as the polemic developed, much as it had done during an earlier resurgence of the episcopacy in the ninth century. Thus the fundamental binarity, which the trifunctional ideology had overlain, and which remained in the background of Raoul Glaber's utopian eschatologies, returned to center stage, eclipsing the other figures, deepening once again the division between all churchmen, including monks, and other men, a division whose line of demarcation had been insidiously shifted by monasticism. When in his *Treatise against the Simoniacs* Humbert of Moyenmoutier maintained that the "vulgar" might at once be subjects of both the "clerical order" and the "lay power," thereby distinguishing three social categories, his words are reminiscent of those of Garin of Beauvais and the prelates who favored the peace of God. In reality, his attention was focussed entirely on the distinction between the *ordo* (spiritual) and the *potestas* (temporal), on the unbreachable gulf, pointed to

208

by Gelasius, between the two fields of action: "just as clerks are forbidden to undertake secular affairs, so laymen are prohibited from ecclesiastical ones . . . just as within . . . basilicas the clerks have their place and their function and the laymen theirs, so outside the church they must be considered separate, having different places and functions. Accordingly, laymen should occupy . . . themselves only with secular affairs; clerks only with- . . . ecclesiastical affairs."[1]

During the last quarter of the eleventh century, the canonists were working on the idea of a simple distinction between two kinds of function, while a parallel effort went into a reconsideration of the sacerdotal ministry. Cluny had viewed the latter, sublimated in liturgy, as a sort of culmination of the monastic profession; clerical thought brought it back to earth, assigning it the task of influencing the populace through the sacraments and through preaching. In the *Decretum*, that compilation of canon law set down by Gratian in about 1140, and still cited six centuries later by Charles Loyseau, a sentence backed by the authority of Saint Jerome[2] declares: "there are two kinds [*genera:* the word is from Saint Augustine] of Christians;" one of them is assigned the "divine function": this was the clergy, which included the "lay brothers," those monks who were not priests; the members of this superior category were truly kings; they reigned; no temporal power could compel them to take action of any kind; they used their power over other men to guide them towards the truth (indeed, this was the purpose of the Gregorian struggle: to confer the *regnum* on the priesthood and relegate the kings of the earth to the other, inferior "genus"); in fact, "there is another kind of Christian: the laymen. . . . To them it is given to cultivate the earth and take a wife." At no time does this meditation on the social order treat nonmales: the feminine remains out of bounds, confined in the household to those dark, closed places where men and women coupled and procreated, where children were raised, food prepared, and the bodies of the dead washed. To the masculine portion of the laity, moreover, the ecclesiastical reformers granted a license—a permission afforded condescendingly, it is true, in itself instituting inequality, disparaging, subordinating, degrading in the strict sense of the term, any creature weak enough to avail himself of the authorisation thereby granted: the permission to soil oneself through the sexual act and through manual labor.

At the center of his poem, Adalbero asserted the existence of two laws, divine and human, and further maintained that the former, whose dominion embraced the servants of God, was the source of the fundamental division between the *ordo* and the rest of mankind. At the start of the twelfth century, the victorious Gregorians used the same argument. But they overworked it somewhat. As though impatient of opposition, they toughened the model's features. There was a need to confront the enemy forthrightly, to mark clearly the distance between the categories: "Whoever attempts to

leave his *ordo*," Anselm of Laon now said, "commits a mortal sin"[3]—
henceforth a definite misdeed, punishable by specific sanctions which the
priests were charged to impose. Above all, there was a need to avoid making
the hierarchy of conditions in the enemy camp too evident. The enemy drew
part of its strength from that hierarchy.

Accordingly, the bipartite schema gained the upper hand everywhere. In
Poitou as in the Ile-de-France, the scribes of charters took to the habit of
classifying witnesses into two groups, clergy and laymen, and the word
laicus is encountered with increasing frequency in their vocabulary. Painters
and sculptors also represented society in a binary form. Nothing of their
work remains but what was done in and for the Church. In the lush iconography of the early twelfth century, still much under the sway of fantasy but
employed in the service of a power undergoing secularization, whereby it
was gradually drawn closer to concrete reality, one searches in vain for
sign-complexes reflective of the trifunctional concept. When the image pur-
posed to depict heaven, it was deliberately based on Dionysian triads. But
when a representation of earthly society was desired, the image was resolutely dualist, setting to one side—the good, righthand side—the clergy,
lined up behind Saint Peter, Saint Paul, the popes, the bishops, and all the
reformers, while relegating to the other side all laymen, including kings,
with the women in their midst.[4]

In fact, in the new law, in the new morality forged in the course of the
Gregorian battles, the dichotomy *clerus/populus* verged on another binarity:
chastity/marriage. Fundamentally, the nature of the gap between the two
"orders" was perceived as sexual. All the clergy must be wifeless. This rule
was laid down by divine law. For the laity itself to become an order, it, too,
must follow a rule, symmetrical with the former, hence impinging on sexuality. The rule for laymen was to have women—legitimately: through marriage. Thus the ideology of the so-called Gregorian reform reduced to duality
another ternary hierarchy, that of merits, which set virgins above the continent, and the continent above the coupled. In fact, the dream of the
reforming bishops was to merge the top two grades in this hierarchy, to
impose a monkish virginity on all the clergy. Bent on controlling monasticism, the bishops wanted not to disparage but, on the contrary, to equal
it. All, or virtually all of them had had experience of a monastery; they
hoped one day to retire to one. For them, monastic life represented perfection. Their ideal was to rival the purity of the best monks, but without
abandoning the world, choosing instead to participate therein, in order to
purify the laity, and above all the kings. What was the Gregorian system if
not that of Adalbero and Gerard but stiffened, as it were, in the vicissitudes
of a struggle which in its decisive phase had been antiroyal? Accordingly,
that system rejected the king's claim to be at once *rex* and *sacerdos,* to
occupy the place of Christ, a place it reserved instead for Saint Peter and his

successors, consequently excluding sovereigns, their anointment not-withstanding, from the group of *oratores*. As a result, Gregorian ideology did not adopt the trifunctional postulate. To have recognized the existence of two functions in the laity would have amounted to exalting the military function, hence to conceding some advantage to reform's most adamant enemies, to the custodians of the temporal sword, to kings and princes, to the *bellatores*. Not to distinguish them from the subject populace was a matter of good tactics.

The renovation of Church structures completed in the first quarter of the twelfth century was quite obviously fostered by certain deep-seated changes, the same changes that were slowly pulling Western civilization out of the rurality in which it was mired. In northern France around 1120 we begin to see two developments, both stimulated by the expanding growth process, which directly or otherwise influenced the way that cultivated men conceived of the social organization. The first of these changes bore on mental attitudes. It affected the way men looked upon the things of the earth, and consequently the way they regarded the human condition. What brought this change about was, first of all, the agonizingly slow, dimly perceived, but inexorable movement that turned back the tide of *contemptus mundi,* overcoming little by little the feeling that the visible world was a despicable place, that it was to be shunned, that the true riches lay elsewhere. Disgust with the world had spread in a society convinced that earthly things were inevitably inclined to decay, destined to grow corrupt, to regress. Now to contradict such a belief came the vitality of the progressive spirit, the surge of production intensified by seigniorial coercion, and, arising out of the furrows plowed in freshly cleared land and from the newly planted vines in the vineyards that formed a steadily widening halo around every city in the Ile-de-France, the awareness of the following axiom: that man was capable of mastery over nature, capable of forcing nature to yield in greater abundance, and that by changing the course of rivers, adjusting the rotation of crops, and regulating the migrations of his flocks, he might use his strengths of body and mind to help dispel some of the disorder that had crept into creation. At the same time that the value attached to *operatio*—the efforts devoted to making the garden of Eden bloom and bear fruit—was rising steadily, and the attention of intellectuals was slowly turning toward the nature of things, toward physics; the idea that the kingdom of God might also be of this world was taking shape. What this meant was that men were emerging from the world of fantasy, that they were more openly than before repudiating the temptations of other-worldliness, and manifesting a new impatience with analogies and symbols. They were opening their eyes, comprehending that man worked in God's employ, and that procreation and manual labor were less degrading than had been said. A sure and decisive change affected the way that the flesh was seen, a change in the intensity and quality of the gaze upon the carnal, which was enough to restore the clerk's preeminence over the monk, to rehabilitate holy wedlock—which, transformed, became the basis of secular morality and the framework of the lay order—and to raise the laborer's function slightly higher in the hierarchy of social functions.

The other modification was tangible and touched the social fabric itself. In the first decades of the twelfth century, economic growth in northern France had reached the point where money—i.e., commercial transactions, hence cities—regained a role in the social structure comparable in importance to that which it had played a millennium earlier. As a result, the classificatory systems underlying the various social ideologies had to make room for a new category. Distinguished from the mass of men destined to support, to feed, and to serve the few—from the "slaves," as Adalbero of Laon said, or the "men of toil" (no doubt the best translation of the word *laborator*)—was a new group. This did not consist of the "ploughmen," as they would later be called, the peasants who owned plow gear. It was made up of "ministers," specialized underlings, charged with those tasks, those "occupations" (*ministeria*) that had acquired a certain distinctive individuality within the staff of the great aristocratic houses—occupations made increasingly indispensable by the growing importance of money. Some of them fashioned or fetched from afar finery and potions unlike anything produced in the peasant hovels, luxuries desired by their masters because they now wished to live not like rustics but nobly, because they wanted to dazzle their guests, as kings did, to regale them, and because they were less in want than they had been of cash to buy what the land did not provide. Others, no less desirous of distinction from mere villagers than their masters, collaborated in the management of the manor, insuring that it brought in ever greater amounts of the much-needed deniers. In both cases the ministers were domestic servants. But little by little we see them gaining freedom for themselves, we see them cease to carry out the third function of supply solely to satisfy their lord and begin to work in their own behalf, enriching themselves, keeping for their own use a portion of the taxes they collected or of the value of the commodity they were furnishing. The jobs they were assigned stood close to the sources of the new prosperity, a prosperity fostered by heightened circulation of money in the economy.

By this time the numbers of such men had grown too large, and their importance too great, for the want of distinction between them and those who labored in the countryside to continue. A place apart had to be set aside for them, a niche etched in the gridwork of the imagination through which the diversity of social conditions was conveyed to minds seeking to reduce variety to intelligibility. But what place? What word could be found to characterize these people? "Rustic" was no longer appropriate: most of

212

them lived and worked in the new quarters of the renascent cities, around the markets and fairs. Was "slave" any better? Here indeed were men subject to a lord's power, exploited, judged, punished, compelled to pay taxes; but they were not men whose backs one saw bent over the soil. In the squares they sang freely and shouted the word "liberty." Though they often bore arms, could they be classified as "warriors"? These questions had already been raised in the early days of the peace of God, i.e., in the time of Adalbero and Gerard. The two bishops had evaded them. But their colleagues from Beauvais and Soissons had not, out of concern lest this not poor but still vulnerable segment of the populace be abandoned to the brigandage of the knights; accordingly, these bishops took care to see that the wording of the peace oaths mentioned "merchants" and "wine carriers." But was the activity of this rising class accurately defined by the wine trade, or by trade in general? Finally, at the end of the eleventh century, in the time of the first crusade, the scribes included a new group between the knights and the peasants in the lists of witnesses, a group dominated by the former and dominating the latter and categorized as consisting of "bourgeois and sergeants."[5] It should be noted that these two terms had no functional connotation. First seen a century earlier in Cluny's charters, the word "bourgeois" evoked the place of residence, the "bourg," that cluster of buildings whose appearance was not altogether that of a village and whose vocation was not purely agricultural. Standing outside the walls of a city, below a castle, or at the gate of a monastery, the bourg seemed to be an outgrowth of the seigniorial residence. The word "sergeant" indicated a certain form of service. What both terms conveyed was a complex situation, compounded at once of domestic subjection and autonomy with regard to the traditional constraints of the rural community or the kinship group. Ambiguity. This should not surprise us: the belated, stealthy emergence of this category in the written sources, in the acts whose purpose was to establish rights in a definitive form, was a particularly disturbing occurrence. Indeed, it did confuse in several ways the traditional view of the social organization taken by men capable of detached reflection.

To set the "bourgeois" apart as a distinct group in the classificatory scheme was to admit that the countryside was no longer everything, that there existed another kind of social space with its own peculiar structure, the urban environment, wherein one found men specialized in the third function, albeit not practicing it in the traditional manner, and that this had to be taken into account in analyzing society in functional terms. Thus in Laon, Adalbero's city, swollen in the meanwhile with suburbs, the trifunctional schema reemerged, but in a new form in an ordinance pertaining to peace issued in 1128, concerning those who might do harm "to clerks, knights, or merchants." Three functions, the third being trade. But this ternarity did not extend to the entire body social. It pertained only to that islet, the city, in which already we see a concentration of what was important in society: power, wealth, prestige. Even then, did it pertain to the whole urban population? Did it not omit those people, of whom there were surely many in Laon, who worked the earth, who performed what henceforth was looked upon as a fourth function, the peasant's—already passed over in silence, neglected? As disconcerting as the acquisition by the bourgeois and the seigniorial agents of a social personality was in itself, perhaps still more disconcerting was the fact that some of these men, who not long before were still to be found mingling with the domestics of the bailey, had found ways to enrich themselves with salaries, pledges, percentage deductions, and "benefices" (notice how expressive the vocabulary is: the same word also denoted the fief; it was a "benefit," a gift of the patron, and in fact the deniers amassed by certain bourgeois and sergeants came straight out of their master's privy purse; yet this money was not given to them, but rather earned, and it accumulated because those who earned it were not nobles, not generous, and held on to their cash with tightly clenched fists). In this period the only discernible social trend with any force to speak of was the irresistible attraction that the aristocracy exercised on the boldest gamblers among the *ministeriales*. Prepared to do anything to win the friendship of the knights, eager to shed any remaining traces of servitude and to win access to respectable society for themselves as a body, they stalked about in arms, rode in cavalcades, and built stone houses in the city in imitation of the great lords. They were eager also for spiritual advancement. Imperceptibly, the Carolingian system of values, wherein no virtue or charisma not carried by noble blood was imaginable, was disintegrating. In the bourg one persistent question was heard: could a man with base blood be holy? And coupled with this question was another: could a man up to his elbows in treasure be a saint?

There is one further reason why the inroads made by money, the expansion of trade, and the attendant social mobility worsened the fit of society's ideological cloak: in the city not everyone was successful. Urban wealth was compounded of fortune and adventure: of instability, in short. Some were winners in the game, others losers. The new social locale turned up a novel and shocking phenomenon: inequality attended by misery. No longer was destitution shared by the entire community, as during the great famines of the year 1000. Now it was individual, and revolting because it rubbed shoulders with extreme opulence. In the urban setting the notion of poverty underwent a transformation. The notion of indigence appeared. For here the poor were no mere figureheads but were actually suffering. Also discovered was a new form of almsgiving, a different conception of charity. When did this occur? In northern France the discovery came between 1120 and 1150. Consider the behavior of princes. Charles, count of Flanders, assassinated in 1127, was immediately held out as model of sanctity: he had died a martyr, among the canons of his collegiate church at Bruges, while praying, while reading a book like a clerk, and while giving generously, like a king. But ritually: designated representatives of the poor, like those maintained by Robert the Pious, marched in procession past his throne, and each received at the appointed hour a denier, a symbolic donation. Charitable works were still no more than a figure in a ballet staged in the grand theater of sovereignty. Twenty years later at the court of Champagne this was no longer the case. Count Thibaud had heard Saint Bernard say that the "great" ought to humble the proud, defend widows and orphans, and punish the wicked, thus assuming the functions of the Carolingian king, but also that they ought to distribute food and clothing to the wretched from their own hand, in personal visits to the places of suffering. To this unpleasant chore Thibaud submitted, renouncing luxury and giving away the treasure that had been the glory of this house. The prince may thereby have succeeded in forestalling the movements of voluntary poverty then on the rise, particularly in the cities—whether or not he consciously intended to head off their aggressive challenges to his authority. These movements criticized the Church of wealth—the seignorial Church—and impelled laymen to accept responsibility for the tasks of distributive justice that were being neglected by God's servants, too often guilty of insufficient meditation upon the word of the Gospel. Count Thibaud inquired as to how he might aid the poor, using as his agents two Premonstratensian canons—men of great purity who obeyed a rigorous rule and yet were not monks closeted away in a cloister, but men living and acting in the world. On his behalf, the count's almoners made a round of visits to the indigent. Rather than scour the countryside, their search focussed on the bourgs: in the city streets and squares they gathered the sick, the leprous, and shared out food and money among them. Judiciously: the gifts were proportioned to need, but also to rank. Indeed, even in practicing charity, the count of Champagne—as well as the Cistercian who in recounting the life of Saint Bernard praised in passing his love of the poor—remained a prisoner of the ideological system that looked upon inequality as necessary. Throughout the twelfth century, the hierarchical conception that men had of society continued to influence their concept of poverty. This was judged to be relative.[6] A knight a hundred times as wealthy as his tenant farmer appeared nonetheless far poorer if his means were insufficient to the maintenance of his rank; in that case he was acknowledged to have a right to aid, a right to receive one hundred times as much as a poor man of the "people." It was important that the redistribution of wealth through alms given by the wealthiest members of society be effected in accordance with God's justice, in keeping, therefore, with the order that he had established, thereby instituting ranks among men. Princes and prelates were convinced that charity should not call the hierarchy of dignities into question. Anyone who wished for a leveling charity was a heretic. Now, in the cities, specifically, the compassionate feelings awakened by the spectacle of indigence bore within them the seeds of heresy. In the form of an aspiration to justice, a justice that would bring about equality, heresy was undergoing a revival.

This desire to abolish differences and to live among equals in friendship was exploited by the wealthiest and most active inhabitants of the cities, whose initiatives were hampered and whose accumulation of wealth was slowed by the seigniorial system. They loudly voiced egalitarian claims in their struggle against the urban lords. With an oath of mutual aid they attempted to unite all the town dwellers in a "commune." One oath for all—analogous to the one that had rallied the soldiers of the peace of God around Aymon, archbishop of Bourges. This was a model society, composed of "friends," of "brothers," a sort of family that had ostensibly rid itself of its father, analogous to the bands of young knights expelled from the ancestral abode to seek adventure, or to the colonies of hermits who lived by gathering what they could in the forests or by selling charcoal to the ironsmiths in the expanding cities—analogous to the heretical sects. In the communal movement in Cambrai in 1101 and simultaneously at Aire-sur-la-Lys, the very same egalitarian expectations that bishop Gerard had combatted seventy-five years earlier showed signs of renewed existence. But the nature of the equality to which the communal movement laid claim was different. Rather than a spiritual preparation for passage over into eternity, as in the preaching of the heresiarchs of 1025, the equality now envisioned was tangible and terrestrial. But its proponents, too, denied the existence of differences of condition. "Citizen respected citizen, the rich did not despise the poor; they felt the greatest repugnance for rows, lawsuits, discords; they competed only for honor and justice." Such an idyllic picture of communal society was reconstructed after the fact, in 1153, by the author of the *Annals of Cambrai*, Lambert, canon of Waterloos. The "friendship" in reality lay only on the surface. In no respect did it diminish the blatant contrasts between the wealthy bourgeois and the poor. Still, in condemning all forms of violence and declaring null and void all social distances due to fortune, the leaders of the movement perpetuated an illusion that they hoped would entice the wretched to join their cause, an illusion that harked back to the dream of the heretics of Arras. For reactionary chroniclers to identify the spate of communes with the resurgence of heresy was not without justification. The links between the two were quite plainly indicated.

Also a result of economic growth, and inextricably bound up with the revival of trade, was one further change of considerable importance, the simultaneous rise in the status of both the bishop and the lay prince, i.e., the two most prominent figures in the Gregorian struggle. Both owed their rise to money, and sought financing from the sources where it was most abundant; rather than scour the huts of peasants for a hidden coin or two, they took gold by the handful from the places where streams of it now flowed, in the markets and fairs, and from the merchants' stalls in the *faubourgs*. Tied to the city, both bishops and princes had the support of the sergeants and the bourgeois. Thus in Paris, cathedral and palace stood face to face—on one side the bishop and his clerks, on the other the king and his nobles. Adalbero's heir and the heir of Robert the Pious advanced in step to center stage. Once more we find binarity, antagonism coupled with complicity. But the scenery is no longer the same. The landscape has become urban. This gave rise to a second binarity. The gap between city and countryside had been reopened and would never again cease to broaden. Growing steadily, the city established its foothold. Still, prior to 1180 in northern France it had not yet emerged victorious. During the second and third quarters of the twelfth century the centers of growth were still rural. This explains why monasticism, bound to decline in the wake of economic development, continued to show considerable signs of strength. This period, when the first Gothic cathedrals were going up, was also the time of the extraordinary expansion of the Cistercian monasteries. What monks had to say about society was still important. We must hear them before turning our attention to the clergy.

18

MONASTICISM'S LAST LUSTER

I shall consider three abbots: Guibert of Nogent, Bernard of Clairvaux, Suger of Saint-Denis.

A man of the old era, Guibert stands astride the dividing line between old and new. He was born in the Beauvaisis in about 1065,[1] among the knights who garrisoned the castle of Clermont, thus into the lower strata of the aristocracy. He was nevertheless given a tutor who initiated him in the art of words. This would not have precluded his becoming a knight: in this region the custom of giving instruction in letters to all the sons of the nobility was already gaining a foothold. His elder brother wished to place him in the Clermont castle's chapter of canons. At the age of thirteen he was offered to the monastery of Saint-Germer-de-Fly, of which his maternal grandfather had been protector. He ended up as abbot of Nogent, near the border with the Soissonais, but within the diocese of Laon. Then beginning to weigh more heavily upon this tiny country monastery was the cultural domination of the vital, properous episcopal city, where in the neighborhood of the cathedral the books earlier annotated by Adalbero were again being read. This stimulated Guibert's taste for writing. He followed the customary pattern of monastic writers, first meditating upon the Scripture, then turning to the elucidation of those other signs from God, current events. He wrote the history of his times, the history of the crusade, in the *Deeds of God through the Franks,* which he completed in 1108. In 1115 he wrote his *Memoirs.* In one sense these writings enter into the same universe as Raoul Glaber's. They are replete with ghosts, demons, and angels. The marvelous tends, however, to center on the Virgin and the crucifix: even in abbeys as miserable as this one, Christianity had over the past seventy years taken a more evangelical turn. Men Guibert saw with the same eyes as Raoul. Peasants did not interest him. He regarded them as a sort of tool, useful for the upkeep of the monks and the castle knights. He was caught in the toils of seigniorial ideology. Yet the ideology of the peace of God also continued to exert an influence on him. Accordingly, when he paused to describe the battle against the "tyrants," the wicked lords—those detestable neighbors, the nearest and most troublesome of whom was Thomas of Marle, the lord of Coucy—Guibert felt bound to celebrate the "people." Thus in describing the host recruited by the bishops for a veritable holy war, with promises of indulgence such as the crusaders had received, he recognized the presence of knights but regarded their contribution as insignificant; the bulk of the credit for success fell to the populace. Still, as specified in the oaths of peace earlier administered in the same region by Garin of Beauvais and Béraud of Soissons, the people were led by the king,[2] for—and here lies the essential point—even though this campaign was quite similar to one waged in 1038 by the archbishop of Bourges, the upshot of which was the disorder denounced by Andrew of Fleury, the result here would be different because this time the action would be carried out in an orderly fashion. Order, it should be noted, was once again said to derive from the state, whose renaissance was in progress as Guibert wrote: the monarchical state, that is, guarantor not only of peace and justice but also of the necessary inequality.

Indeed, for Guibert of Nogent as for Adalbero, a major breach divided men into two categories: the "slaves" (or "serfs," *servi*) and the others. This accounts for the outrage the "liberties" conceded to the people of Laon provoked in him. Everyone knows his vitriolic invective "against the execrable institution of communes, in which contrary to all justice and all law slaves [serfs] may be seen escaping the legitimate authority of masters [lords]." These words Guibert put into the mouth of the archbishop of Rheims, come to purify the cathedral of Laon in the wake of the communal upheavals,[3] but he based them on the first epistle of Peter 2:18: "Servants, be subject to your masters with all fear, not only to the good and gentle, but also to the froward." He also claimed a basis in law, specifically, the canons prescribing anathema against those wicked men who counseled slaves to disobey or flee. Guibert was familiar with all the judgments that Gratian would one day collect.[4] He made use of the whole juristic arsenal then in preparation so as to assure the Church a predominant place within the seigniorial mode of production. The jurists were convinced of one thing, that human society necessarily consisted of two parts. Certain men—including the bourgeois—were born to servitude. Others were well-born.

Concerning the latter group, Guibert of Nogent, who might have taken horse and sword had he not preferred to serve God,[5] shared the opinion later held by M. de Torquat, that two possible courses, two vocations, lay open to its members: arms and prayer. The superiority of the latter was beyond doubt: were a clerk to embrace the knightly estate, according to Guibert, he would be committing "a shameful act of apostasy."[6] The status of knights was indeed the lesser of the two, for the knight was irremediably corrupt. What was the source of this corruption? Not the blood that he might be bound to spill, but rather the use he made of sex. To hear Guibert tell it, a certain monk was deemed shockingly wicked because he had entered the monastery after puberty: converted belatedly, "he had spent his whole life amidst knighly habits, debauchery, and whores."[7] This is not the place to examine at length the obsessions that haunted the abbot of Nogent. The fact of the matter is that to him all knighthood—and heresy as well—seemed in the grip of a frenzied sexuality. Nor did this delirium spare kings. It had destroyed Philip I's thaumaturgic powers. On the one side were the subjects—enslaved and contemptible; on the other, the knights—salacious and corrupt; and some clerks were no better, like those wicked bishops, Manasses of Rheims, too enamored of the men of war, and Adalbero—our Adalbero—the perjuror, the consequences of whose sin still beset the city of Laon. Only the monks were truly pure; the good monks, that is, those who had quit the world as virgins and had not succumbed to temptation. Shut up in his tiny cloister, Guibert of Nogent classified society as of old, hierarchically, according to the traditional norms of inequality, Gelasian duality, and a scale of merits along which ranking was determined by the greater or lesser degree of sexual purity.

Guibert was not blind, however. He saw the power of another agent of corruption, money, those pieces of silver which tempted even monks[8] and were hoarded by usurers, "bloodsuckers of the poor."[9] This accounts for his hatred of the new, urban society, and particularly of the members of the Laon commune. In the bloody events of 1112, still horrifyingly fresh in his memory, wherein the "people of the lower levels," those "inferior beings,"[10] had offended by attacking their lord, the bishop, he saw all the defilements combined. Had not the bourgeois, rebellious and filthy rich, taken for their ally Thomas of Marle, pillager of pilgrims and paupers, a man capable, according to the nasty gossip spread by Guibert, of erotic perversities of the worst kind? There were three causes for the outbreak of disorder: the first of them, quite remote, was Adalbero's betrayal—Raoul Glaber's idea that guilty prelates were responsible for the sins of their people was again current; second, the greed of the archdeacons and the lords of the city: they had sold liberties, daring to diminish inequality in society in exchange for money; finally, the bestiality of the "serfs": the one who killed the bishop—a bishop deemed unworthy by Guibert, yet anointed of the Lord and hence untouchable—was a wolf, Ysengrin; of popular origin, a fine representative of the rising class, he had climbed to the highest rank by aiding the lord of Coucy in the collection of tolls. Because this was an uprising fomented by the knaves of "tyrants," by upstarts grown wealthy at the expense of monks, and by clerks and foreigners in transit, worse than the worst castellans and bereft even of their excuse of being of noble blood, it had swollen like a purulent wound in which all the infections of the carnal world were concentrated. When finally the abcess was drained, the wound cauterized, purified by fire, this riotous incident, which began—was it by chance?—in the gold-laden house of the paymaster, had come to symbolize the ills of society. Indeed, riot had not arisen in the peasant populace, but had rather sprung from that ignoble place, the city, whose power lay not in wealth passed on, peacably, through inheritance, but rather in wealth earned, amassed, stolen, wealth that represented an insolent attack on the privileges of the well-born, on Guibert himself and all his cousins. Against this rot there was only one source of comfort, one hope of salvation: the values kept safe on those two islands that constituted the last refuge, as it were, of the good, in those two brotherhoods whose virtue pitted them against that other, accursed brotherhood, the commune: the community of monks—albeit the monasteries faced the constant threat of contamination, particularly from those mangy outcasts, the former knights, who had made love before being received into the monastery and so carried with them the leprosy that was in the world; and the community of crusaders, molded like monasticism by a movement of retreat, renunciation, and conversion.

As the scales fell from other eyes, Guibert actually continued to stare in wide-eyed amazement at the mirage of the great migration to Jerusalem. Came the departure: the pilgrims marched off in bands, like the locusts mentioned in Proverbs 30:27, "touched by the sunshine of justice, abandoning their father's house, leaving their king, sanctified by their goal," single-minded—and yet "they had no king, each believer guided by God alone, each considering himself the ally of God."[11] For unlike Adalbero, when Guibert dreamed of the perfect society he deemed royalty superfluous on earth, even though he portrayed the king leading the men of the parishes against the wicked lords. Nor did he look upon the kingdom established in the Holy Land as having any but a disincarnate value. He makes a point of saying that King Baldwin had sent his wife to a convent so that thus protected against inflamatory desires, "emancipated from the necessity to fight against flesh and blood, he could devote himself entirely to the struggle against the princes of this world."[12] First with no king, and later under a sexless king, crusading society might well count both great men and small, rich and poor, among its number, but all were like brothers. "Wearing the same yoke, under the authority of God alone, so that the slave [the serf] no longer belonged to the master [to the lord] and the master no longer taxed the slave but for the dues of the confraternity."[13] With inequality and seigniorial domination done away with, only one sign remained, the cross, like the cross-belt of a new knighthood.[14] Dazzled as he was by the splendors of a paradise whose gate seemed to stand ajar, Guibert was not unaware, as he wrote in 1108, of the widespread disillusionment. Chaff had been sown among the pilgrim converts. Who was spreading the corruption? Obviously

221

women, above all; but also the foot soldiers, the nonnoble element of the campaigning forces.

Still, the crusade cleansed knighthood of its impurities, and this was for Guibert the essential point, the function of the undertaking. When a knight took the cross, he was at last pledging to respect the moral code that justified his preeminent worldly station, a code that he was constantly forced to violate by the power of worldly temptations; in perfection, he was accepting the duties associated with his specific function. God had need of knighthood. He wished it to be good. Now he had stirred up holy wars "so that knights need not, in order to renounce the world [this is the point: the monk Guibert deemed the world a wicked, contemptible place], embrace the monastic life, but might instead, while keeping to their customary habits and fulfilling their customary obligations, make themselves worthy, to some degree at least [monasticism was of course superior] of his favors." The crusade thereby restored order. It dissuaded from entering the monasteries men who, because their conversion had come too late, might have threatened those places of purity with corruption. For, ensconced in his rural abbey, Guibert was convinced that one thing was essential: the preservation of that redoubt of righteousness, that halfway house to the world, wherein the good monks dwelled. The rest of society played out its roles in one or the other of two quite distinct theaters. One was vast, tenebrous, obscured by brush, thronged with hordes of peasants and herds of beasts rubbing one another's flanks. The other stage was set with a decor strictly urban, with market, rampart, and cathedral for props. Amidst this scenery three actors played their parts: the wicked—bourgeois and sergeants, who shared the characteristic arrogance that impelled serfs to acquire riches; the clerks; and finally the knights. The latter played the lead, provided they had the wisdom to shun *cupiditas* and *libido*. All the elements of what would later be the view of Saint Bernard are already in place.

Bernard and Guibert share similar origins. Bernard's parents came from slightly smarter society; his father was lord of a castle, his mother related to minor counts of the duchy of Burgundy. They differed, first of all, in the quite different spiritual qualities each possessed, and secondly in that Bernard belonged to the succeeding generation. By his day the world had changed: monasticism was now firmly integrated in the new structures of the Church. Bernard joined the Cistercian order, whose tenets were based on the rule of Saint Benedict, albeit revised and adapted to the exigencies of a new age. No longer was the order's poverty to be symbolic: the Cistercians chose not to live by the labor of other men, and so took a stance outside the seigniorial mode of production. Cîteaux bowed to the preeminence of the bishops: the order refused to have anything to do with exemption; this won for it the favor of the popes, but more than that, it explains the powerful resurgence, just as Bernard's thoughts were turning to the social structure, of the tripartite schema, of a three-tiered hierarchy.

This schema was not, however, that of Adalbero and Gerard. The ternarity it invoked was that which Saint Augustine and Saint Jerome before him had used to classify tasks and merits. On several occasions Bernard repeated virtually verbatim the Augustinian formulas. "We are used to distinguishing three kinds of men." In the triad consisting of Noah, Daniel, and Job, he saw the symbol of the "three orders"—prelates, continent, and married.[15] He thereby expressed his wholehearted acceptance of the Gregorian program, his conviction that all the servants of God should, under the direction of the bishops, "follow chastity and the virginal way of life and scorn the pleasures of the world,"[16] and that the married estate constituted the layman's rule of life. For the Cistercians there was, of course, no question that the monastic way was the more arduous, that "the clerk in becoming a monk submits himself to a greater humility, obedience, and abstinence."[17] Accordingly, the monks of the order, more stringently regulated than the clergy, in certain respects held dominion over it. In any case, as penitents they refused to countenance taking action of any sort in the world. As Saint Bernard put it, "the function of a monk is not to teach but to cry."[18] Cîteaux stood markedly apart from the world. Its abbeys were founded in the "desert"; no portal pierced their walls; they were closed in on themselves; a girdle of uncultivated land isolated them, protecting them from any worldly disturbance.

Without being aware of it, however, Cistercian society was itself caught up by the deep-running current stirred by the agrarian conquests of the second quarter of the twelfth century, which led to the world of flesh being afforded a higher value than hitherto. On the fringes of the clearings pushed ever wider by their own handiwork, the monks—like pioneering peasants, artisans, and merchants—were snatching up the stuff of nature by the armful and shaping it to their desires. The allure of the other world was thus diminished in their eyes. In Cistercian cloisters meditation centered on the mystery of the indissoluble bond between body and soul, on the incarnation. No longer was the inescapable carnality of the human condition denied, as it had been at Cluny. Cîteaux accepted this condition as its own. As it found it. And took also as it found it, with its differences, its insuperable distinctions, and its classes, human society. More imperious, perhaps, than with Guibert of Nogent or Andrew of Fleury, aristocratic prejudice ruled Saint Bernard's thought. Railing against heretics in his inimitable manner, passionate, vehement, and extremist, he could think of no insult worse than to call them workers. Indeed, in the abbeys of the order, the choir monks, sons of noblemen, set to work clearing brush and swinging the sickle, but their purpose was to humble themselves even further. For they had no doubt that manual labor was the work of contemptible louts, particularly the lay brothers, those sons of peasants who worked shoulder to shoulder with them, whom they called brothers, but whose existence they could not really bring themselves to share, relegating them instead to a place apart, to special quarters, because they were not well-born. Like all the Cistercians of his day (and this is perhaps the place to look for an important reason for the differences of opinion over social structure between Cluny—most of whose inmates had been raised from childhood in the monastery, in the shelter of the cloister—and Cîteaux), Bernard was an adult when he "converted" in 1111; he knew the world; he knew what place was his by birth in a hierarchy which seemed to him necessary and immutable, whose derangement by the newly rising categories he perceived but dimly. With iron-clad certainty he believed that the order according to which men were ranked in the world would not be disturbed until the resurrection of the flesh.

This he once stated in no uncertain terms to the clerks of Cologne:[19] "When men begin to come back to life, every man in his own order[*unusquisque in ordine suo*—Paul, 1Cor. 15], where do you suppose that [your] kind [*generatio*] will be lodged? If peradventure [you] go with the knights, they will drive [you] out for having lent them so little support in toil [*labor*] and peril. The peasants [*agricolae*] and the merchants [*negociatores*] will do the same, and every order [*ordines*] of mankind will thus exclude you from its territory. What will be left then for those rejected and at the same time accused by every order: to them will be assigned the place without order, where sempiternal horror dwells." The admirable rhetoric of this invective throws a clear light on the abbot of Clairvaux's judgment of human society. He regarded it as ordered by its very nature and by that irresistible force that raised it toward the good. For him order was an attribute of heaven, disorder of hell. Then again, were new proof needed, this text would provide irrefutable confirmation of the fact that in the minds of intellectuals then dreaming of social perfection, the word *labor* signified not manual labor but physical suffering, fatigue—painful (*labor* and *dolor* were linked by Bernard as they had been by Adalbero), hence redeeming. A knightly "toil" existed, which, like the confrontation with danger, redeemed the sins committed in battle. By pampering their bodies some clerks fell into dissolute ways, and it was for this reason, not merely out of humility but in order to be worthy of their estate, that the Cistercians reserved a large place in their lives for *labor,* for physical exertion in field, forest, and forge. Note, finally, that among laymen Bernard distinguished categories he called orders. Not two, but three. Bernard was witness to the new age: to the "knights" and "peasants" he added—he was speaking in the city of Cologne—"merchants." He placed them at the bottom of the list, perhaps because he shared the judgment of Guibert of Nogent that these money-men who went about with their heads held high were the worst of all. These orders were functional. We thus observe the resurgence of the idea, still vital, that the function a man served determined his place in the order, whether through military action or provision of foodstuffs—the latter activity being split henceforth into its agricultural and commercial components. Still, the real rift fell between the provisioning function and that of the warrior. This barrier was inherent in the mode of production, and it was by no means the intention of the Cistercians to abolish it: though they refused the profits of the seigniorial system for themselves, they nevertheless strictly separated two areas within the confines of the monastery, the one reserved for the monks, whose toil was primarily spiritual, the other for the lay brothers, who by birth and the inviolable laws of procreation were destined ineluctably to suffer, especially in their bodies.

This division within the Cistercian community was to be further accentuated: in 1188 the chapter general of the congregation decided to forbid "noble laymen entering the monastery" to elect the status of lay brother out of humility: they would derogate if they did not become choir-monks.[20] Resolutely committed to the carnal world, employing the most up-to-date methods of farming in their domains, the twelfth-century Cistercians thus refused to blur the distinctions between the *ordines*, even for men set apart from the world by the cloister wall. Indeed, it was God's will that class distinctions endure until the end of the world. Aiming at perfection, at an organization in keeping with the will of God, the Cistercians, the monastic order best adapted to the imperatives of the age, established their abbey in the conviction that men of different blood ought not to mingle. This was expressed by no one more forcefully than Hildegard of Bingen, who died in 1179. The abbess of Andernach had expressed her surprise that only daughters of the nobility were received among the nuns, whereas, according to the Apostle (1 Cor. 1:26), God did not distinguish between persons. Hildegard answered that it was "the will of God that the inferior estate not rise above the superior as Satan and Adam had done. What man would gather all his herds in one stable, cattle, asses, and sheep together? Respect for custom would thereby be destroyed." This is followed by a resounding reference to the words of the pseudo-Dionysius, reflected from the Germanic depths as though in echo of the ancient and very "French" pronouncements of Adalbero and Gerard: "God orders persons on earth just as in heaven, where he distinguishes angels, archangels . . . [etc.]."[21]

The result of all the progress made in the world was that in the judgment of the dominant culture in the mid-twelfth century the class barrier seemed more essential than ever—an impression reinforced by the fact that tremors in the underlying structures were then beginning to undermine that barrier as a line of defense. Efforts were made to fortify that line even in the domain of the spiritual. Cluny followed suit: in reforming the statutes in 1146, Peter the Venerable issued a warning not to allow in "among the monks too great a number of old men or cretins," to be sure, nor "too many peasants" either.

The cause of inferiority was no longer ascribed to servitude (serfdom was declining rapidly in many northern French provinces), but rather to non-noble birth. This was now held to be an indelible stain. In a period of social unrest provoked by economic growth, which had already seen a few instances of merchants becoming lords, along with the assassination of the count of Flanders, a murder that certain very powerful personages had not hesitated to commit to keep the fact that their father had been a serf from coming to light, the important distinction in the laity was no longer based as it had been a hundred years earlier on the relations of production. These relations were undergoing certain shifts, and the line of demarcation tended to waver ambiguously. Men who stood on the favored side of the line thought it important to firm it up, to change its basis from seigniory, from power—because these qualities, one now knew, could be bought—to birth, nobility, gentility. To put it another way, from the time of Saint Bernard on, distinction was made a concomitant of chivalry.

Like Guibert, Bernard of Clairvaux was really interested, apart from monks, only in knights. To their salvation he devoted all his ardor, and he, too, regarded the crusade as the means by which it could be achieved. For those who had not the courage to fly to that other, preferable Jerusalem of renunciation, the monastery, he deemed the crusade the surest instrument of repentance. This was a point he made in his *Praise of the New Knighthood,* the title referring to those nobles who without renouncing their arms had taken up the life of the monk, submitting to obedience, chastity, and poverty: the Templars. After this company was accorded its rule at the council of Troyes in 1128, a momentarily hesitant Bernard undertook to offer it comfort and support against its critics.[22] Accordingly, he wrote a eulogy to this host, at last purged of lust for riches and vainglory, purified, its forces joined with the heavenly armies, protected against the two dangers inherent in combat: the danger of killing one's soul along with the enemy, and the danger of being killed in both body and soul. This protection they owed to the fact that what the Judge took into account—on this point Bernard found himself in agreement with his enemy, Abelard—was the intention behind the act, the aim, the cause one served, the "disposition of the heart": when "the knight of Christ . . . kills a malefactor, his act is not homicide, but if I may say so, malicide; he is none other than Christ's avenger against evildoers."[23] Here the abbot of Clairvaux was following the lead of Peter Damian, who fifty years earlier had exhorted the "warriors of this world" to convert and become "warriors of Christ," as well as the example of the last great abbots of Cluny, who had tried to eliminate the demonic elements from knighthood. It is true that in celebrating this "new" knighthood (new in the same sense as the Cistercian monastery, having battened on the old), he inveighed against knighthood in general. But when he preached to the great military religious orders—all that remained of the grand dream of 1095, wherein monks and crusaders were combined indiscriminately into one community—he himself came to dream of a new "type of man" epitomizing the highest values of earthly society: for in such men the preeminent "orders" would be joined together, the one spiritual, monastic, the other corporeal, chivalric.

Nevertheless, until all knights had been converted, made obedient, humble, chaste, and poor without sacrificing an iota of their gallantry, the social order must not be tampered with by anyone. In sum, Bernard pictured a society built on the plan of the Cistercian cloister, square in shape—symbolizing the realm of the incarnate: 1, the monks; 2, the knights; 3, the clerks; 4, the rest. On this chessboard, several moves were possible: 1 + 2: the knights of the Temple; 1 + 3: the choir-monks; 1 + 4: the lay brothers (and in the Templar order, the sergeants); 1 + 3 + 4: the Cistercian monastery; 2 + 3 + 4: the secular world. The pattern in the carpet was still a checkered one. And would remain so until the day of the trumpet blast, when the dead would rise from their tombs and form up in ranks, "every man in his own order."

A contemporary of Saint Bernard, similar in social background (of "humble origins," it is said, which is not to be interpreted to mean that he was born of peasant parents, but rather that his family were not cousins of kings, in contrast to Hugh of Cluny or Peter the Venerable), Suger stands at the opposite extremity of the monastic world. Where Bernard fulminated furiously against luxury, Suger's only thought was for the embellishment of his church, and it was he who was the object of the attack in Bernard's *Apology to William*. Where Bernard supported the count of Champagne, a feudal lord, Suger's backing went to the Capetian king, and he subordinated knightly values to royal authority. Suger was abbot of Saint-Denis, a royal monastery earlier reformed by Cluny. His function was to watch over the crypt wherein the tomb of the Frankish kings enclosed a sepulchre thought to be that of Dionysius the Areopagite. In the gorgeous abbey church he therefore staged sumptuous liturgies, whose ordering reflected the triads of the celestial hierarchy—three porches were opened in the new facade of the basilica, and the multitude was divided into three groups for the consecration ceremonies: the clergy, the great, and the people. Though intended to reflect on earth the sumptuousness of heaven, this festival, as organized by Suger, centered on a monarch, like God in his glory perched atop a pyramid of various forms of devotion and reverence. Because he served the king of France, Suger agreed more nearly than anyone else with what Adalbero and Gerard had once maintained. Like those two prelates intent on fortifying Capetian power, he reverted to the Carolingian model, to Charles the Bald, to the image of a sovereign aided by underlings of two kinds—those who pray and those who fight. Like them he also borrowed from

Dionysian concepts. Times having changed, he chose to base the political order on the feudo-vassalic engagement, but this he made the backbone of a hierarchized structure, all levels of which were unified by exchange of affection and submission. At its summit stood the royal person—or rather the crown, the emblem of a sovereignty that survived each individual monarch. When at Saint-Denis the crown was placed at the center of architecture designed to give visual representation of Dionysian theology, that golden object indicated the focal point from which power, peace, and justice radiated, thereby projecting the monarchy's image from echelon to echelon down to the lowest depths of the kingdom's populace.

Suger, though, was a collector: to restore the unity of the realm he was bent on transporting to the banks of the Seine samples of the south's every aesthetic achievement, there to mingle them with what remnants of the greatest Carolingian art the north was yielding to his researches. And to polish off his work he also took elements from Cluniac tradition—southern and Gregorian—such as found imposing expression in the biographies of Saint Hugh. The *potestas,* delegated to the king (through anointment, but also through the crown, placed on his head by the monks of Saint-Denis charged with its safekeeping, and not charged with the safekeeping of the Holy Ampulla, the mysterious receptacle, as it were, of power), was to be used primarily to defend "liberty" against "tyrants," i.e., as Hincmar would have put it, to defend the "poor" against the "powerful." Suger reiterated this idea in his *Life of Louis VI,* written between 1138 and 1144, in which he depicted that sovereign—already anointed but in view of the fact that his father was still alive the embodiment of the latter's "youth," strength, and impetuosity—in an exemplary role as "illustrious and ardent defender of the churches of his father's kingdom, caring for those who pray, those who toil, and the poor."[24] Defender of churches and the poor: the formula is banal. And yet this phrase was the first in France of which any trace remains wherein we find the two terms *orator* and *laborator* linked together. I would also point out that here *laborator* was distinct from *pauper.* Indeed, Suger was well aware—the fact was strikingly apparent in the byways of the bourg of Saint-Denis—that economic vitality had by this time put quite a considerable distance between the worker's condition and penury.

Orator, laborator: the two functions are evoked in a panegyric to the Capetian monarch's earthly activities. Suger has openly moved away from Helgaud's position. Far from wishing to see his sovereign monasticism's prisoner, relegated to the domain of angels, he rather brings him down to earth, to men eagerly awaiting the support of his forces. He is enjoined to fight on their behalf. No longer is the king half-monk or half-bishop. He is the *bellator.* The military function is essentially royal. "By right and the vocation of their function, it is given to the most powerful right hand of kings to put down the impudence of tyrants who tear all the earth asunder in warfare or take pleasure in pillaging and ravaging the poor and in destroying churches."[25] When war was not spoiled by money (Suger contrasts the virtue of Louis, victorious by virtue of his unaided courage and his full employment of his office with the evident depravity of King William Rufus of England, who dipped into his treasury to pay for mercenaries), when it was waged by the king, and to the end toward which Adalbero had tried in vain to impel Robert the Pious, then it was good. In Suger's estimation the struggle to restore order to the Christian people was as salutary as the crusade; no doubt he was not far from thinking it even more salutary. Louis and those who served under his banner were in Suger's eyes what the Templars were for Saint Bernard, Christ's avengers. When in 1127 the king of France led his host to Flanders to punish the murderers of the good Count Charles, "by diverse manners of vengeance and by the shedding of much blood, Flanders was cleansed and, as it were, rebaptized."[26]

Waged in this world rather than as some sort of dramatic prelude to the end of time (Suger's eschatology was as serene as that of Adalbero and Gerard), the sovereign's military efforts were to be carried on within the framework established by the institutions of the peace of God. For Suger—and here we see the southern influence in his thought mingling with the Carolingian legacy and driving a wedge between his view and that of Gerard and Adalbero—the ideal society was organized along the lines dreamed of in the peace councils of the early eleventh century: the prelates and the populace allied against depravity. But Suger proposed as their guide the king, barely tolerated by Garin of Beauvais, and, deeming knightly unrest the main obstacle to the establishment of the king's authority, he chose to exalt the military role of the populace, mobilized in communal regiments. Earlier, the abbot of Nogent, arguing in his memoirs the opposite view to Andrew of Fleury, had allowed the possibility of popular participation in the administration of justice, on condition that the king remain its guiding spirit. Suger went farther. The troops he showed accompanying Louis in his campaign against the lord of Le Puiset were, like those raised by Aymon of Bourges, a peasant militia officered by priests. No trace of the grotesque attaches to them in Suger's account, nor do they suffer defeat. Another monk, who shared Cluny's cast of mind, Orderic Vital, looked upon the same events from the vantage of Normandy—a country boasting structures different from the French (not different social structures: like Saint Bernard and Guibert of Nogent, Orderic was convinced that there were four orders: "monks, clerks, knights, peasants, men of all the orders," as he put it;[27] but rather different political structures: a country ruled by the duke alone, surrounded by his knights). Orderic found this peasant army more surprising, but he, too, refrains from condemning the "priests who on order of the bishops accompanied the king in siege and battle with banners and their parishoners."[28]

Here, then, we see armed priests and workers, but the want of discrimination between the orders that had horrified Andrew of Fleury in 1040 was now no longer scandalous. This was because of the *affectus cordis,* as Saint Bernard put it, because the cause was good. And above all because the king, God's lieutenant, made sure that no one would transgress the fundamental boundary line setting the nobles apart from their subordinates. The people of the communes actually constituted only one contingent in the royal army, and a lowly one at that. "Let the bishops, counts, and other powers of thy kingdom gather round thy person, and let the priests and all their parishoners go with thee wherever thou shalt order them [the argument here very graphically draws a horizontal line across the two vertically aligned parallel orders envisaged by Gelasian doctrine, the *clerus* and the *populus,* in keeping with a necessary inequality that set the leaders apart from those who follow and obey, the powerful apart from the paupers, the lords from the subjects] so that a common army may exact a common vengeance from the enemies of the people."[29] In the state of which Suger dreamed and upon which the Norman Orderic looked with a skeptical eye from afar, was not the perfect society envisioned as the commune? This would of course have been divided into orders, into functional categories, but as in crusading society its divisions would have been sublimated in unanimity. Ultimately, what was the image of perfection but a reflection of the crusade—albeit a crusade aimed not at a mirage but at reality, different from the locusts of the Bible in that here there would have been a king, firmly in charge.

To be an abbot was Suger's pride. The monastery was in decline, however, caught up in the workings of a power whose seat lay in town, close to the cathedrals. For the public good, for the commonwealth, Suger placed in the service of the monarchical state the monastic conception of the social order, the conception of the peace of God, consolidated by Cluny, and in doing so adapted it to the resurgent elements of the proclamations of Adalbero, Gerard, and Hincmar of Rheims, i.e., to concepts predating the feudal revolution. In the picture of society that he evolved at mid-century, knighthood occupied the central position. Like Saint Bernard, like the proponents of the peace of God, and like Adalbero, Suger consigned knighthood to a place among the accursed. Its unruly ways impeded the prince in his efforts to secure a lasting peace. Its vocation was disorder. But Suger, like Saint Bernard, was intent on rescuing it. He was a monk. Yet since his monastery was neither miniscule like Nogent nor swallowed up in solitude and silence like Clairvaux, he did not dream of making the knights monks. Instead, order would be imposed upon them by the state. What political form should this state take? Saint Bernard was inclined to favor a principality. Suger defended the royal office. By the middle of the twelfth century, at which our account has now arrived, every social ideology again had to be put together with an eye to secular power, which monasticism had hoped to arrogate to itself, if not destroy. This secular power was served by clerks, who were making a powerful comeback.

19

IN THE SCHOOL

Suger, abbot of Saint-Denis, died in 1151; Bernard, abbot of Clairvaux, in 1153; and Peter the Venerable, abbot of Cluny, in 1156. They were the last great abbots of medieval France. Deprived of these imposing figures, monasticism remained robust enough: in northern France, men by the thousands and women by the hundreds left home each year, altering the course of their lives, shutting themselves up in a cloister; the choir of Cluny still boasted of four hundred monks, and the Cistercian order was undergoing rapid expansion in the royal provinces. Yet the permanence of the institution must not be allowed to hide the fact that ever since the third decade of the eleventh century the monasteries in this region had been reduced to mere remnants of their ancient forms—like Nogent and the numerous other tranquil little cells that dotted the countryside—living on in a state of dormancy, or else had been caught up against their will in the changing world, forced to adapt, accordingly being torn in two directions, represented by forest and court. These furnished the settings for those adventure tales then being composed for the pleasure of the lay aristocracy, tales whose impressive harvest reveals the youthful vitality of another culture, that of chivalry—evincing knighthood's triumph, at a time when the rise of the bourgeoisie had hardly begun, when the grandest bourgeois achievements led nowhere but to an unfeigned longing to mingle with the knights, and when changes in the monastic institution were in reality designed to answer the challenge of chivalry. The forest of Merlin and Lancelot; the court of King Mark and King Arthur. The desert or politics? Some of the best monks dreamed of removing themselves still farther from the world, and of taking with them to a place remote from turmoil and corruption as many peasants, clerks, and, above all, knights as possible—Saint Bernard, for instance, inviting men to take part in a spiritual wedding, bidding them abandon themselves and be consumed in divine love's embrace, but far from all that was worldly, thus leaving to the secular Church the concrete forms of charity and the concern to improve the populace. Other monks dreamed instead of riding the crest of the wave that was carrying the state to new heights, even as the pace of monetary circulation increased and roads and cities bustled with activity; they dreamed of improving the administration of civil society—Suger, for instance, magnificently equipping Saint-Denis with its triple portal, exhuming the relics from the crypt, hedging them about with gold and gems to make them even more awesome: the abbot was the mystic firebrand who some hoped would rekindle the fires of royal power.

In the twelfth century the roots of every earthly power struck into the supernatural. Accordingly, the renascent state naturally sought to base itself on the solid structures of the Church. Not without difficulty. Everything then written about what we now call politics treated the relations between the Church and the lay princes, and every vision of society was based on a certain conception of those relations. Like their ancestors in the year 1000, heads of state expected the abbeys of which they were patrons to provide funeral services, liturgies. For the salvation of their subjects, a responsibility they felt was theirs, as well as for their own salvation, these rulers preferred to place themselves in the hands of the purest monks—take Louis VII, for example, who out of religious fervor refused his mortal remains to Saint-Denis, ordering instead that they be taken to the Cistercian abbey he had founded; or again, to take a much latter example, Saint Louis, who carried stones on the work sites of Royaumont and bullied his brothers to take part without undue complaint in the manual labor to which the monks submitted for their greater humiliation. But without violating their vow to remain fixed in one abode, it was difficult for monks to provide all the services, overt and flexible, now required by the sovereigns. Clerks were far more useful: they were not cut off from the world. In the twelfth century it was natural for the clergy to become the auxiliary of temporal power, on an equal footing with the knights. It lent its assistance in three ways.

In the first place, through moral exhortation, tirelessly urging respect for the virtues that contributed to the maintenance of the public order, reproving the sins which were generally supposed to be injurious thereto. Was there a better instrument for checking the insubordination of a vassal than excommunication or interdict, fulminated against the violators of the peace by docile prelates? Was there a more effective way to muzzle the populace than to rely on the curate's day-to-day authority in his parish, at a time when gradual progress of land clearing made parish boundaries stand out with new prominence? Gradually, during the course of the twelfth century, the parish in northern France became more and more the basic cell of the seigniorial organism, of the system of exploitation and repression neatly laid out over the expanse between court and forest, the zone of cultivation and light, of established and continuous order—a cell that constituted one mesh of a net thrown over all the villagers to keep them quiet. But the custodians of public power expected more from the bishops, canons, and curates than just sermons, anathemas, and instructions issued in the confessional. The clerks knew how to write, count, keep books. Everywhere available for service, they alone could effectively run the brand-new administrative machinery, and appropriately channel into the coffers of the state the surplus product generated not only by agriculture but also, in steadily increasing amounts, by vineyards, pastures, and forests. Lastly, no prince bent on having a theoretical justification of power elaborated on his behalf could dispense with their services. Stimulated by the economic growth, the renaissance of the state and that of the clergy were mutually beneficial. As much as the expansion of the cities, the strengthening of the authority of the greatest lords rescued the episcopate from oblivion and restored to the clergy its leading role in the cultural sphere. After the first quarter of the twelfth century, we find the great creative workshops in Autun, in Sens, and soon thereafter in Ile-de-France; in the cities. There cathedrals were rising. Throughout northern France the cathedral chapters became the most active centers of literary production. At the heart of this literary output we find reflective treatises concerned with the nature of society.

These works pursued two distinct lines of thought. According to one, the *orator* stood aloof from secular power. He defended the positions won during the Gregorian struggles, continuing to maintain the superiority of the spiritual over the temporal and to hold that the mission of the clerk was to help keep the prince from straying from the path of righteousness. Lay society was said to consist of the followers of the king, the duke or the count, and the orator's sermons were addressed both to the ruler and to the attendant multitude. Like his Carolingian predecessors, with their "mirrors," he analyzed the social organism in order to lay the groundwork for the establishment, or, rather, the restoration of a moral order. According to the second line of thought, on the other hand, the *orator* deliberately enlisted in the service of the state. He thought for the prince. His intention was less moral than political. What he divulged about society would show how to establish the public order on a more solid basis. These two postures, or points of view, need to be considered one at a time.

Ever since the final decades of the ninth century, the clergy had been receiving suggestions that in order to attain perfection and achieve superiority over the monastic condition, it should adopt the "apostolic way of life," wherein action and contemplation would be coupled, and the "practical" path identified with the "theoretical." (Dudo of Saint-Quentin had not yet advanced to this stage, for he still had Martin of Jumièges distinguish these two paths, in order to establish a parallel between them.) The advice given the monks was not to make themselves into angels or to emulate the desert fathers. The example held out to them was rather that of the apostles, men as pure as monks, but who bent their backs to whatever work there was to be done, men who were committed to discharging the lowliest of tasks. The rigors, renunciations, and outpourings of the spiritual life served only to make them more ready to carry out a wordly mission: to guide laymen toward the good, to wrest them from the grip of evil. This they were no longer to do by turning their charges from the world, luring them into the crypts where they would prostrate themselves before the reliquaries, amidst flickering lights and liturgical ceremony, awaiting a miracle. Instead, they were to carry the sacred to laymen everywhere, even on the battlefield and in suburban hovels. Of course, the sacraments were still deemed the proper means for accomplishing this dissemination of sacredness, and the mission peculiar to the clergy was still held to be that of calling men to life through baptism, feeding them on the eucharist, correcting them through penitence, and regulating the perpetuation of the race through marriage, which in the last third of the twelfth century took its place among the seven sacraments of the Church. The clergy was above all a body of "professionals," "ministers" of God, paid, just as the agents of the temporal power were, out of taxes, oblations, and a portion of the tithe. In the twelfth century, however, in a region as highly developed as northern France, this highly formal and strictly detailed manner of parceling out the sacred was tending to decline in importance. Its value was being challenged by heresy—once again proliferating, while the weakening of monasticism became more apparent. Most important of all, ritualism—that residue of magic in ecclesiastical ceremony—was undermined by the advance of culture, which gradually penetrated the laity, infiltrating strata ever lower on the social scale; this had the effect of refining religious sensibility and of arousing a desire for religious practice intended to serve not merely the needs of the body but also those of the heart and mind. The slow ebb of the liturgies is a constant feature of the era we are examining. Accordingly, preference was shown for the other means of rendering God present unto mankind: through the word.

Indeed, the sacrament was only one sign among others, one of the manifestations of the Word. Logos was what counted. Why not divulge it directly and fully through language, in oratory, whether public—in the form of sermons—or private—in the counsel of the confessional? To raise this question was to suggest that the art of speaking—rhetoric—and the art of proof—dialectics—be restored, after a century-long eclipse, to a prominent place in the educational curriculum followed by cultivated men. At the same time it was to fall in step with the general march of Christianity toward greater internalization and personalization. Bernard of Clairvaux and Abelard had both insisted that the important thing was the intention, not

235

the act, the heart and not the outer shell, the pith and not the rind. In the forefront of those clamoring for a new religiosity, the heretics were not alone in believing that sin could not be cleansed away by means of an act—charitable works—still less by an act performed by others—the prayer of monks; they held instead that the way to salvation was to put God's word into practice. At that time laymen were moving into positions of responsibility and acquiring the capacity to pursue spirituality on their own. Accordingly, there was a newly-felt need to prove that anyone who wanted to remain orthodox needed the guidance of men specially instructed in the meaning or meanings of Scripture and uniquely skilled in imparting the sense of the biblical text to others. The clerks thereupon moved in to relieve the monks in the front lines of the war against evil—still raging, as it would continue to do until the end of time.

For the battlefield had changed location: no longer did the combat take place in the cosmos (although the naive idea—the one that inspired the crusades—was still current, and would long remain so, that to expand the kingdom of God the infidels must be slain and the Jews expelled). Now the *opus Dei,* the labor for God, had a new form; the battle raged within that microcosm, the individual soul: within, there was territory to be reclaimed, cleared of underbrush, rid of demons, sanitized, drained, made free of pestilence—mirroring the tangible labors being carried out on the fringes of the Cistercian clearings by the lay brothers, who were bringing order to the land and restoring it to rectitude. For the work to be performed properly, however, a master plan was needed. The drawing up of such a plan was the task of those who had achieved a thorough knowledge of the truth thanks to rhetorical and dialectical instruction together with (a reversion here to Carolingian conceptions, i.e., to Adalbero and Gerard) a mysterious gift, wisdom, conferred upon bishops by anointment and diffused by the rites of ordination from echelon to echelon within that hierarchical *ordo,* the Church. By the twelfth century, moreover, men had taken to imagining that the faculty of imparting righteousness through the word had even penetrated the rural depths and made its way into the parish, that basic social cell. One day, they hoped, *sapientia* might even come to that mediocrity, to that petty, meddlesome authoritarian, the village curate, butt of the mockery of the *fabliaux.* In any case, the conviction took root that order, moral order—from which social order was inseparable—depended on the ability to speak in a particular manner and that it was consequently the responsibility of those whose function was specifically to express themselves in speech.

This was soon acknowledged to be the rightful function of the clergy. At the turn of the twelfth century, this question had not yet been settled: in 1096 the council of Nîmes deemed priest-monks more fit to preach than clerks, the latter being corrupted by the world in which they were too deeply involved; Honorius Augustodunensis, whose oratory continued unabated, was probably a monk. But the question of "distinctions" was taken up by Anselm of Laon, who, as we have seen, maintained that to step outside one's order was a mortal sin, and on this particular point he was categorical: "The clerks are chosen to preach and to teach those who are subject to them [in passing, the question of a necessary subjection of the laity is touched on lightly], the monks to pray."[1] Saint Bernard concurred, having condemned a certain Rhenish hermit who had been known to harangue large crowds. Thus in the course of the twelfth century, a new kind of relationship was established between the regular and the secular clergy. In the meditative silence of the cloisters—even those of the most isolated order, the Cistercians—sermons were composed; copyists would then disseminate the text among the spokesmen, the priests. Even the humblest priests were thus supplied, and the Cistercians were thereby induced to employ the vulgar tongue, not because they were addressing the laity directly but rather because they labored on behalf of clerks whom fine Latin would have baffled.[2] At the same time, the bishops—the good bishops turned out by the reform—were well aware that it was primarily up to them to train preachers. To that end they endeavored to equip each see with a school. Since the goal was effective preaching, the bishops encouraged their scholars to analyze the audiences for which the sermons were intended, the multitudes that the orators hoped to move with their words, i.e., profane society.

This was taking place at a time when the clerks brought together in the cathedrals were agreeing to respect a rule, as monks did, and withdrawing, in order to facilitate their prayer (now their function as well as the monks'), to within an inner sanctum in the nave of the cathedral or collegiate church, walling off the choir and accessible through a sort of interior porch, the rood-screen (does this new arrangement not prove that laymen were entering the church more regularly?).[3] Meanwhile, those phalanxes of scholars, the *scolae,* were applying themselves to study, assiduously. This they did under the tutelage—for the *scola,* in the proper sense of the term, was a group that fulfilled a function in a disciplined way—of the most knowledgeable of their members; on occasion this might be the bishop himself; more often the prelate delegated this responsibliity to other men, to teachers referred to as "masters." *Magistri:* this word—still suspect in the eyes of Adalbero and Gerard, who had applied it to the heresiarchs, as well as to the usurper and false prophet Odilo of Cluny—toward mid-century came to be used as a title that bestowed upon its bearer a rank, a place—a new place—in the clerical hierarchy, an honor, and a responsibility. It was a title conferred by the authorities of the Church, which selected teachers, issued credentials, and granted the license to educate those students who would in turn instruct the laity. During the first half of the twelfth century, the abundance of writing by these masters grew steadily, at first supplementing the writing of the monks and soon outstripping it.

The best schools were located in northern France, in that region wherein the teaching of Rheims had sown its seed during the ninth century, and wherein a hundred years later a new growth had germinated, making possible the work of Adalbero and Gerard. In these same locations, at Orléans, Le Mans, Chartres, in the shadow of the same cathedrals, a renaissance took place—and particularly at Laon. Toward these fountains of higher learning pupils hastened from every corner of the world, as they had been wont to do in the time of Hincmar or John Scotus or in the year 1000; the bulk of them came from Lombardy or the British isles, in ever increasing numbers as travel grew less and less arduous. Work was resumed on the same fund of resources (the books used by Adalbero) precisely where it had left off two generations earlier, at which time it had been interrupted by the simultaneous collapse of the episcopacy and the monarchy. Now further advances were made, moving beyond the first two disciplines of the *trivium,* grammar and rhetoric, toward research into the laws of nature, particularly at Chartres, and toward elucidation of the text of the Bible, particularly at Laon.

The Masters of Laon

Thus it happened that at Laon in the first decade of the twelfth century, Anselm and his brother Raoul reread what the Carolingians had had to say about the Bible: both the glosses (or word by word explications) and the commentaries (or sustained discursive explications). Referring to themselves as *ordinatores glosae,* they felt the need to bring some order to this legacy. Since the intuitive approach, using analogy, symbolism, or a kaleidoscopic shifting from one meaning to another in the imagination (which had been Cluny's method and would again be that of Suger and Saint Bernard), no longer satisfied their desire to understand through deductive reasoning, they attempted to isolate the various meanings of each word of Scripture in a rigorous way *(distinctio).* But they also felt obliged to revise and extend the commentaries. There were three reasons for this. First, the meaning of the divine word had now to be made clear to men preparing for careers as preachers. Second, the goal of dispelling the obscurities in the Old and the New Testament was henceforth to elaborate a moral teaching, useful for supervising the way men behaved in the world. Finally, the glosses and commentaries inevitably led to a theory of the social order, to an ideology of society. This incursion into the social domain was as yet quite limited, having advanced no more than a hair's breadth in Anselm's day, in the early days of scholasticism—at least so far as we are able, for the time being, to make out amidst the dense underbrush of manuscripts—most of them unpublished, difficult to read, poorly catalogued—into which no one else has yet looked for answers to questions of the type raised here.

In view of the paucity of research in this area, what I am about to say about the traces of the trifunctional figure in these writings must be regarded as a mere preface to work yet to be undertaken. For even this much I am wholly in the debt of Guy Lobrichon, whose work has led him to look closely at just one of the sacred texts commented on by the masters of Laon, an important one to be sure: the Book of Revelation, or the Apocalypse. A fiery book, on which attention was still focussed in the time of Anselm and his disciples, since the dream of the crusade had not yet met with disappointment, the immense theater had not yet been dismantled, and Christendom still awaited, anxiously, the harbingers of the Second Coming. One fact begs our attention: among these glosses and commentaries on the Apocalypse, we find a tripartite figure. Is it not the very same one that was used earlier by Adalbero, and that the cathedral clergy at Laon in the early twelfth century retained in its memory?

The figure in question was pressed into service to explain verses 9–10 of chapter 5 of Revelation, the "new song" sung before the Lamb by the four beasts and the four-and-twenty elders (the very same scene was chosen during this same period to adorn, in sculpted form, the tympanum of Moissac, as the symbolic representation of the two Christian mysteries of the Incarnation and the Redemption): "For thou wast slain, and hast redeemed us to God by the blood out of every kindred, and tongue, and people, and nation; and hast made us unto our God kings and priests and we shall reign on the earth." Heaven stands open, ready to receive humanity. Mankind, cleansed for the ascent, delivered from sin, hence from inequality, had returned by way of the priesthood to the original unity of the children of God. "Kindred," "tongue," "people," "nation": these terms, reflecting the diversity of the human species which would be abolished in the final moment, were in John's text massed in support of the statement that all men, of every kind, were called, were redeemed by the sacrifice of the Lamb. In a discursive commentary said to be the work of Anselm of Laon himself and ostensibly dating from 1100–1110, we find an explanation of each of the above words from the Vulgate. In particular of the word *tribubus* (which in the *Bible de Jérusalem* was translated as "race" [and which appears here as "kindred," from the English of the King James version—Trans.]): "*Ex omnibus tribus*,"—"let us understand," says Anselm, "the men of prayer [*oratores*], the knights [*milites*], and the peasants [*agricolae*]."[4] The same explanation is repeated each time the word *tribus* in John's text evokes the real, tangible divisions of human society (Rev. 5:9, 13:7, 14:6), whereas on other occasions, where the term occurs in a different sense, the explanation changes as well, invoking instead the venerable tripartition of virtues: Noah, Daniel, and Job; the virginal, the continent, and the married. In a gloss elaborated again by Anselm himself or perhaps by a member of his group, the figure recurs in virtually the same form: "knights [*milites*], laborers [*laborantes*], celebrants of the rite of sacrifice [*sacrificantes*]."[5] And to take one final example, the same formula appears again a little later, in about 1120, in a more pedantic form that is even more reminiscent of Adalbero (*oratores, defensores, agricolae*), as an explanation of the same biblical passage, this time in the commentary contained in a manuscript of the *Liber Floridus* by Lambert of Saint-Omer.[6] The fact is striking. For a time we had ceased to hear the clerks. The moment they become audible once more, we find them repeating words uttered a century earlier by Adalbero. Hence these earlier utterances had not disappeared into oblivion. Trifunctionality is mentioned in commentaries on the *divina pagina* originating in only one place—the very city in which Adalbero had worked. Moreover, the formula first uttered in Laon is echoed only in northern France; as Guy Lobrichon has established, it was not adopted by commentators on the Apocalypse then working in Germany or Italy. There is nothing to confirm—but then again, there is nothing to refute, either—the hypothesis that Anselm and his followers (did they share Guibert of Nogent's animosity toward the "old traitor"?) may have looked into the unfinished manuscript of the *Carmen*. Our first impression—and a profound one it is—is that of a continuity of the trifunctional image in the memory of the northern French clergy. Must we reject the idea that Adalbero was shouting in the desert? Have we not been misled by the circumstance that only monastic writings have come down to us from the period prior to the early twelfth century?

Let us take a closer look at the matter. Can we establish whether or not the formula in the commentaries and glosses stems directly from either Adalbero or Gerard? As a preliminary, consider the following question: Are the words really the same? As for *orator,* there is no doubt; *agricola,* too, and even *laborans* can pass muster. But there is one important difference— extremely important in view of the meaning attached to these terms by the prelates of the year 1000—in the substitution of *miles* for *bellator* (or *pugnator*). Thus the vocabulary in use in the school of Laon in the early twelfth century does not precisely coincide with that used in the earliest formulations of trifunctionality. The language is rather that of the peace oaths and charters. Like their comrade, Guibert of Nogent, as well as the many scribes then employed in drawing up public and private documents, the masters did not look upon the military function as the province solely of the prince, wielding the royal sword. Their glance embraced knighthood as well. They therefore adapted the Adalberonian schema to the palpable realities of social organization. Unless, perhaps, they drew from another source—possibly English? The ties that at that time bound Laon to the cities and monasteries on the other side of the Channel are well known: had not Anselm himself visited them? The methods used by Anselm and his pupils in their work should be borne in mind. They were taking up the baton handed them by

240

their predecessors. They started with older commentaries on the Apocalypse and improved on them. These were Carolingian commentaries, all of which defined *tribus* in the same naive manner, deriving from a chance similarity, an assonance that was virtually a play on words: *"tribubus id est tribus ordinibus"*—"the tribes are the three orders." The masters of Laon might have read this phrase, but by their day its meaning was no longer clear. Three orders? What might that have meant? Conscientiously, they added details, indicating that in this case there could not possibly have been a reference, as there was in other passages, to the three orders of Saint Jerome that would immediately have sprung to mind. At issue here was rather the living, tangible society, which existed in the realm of the temporal, of flesh, of history; the "three orders" *(tribus)* referred to the social, and not the moral, sphere. Hence they reverted to the trifunctional figure: there were those who pray, those who fight, those who work. Is there any way to avoid drawing the conclusion that they found this particular formulation of the tirpartite image in one of the Carolingian commentaries kept in their library, one of the commentaries they were bent on improving? This was in fact the case. As we saw earlier,[7] the image may be found in the writing of Haymo of Auxerre, in whose work the clerks of Laon might have read a gloss on the word *tribus* that mentions the three words *sacerdotes, milites, agricultores*. That is enough to convince me that Anselm and his disciples borrowed their explanation in terms of trifunctionality not from Adalbero but rather from Haymo, merely shifting it from Revelation 3:7 to 5:9—and what is more, this particular text was very likely one that Adalbero himself had read: it numbered among the books in his collection. We may look upon the commentary written in the Laon *scriptorium,* not far from that collection, shortly after the composition in nearby Lotharingia of the life of Saint Dagobert, as the last echo of a notion first conceived by a monk in the favorable climate of the Carolingian renaissance—a monk who appears to have been the original source, at least within the boundaries of the particular cultural region we have been examining, of the classificatory schema whose fate we have been attempting to trace.

Two further points. In the writings of the Laon school, only passing mention is made of trifunctionality. No one felt the need to use trifunctionality in arguing for reform aimed at restoring earthly society to the perfection envisaged in the divine plan through a new balance of power and a different assignment of roles. On the contrary, the trifunctional theme was used to account for the imminent withering away of earthly society. Time was coming to an end; all disparities among men were vanishing; the old social structures were now devoid of sense. John's text brought them to mind just at the moment they ceased to be of consequence. So far as we know, this was the only time that the masters of Laon alluded to trifunctionality. And a fleeting allusion it was. How can we fail to note the striking fact that men resorted to the trifunctional theme as they were being blinded by the splendor of their eschatological fantasies, and as the verses of the Apocalypse sent their imaginations wandering far from earth and the provinces of the rational, into the realm familiar to John Scotus Erigena, and so to Dionysius? Then, too, it is worth noting that as the twelfth century wore on, commentators in this particular region gradually abandoned this way of explaining the word *tribus* as it is used in the verses in question. To my mind, this confirms the hypothesis that the trifunctional image underwent no revival in the Laon school in the early twelfth century, and that we are merely hearing a muffled echo of the past, about to die out entirely. After the middle of the century, they dropped it altogether in favor of either Jerome's three orders of merit and the symbolism of Noah, Daniel, and Job, or else the three "peoples"—Greek, Hebrew, and Gentile.[8] Their choices are most enlightening. If other ternaries came to the fore, in particular the ternarity of cultural influences—the synagogue, the Greek church, and the Latin church—and above all the ternarity that formed the backbone of the moral value system, can we escape the conclusion that the school's masters thought thereby to improve the instruction they were offering to fledgling moralists in fulfillment of the mission with which they were charged? Improvements in the techniques of instruction led to the rejection of definitions handed down from venerable sources but no longer suited to the realities of the day. Such definitions might confuse the students, men who would someday need to speak clearly and so would have to be able to identify the social status of their auditors with precision. Indeed, the research being carried on in the cathedral schools was directed toward a science rather than an ideology of society. Accordingly, the inadequacy, uselessness, and even worse, deceptiveness of the trifunctional schema with its crude distinction between warriors and peasants loomed ever larger in the eyes of the masters. This was an advance of major importance. Let us next try to take a closer look at the course it followed.

HUGH OF SAINT-VICTOR

To that end, let us now leave Laon and head for Paris, following the current that slowly carried the boldest truth-seekers toward the banks of the Seine. Hugh of Saint-Victor is an excellent observer. He was some thirty or forty years younger than Anselm. Having come from Germany to attend the lectures of William of Champeaux, whose teaching was directly inspired by the Laon school, he stayed on in Paris, teaching there himself from 1125. The group, or *schola,* that he led was affiliated not with the cloister of Notre-Dame but rather with its purified offshoot, so to speak, the collegiate church of Saint-Victor. There, at some distance from the city to insure the necessary isolation, but at its gates so as not to be cut off from the most vital of secular doings, William of Champeaux had established his own version of an ordered, exemplary environment wherein men tried to emulate the apostles in abstinence, while at the same time delving into the sources of knowledge. In Hugh's time Saint-Victor offered a natural counterpart to Saint-Denis, which with each passing day grew more ornate; at Saint-Denis one found liturgical pomp, while at Saint-Victor asceticism was coupled with intellectual striving. It was the major center of pastoral, hence of educational, research: the school of the masters. How was one to be a good *magister?* What texts could most usefully be read and explained to students who would one day repeat what they had learned? These questions were on the minds of all the intellectuals who were rising steadily in the Church hierarchy, who were bit by bit taking over from the bishops the most luminous aspects of their role, and who were led by pride to identify themselves with Christ. Take Abelard, for instance, who scrutinized the mystery of the Trinity; he reverts to Augustine's notion of correspondences among the three persons and the three categories—*mens, notitia, amor*—which he alters by substituting another triad for the latter: "power," "wisdom," and "charity."[9] Here "wisdom" is the attribute of the second person. The image of Jesus in the West has its history. In that history the present period was one of preparation for the replacement of the image of the Lamb of the Apocalypse and the Redeemer of the Synoptics by the new image of the Teacher, at least in intellectual circles. Could one ask for a more striking sign of the rise of the masters, who, during the first half of the twelfth century, made up for the decline of monasticism by bringing down the temples of the old high culture?[10]

One portion of the work of Hugh of Saint-Victor was designed to answer these questions. In his *Didascalicon* we find a superb plan for the reform of the educational system. It envisaged a considerable broadening of the basic curriculum, handed down from Roman antiquity through the Carolingian pedagogues; henceforth the *trivium* was to serve as a mere propadeutic, giving access to an immense edifice that surveyed the twin panoramas facing the contemporary clerk: contemplation and action. Hugh's first concern was to distinguish the disciplines of learning, which he classified logically, which he "ordered." It is noteworthy, I think, that in his proposed classification knowledge expands in scope by proceeding through a sequence of ternarities. As in all teaching, the progression was from the elementary, the simple, the schematic, to the complex. This progress paralleled the gradual broadening of the clergy's view of the social world during this same period: the initial, unsophisticated triangular figure gave way to a more complex vision, necessary to encompass the variety of phenomena that were encountered once the observer left the cloister to venture onto the city's byways and gaze upon the diversity of a flourishing civilization, a turbulent and growing world. The educational edifice was actually a three-storeyed structure, whose three levels represented three stages in an ascension, a sublimation of the material in the spiritual. The learner's itinerary began with the "mechanical arts"—physical activities which included agriculture—on the lowest level; the student then moved on to the second storey, which sheltered the venerable *trivium*—there the techniques of speaking and reasoning were taught in three phases; finally, he moved to the highest level, the stage of true higher learning, which was itself split into two segments, one placed above the other. Each of them was tripartite: three applied disciplines trained the student for the "practical" life, namely, ethics, politics, and economics (the latter a useful preparation for service to the *res publica*, hence to the prince); these led on to the three "theoretical" disciplines whereby one could grasp the laws of the world and the reason of God, namely, physics, mathematics, and lastly, culminating the ascent, at the summit of all education, theology.

In parallel with the proposed course of study, Hugh's coherent vision extended to a symmetrical discussion of the "profession," or office, of master; at the same time, his efforts at classification reached outside the framework of the school, to lay down the organizational outlines for an analogous process of initiation involving man and his position in the universe. Hugh's teachings to aspiring preachers are summarized in *On the Sacraments of the Christian Faith (De sacramentis christianae fidei)*. In reading this work, we are struck by the force of his eschatological concerns: the whole argument is constructed with ultimate ends in view, on the basis of that life which begins with death. This would serve as a reminder—were any necessary—of the spiritual dimension of the school, in which periods of reading, meditation, and prayer alternated and ultimately merged. The men I am discussing now are my brothers, fellow professors. I must be careful lest I forget that their actions were always the actions of priests, their words always the words of liturgy, and that the *schola* was first and foremost a gathering of pious men: the goal of education was inevitably eternity. Therein lies the explanation for the truly *essential* relationship between the didactic works of Hugh of Saint-Victor and the mystical works of Dionysius the Areopagite that Hugh, in his Parisian haunts, never stopped reading and glossing. Indeed, the ternary hierarchies of Dionysius influence the thought of Hugh of Saint-Victor as strongly as they did that of Adalbero and Gerard, particularly when Hugh turns to investigating the social order in order to be in a position to act as mentor to men who one day would have to go out into the city among the people to make speeches, hear confessions, and bring salvation through the word.

As a first example, consider the following definition of economics, the highest of the three practical disciplines, which is taken from the *Didascalicon:* "Here we stand at the gateway to man's fatherland. Here the estates and dignities are settled, here the functions and orders are distinguished. . . ." This might be mistaken for Loyseau—in any case, what Hugh calls economics was nothing less than the effort of intellectuals to replace the fantasies and oversimplifications that erstwhile scholars had deemed acceptable images of society, and that still influenced current opinion, with rational, scientific knowledge based on a new classification, more lucid, more precise, more fine-grained and thorough than the old. But above all "men hastening to return to their fatherland are here taught how, in keeping with the order of their merits, they may enter into the angelic hierarchy." The first step, then, was observation—and therein lay the novelty for the twelfth century. Immediately, however, this first step was hampered, caught in the trap of its preconceptions, in its respect for the *auctores,* for the venerable books—the same books used by Adalbero and Gerard still held sway over men's minds. And so we meet with Augustine's notion of men hastening in procession, and Dionysius's recursion to the celestial model, along with the idea that the absorption of human society by its true "fatherland," beyond the veil of appearances, beyond change and corruption, might be facilitated insofar as society conformed beforehand to a hierarchical order based on the model of the more perfect society of angels. When it came to laying down a pragmatic moral code, the master looked first to heaven, and considered reality only afterwards. Fantasy reigned no less imperiously than before, and since Hugh's imagination remained under the influence of Dionysius, the triangular, trinitarian schema is a prevalent feature of his work.

For a second example, we may turn to the treatise *On the Earnest of the Soul.*[11] In this book the Church—the society of Christians—is compared to the *triclinium,* or nuptial banquet hall, with its three beds, each of which, following Roman tradition, Hugh of Saint-Victor envisaged as containing three guests. According to him, the metaphor was chosen because the Church consists of three "orders"—these being in this instance the three orders of merit, the orders of Jerome and Augustine. In the *Moral Ark of Noah*[12] (a title that reveals scholasticism's aim: to move from Biblical commentary to the elaboration of an ethical code), Hugh mentions three houses because, as he tells us, there are three "orders of believers"—and once again these symbolized three degrees of emancipation from carnality: "the first make legitimate use of the world [these were "married people"], the second flee the world in the hope of forgetting it [these were the "continent"], the third have forgotten the world, and it is they who stand nearest to God." Three degrees of detachment. Note the close correspondence between Hugh's ideas and those of Bernard of Clairvaux (as I have been forced to treat clerks and monks separately in order to give a clear analysis of the historical situation, I should like to stress a point that might otherwise be overlooked, namely, that clergy and monastery throughout the twelfth century both belonged to the same tightly knit community of thought).

Since, however, Hugh's efforts went to equipping his disciples to reform carnal society, the concern to consign the world to oblivion did not prevent his turning his gaze upon the earth. This is what he does in that encyclopedic work, the *De sacramentis*. There he managed to extricate himself from the tyranny of the triad, but only to fall under the sway of another ideological formalism, the Gelasian concept of binarity. In discussing reality and the tangible world, Hugh maintained along with Cardinal Humbert and all the Gregorians that there were two *potestates*—a "terrestrial," "secular" power, and a "spiritual" power: "there are, indeed, two lives, one on earth, the other in heaven, one corporeal, the other spiritual." [13] "In each of these powers there are several ranks [*gradus*] and orders [*ordines*] of power." How many? Seven. Seven in each; seven among the clerks, because the sacraments of the order were seven in number; seven among the laity for the sake of symmetry. Of what was going on outside the collegiate church, Hugh saw nothing; rather than observe, he reasoned, convinced that because the social organism originated in the mind of God, it was rationally constructed, based on a system of checks and balances. Again we note the strength of preconceived notion, of an inveterate taste for symbolic correspondences. As in the *Didascalicon*, however, we find here a simple structure made diverse, developed in harmonic sequences. But here ternarity has been wholly expunged from the exemplary social image.

The attendant fear, however, was that this proliferation of roles might be taken as an indication of dissolution, disintegration. Accordingly, Hugh of Saint-Victor reverted to the metaphor of the body as a way of restoring overall unity. "The holy Church is the body of Christ, called to life by one spirit, unified by one faith, and sanctified." Christ, metaphorically the head wherein the two powers were joined, coordinated the various ranks. "The two sides are both ranged under a single head; they are deduced, as it were, from a single principle [logic once again] and referred to the one." The use of this metaphor at Saint-Victor is clearly related to speculation there on the incarnation, speculation stimulated by the spectacle of a world wherein thanks to the combined efforts of all mankind nature was slowly being subdued. As in Christ, in man also two natures were entwined. Similarly, in human society there were two orders, closely intertwined. The two orders of laymen and clerks are knit together in a homogeneous whole "like the two sides of a single body." [14] For order to be maintained, though, one would have to obey the other. It was common knowledge which side was superior: the right-handed side. Laymen were accordingly placed on the left, the sinister, subordinate side. This arrangement of matters was depicted (if not precisely when Hugh was writing then shortly thereafter) on the sculpted tympanum of Notre-Dame (subsequently replaced by the new facade, the present one): the Virgin was flanked thereupon by two personages representing the two "powers"; King Louis VII was placed to the left of this female figure (who, as God's flesh, the instrument of his incarnation, symbolized the superior power, wisdom and strength); the king knelt, attended by symbols of the world drawn from the Gospel account of Christ's infancy—the shepherds, the three magi, Herod; on the right, standing tall and erect in a clear posture of superiority, was the bishop.[15]

To complete his picture, though, Hugh abandoned duality and returned to ternarity. On earth, to be sure, two lives existed, "one in which the body lives by the soul [and it was the function of the clergy, of intellectuals of the utmost purity like the canons of Saint-Victor, to sustain that existence by distributing the eucharist and delivering sermons], the other in which the soul lives by God."[16] This implied first of all the existence of a third, atemporal sphere, and, second, that the clergy, which occupied the intermediate zone and communicated with the angels via the hierarchical network described by Dionysius the Areopagite, played the role of intercessor between heaven and earth. We have thus come full circle back to the old ideas of Adalbero and Gerard. What is more, a major element of their ideological system has once again been pressed into service here, namely, the fundamental idea of mutual service derived from the notion of incarnation and perfectly illustrated by the bodily metaphor: "just as in the human body each part has its function, specific and distinct—and yet none acts alone and for itself only," so in the body of the Church "it is one for all, and all for one." Quite obviously, exchange, charity, and the foregoing idea, taken together, bring us back to the concept of functionality.

The thought of Hugh of Saint-Victor has been examined closely. Reflected therein I see something in the nature of mental disarray. The decisive turn has been taken both in the school and in the sculptor's studio: now the imperative has become to extricate oneself from the grip of the imaginary, to uncover what good might lurk in the flesh. The taste for the bodily metaphor is also indicative of a very slow, imperceptible, unconscious rehabilitation of the flesh. This image was not invented by Hugh. He had read of it in treatises once again drawn from the Carolingian legacy. In 841 it had been employed by Walafrid Strabo.[17] For three centuries it had been consigned to oblivion out of a kind of distaste, of shame at the sight of the body. Hugh dared make use of the metaphor before his students, at a time when the *scholae*, disciplined research teams, were showing a greater interest in nature, and, what is more (for this seems to me to have had a far more determining influence on the evolution of high culture), were seeking to penetrate the mystery of the incarnation. Turning to new concerns, scholars were making prodigious efforts to classify men as well as plants and stars in a more precise and rigorous manner. What might come to pass if this application of lucidity and intelligence to society were to reveal the inadequacy of the traditional social taxonomies, those backed by the authority of the Church Fathers? Anxiety. Hugh of Saint-Victor lived among books. From these came a number of quite rudimentary symbolic systems, which took firm root in his memory. He was unable to work free of their influence. And yet he saw the superabundant complexity of reality, and knew that no one of those systems by itself could reduce life's sensuous profusion to order, whereupon he attempted to bring all of them into play at once, seeking to combine one with another. Accordingly, at certain places his teachings resemble Adalbero's. He was drawn to Adalbero's system by what he had found in Dionysius, namely, the hierarchies, and by Walafrid Strabo's assertion that order originated in reciprocity of service. The concept of function, or office, occupied a central position in his mind. But his knowledge of a society in which his students would one day have to play a leadership role had convinced him of one thing: it was impossible to reduce the number of these functions to three. Thus for him the trifunctional figure was useful only as a pedagogical device.

HONORIUS AUGUSTODUNENSIS

Mental disarray. After all the books had been scrutinized, memory explored, the various systems of classification put to the test, combined, rearranged, and all had proved futile, men were still faced with social relations grown clearly too complex to be easily grasped or understood. There is undoubtedly no better expression of the perplexity of the masters in the early decades of the twelfth century than that teeming and ill-assorted work that is collected under the name of one man, Honorius Augustodunensis.

According to the specialists, he was not from Autun—and yet, at the time this man was completing his work, during the episcopacy of Étienne of Bâgé, in 1135 or thereabouts, when sculptors of genius were transcribing to the stone of tympanums and capitals what seems indeed to have been the flower of the new humanism, Autun represented the most refined expression of a meditation on the brotherhood of man and Christ and on personal responsibility. Of Honorius virtually nothing is known.[18] Not even whether he died in 1125–27 or lived until 1158. Was he a hermit or a Benedictine monk? If the latter, he was a monk who traveled the world, roving farther afield even than Raoul Glaber, claiming for monks the right to speak, to teach, to come to grips with the world as the clerks were doing, a proponent of a sort of liberation of monasticism from the cloister, which would have joined monks and clerks together in pastoral activities. He may have been an Irishman, drawn to the continent like so many inhabitants of the isles by a thirst for knowledge, probably spending the latter portion of his life in Germany, where some think he entered the monastery of Saint James of Ratisbon. In any case, particular attention was paid to his teachings in Germany. It is probable, however, that Honorius for a time took a part in the schools of northern France, and that he was familiar with what was being taught at Laon and Chartres, i.e., at Paris, at the beginning of the century. Accordingly, this elusive personage does not fall entirely outside the purview of our study. More than that, he is of interest because his writings enjoyed a considerable and lasting success in northern France; more than eighty manuscripts of his *Elucidarium* are preserved there, for example.

His work is profuse, overabundant. Honorius was certainly not responsible for all the works that have been fathered on him. But there is no reason he could not have written the bulk of them, provided that one is inclined to accept the later date of death and stretch out the chronology of the manuscripts. At the end of his life, his efforts were directed exclusively to commenting on the Bible. In his younger days, however, in the time of his travels in France among the *magistri,* prior to the great summas of Hugh of Saint-Victor, his taste ran to composing sermons based on his lecture or reading notes. This he did in order to spread his teaching in a convenient form, within reach of the ordinary clerk, and tailored so as to be useful for the purposes of preaching. He succeeded: his books were everywhere read, copied, and passed from hand to hand, and were also widely used as manuals.

The names given them are revealing. *Elucidarium:* Honorius' purpose was to enlighten, to spread illumination; *Speculum ecclesiae:* like the Carolingian bishops, he held out a mirror which enabled men to know themselves better, to correct their behavior, and compose their features; but he hoped that his mirror would be held up not only before the prince but rather before the "Church," i.e., all of Christian society—that at the very least it would be held out to the multitudes gathered in the urban churches to hear the oratory of his readers, the clergy. In this we see how during the second "renaissance," that of the twelfth century, the mission of the *orator,* or rhetor (Honorius was thoroughly inbued with the *Rhetorica ad Herennium*), was enlarged. The format was still one of dialogue between master and disciple—the level of educational technique was still quite primitive, like Alcuin's: the *Elucidarium* is a series of brief questions and answers, like a basic catechism in miniature. Now, however, the disciple was no longer Charlemagne but rather the segment of the laity just emerging from rustic simplicity, the clergy being charged with the mission of guiding these laymen towards salvation by means of the word. From this period of his life, during which he busied himself with the work of vulgarization, standing between the learning of the school and the thought of the ordinary man, Honorius left as his legacy to us historians of ideology an irreplaceable record: through him we can gain access, we think, to what the average clerk, the journeyman of the pulpit, might have known of the discussions of society being carried on in scholarly circles in northern France during the lifetime of Anselm of Laon. Our impression that this was a period of hesitant searching, during which various classificatory systems were tried out one by one, is thereby reinforced.

In the *Elucidarium,* written before 1101, the proposed classification was of the most commonplace variety.[19] There were two intersecting dichotomies. One, horizontal, separated those who led from those who must obey; the other, vertical, divided clergy from laity. But matters were arranged in this way in order to answer the question on the mind of every leader, of all the *prelati,* or guides, particularly those "prelates" of third or fourth rank who preached in the *faubourgs,* namely, the question put by Duke William I of Normandy to abbot Martin: Who would be saved? Could a man find salvation in his order? What dangers and what duties were specific to each? To improve the instruction of the faithful, Honorius taught his listeners to distinguish categories, which were also ranks, among the *subditi*—i.e., among the flock shepherded by his pupils. These were not three in number, but rather four. The clergy led the way—they were treated separately; for them the important thing was to be pure, to stand aloof from the world; priests, other "ministers," and monks were all equal in this respect. Next came the *milites;* they, too, were subjugated—to the prince, as priests were to the bishops and the masters; the men of war had only the slimmest chance of being saved: the temptations to pillage and vainglory were too strong; God's wrath was upon them; this Honorius proved by citing several verses of Scripture; these were intended to be used as themes for appropriate sermons. Such was the technique of the pastoral mission, which a book of this kind was designed to aid: it consisted first in making a diagnosis of the malady, the infection, which took on forms peculiar to each social estate; and second in administering care, in purging the purulence, in forcing every man to examine himself lest he incur the promised punishments, of which reminders were issued. In any case, Honorius looked upon knighthood much as the proponents of the peace of God had done: it was damned; it was the devil's lair. As for the men of the third function, the *Elucidarium*—like Saint Bernard—distinguished between two kinds: some lived in the city, e.g., merchants, artisans, and entertainers; all of them were utterly and equally condemned, because they swindled and lied—the troubling new world in which those disquieting, unpredictable forces that threatened to disrupt the established order could be sensed festering frightened Honorius, as it had frightened Guibert of Nogent; the others, the *agricolae,* or peasants, were by contrast noble savages, the only human beings (apart from infants under three years of age still unable to speak) assured of reaching paradise: "for the most part, they will be saved, because they live in simplicity, and because they feed the people of God by their sweat." *Suo sudore*—*labor, dolor:* to work for others was a work of penitence, an instrument of personal redemption. Thus one of the key components of the ideological system of Adalbero and Gerard remained in place, justifying the seigniorial mode of production through exchange of mutual services, and inundating with hope of heavenly recompense the rancor and rebellious spirit present, it was sensed, to a fearsome degree in the laboring class. More than that, to depict the peasantry routinely escaping perdition was to provide all those clerks whose tastes inclined them to keep to the towns with an excellent alibi: what was the use of wearying oneself in villages and fields, of wallowing in filth? The front lines in the war against Satan lay not in the countryside, but rather in the castles and their marauding garrisons, and above all in the cities and towns. Thus the specialists in the *cura animarum* were led for a time to regard the trifunctional schema as obsolete and ineffectual: the "people" were to be found in two distinct zones in which the mission of preaching and granting absolution had to be carried out in very different ways.

In the *Speculum ecclesiae,* no doubt of more recent composition albeit prior to 1105, the same question is raised, but its object has now shifted.[20] Here the focus is on certain prayers said at mass, during the offertory, which provided the priest with an opportunity to indicate for whom the suffrages were intended and thereby to inveigh against the traps laid by the devil, and accordingly to moralize. For whom were special prayers to be offered up? The peasants were no longer of concern: they had no need of special help. The dead, on the other hand, were in this respect foremost, for their need was greater than anyone else's. Next came all among the living who suffered in tribulation: among them we find monks, pilgrims, seafarers, and captives. Finally, attention turned to those who led, charged with the mission of guiding the rest. For this group, the treatise merely adopted the Gelasian classification, erecting two parallel hierarchies in the manner of Walafrid Strabo: on one side, the pope, the bishops, the priests, all men "comprised in the sacred orders," the Church—the secular Church, exhorted to do its utmost to carry its light to the world; and on the other, the dukes, the counts, lords of every kind, ranged behind the king instituted by God as his "namesake," exhorted to treat the "subject people" mercifully. In all this there is nothing new, save that the monks are treated as a group apart, coupled with those who face the greatest danger and suffering.

Once again we find various criteria being used on a trial basis in an effort to arrive at a usable classification. In the main body of this work, this epitome of effective preaching technique wherein the clergy found what it was looking for, that effort is carried to even greater lengths. To carry the message home, to insure that the seed being sown would fall on fertile ground, the mirror—that tool of reformation—had to be tilted at the proper angle towards each of the many faces in the crowd of listeners. Accordingly, a refined social analysis was needed. It was also apparent that the four categories were no longer adequate. One by one, therefore, the *Speculum* focussed its attention on the following groups of laymen. First, the lords, who were enjoined to secure a righteous administration of justice. Second, the knights, who were to cease their pillage (we thus observe the continued prevalence of this image of the warrior class, terrorizing the populace with its cavalcades, or patrols, enforcing the collection of taxes—whereby this group came to be seen as the agent of seigniorial collections and confiscations, whereas justice, i.e., redistribution, was exercised by the "potentates" whom they served. Honorius accordingly saw the lay aristocracy as consisting of two strata, one set above the other in rank). Third, the rich, who were to give alms. Fourth, the poor, who were to be patient (disparities in economic condition were beginning to command attention). Fifth, the merchants, enjoined not to defraud their clients. Sixth, the peasants (notwithstanding): "they shall obey the priests, they shall not exceed the limits, they shall pay the tithe" (this counsel says a great deal about the fear inspired by the peasantry, that alien and dangerous group; in a negative sense, it sheds light on the theater of class conflict in the Church domains, in a rural world felt to be restive and wracked by anticlerical and antidecimal "heresy"). Seventh, the married—this was where women wormed their way in among society's representative figureheads—at the very end of the line.

Because its purpose was exclusively practical, such a classification is reminiscent of the systems used by the charter writers, and accordingly shows less affinity with the theoretical models constructed by ideologues like Gerard and Adalbero. The aim was to adhere closely to society's tangible contours, to take in reality—that which the senses could reveal about the world—by touching, listening, and looking; a product of the school, this desire to get a grip on reality soon impelled culture generally to move very gradually towards realism: Honorius eschewed speaking of collectivities, of an *ordo* that could not be observed or deduced from sensory experience but rather had to be postulated or revealed through mystical experience. This led him to take up a position with regard to the problem opposed to that taken by the Carolingian *speculatores:* what they wanted was to use the princes as a medium through which the image of an internal order, established in the king's palace and modeled on an invisible organization, mysteriously divined—that of celestial society—might be projected externally onto the entire body social; whereas Honorius, like a confessor engaging his penitents in dialogue one by one, began instead with the singular. Less attentive to structures than to cases, he applied general evangelical precepts to particular situations, one at a time. We do not know what teaching his *Speculum* reflected. At all events Honorius seems in this work to have been less dependent on the schools of *Francia*. If he was following a tradition, was it not rather that of the countries of the Empire? Is he not a member of the family consisting of Bonizo of Sutri, Ratherius of Verona, and Isidore of Seville?

But now that empirical methods had at last succeeded in laying bare the obvious fact that in society nothing was fixed and everything changeable, that it was idle to look for neat pigeonholes and categories, this popularizing writer became concerned—like Hugh of Saint-Victor before him—with the necessity of restoring some semblance of unity, with the need to organize. With the analysis complete—or, rather, even while it was still under way—Honorius accordingly felt the need to synthesize. How? This is what I find interesting about him: his uncertainty over what means to choose, a trait he shares with all the schoolmen of his day. As a first solution he tried number symbolism—was the universe not musical, a great cithara, and were harmonies not omnipresent? Honorius accordingly shuffled and reshuffled the deck. As key to the social order, he first took the figure nine, following Dionysius, with his nine choirs of angels.[22] Next, he tried seven, the seven virtues; or eight, the eight beatitudes. He identified four "orders"—the orders of the elect—or five—the orders of the faithful (married, widows, virgins, monks, and priests). One number, however, recurs constantly: three, naturally. All the triads reemerge.[23]

One of them seems to have been invented by Honorius. In the treatise *On the Image of the World*—of the two extant versions, I shall use the second, which dates from after 1133—he says that "mankind [what remained of it after the flood in the world's second age, a father and three boys] was divided in three, among the *liberi,* the *milites,* the *servi;* the "free" descending from Shem, the "knights" from Japhet, the "slaves" from Ham.[24] In all of Honorius' work, the prolixity of which has been mentioned, this is the only appearance of a figure resembling that used by Adalbero and Gerard. It is much distorted, moreover: the classification is not traced back to the origins of the species but is rather part of history, being assigned a date; more than that, the functions have been replaced by legal categories of status, or, more precisely, by degrees of freedom. Yet if we read carefully, we find that the image is really a trifunctional one. "Slaves," *servi:* the word is Adalbero's, applied here to the descendants of Ham, who are damned, sunk in servitude as a result of his sin: Saint Jerome had earlier meditated on the sin of Noah's son and its consequences. Of course, neither Adalbero nor Gerard spoke of "free men"; they used the word *oratores;* they also used *bellatores* rather than "knights." Nevertheless, Honorius was merely using different words to express an idea identical to the one the two bishops had had in mind in 1025. This is proved by a passage in another of his books, the *Summa gloria.*[25] We read there that Shem prefigured the "priesthood"; Japhet, the "kingdom"; as for the third son, "who is placed in the service [or 'in the servitude'] of his two brothers," he is to be understood as representing the "people [*populus*], subject [*subjectus*] to the priesthood and the kingdom, and [like?] the Jewish people serving [or 'in bondage to'] both." Thus Noah's two eldest sons represented the two parts of the Gelasian binarity, respectively custodians of the two powers, the two swords. Liberated by divine law, the "free men," the sons of Shem, were consequently members of the sacerdotal order, as the *Carmen* explains; the "knights," sons of Japhet, those who administer the kingdom of this world by the sword, were (as they had been for Adalbero and Gerard) the princes, of the blood of kings, but here attended by their underlings—on this point, Honorius parted company with the two prelates and adopted the views embodied in the peace of God; the slaves, for their part, were men "in bondage" by dint of their labor, together with the Jews, the opposition clergy/laity being superimposed upon that of church/synagogue.

To bring everything together, Honorius also made use (literally everything is to be found in the work of this compiler) of the twofold metaphor of architecture and the body. In the treatise entitled *Jewel of the Soul*,[26] he sought to use architecture (in a period of construction on the most vast and ambitious scale imaginable, the time of that grandiose endeavor to symbolize the Christian people, the universe, knowledge, and God himself in stone) to make manifest the complementarity of functions. As the principle of authority stood at the center of Honorius' thinking (as it did also for Adalbero, Gerard, Hugh of Saint-Victor, and all his comrades, the masters, who kept firm control over the group, or "school," that they headed), the leadership constituted the structural members of the great edifice: the bishops were its pillars, on which everything rested; but they were aided by the princes, who formed the arches. Light—and all of ideology's glimmering reflections—entered through clerestory windows symbolizing the "doctors," these being solidly framed by the arcatures of power. Overhead, the knights formed the protective roof. The *laboratores* were left to prostrate themselves, to press in upon one another at the very bottom of the structure, huddling together to form the floor that the others trod underfoot. Powerful imagery. The bodily image was earlier and more frequently invoked: the *Elucidarium* and the *Speculum*[27] had already made it familiar by the time Hugh of Saint-Victor wrote his *Treatise on the Sacraments*. Honorius was thus the first to make use of Walafrid Strabo's metaphor, which he completed, notably by adding feet to the organism: the peasants. The image obsessed him constantly. At the very end of his life, perhaps in 1153, when he was shut up and no longer able to move, composing commentaries on the *divina pagina,* he reverted to it one last time in connection with the *Song of Songs,* a book that enchanted the amorous twelfth century—regardless of whether that amorousness was profane or mystical in nature. It occurs twice. On the first occasion,[28] the image takes the same form it had earlier in the *Elucidarium.* But the second time,[29] the body social is compared not to the body of Christ but rather to the bejewelled body of the bride, the Sulamite. Honorius was dreaming: he saw more differences, more divisions than he had noticed before: now the peasants were not the feet, but the thighs, and conjugal partners the stomach, which was adorned with ivory and sapphire. In this somewhat delirious dream image, the *ordo* was seen as embellishment of the female body, as it were. No other bodily image in

Church literature makes such allusion to sex—fleeting, ambiguous, and yet direct.

Digressing (was it really a digression?) to consider Honorius Augustodunensis was not wasted effort. It has helped us to understand why the masters, in the first half of the twelfth century, dropped the trifunctional system of classification used by Gerard and Adalbero, and why the restoration of the clergy, the episcopate, and the writing workshops associated with the cathedrals did not rescue the system put together by the bishops of Laon and Cambrai just after the year 1000 from the oblivion into which it had fallen in the schools. In northern France, the enthusiastic groups of researchers that took the lead in the battle for knowledge still looked to tradition, to the "authors"; they were nevertheless learning to take the complications of the body social into account—and particularly the complications of their own ecclesiastical society. The Church was agitated by the rivalry of the "diverse orders," whose numbers were constantly multiplying. Its monastic contingent was fragmented by the variety of observances, and its canonical contingent by the unequal strictness of the rule. It is conceivable that experience of many new distinct "professions" within the Church increased the skill of the clergy in "making distinctions," and made them more attentive to the similarly increasing complexity of profane society. They cast about for formulas that would make it possible to describe the diversity accurately without curtailing it too drastically. At the same time, the need to gain mastery over the seething society with which they were confronted led them to give the concept of "office," or function, a prominent place in their thinking, in light of the principles of "concord," solidarity, mutuality, and "charity" to which they attached great value owing to the new diligence in meditating upon the Gospels. But how many functions were there in this world in flux wherein city and country each day stood in starker contrast, as the division of labor proceeded apace on every level of society? Then, too, the importance of categorizations other than the ternary variety had increased, as these had proved useful, and were continuing to be used, in the struggle for the independence of the spiritual and for the purification of the clergy. The upshot was that a quadripartite classification gained favor. This differed, however, from the quadripartition ordinarily used by monks: it stemmed from the intersection of two binarities—one of them proposed by Pope Gelasius, separating the ecclesiastical from the lay power, the other by Pope Gregory, setting the rulers apart from the ruled. Overlaying this intersection was the triad virgins-continent-married, more potent than ever. Invoked more than any other metaphor by the masters of Laon,[30] this latter figure owed its power to the fact that it was especially well suited to the elaboration of a sociology of

255

sin—sin experienced primarily as sexual—and still more to the fact that it was uppermost in the minds of prelates preoccupied with marital problems, the most pressing of the difficulties faced by men engaged in the pastoral mission.[31] Indeed, in the eyes of the Church the entire moral order now rested on marriage. Its own officials were forbidden to marry. By contrast, the Church proclaimed that for anyone who was neither priest nor monk, no decent life existed outside the context of matrimony, home and "hearth"—the finest mesh in the net that held the populace captive in parish and manor. In the end, quaternity, ternarity, and the like all proved too simple. The trifunctional schema, at any rate, was discarded, cast aside to languish in a forgotten corner of the workshop.

Of course, not all clerks whose writings have come down to us were employed in improving implements for use by the agents of the pastoral mission. Some had chosen instead to serve the lay state. They, too, faced organizational problems. They, too, had to adapt classificatory models to meet new requirements. They, too, were called upon to come up with an image of society—and no doubt the need in their case was far more urgent. What they were asked to provide was a pragmatic tool, designed to meet the needs of the temporal princes.

20

IN THE SERVICE OF PRINCES

With the great leap forward made by material civilization and culture, the twelfth century witnessed a diversification of "occupations." Teaching was one of the new professions. But among the clerks who attended the lectures of the masters, there were some who eyed another *ministerium*, another office even more readily accessible, and even more profitable, wherein a man born with nothing had a good chance to rise rapidly if he was competent and loyal: the service of the prince.

A fine instrument very quickly brought to a pitch of perfection, the school was not really designed to prepare students for a civil profession of this kind. Normally, the school trained the servants of God. By the second third of the twelfth century, the bishops—soon to be followed by the popes—had begun to worry about the diversion of a segment of the student population into profane employments, a secular "brain drain" that they looked upon as a waste. They condemned the *litterati* (some of whom even boasted the title of master, and might have applied their knowledge to divine tasks, to the elucidation of God's messages) who no longer cared about serving in the Church. For their part, these turncoats had no trouble with their consciences. For them to serve the great men of this world in their households, and to carry the good work therein, was a salutary thing, was it not? What conceivable way of improving lay society was better than to live in familiarity with its rulers so as to castigate their wrongdoing and point out the path of righteousness, since the spiritual uplift of the populace depended on its leaders, and since the wickedness of the lay "prelates" redounded to their subjects as well? There was general agreement that the most urgent task was to convert the noble households, the breeding grounds of *potentes* and *milites*. It was there that a beginning had to be made. With the head. In keeping with the general trend toward dispersal of the powers and attributes of royalty, chapels proliferated in the eleventh century. At first, dukes and counts established their own; by the period we are now considering, every aristocratic residence of any size harbored a staff of specialists in liturgy and literature. Most chaplains had been through the school; they had advanced beyond the elementary level. They taught the master's sons to read and write Latin, regardless of whether or not the boys were destined for the Church—and the proliferation of such tutors contributed to the decline of the elementary disciplines of the *trivium* in the episcopal schools. Adapting the precepts of the Bible to the secular aristocratic value system, mingling what they remembered of the teachings of the *auctores* with legendary epics and courtly tales, the chaplains preached sermons to the lord's entire family. With this domestic teaching and instruction, the upper strata of profane society gradually assimilated a little of what was being studied in and disseminated by the schools. In princely courts great and small, the two cultures—chivalrous and sacred—intermingled.

There were also clerks (usually the same ones) who helped improve the seigniorial administration of the patron who provided their meals. This was one of the functions of the chapel. To theirs the dukes of Normandy had once attracted adventurers from every corner of Europe—from Scandinavia, Britain, and Italy. By the late eleventh century they were already at work laying the foundations of an efficient state apparatus. During the twelfth century this role was often filled by the collegial, the community of canons that was attached to every seigniory of any size. Distinct from the princely household, these institutions were nevertheless closely tied to it: the lord customarily had his place in the chapter, sometimes the most eminent one; he participated in the offices: close by the residences of the high nobility, the collegiate church was essentially the perfected form of the chapel. The canons did the work of notaries, revising the charter formularies, bringing a strict and rational new order to the arsenal of social terminology therein compiled for better or for worse by preceding generations, thereby helping to classify and rank the population at large. In this way they did their part in arranging the pleats in the ideological garb. By considering how they rated a man's quality, chose new terms to characterize the proliferating social subgroups, and ranked the hierarchical echelons in their lists of witnesses, we can gain an understanding of the outstanding features of their image of society—the most basic and widely current image, adapted to the practical demands of everyday life. At other times, however, these administrative officials and legal experts indulged in other, more literary forms of writing. They might do so on commission, or perhaps of their own volition, to advance their careers—not in order to detail a plan of reform (like Adalbero, Gerard, and to a certain extent the school masters) but merely to recount a sequence of events. This they would undertake as observers of the utmost

258

lucidity, skilled in the art of setting down each happening precisely in its proper place. In such a context they would delve more deeply into the conceptual models that they used in order to achieve intellectual dominance over the complexity, changeability, and nebulousness of the social realm, so as to be in a position to aid the prince in his worldly activities. Accounts of this sort are of exceptional interest. I have chosen a particularly fine example that happens to be pertinent to a period and region on which the present study is focussed. Its author was Galbert of Bruges.

GALBERT OF BRUGES

Galbert was a man of the city—in a country, Flanders, in which urban ferment had begun particularly early. He was a clerk, closely tied to the collegiate church of Saint-Donatien, which he knew well from within. He was also one of the count's notaries. In the very lively Latin of the chancelleries, midway between rhetorical language and the Latin of daily intercourse, he gives a day by day account of the troubles that befell his country following the assassination—the sacrilegious murder—of the count, Charles the Good, by members of his own family in the midst of the canonical chapter and while the liturgy was in progress. From this account, *Of the Assault, Betrayal, and Murder of the Glorious Charles, Count of Flanders,* [1] he hoped to draw material for composing a hagiographic work to the glory of the martyr, for which he anticipated bountiful recompense. A canon of Thérouanne unfortunately got the job done ahead of him. The fruits of Galbert's journalistic efforts remain in their raw state, unadorned, admirable in their directness. They are infinitely precious because of what they disclose of the latent structures, of the vast range of things about which ordinarily nothing is said. More than that, though, they reveal the ideological apparatus superimposed upon those structures in order to justify them, to impose order on them.

A practical man, Galbert believed that the *ordo* in the social organization resided neither in the heavenly Jerusalem nor in the *ecclesia* nor in the Christian people, but rather in the state. A *regnum,* a "fatherland": Flanders. Therein lay the novelty: in this case the foundation of the ideological edifice was a "feudal principality" (as it is still often called), a foundation laid early and built of sturdy timber. Looked upon as a body, it was governed (like the Church and the Kingdom of Heaven) by one man alone—the head, the "chief"; this was the count, the *princeps,* responsible by hereditary right for seeing that prosperity was attended by order. Implicit in this responsibility was the necessity to maintain constant communication with the invisible, as well as to spend a portion of his time—the most useful portion—among his fellow canons, performing along with them their customary ritual actions, and reading from the usual books the customary

259

words. The happiness of all depended on his physically taking part in the *opus Dei.* He prayed. Like King Robert an *orator* in one aspect of his person, the count of Flanders was thus a prince of the first function. Even more, however, he was a *bellator.* By the sword above all did he maintain peace and justice. His mission was to ward off attackers and make the Flemish homeland a formidable fortress. Each spring, therefore, he gathered all the warriors of the principality together and led them from tournament to tournament—to inure them to the hardships of war, to make a display of their valor, and to add to the glory of the fatherland. In these athletic outings their aggressiveness found an outlet, much like that provided by the crusade—a trial undergone by Charles himself, the crowning achievement of his "childhood," whereby he received initiation in the chivalrous virtues. From such seasonal debauchery the count drew authority to impose limits on the use of arms within the confines of his state, for the settlement of disputes relying instead primarily on discussion, law, and wisdom. By thus relying on these regular outings to banish the practice of the second function from within his own borders, the count could presumably depend inside his country on the first function—on law—instead. But not only on the first: the third—the providing function—was equally his responsibility. His people looked to him as a source of gifts and alms, and expected that in times of famine he would regulate the cycle of planting so that all, even the poor, might have enough to eat. "Prince of the earth" *par excellence,* unique in his rank, the count occupied in the "feudal" system of social imagery the place reserved for the king and his heavenly counterpart—Christ—in the Carolingian-derived monarchical system, which Adalbero and Gerard had taken it upon themselves to interpret.

He was not, however, the only *prelatus.* Other men stood with him up front, leading the way. Galbert accordingly referred to these men as *proceres, primates, primores.* These men of the first rank called themselves the "peers" of the count—his equals. They wielded power along with him on a footing of equality, as commanders of fortresses or rulers over a portion of the countryside—independent, immune from restraint. Together with the count they constituted a college. Just as the "thrones," the highest order in angelic society, surrounded God in heaven, so they surrounded the count. Charles' great merit, in fact, was to have governed at all times *judicio principum,* "with the advice of these princes." In Flanders, accordingly, the major rift—the breach between *prelati* and *subditi*—did not, in 1127, with the renaissance of the state still in its beginnings, pass between the count and his subjects. It rather set apart the miniscule group of "peers" from the ranks of the knights.

In fact, the "knights of our province" constituted a specific body, a subordinate echelon (*gradus*), compelled to render a certain kind of service and invested with an *officium,* a function: to aid in protecting the poor and the churches by means of arms. Chivalry therefore required the display of specific virtues, both moral (fidelity) and physical (valor—the lame were excluded from knighthood, relegated to the monasteries; this was also one of the uses of monasticism, which served as a repository for the aristocracy's deformed offspring, unfit for the game of war). But it was equally recognizable by its specific vices: treachery, greed, cowardice. The services that knights were supposed to render were compensated by privileges: they did not have to shoulder the burden of seigniorial taxes and they shared in the profits of their military exploits. Like their lords, the "princes," they were entitled to two intertwined advantages: nobility and wealth. Yet theirs was a lesser share, and decreased in size as one descended from echelon to echelon within the hierarchy: knights were not all of the same rank, and Galbert, who knew how to weigh his words, always used comparatives whenever he mentioned nobility and wealth. Still, these two qualities were diffused throughout the body of knights to the point marked by that other social boundary—the most rigid barrier of all, which stood between knighthood and the populace.

Beyond this frontier a different law held sway, and one came under a new jurisdiction. Ideology in this case actually played the role of infrastructure:[2] it molded society, transforming the hazy no-man's-land that the relations of production by themselves determined into a strictly delimited and well-guarded frontier. By laying down a system of values, ideology first aimed to conceal—with dubious success—the greed, turmoil, and mortal jealousy that wracked the clientele of vassals surrounding every great man, as well as that constant conflict, so difficult to subdue, that stifled the virtues of generosity, fidelity, and friendship on which the knights prided themselves. Of such turmoil we witness a sudden outbreak in the spring of 1127 on the death of the count, on the pretext of loyalty, of vengeance for his murder—this predilection for violence in fact lay at the very heart of the affair. Ideology was also used to mask the venerable rift between liberty and servitude, which the concept of knighthood concealed. This rift had apparently been forgotten in the rest of lay society, but had yet to be entirely plastered over within the aristocracy itself, where the competition for power kept it gaping wide. We see this clearly in the episode recounted by Galbert, in which in order to get rid of a rival rising too rapidly through the ranks of the *militia* and on the verge of worming his way among the "princes" themselves, his enemies accused him of being the son of a serf, a denunciation which drove those offended by it to kill their lord, the count, rather than face a public trial. If this account offers so clear a view of the ideological apparatus that Galbert, like all the scribes in the service of power, was working so hard to reinforce, we may attribute this to the fact that the crisis had shaken the foundations of the state and forced into the open the disorder that ideology was supposed to repress.

The same weakness of the state contributed also to the disclosure of another role of ideology: to denigrate anyone not belonging to the dominant class, i.e., the high nobility and its underlings, the knights. Relegated to the lowest depths—so far down that they were looked upon as a homogeneous mass in which making distinctions would have been unwarranted—the "people" relied on the count to meet all their needs. Still, wanting to be a keen observer, Galbert could not ignore the contrast between town and country that in Flanders was always quite stark, and in the thick of the troubles even more so; nor could he confuse the peasantry with the "citizens and bourgeois." He could not hide the fact that in the cities the barrier separating the latter group from the aristocracy was in reality quite porous. Marriage, wealth, and military training brought together in a middle stratum the elite of the common people and the least prepossessing specialists in combat. Thanks to the damage it did to the organizational structures of the military, the murder of the heirless count brought windfall profits to the bourgeoisie. On pretext of avenging the martyr, they, too, pillaged and sacked—on foot, on horseback, under arms. Arms they were fully capable of using—even as adolescents, they had lined up in battle order in what was left of the forest to undergo ritual initiation in archery.

Beyond a shadow of a doubt, armed combat could not have been looked upon as the monopoly of one "order" of society (was it really thought to have been?) had it not been for the interplay of carefully arranged deceptions, theoretical proclamations and the summertime pageantry of derring-do in the tournaments. Here we stand face-to-face with reality in all its nakedness, with its belligerent commoners and its men of ignoble birth whose "occupation" was warfare—the so-called *cotereaux,* the dregs of the military, a "rabble of brigands." And ultimately we see the power of money, which in fact called the tune. This episode gives an indication of the distance between reality and fantasy, between what social relations really were and what words, acts, pomp, and ceremonial depicted them as having been. The count's notary was convinced that there were three functions and that it was essential to be able to tell them apart. That the trifunctional schema was no longer serviceable for defining the relations of man to man was to him the most unmistakable symptom of a disorder that he deemed accidental. Reacting to his disorientation, he realigned the model on the person of the *princeps,* the chief of state. Striking proof of the count's preeminence was provided by the virulence of the turmoil precipitated by his death: he had been the ultimate judge, the supreme guarantor of order. Although Galbert's account never refers explicitly to trifunctionality, it is suffused throughout with nostalgia for an order—the dream of Adalbero and Gerard—impervious to the nefarious influences of money, commerce, and urban life; under the aegis of a monarch who would chant psalms alongside his canons, lead his knights into the lists, and protect the peasants whose labor fed his entourage, this order would embrace three functions, standing in perfect equipoise.

JOHN OF SALISBURY

Had Galbert troubled himself to couch his eulogy in a more rhetorically polished form, would he have based his argument on an earlier formulation of the trifunctional principle? He wrote as an amateur, not in response to a commission. No schoolmaster, he had no intention of producing a disquisition on power. Other clerks—of higher rank than Galbert—did work to this end, addressing themselves not to aspiring preachers but to the rulers of the state. They hoped thereby to contribute to its strength—not by lending technical administrative assistance, but rather by theorizing, much as Suger was doing, and as Adalbero and Gerard had done. Indeed, social theory was actively pursued in sovereign entourages during the second third of the twelfth century. Out of these efforts came an authentic political treatise, the *Policraticus,* completed in 1159 by John of Salisbury.

Drawing on the teachings of the schools—the Parisian schools, among the best there were—the *Policraticus* was a product of the highest reaches of culture and learning. Its composition conformed not only to the dictates of reason but also to the laws of fine rhetoric. It embodies the full vitality of a renaissance, as well as a fervor for revived antiquity that was quite keen among prelates who—a century before Frederick II and the laureate Capuan effigies—were bringing back from Rome statues and cameos that they admired, and who in writing sought by choice of words and turns of phrase to recapture the antique style. The work was dedicated to Thomas Becket, whom John then served as secretary. At the time, Thomas, chancellor of England, was a faithful retainer of Henry Plantagenet. Over and above his officer, it was in fact to the king that this plan for a society on which the lay power would impose a fitting order was addressed. The work is an example of a genre established by the "letters of instruction" that the bishops of western France circulated in the early twelfth century and by the innumerable "mirrors of princes": in book 4 we find, in the Carolingian manner, a biblical commentary to support each point in the statement of the duties of the sovereign. But the *Policraticus* went even further. It backed its advice to rulers with a theoretical account of the armature of the state, whereby order might be maintained.

This picture of society was the work not of a practical man but of an antiquary, an intellectual in thrall to the beloved authors of the classics he had read. He, too, spoke of *renovatio,* of returning to a better age, of reform. But for him the model age was the Roman. The difference between him and Gerard and Adalbero was that he invoked not patristic authority—Augustine and Gregory the Great—but rather the authority of the pagans, of Plutarch. John of Salisbury mentions his source by name: the *Institutio Trajani*—a text which no longer exists and which, incidentaly, was not by Plutarch. Was it a forgery of John's? Or was it rather—as the administrative vocabulary that shows through the text of the *Policraticus* as though it were a palimpsest might incline one to believe—a lost treatise from fourth-century Rome? In any case, it was an antique decor that set the stage on which the scholastic writer attempted to place the actors of twelfth-century reality. Was this archaizing *mise-en-scène* designed to whet the appetite of the audience? Self-effacing, John of Salisbury hid in the shadow of Caesar Augustus, of Trajan, the good emperor. Artifice: a "pernicious classicism," says John Baldwin. Indeed, in contrast to Galbert, all that is tangible has vanished beneath this cultural costumery.

In no sense, however, does this diminish the author's originality. John of Salisbury transferred the bodily metaphor—Walafrid Strabo's—from the Church to the *res publica,* to the state. His is a work of secularization, of profanation. The head of the body is no longer Christ, but rather the prince. This I regard as the crucial change. The *Policraticus* is the first systematic formulation of a secular ideology of power and social order. As it was the work of a clerk—and not a servile one, but a man convinced of the superiority of his estate—the system it proposes is, of course, strongly marked with the imprint of ecclesiastical thought. Its outlines are derived from Gelasian duality. John of Salisbury's innovation (a bold stroke of the utmost importance) was merely to separate the two "sides" of the organism that even as late as Hugh of Saint-Victor the unitary *ecclesia* was thought to embody; once this unity was destroyed, he proceeded to substitute two bodies for the formerly homogeneous one. Events were in fact leading up to such a fission. The Gregorian triumphs had inaugurated an evolutionary process which, by the mid-twelfth century, had increased the separation between the two powers, with the lay power gaining thereby in strength and independence. The *Policraticus* was written eleven years before the murder in the cathedral, and five years before the Constitutions of Clarendon which presumed to subordinate ecclesiastical to royal justice—a presumption at which Becket balked, reminding Henry II from exile that "there are two orders in the Church, the clergy, responsible for salvation in the hereafter, and the people, which includes the king."[3]

Temporal and spiritual, body and soul—with the soul, quite clearly, dominating the body, inspiring it: the composition of the *Policraticus* in 1159 actually observed this hierarchical distinction. When, moreover, John of Salisbury used bodily imagery to sharpen his depiction of the organization of the secular state, it was not with the intention of representing that state as autonomous. On the contrary, the metaphor lowered the lay power to the level of the carnal, thereby throwing its dependence into relief. "The *res publica* is a body," he wrote;[4] but in relation to that body, the priest-hood was the soul. "Caesar Augustus was subject [*subjectus*] to the pon-tiffs." John, therefore, had not quit the Gregorian party. His stance was identical to Adalbero's: in order to reform earthly society, to bring it into closer conformity with the intentions of its Creator, to make it ready for the Second Coming (still awaited), it behooved the sovereign to heed the leaders of the Church whose wisdom would make the truth known to him. In the hierarchy God-soul-body, the princes played the role of "ministers of the priesthood." Nevertheless, the bodily metaphor was useful in that it made possible an analysis, if not of society, then at least of the mechanisms through which the power of the prince could be brought to bear.

The analysis was not really carried any farther than Honorius had taken it: the hands—or, rather, *the* hand that brandished the sword—symbolized the knights, while the feet represented the peasantry. There, again, is a hidden trifunctional image—recall that the priests, the *oratores,* have been set apart. At the same time, John of Salisbury was perceptive enough to see reality as it was, and a writer skilled enough to describe it. Consider the *militia,* for example. In the classics he had found the phrase "military oath." He provides a gloss on this terminology, though, in which he alludes to previous training and to the practice of dubbing procedures. These he evokes in his antiquarian manner with the term *adscriptio,* perfect for de-noting the process of initiation whereby an individual entered a body or "order."[5] When he comes to discuss the corruption that constantly threatened the well-being of that carnal creature, the state, John denounces the "violent warriors whom Cicero called brigands." Now this happens to be the word then applied to the mercenaries—the *cotereaux,* or Brabantines—to distinguish them from the good knights. He further sketches a military code of ethics—one that owed a great deal, incidentally, to Bonizo of Sutri. The major vice—to be shunned by the *miles* above all others because it was injurious to order—was violence. The duties of the knight were "to protect the Church, fight against perfidy [meaning heresy], venerate the priesthood, combat injustice that victimized the poor, secure peace for the homeland, and if necessary to shed his own blood on behalf of his brothers, as the oath bade him."

Turning his attention to the "feet," representing the "humblest" func-tions, the perspicacious John did not limit his discussion to agriculture. He made room for the "several ways of working wool, the mechanical arts whose domain is wood, iron, bronze, and all the metals," and went on to mention "servile chores and the various other ways of earning one's living." He thus recognized the diversification of the category of *labor.* Without forgetting the peasantry, he first treated the town, aware of the fact that the functions were "so varied in form that no one who has written about them has yet set forth the precepts peculiar to each of these species." He thus called for a continuation of the effort to analyze society for moralistic purposes and gave encouragement to the masters working in his own Paris to produce a new system of classification. Indeed, the body that he was attempting to describe did not have two feet, or even eight like a crab, but "surpassed the centipede in the number of its legs."

Perhaps even more novel was the discovery that the social machine was run by a motor organ, itself complex: the court. No doubt it was this observation that led John to adopt the bodily metaphor: it made possible an explanation of the dynamics of power in terms of the interaction of the several departments of the restored state aparatus. Critical scrutiny centered on these departments. To redress their ills, a civic code of ethics was set forth. To foil the devil, John of Salisbury played his hand skillfully. He put his finger on the sore spot. The mirror that he fashioned was designed neither for the prince nor for laymen in general; it was rather an example of a *speculum curiae,* a mirror of the court—of a court that was witnessing a "polycratic" proliferation of power. The sovereign was not in fact the sole person to wield power. Sharing responsibility were his agents, to the extent that they had gained autonomy of action. Still prevalent was the old notion that decay of the body began with the head—this being the case, for instance, when the chief ceased to be the image of God and became rather the "image of the devil."[6] To this, however, was added the new idea that appendages could also be sources of contamination: if one of them was injured, the repercussions affected the head.[7] The ruler accordingly suffered from weakness in any of the organs of his power. It was his duty to detect whatever might be amiss and to remedy it: here we see the first signs of the tendency to divert the subjects' resentments from the sovereign to the officers of the state. The effects of any injury were felt throughout the microcosm, whether they first touched the "heart"—the council—susceptible to iniquity; the "unarmed hand" which might commit an injustice; the "armed hand," which could be inflamed by violence; or the "tongue" and "ears," the instruments of law enforcement, which might be thrown off the scent by the propensity to lie. The primary targets of John's admonitions were the "stomach" and "intestine," i.e., the financiers and money-changers, whose services were increasingly indispensable, and also the "flanks," or *curiales*—the intimates of the prince, the closely knit group that surrounded him in his household or bedchamber and screened him off from the rest of the world.[8] The members of this latter group were prey to the vice of selling themselves. Criticism was also focussed on what was, in the time of the *Policraticus,* the dominant structure of the renascent state: the *domus,* or household, i.e., the court; John's strictures were intended to demystify the sham values of generosity, honor, and courtliness that were flaunted at court.

John belongs among the forerunners of political thought. With perspicacity, he was the first to discern the beginnings of the duel within the princely household, at the source of power and wealth, between clerk and knight. As a Parisian schoolman and domestic of the English chancellor, he himself belonged to the antichivalric camp. Graced with the sacerdotal dignity, flying the tattered Gelasian banner, he launched his attack against his triumphant rival, the knight—denouncing, in the name of Roman virtue, the vices of the new "order" and the swaggering *militia,* with its vain braggadocio.[9] Against all this, he invoked the monarchy and forged a morality based on voluntary acceptance of—as well as respect and veneration for—authority. In the *Policraticus,* only the limbs of the body social are taxed with blame. The head remained guiltless so long as it ruled the body justly, controlled its several organs, and compelled them to render lawful service, while showing indulgence toward the most vulnerable, beneficiaries of the charity of the ruler—thanks to which the "feet" were "shod." This is the central theme of the whole work, to which Gregory the Great's venerable assumption that all order was based on hierarchy and on an exchange of respect and love was adapted: "the inferior must obey the superior, who in return must provide them with all that they need"; "in this way the inferior and the superior will be made to cohere, and so will all the limbs submit to the rule of the head, whereby Christian morality may be defended." Most important, every person was to remain in his station, satisfied with his fate: "let every man be content with what he has and with what he does, with the place and role assigned to each, residents of the cities and suburbs, tenants on the land and peasants...."[10] A regimental code of ethics.

How had John come to conceive such a code? In the first place, he had spent twelve years of his life studying with the masters of Paris, learning from them how to use analytic distinctions to reduce the complexity not only of theoretical argumentation but of reality as well. He had lived in the presence of an important ruler, and entertained the hope of one day becoming a bishop himself—he was thirty-eight years old, well placed, and still had seventeen years to wait before he would at last accede to the episcopal throne of Chartres. He affected aloofness from the things of the world, and was contemptuous of those misguided clerks among the *curiales* who comported themselves as valets of state power. With keen insight he took care not to cast the military function in an imprudently favorable light. Most important, his purpose was to extricate the clergy from the jurisdiction of the temporal authorities, to which he would have granted dominion only over profane offices. He appreciated the full consequences of the Gelasian duality. For all these reasons he was careful not to couch his ideological scheme in trifunctional trappings, which seemed to him threadbare. As Loyseau was to do after him, he relied instead on Gregory the Great. In contrast to Loyseau, however, he drew nothing of what he had to say directly from Gerard of Cambrai. Nor was trifunctionality explicitly invoked in any scholarly discussion of man in his social context from the period between the second third of the eleventh century and John's day, whether by monk or clerk—at least among the documents that have come down to us. In John's mind—as in the minds of all these men—the trifunctional image was present, one among many linguistic and mental formalisms. He eschewed its use.

Unconsciously, though, was he not laying the groundwork for the resurgence of that image when, in his investigation of the government of the English king, he chose to secularize the older ecclesiastical theories of the social order? The resurgence did in fact occur outside the theater of the sacred, in the universe of courtly culture. Like the earliest formulation of the trifunctional theme, its resurgence can be pinpointed with accuracy (as accurately, at any rate, as one can hope for in dealing with documents so ancient): in the court of the Plantagenets—John's own court—in about 1175–80, only twenty years after the publication of the *Policraticus*.

PART FIVE

RESURGENCE

21

THE TRUE DEPARTURE

THE THREE ORDERS

In the *Estoire des ducs de Normandie* that he wrote between 1173–75 and 1180–85, Benedict of Sainte-Maure placed the figure of trifunctionality at the center of a picture of the perfect society. The vestiges of the written record of northern French thinking yield no older trace of an explicit attempt to reinstate this conceptual model in a coherent ideological system.

Sainte-Maure lies in Touraine between Loches and Chinon. Benedict may have been trained in the episcopal schools of the Loire valley, in which the bulk of the work consisted in commenting on the poets. He had made his talents available to the counts of Anjou, perhaps as early as Geoffrey the Handsome, and surely by the time of Henry Plantagenet. A typical representative of those men of letters who worked as retainers of a great prince, he was responsible for entertaining his patron's court—that new public consisting of literate knights, of *illiterati* nonetheless capable of following the reading of a lengthy rhyme attentively, and, last but not least, of women. These people understood Latin poorly, if at all. Yet they coveted familiarity with the contents of the book-chests in the monasteries and cathedral chapters. Accordingly, the writer's role was to translate—albeit without eschewing invention—from Latin into the Romance tongue, into "romance." Benedict was a celebrated "romancier." In about 1160 he dedicated the *Roman de Troyes* to Eleanor, thereby associating himself with the vast literary undertaking of which the Plantagenet king was the most energetic sponsor in northern France. To the high clergy the grammarians and rhetors held out the great antique narratives as models of fine writing, and courtly society hoped to gain access to this literature through romance. For his part, the prince whose largesse paid for that society's entertainment—count of Anjou, duke of Normandy, and by marriage duke of Aquitaine—hoped that it would withhold its favor from the *chansons de geste:* they were altogether too loquacious on the subject of Charlemagne—i.e., the king of France, the duke's lord and rival for prestige. Some years earlier, Wace, another "reading clerk" of his household, had presented the same Eleanor with his *Roman de Brut,* an adaptation of Geoffrey of Monmouth's Latin narrative recounting the fabulous exploits of the ancient kings of Britain. To the clergymen whose careers brought them into the entourages of the great, these many commissions seemed also to provide an opportunity for accomplishing their pastoral mission—a chance to educate while entertaining, to use heroes of virtue as exemplars of moral teachings. Benedict fit the bill perfectly. In approximately 1173 Henry II was in difficult straits. The pope had finally forgiven the murder of Becket, but had canonized the martyr of Canterbury; Eleanor was leading a rebellion against her husband, and his sons against their father. He asked Benedict to write a panegyric to the dynasty similar to the *Roman de Brut,* i.e., based on Latin epic but done into Romance. The idea was an old one: a decade or so earlier, Wace had sketched a eulogy of the first Norman dukes. Benedict picked up where he had left off, gathering up his predecessor's drafts, together with whatever he could use from the several Latin works earlier dedicated to the glory of the lineage by William of Jumièges, William of Poitiers, and Dudo of Saint-Quentin. He scoured all the books, abridging and translating as he went.

In fact, it is in a passage translated from Dudo's *De moribus* that the trifunctional image figures as an exemplar—a fortuitous happenstance as far as we historians are concerned. We may compare the original text—a century and a half old and, as mentioned earlier, contemporary with Adalbero and Gerard—to the adaptation made of it to suit the tastes of King Henry's courtiers. Accordingly, we can identify what changes Benedict thought it worthwhile to make in order to enhance his audience's pleasure, and particularly to please his patron, the prince who commissioned the work. In an altered form the trifunctional figure does in fact appear, revised, adapted to the transformations in authoritarian ideology that had come about with the passage of time and shift in locale—from Saint-Quentin, Laon, and Cambrai to the lower Seine and Loire valleys.

With verse 13,229 of the *Estoire* begins the account of an episode of which mention has already been made: Duke William's visit to Jumièges. From the outset Benedict embroiders upon his source: two monks receive the prince and offer him something to eat; he refuses; the following night he is injured by a boar. Was he being punished for not having accepted the gift? For not having entered personally into the reciprocal engagement, the mutual exchange of service? Is it absolutely necessary to attribute significance to what may have been a mere stylistic flourish? William returns to pray, repentant. At this point he asks the abbot Martin—just as before—the same question that he raised in Dudo's work. But he is far more talkative than Dudo had imagined: the speech attributed to him by Benedict takes up sixty-three lines of the poem. What does he have to say?

To begin with,

> Three orders exist, each one for itself,
> Knights and clerks and peasants.[1]

Just as in the *De moribus,* we find here tripartition. But not the same tripartition. Dudo had maintained that there were three courses: one followed by monks, another by canons, and still another by laymen. Benedict intends something quite different. He does not set the monks apart in a separate class. He does not mention them at all, for they have been relegated to the periphery of the world they have chosen to flee, or else swallowed up by the clergy, whereas the laity has been divided into two bodies. Such a categorization is reminiscent of the practice of the notaries, and also of the way that Gerard and Adalbero set up their classification. Now we can understand why the ternary pattern should have been altered in this way. Rather than being based, as it had been, on life's various purposes, it now referred to distinct functions. What is more, this is the first time—in France—that we find the three functional categories called orders:

> One of the orders prays night and day,
> In the other are laborers,
> The other does justice and keeps it.[2]

(note that knighthood is characterized not by the military function, but by the judicial, which Adalbero had attributed to the "nobles," and which, properly speaking, belonged to the king).

Together, the three orders constituted the Church,[3] which was looked upon as

> By its orders severally honored,
> Made, exalted, and administered.[4]

Here once again we find a basic feature of the system of Adalbero and Gerard: the complementarity of services, and their reciprocity:

> The one order sustains the other,
> And the one order maintains the other.[5]

Each order has its particular joys and sorrows, its peculiar difficulties to overcome, and its own rewards to win. Each has its specific morality. Here Benedict is following Dudo quite closely, but the point is one on which Dudo's ideas themselves were similar to those of Gerard and the Carolingian "mirror" literature. Then, too, Benedict was in accord with the concern of contemporary preachers to preach to each social category in a manner best suited to it.

273

As for the clerks, Benedict—a member of their order—wanted particularly to justify their way of life—seigniorial—and their wealth.

> They have to eat
> To dress and to shoe their feet
> Far more lavishly
> More peacefully and more securely
> Than those who work the earth.

But the comfortable security enjoyed by these lords, "glutted by the workers," "supported" and maintained by them, was in fact paid for by self-abnegation.

> To them alien and remote
> Is every earthly pleasure.

They did not make love. Was love not "pleasure," the greatest delight this world had to offer? Voluntarily to forego such a pleasure was a sufficient price to pay for the right to live in peace and plenty.

By way of contrast, Benedict followed this immediately with a verse stressing the "pain" that was the lot of the "peasant." Like Adalbero, whose somewhat sanctimonious lament he repeated, he looked upon *labor* and *dolor* as one and the same thing: if he attributed any value at all to labor, it was one of penitence. Such a judgment was in keeping with the parallel traditions of contempt for the world and contempt for servile labor.

> They bear so much pain and suffering
> They endure the great scourges
> Snow, rain, and wind
> Working the earth with their hands.

(This passage offers further proof that the word *laboureur* [peasant, worker of the earth] did not, in any of these theoretical treatises, have the special meaning attributed to it in one early tenth-century charter, where it was applied only to the leading peasants, or ploughmen, who were seen as the primary artisans of agricultural growth; it commonly referred to all who worked with their hands.)

> Terribly uncomfortable and hungry,
> Their lives are most bitter,
> Poor, destitute, and beggarly.

Benedict felt no compunction to indicate that anything whatever mitigated the suffering of these creatures, unless—and here again we catch an echo of Adalbero's words—it was the absurd gratification of being useful: without them order could not endure.

The guardians of that order, finally, were the knights, whose mission was to check the damage done by the greedy.

> They whose desire knew no limits
> Wanted even more might and power,
> And neither sanity nor reason,
> Neither right nor measure would exist on earth.

It is worth pointing out that the function of the knights was none other than that of the Carolingian king—working tirelessly to restrain the appetites of the *potentes*. Now in the service of the prince, knighthood encircled the last stubborn vestiges of feudal violence within the state in order to subdue them—or so it seemed. The knights also took over another of the king's missions: God and "country" relied on them to keep the peace:

> This order defends the country
> From the blows of its mortal enemies
> And to protect others
> These men offer their own heads
> And so often lose them.

In compensation for risking their lives, the knights enjoyed privileges—about which Benedict is silent. At this point, William raises a question concerning all these people, who live such diverse lives:

> Will they partake equally
> Of merit and reward?

As in Dudo's account, the abbot Martin answers this question by saying that on Judgment Day, every man will receive his due. But this answer is preceded by an entirely new argument. Its purpose is to justify the seigniorial mode of production, the foundation on which the state was built. Once again social trifunctionality is invoked to prove that the distribution of services and privileges is equitable, and accordingly that the foundation of the *respublica* is stable. The aim of this discussion—unlike the work from which Benedict of Sainte-Maure was translating—was to establish not a religious moral code, but a civil one.

For the edification of his retainers, King Henry expected a panegyric that would celebrate the history of his predecessors—his maternal ancestors, the dukes of Normandy—and describe the roots of his power. The adaptation made by Benedict was not merely a matter of replacing the old model of three ecclesiastical orders (which had preoccupied Dudo at a time when the Norman clergy was undergoing reorganization) with the model set forth by Adalbero and Gerard. The latter was in fact subjected to far-reaching revisions. The trifunctional schema was retained, but only after being desacralized, as evidenced by the way Benedict has twisted around the dialogue between the duke and Martin of Jumièges. In the original account, it was the clerk—the abbot, the contemplator of invisible things—who described the ideal order to be imposed on earthly society. In Benedict's version, the description is given by the duke himself, who from the height of his princely power utters an "edict"—a judgment whereby justice is established and the law laid down. A human law—which is enough to make the social order independent of providence, hence of the ecclesiastical institution as well. Accordingly, the task of divulging the structure of that society no longer falls to a personage imbued—by anointment—with *sapientia*. Indeed, the prince who happened to be speaking was not sacred; holy oil had never been poured over his body; he had none of the attributes of either bishop or rhetor, nor was his gaze directed heavenwards. It would be an idle exercise to search his pronouncements for traces of the idea—central to Adalbero's system—that the ideal earthly distribution of functions and dignities should reflect the organization of the heavenly city. For the earth is here the be-all and the end-all, and responsibility for insuring stability rests entirely with the *princeps*—independent and secularized. This is the fundamental, the tragic change—this fall, this plunge from the dizzying heights of theology, to which the bishops of the year 1000 had been raised by the imaginings of the pseudo-Dionysius, toward the abysmal depths of that petty, trivial thing that we call politics. The word, the concept of *ordo* remained, albeit in a form that amounted to desecration. The *ordo* no longer reflected the distribution of grace according to a divine plan of redemption, but rather was shaped by the purposes of the ruler in assigning the various roles within his state. In one northern French principality, the orders were now looked upon as stanchions, as pillars upholding the state.

Once the prince had taken it upon himself to utter the incantation out of which order was produced, he became the organizer of a contest in which he no longer took part. Instead, as umpire, he insured that the rules were observed, duties carried out, and rewards justly meted out. He supervised the exchange of services. Thus the prince arrived at that commanding height where once the monk—Raoul Glaber or Saint Bernard—had stood in judgment over the world. Another change of considerable consequence also took place. Neither Adalbero nor Gerard had looked upon the king as standing above trifunctionality. Within the functional categories he occupied a particular place and rank of his own—whether, as for Gerard, the first of the *bellatores,* or, as for Adalbero, at the seam where sacred and military functions were joined. Benedict of Sainte-Maure, on the other hand—along with the master he diligently tried to serve—believed that the prince must dominate the three functions; they supported the monarchy, and watched over them in turn. This was essentially also the view of King Alfred and Aelfric. Yet these functions were not seen as the projection onto the body social of the virtues of the sovereign. It is very likely that the three values embodied in the system whose structure was described by Georges Dumézil were combined, owing to deeply rooted mental habits, in the person of the sovereign, wherein they reached their culmination. If one cared to, it would be possible to interpret in the light of that system the eulogy composed by Benedict of Sainte-Maure (in this instance translating William of Poitiers) to the young William the Conqueror,[6] in which the hero's beauty, courage, and intelligence were celebrated in turn. But the mirror of morality was held in the prince's own hand, together with the reins that guided and if necessary steadied the pace of the team of three that strained in harness to his power.

The prince, however, was bent on forging a solid alliance between himself and one of the three orders: knighthood. As we have just seen, the knightly order had been made responsible for tasks that had once belonged to the Carolingian kings. In speaking of the knights, Benedict of Sainte-Maure repeated almost verbatim what Dudo had written about the function of the duke—that his office was to maintain peace and "uprightness" in the country. In terms of ethics and obligations, knighthood was thus represented as a sort of extension of the monarchical function; it was a many-faceted mirror in which the image of the prince was reflected. The coalescence earlier observed by Galbert of Bruges, which attached the humblest of the *milites* to the sovereign, was raised in the *Estoire of the Dukes of Normandy* to the status of a principle.

Not a history written to be read out in public in the city squares, the *Estoire* was intended for the edification of the court. The real subject expounded by Duke William—the thing that Benedict of Sainte-Maure was seeking to describe through his princely spokesman—was not so much all society as it was that select society that inhabited the household of the prince. The order he discusses here was—as it had been for Hincmar—that of a well-run palace. That residence should set an example for the entire country; indeed, the country was like a remote wing of the palace. Its populace was exhorted to model its behavior on that of the retainers of the prince, their common master, and share in performing the various required services. The peasantry figures in this passage of the *Estoire,* and its condition and doings are realistically described. The ideology expressed in these lines is seigniorial. Accordingly, the exploitation of the peasantry is claimed as a legitimate right—and, in passing, the agitators who went about preaching that the clergy would do well to live in greater poverty are denounced. Above all else, the prince insured that the seigniorial machinery ran smoothly. Later in his romance, Benedict of Sainte-Maure made use of Wace's account of the Norman peasant uprising that occurred in the year 1000 or thereabouts, as the seigniorial mode of production with its attendant rigors was being put into place. He castigated the peasants who had dared abandon their order, who had thrown off the yoke and refused to bear the burden of taxation. Dreaming of equality, they had organized communes—scandalous behavior. In chorus the court took up the old anti-egalitarian refrain that first Gerard of Cambrai and later Guibert of Nogent had sung many years before. The trifunctional figure was used in combat to

277

defend positions occupied jointly by clergy and knighthood as a class. It was flaunted as a standard symbolically planted at the front lines in a battle that in 1175 was growing increasingly bitter, as the most perceptive observers saw clearly—a battle which helped revive after some two centuries' dormancy memories of the old insurrections, of the resistances to the "feudal revolution," and of the repression that broke them.

Was it not also the case, however, and perhaps of even greater significance, that this same figure was employed at that time to consolidate other barriers—within the princely entourage itself—and to maintain divisions within court society on which the patron capitalized in order to insure obedience to his orders? Refurbished by a clerical retainer and set forth in the vernacular so as to be comprehensible to all the intimates of the palace, no sooner was the trifunctional theme desacralized than it took on the appearance of a *courtly* model, in the strict sense of the word. In his statement of the formula, Benedict of Sainte-Maure used the word "villein." In elaborating on the group thus set apart from the knights and the clerks, he referred in fact to men who "worked the earth" (*laboureurs*), "kissing their own behinds," as an anonymous poet was to put it much later, in the sixteenth century. It is worth noting, however, that this was not the primary meaning of the word "villein" for Benedict's audience. Its true significance is disclosed by another passage of the *Estoire,* in two verses that echo each other:

> He was neither a fool nor a villein . . .
> But deemed courtly and wise.[7]

Wise/fool, villein/courtly: these pairs of terms were the cornerstones of a value system built in effect on an opposition between courtliness and baseness (*vilenie*). This was of course an opposition between two domains in social space—the court and what lay outside it, the latter stretching into those dark reaches, "strange and alien," wherein lay the fields and villages of the realm. But more important was the far more clear-cut opposition arising out of daily experience within high society itself—an opposition between two forms of behavior. Within himself every individual could sense a battle raging between his base and courtly qualities, as between wisdom and folly. In particular, it was possible to identify those members of the princely household in whom baseness predominated by nature, as an inescapable fact of birth. This difference was the foundation on which Benedict built his work, and on which all chivalrous literature was based. Read, for instance, the eulogy of Duke Richard in the *Estoire:* he tolerated no villein in his court; he granted access only to sons of knights, cherishing no others, treating clerks and warriors alike. This social barrier was fundamental and played a decisive role in the last quarter of the twelfth century, as the spate of Romance literature from the period makes unmistakably clear. It reflected the enormous difference between men of the first two "orders" and intruders from the third within the households of the great; the presence of these intruders was nonetheless real, and the admonition to the prince to segregate them from the rest of the company would have been less vigorous had they been less powerful, less useful, and less favored. Another work contemporary with the *Estoire,* the *Romance of Alexander,* pointed out that it was indecent for a ruler to accept the advice of "serfs," and that he should pay heed only to "the gentle knights" (those of good "genus," well-engendered, of good stock), to "the wise and good clerks" (stout of body and, thanks to wisdom, enlightened of mind, with body and mind kept in equilibrium by "uprightness"), and, finally, to "the ladies and maids." In about 1215, moreover, Thomasin of Zerklaere dedicated the *Wälcher Gast* "to the stout knights, good ladies, and wise clerks."[8] Anyone interested in detecting instances of the Dumézilian tripartition will take note of these three adjectives. Does the way in which they occur here indicate a tendency to feminize the third function? Has not another triad wormed its way to prominence on the courtly stage? This ought not to surprise us: courtliness also signified making way for the fair sex—for womanhood.

To evoke the peasantry, then, in 1175 was first of all to issue a reminder that the gateway to the court was shut. But everyone knew that it could be forced open, that money had that power, and that large numbers of merchants were even then making their way inside. This accounts for the great pleasure taken by the audience of the new romance in hearing condemnation made—in this instance by Chrétien de Troyes—of

> that base rabble,
> Those rabid dogs, those whoreson lackeys,

i.e., of those upstart bourgeois who must at all costs be held at arm's length. For they were represented in the assembly that the prince contemplated daily, toward which he held out his mirror so that he might see himself as he was, and also as he ought to have been. For the prince, the trifunctional formula, with its distinction of peasants from clerks and knights, was a way of letting it be known that he would insure that the barriers remain intact, and that orders, dignities, and ranks would be kept distinct. This was also broadly advertised in public ceremonies, through the order imposed on processions that the prince led—take Robert the Magnificent, for example, in the monastery, for the great festival, leading the offertory procession, *prelatus,* steering his carefully arranged cohort towards the Lamb:

> Next, the wealthiest and the best,
> Followed by the second, and the last.[9]

As it became secularized, severing its ties to the grandiose cosmological vision of which it had been an integral part, the schema that had been used by Gerard and Adalbero was sufficiently diminished in scope to be compressed within the closed universe of the princely household, where it was superimposed upon another schema, profane and domestic. No longer were the three orders homologous to the companies of angels in the service of the Almighty, being now rather departments of the court, responsible for prayer, defense, supply. Benedict took note of this circumstance in another anecdote, this time celebrating the patron's largesse (a most important virtue, since it was by making judicious distribution among his people of the wealth that his power brought him that the lord insured his authority). This was the story—most curious for what it had absorbed of material that came streaming in through the fissures in high culture from a reservoir of folklore—of the gifts offered by the duke. To a knight, a clerk, and lastly to a cutler, a master craftsman, a "laborer," who worked, who toiled with his hands, but whose function was the indispensable one of keeping the duke's household supplied with fine and handsome objects.

John of Marmoutier and Stephen of Fougères

Benedict's book is a useful marker along the path we are following. It fixes a point in time. It dates the resurgence. But it was by chance that this particular treatise survived, and it should not be forgotten that it has a place within a larger context. Late in the eighth decade of the twelfth century, in these same circles (the Plantagenet entourage) and still in the same quarter (more Angevin than Norman) of the same cultural zone, other clerical retainers of the prince were also addressing the court. I shall single out two works for further consideration. Both were presented to Henry II, and both were contemporary with the *Estoire:* one was in Latin, written by a monk, but a monk long employed in celebrating the dynasty; the other in Romance, the work of a bishop.

In about 1180 John of Marmoutier wrote the *History of Geoffrey, Duke of the Normans and Count of the Angevins,*[10] the father of Henry Plantagenet. This was a *vita*, after the fashion of the biographies of Louis VI and Louis VII, and like those works composed in a monastery; but its hero was not a king. A line from Virgil—there we have the "renaissance of the twelfth century"—furnished the plan of this eulogy: it consisted of two parts, war and peace, *parcere subjectis, debellare superbos*. Introducing the "new lord," *novissimus dominus,* describing the bestowal of his function upon the prince, the monk John in the first portion of his work tells three stories. He hoped that the way the young count was shown behaving toward the three "orders"—which he cherished and ruled at the same time—would be taken as a model. Three attitudes. Three virtues: the purpose of the work was to improve Henry's conduct through the example of his forebears, and also (in what was probably a more pressing need of the moment) to help improve his sons' conduct. Three locales: first was the forest, in which like all young nobles Geoffrey took pleasure in hunting. One night, he loses his way in the woods and encounters a *boisilleur,* a man who supplies charcoal to the ironsmiths in the town. The man is black, ugly, disturbing: in him we meet with the populace in its most repugnant aspect. According to John, the count demonstrates his exceptional qualities by showing himself "liberal" toward this savage: "He was not contemptuous of the poor man, as the rich man would have been, but recognizing this man as a man, he lamented in the wretchedness of one individual the calamity common to all men."[11] Geoffrey then thinks of Adam and of the punishment inflicted on him: Thou shalt earn thy bread in the sweat of thy brow. Here we see the very old *topos* of labor-penitence, punishment for the original sin, coupled with the new twelfth-century forms of charity, sympathetic to physical hardship. When the count of Anjou asks to be shown the way out of the woods, the charcoal-burner responds by describing the condition of the people: "there you are sitting on your horse, I do not think that you have to worry about what you will eat or what you will wear," while my family will die of hunger and cold if I do not work with my hands. The story breaks off here to celebrate the prince's "goodness": he was the first to speak in greeting the "rustic"; he asked for his help, when he might have commanded it, and offered to pay, although he was entitled to demand it free of charge; approaching the plebeian from behind, he raised him up to his own level and seated him on his horse, as a brother. And so it came to pass that while riding along, the two men fell into conversation. About what? Popular opinion. Geoffrey wanted to know what the great men and the common people thought of the count. The answer: the count was a good lord, he loved justice, he defended the peace, he warded off enemy attacks, "he was [above all] the benevolent benefactor of the oppressed." Only he was not aware of everything that was going on. He had enemies, hidden enemies, at home: his provosts and stewards. When with his escort the count came to take up residence in one of his castles, these men bought up provisions on credit: they only paid back half what they owed. This meant that the count, without suspecting, was eating the fruits of "rapine." They collected taxes not due. They spread word of some danger to bring all the villagers flocking into the stockades, and then allowed them to return home only after payment of a sort of ransom. As a result, the people suffered (the verb John used here was none other than *laborare*) more grievously in peace than in war. By the time the two riders reach the court, obviously, the charcoal-burner has been laden with gifts and granted exemption, and the prince makes haste to put an end to the malfeasance of his ministers. John of Marmoutier conceived of the state in the same way as John of Salisbury. Its head was by nature healthy; corruption entered through the appendages; the good prince was obliged to maintain a sharp watch over the agents of his power, correcting their errors. John of Marmoutier was convinced, moreover, that the

281

function of the laboring people was to feed the aristocracy; the seigniorial system of exploitation insured that the fruits of labor were properly transferred; the only important thing was that the system operate within the rules; it was up to the prince to see that it did.

The second story is a banal one. It is set in a collegiate church, the chapter of Loches. There, one morning, the count, a "devout listener," attended mass. He offered a prebend to a very poor clerk. The servants of God had need of regular incomes; in order to carry out their task to perfection, it was appropriate that they live in comfort. The good prince, "merciful minister of divine mercy," must deliver them from penury, and offer them a just share of the income of the manor.[12] So much for the first two locales—a forest and a church. Finally, we come to a castle. We meet four knights from Poitou—contemptible, boastful, not very brave, talentless but for their fine singing voices: they are from Eleanor's country—held captive after a victorious campaign. Their fate moves the count to pity. "He has an inhuman heart," he says, "who has no compassion for those of his own profession. Are we not knights? We therefore owe a special compassion to knights in need."[13] John of Marmoutier, as we see here, was repeating the lesson taught earlier by Benedict. Its points were the following. That there existed three functional categories, hierarchically ranked. That the master of the state governed them all. That the prince had the duty "to shoe the feet," that he was obliged to insure that the workers not become too deeply mired in misery. That it was not fitting for either clerks or knights to be poor. That through his liberalities, the master of the state should rescue them from destitution. Therein lay the function of "justice" for which he bore responsibility: to insure stability by making equitable redistribution of the profits of seigniorial exploitation. But, as the count himself acknowledges, his specific "profession" is knighthood, whereby that order rose to preeminence among the three.

The other text, the *Book of Manners* by Stephen of Fougères, is difficult to interpret. The only manuscript, preserved at Angers, is poor; an old published edition is defective,[14] and its vocabulary is shot through with pitfalls for the unwary. Its author belonged to the circle of Benedict of Sainte-Maure. As chaplain of Henry II, he enjoyed greater success than Benedict: he was awarded the bishopric of Rennes (not all bishops now came from the "blood of kings," as they had done in Adalbero's time: the episcopal dignity was the highest reward any good court clerk could hope for). The work is a sermon. Written in the vernacular, it was intended, like the *Estoire,* for a "courtly" audience. Its preaching was inspired by the words "all is vanity," and it concludes with a prayer calling upon God to take pity on this base world. To be worthy of this mercy, let each man fill the duties of his estate, in his own "manner," i.e., in his own "kind" (*maneria*, in Abelard's vocabulary, was the equivalent of *genus*). Stephen accordingly described the various categories, stressing the duties specific to each of them. He classified them in two groups. The first included those who lead: note that here laymen take the fore—kings, dukes, and princes (books 9–52); next come clerks of all ranks (52–134); bringing up the rear are the knights (135–59). The other group consisted of those who obey: peasants, bourgeois, merchants, usurers, followed by ladies and demoiselles. Women—and these are noble women—have their place in this review, but once more it is the last place: the lowest rank among the subjugated.

The plan adopted, a commonplace one, follows a venerable classification, routine since its introduction by Gregory the Great and Isidore of Seville. But allowances have been made for the class division traced by the relations of production. What is noteworthy is that the trifunctional theme supervenes where the two parts of this tearful homily are joined:[15]

> The clerks must pray for all,
> The knights forthwith
> Must defend and honor,

(these are the words used by Benedict of Sainte-Maure)

And the peasants work the soil.

Three verbs: to pray, to defend, to wear one's body out with work. Three nouns: clerk, knight, peasant (*paysan*)—the latter a rare word that Stephen of Fougères preferred to "villein": was this merely for the sake of the line's cadence? Like Benedict of Sainte-Maure (but in contrast to Adalbero) Stephen placed monarchs—heads of state of every kind, whether kings or, like his own master, dukes or counts—above the three "manners," and, this time quite explicitly, above the clergy as well. Under the uncontested authority of these rulers, the seigniorial mode of production set the men of prayer and the men of war apart from those who toiled, who were held down in abject obedience and deprived of all office, in the institutional sense of the word (as women also were, of course). Stephen of Fougères has nothing to say either of "estates" or—with reference to society as a whole—of "order." He recognizes only two orders, which in the Gelasian manner comprise the ordered portion of society, that which is described in the first part of the *Book:* the knights and the clerks—"the ordained." As for the knights, he points out that

> Knighthood was a high order.
> Salvation could well be had in one's order.

Indeed, he looked upon knighthood as an order like the clergy in that one entered into it by ordination, the *sacramentum militiae* spoken of by John of Salisbury. The knight, he said, "has made order" in the church; if he did not accomplish his missions, he was "de-ordained." Stephen's view was more hierarchical, more clerical, and no doubt more primitive than that of Benedict of Sainte-Maure. And he made much more overt use of the trifunctional schema as a riposte to possible peasant rebellions, as support and justification for the seigniorial organization.

The tripartite formula actually serves as introduction to a long *planctus* on the condition of the peasantry, in which the obligations of workers to their masters are recalled. That is its role. This postulate precipitates a discussion not, as in Gerard of Cambrai's work, of peace—the good royal peace—but rather of seigniory. It is addressed to the courtiers, who are told to protect their own positions as *prelati,* as guides, by speaking directly to their subjects and advising them to settle for their lot in life and to be submissive, for the most abject are most certain of salvation. Stephen first gives a crude statement of the "peasant" function:

> Knights and faultless clerks
> Live by what the peasants work.[16]

Then, pretending to take pity on the suffering of the poor, he describes their duties in detail:

> They work and suffer much,
> Pay firstlings, forced labor, and prayers [i.e., tallage],
> And a hundred customary things.[17]

Stephen lastly gives a lengthy discussion of the seigniorial confiscations which left the workers nothing to eat but the "vile" remains—fit only for "villeins." For consolation, they were told that labor was redeeming; the more destitute the common man was, the greater was his merit. What cause had he for complaint?

> As one lived in straits more dire
> By so much was his merit higher,[18]

which redeemed him

> For his sins of wrongdoing.[19]

The condition of this redemption, however, was that he keep to his proper place—honest, needy, abject:

> If he pays what he owes to all
> If he loyally keeps his faith
> If he willingly bears
> His anguish and suffering.[20]

Alas, the peasant "bears nothing patiently," and blames God for his woes. He forgets to thank heaven when what he does turns out well. He is an ingrate, a rebel. He must be bridled.

More aloof from the world, preaching from the exalted height of his magisterium, Stephen of Fougères repeated what Benedict had been saying. His manner was more straightforward—perhaps it owed more to Normandy than to the Loire? In any case, he was perfectly clear. His aim was to consolidate the class barrier, and to quell the incipient rebelliousness roiling the depths of the populace. At court, his purpose was to shore up the ramparts that kept upstarts and newly-rich vulgarians apart from good society. In these final years of the twelfth century, the need for such teaching was great indeed. No sooner had his words been uttered than they were echoed on all sides. The resurgence came not as a trickle but as though gushing from a fountainhead, and from that time on the basin remained full to overflowing.

AROUND HENRY PLANTAGENET

The—rash—attempt to search the remains of an epoch's literary output for clues that would enable us to date and localize the incorporation of the trifunctional figure into an ideology of social order has already, I think, yielded some results. The image first saw the light of day in Frankish territory in about 1025. It then returned to the depths of the inarticulate, only to surface once again a century and a half later—this time to stay. The hiatus corresponds to the collapse of the monarchical state, to the feudal interlude. There is a very obvious correlation between the history of this thought-form and the history of power in northern France. When the postulate of social trifunctionality was first articulated, it was to rescue a foundering monarchy—but the call for help came too late, at a time when the leading figures among the custodians of literate culture were already turning away from the hopelessly feeble Capetian king to set their faces instead toward God—toward the papacy waging its battle for reform, first seeking refuge in the cloisters, and later concerning themselves with the training of effective preachers. For a long time thereafter the theme remained useless. As society grew more complex, it seemed less and less adequate. Thoughtful men looked elsewhere. Was it really forgotten? Was it not still present in parts of the cultural spectrum invisible to us? Is it inconceivable that it continued to play a role, albeit now on the other side of the lines laid down by the Gregorian wars—in the camp of the temporal powers—where it would have been wielded as a weapon to counter the claims of the Church, to cut down ecclesiastical ideologies (such as Gelasian dualism or monastic quadripartition) and to put to rout the notion that society consisted in a body of which the laity, led by the princes, formed the left—the junior—side? Might it not have slipped below the ridge of high culture onto a far slope, hidden from our gaze, into a cultural domain in which nothing had yet found durable forms of expression? Our ignorance is irremediable, and so we must resign ourselves to it. One fact is worth noting: when the model once again came into use, in the 1170s, it was couched in the language of laymen, at court, in the shadow of the throne—and just as the state in this corner of Europe was regaining strength.

In the forefront of this revival was the Capetian state: its growth under the reign of Louis VII is striking. For twenty years it had been gathering strength, ever since the second crusade. The first to be an affair of kings, this adventure was celebrated by Odo of Deuil, monk of Saint-Denis, whose reports to Suger from the Holy Land, intended as panegyrics to royalty, heaped praise upon the prodigious expansion of the French king's role: a monarch whose resources had been sorely taxed a few years earlier by the effort of leading a few communards on a campaign to level the wooden towers of the faithless barons was now directing all Christendom in its wanderings toward the place that symbolized the end of time and the resurrection of the dead. With Suger and Saint Bernard gone, the restoration of the monarchy reached a point where it was plain to see. However pious, however subjugated he may have been by the priests, the sovereign was managing not only to close in on the glories of the hereafter but also to make progress in the more mundane matter of consolidating his political power. In the fifties he dared promulgate peace ordinances applicable to the entire realm. And when, in the sixties, he extended the jurisdiction of his courts to the eastern borders of the kingdom, he succeeded in one effortless stroke in sweeping aside everything that ran counter to his wishes.

When, however, the trifunctional theme appeared once more at the center of an ideological system, it served not the power of the king, but rather the authority of a prince—a prince who had not received the power that he exercised within the French kingdom directly from God through the rite of anointment. He desired complete independence from clerical control. This was Henry, count of Anjou on his father's side, duke of Normandy on his mother's, duke of Aquitaine by marriage, and for good measure—but only for good measure—king of England, although this was of no concern to the country in which he spent the best part of his time. The trifunctional figure was employed by one of his clerical retainers as a series of convulsions brought on by the headlong changes in the structures of the state made it necessary to mobilize every available reinforcement—ideology in particular. To my way of thinking, the fact that trifunctionality, in its profane form, should have come to the fore initially in the Plantagenet entourage can be explained by three main reasons.

First, the principalities of northern France achieved a precocious maturity. While the king of France, the duke of Burgundy, and the count of Champagne were still relying primarily on the monks for assistance in governing their states, already in Flanders, Normandy and Anjou the prince had called upon the clergy to think about society in concrete, empirical terms, without succumbing to the siren-song of bedazzlingly pure theory. Once

Henry had gathered the reins of these states into his own hands, the avant-gardes of clerical thinking on the monarchy and its reconstruction hastened to his side. Was it an accident that the first systematic description of the medieval state machinery and its workings occurred in the *Policraticus* of 1159, or that the *Dialogue on the Exchequer,* written twenty years later by Richard Fitz Neal, contained the first analysis of the operation of public finance?

Second, the roots of Henry's power did, of course, lie in the French kingdom. But that power extended to the other side of the Channel, where the prince was king. In his rivalry with the Capetian monarch, the Plantagenet made capital of his insular base. He deliberately scoured the culture of the British isles for material out of which he might build an ideological edifice to rival the ideology of the Frankish monarchy. We know how the writers in his employ exploited the "matter of Britain," pitting against the image of Charlemagne that of King Arthur. Might not the trifunctional theme have been drawn from the same reservoir? In England it had known no eclipse, at least no protracted one. In the early twelfth century ecclesiastical writers in that country had invoked trifunctionality as a matter of course. If I may briefly step outside the geographical limits I chose to impose on this study at the outset, I should like merely to put down what is common knowledge, contenting myself with summoning four witnesses:

1. First, Eadmer of Canterbury, bishop of Saint Andrew's, who, in about 1115, in the *Liber de sancti Anselmi similitudinibus,*[21] maintained that God had created "three orders of men" to carry out three functions in this world—prayer, agriculture, and defense. *Ordo, officium,* ternarity—a reversion to Wulfstan, Aelfric, and Alfred. No mention is made, however, of the throne or its supports.

2. Gilbert, bishop of Limerick between 1110 and 1130, depicted society in the *De statu ecclesiae*[22] as a hierarchical structure,[23] consisting of two parallel series of seven nested pyramids. At the apex were three heads: the emperor, the pope, and, rather bizarrely, Noah. At the bottom of one of the series was that basic pyramid, the parish—the elementary cell of secular society. Gilbert offers the following commentary: "Those who within the parish church are embraced by these ranks are divided into three. Of these, the ones at the apex of the pyramid must be regarded as *oratores,* and because some of them are married, we shall call them men and women. Those to the left side of the pyramid are the *aratores* [this time—and this time only—the word does indeed refer to ploughmen], both men and women. On the right are the *bellatores,* men and women. I do not say that the function of women is to pray or toil, let alone to fight, but they are married to those who pray, toil, and fight, and they serve them. And since the beginning [*ab initio*], the Church has recognized these three legitimate orders of the faithful, so that within it one part, the clergy, might concern

287

itself with prayer, protecting the others against the attacks of the Deceiver; another, sweating in heavy labor [*labore desudans*], may rescue the others from want of nourishment; the third, devoted to soldiering [or 'to knighthood'], may defend the others against physical enemies." Another pyramid, symmetric with the one corresponding to the parish, represented the monastery. In this place, of course, neither functions nor sexes were in evidence. Gilbert did reserve a place for women—but what a place! Like Gerard of Cambrai, he discussed the origins of the world and of mutual services. He employed some of the same words of Abbo. The order that he followed was that of Eadmer, and of Benedict of Sainte-Maure as well.

3. Let us turn next to John of Worcester. In his *Chronicle,* which ends with the year 1141, he relates three nocturnal visions experienced by King Henry I, who saw himself attacked by peasants armed with their "rustic implements," by helmeted knights wielding lances, and finally by archbishops, bishops, abbots, deacons, and priests brandishing the pastoral crook.[24]

4. In a gloss on the *Canticle,* William of Ramsey arranged "the diverse orders which in the Church are like distinct battalions [indeed, in battle at that time, troops always consisted of three corps, face to face—another ternary figure deeply embedded in the minds of military leaders, their comrades, the knights, and the clerks who accompanied them into the field, whose importunate presence should not be forgotten]. There are clerks, knights, peasants; there are virgins, the continent, and the married; there are the active, there are contemplatives, and prelates."[25]

During the first half of the twelfth century, the trifunctional theme was actively developed only in England, where thinking moved away from royal power to concentrate instead on the structures of the Church (under Gregorian influence), so that trifunctionality was subsumed under the ecclesiastical concept of *ordo.* It may appear paradoxical that the feeling that society had always been strictly divided into distinct classes should have been keener in a country where, particularly in warfare, there was no clear-cut distinction between nobility and peasantry, where the banal seigniory was much less consistent, and where the notion of liberty retained its vitality in courts of public justice; whereas in the Germanic lands, with their more rigidly compartmentalized social hierarchy, this conceptual form was unknown. In any case, nothing prevents us from supposing that this mental representation came into discussions of social perfection after crossing the Channel in order to serve a prince sovereign over both its shores.

A third and final factor in trifunctionality's resurgence in the entourage of Henry II was that his court was a center of literary activity, more brilliant in its day than any other. This vitality was sustained by the generosity of the master, who took care to insure that his was the most diverting of courts, well aware that his glory would thereby be enhanced—and that the more the celebration of the prince and his power and virtues was felicitously bound up with amusing anecdotes and spellbinding tales of the vicissitudes of fortune and love, the greater that enhancement would be. To that end, courtly literature combined two traditions. One of them, a tradition of moralizing exhortation, rhetorical and mundane, came by way of Hildebert of Lavardin and the schools of Touraine from Jonas of Orléans; the other, more profane and domestic, was a tradition of dynastic eulogy, which contributed to the glory of the head of household and his successors by seeing to it that a gallery was stocked with portraits of his forebears attesting to the antiquity and legitimacy of his power—a concern not yet in evidence at the Capetian court, where the king had no need to commemorate his ancestors or to have his own biography written along the lines of hagiography, and where—prior to Philip Augustus, his matrimonial problems, and the threatened restoration of Charlemagne's direct heirs—the sovereign had little interest in having his genealogy traced. By contrast, this tradition had deep roots in Anjou, as well as in Normandy and Flanders. Ever since the late eleventh century this region had harbored the most productive workshops of genealogical literature.

The task of turning out these works had passed from the hands of the monks to the clerks, clerks of the court. These writings disseminated the teaching of the patriarch, or *senior,* to his "dependents," the young. During the twelfth century we witness an accentuation of two tendencies: a secularization of princely morality, and a rise in the values of knighthood, at the expense of those of *clergie,* or learning. Chivalrous values were already much in evidence in the memoir dictated in 1096 by Fulk le Réchin. We watch them undergo further elaboration with each successive revision of the *Deeds of the Counts of Anjou,* which may originally have been written in the monastery at Marmoutier by the abbot Odo, to be taken up subsequently on behalf of Fulk the Younger or, rather, Geoffrey the Handsome, by Thomas of Loches, who, like Galbert of Bruges, was a notary, and, like Stephen of Fougères, a chaplain; still later, it was revised again for Henry II by Breton of Amboise, and, on two occasions, by John of Marmoutier. For instance, the gradual change I have in mind can be detected in the eulogy of Count Fulk the Good (942–60). Thomas of Loches depicted him as canon of Saint-Martin of Tours, chanting psalms in the choir.[26] In reworking this version in about 1155, Breton of Amboise recopied the passage without changing anything of importance: he showed the prince "in the pose and habit of a clerk, the equal of all the others in lessons, responses, and psalmody." To please Henry II, however, he added an anti-Capetian touch in the form of an anecdote:[27] the king of France had laid eyes on Fulk in this devout posture, and the nobles of the royal entourage had laughed derisively: "he is an ordained priest," they hooted (and their sarcasms quite plainly echoed Adalbero's); without saying a word, the count of Anjou had taken up quill and parchment and written this note to the sovereign: "an illiterate king is a crowned ass." The king was compelled to acknowledge "that *sapientia,* eloquence, and letters are attributes thoroughly befitting kings, *and counts,* [italics added]" for they should excell both "in morals and in letters." This moral code harked back to that of Saint Augustine and Gregory the Great: princes were supposed to set the moral example. It was also reminiscent of the morality of the rhetors: rhetoric was conducive to correct behavior. Most important, however, was the assertion that now princes—and not only kings—could rightly take the role of the "orator," even without being sacred. This little story is illustrative of an ideology that may well be called "feudal," since it furnished justification for the appropriation by princely dynasties of the intellectual and religious attributes of royalty, rejecting the idea that the continuing monopoly of anointment by the king entitled him to monopolize wisdom as well.

In the prince, however (and it was this that accounted for his superiority over the king), learning was coupled with the equally indispensable attribute of knighthood. The prince must not be too "pious"—this was the weakness of the king, as evidenced by Robert in times past, and by Louis VII right up to that day. He must not closet himself away with the priests. In speaking of Count Fulk, at once "literate count and stout knight," that consummate lackey of authority Breton of Amboise used these words: "although he received the finest training in the rules of the art of grammar and in Aristotelian and Ciceronian disputation [the whole curriculum of the *trivium* as studied in the cathedral school is evoked here: grammar, dialectic, and rhetoric], he was considered to outstrip the best, the greatest, and the most valorous of knights." Fulk the Good set an example for his distant offspring, Henry: he had equaled the most learned of clerks, he was first among his knights; once, while riding in the company of his nobles "across his lands to secure peace and justice"—thereby fulfilling the function said by Benedict of Sainte-Maure to be the responsibility of the knights—he waited for the opportune moment and then dismounted in order to pray, on both knees, to Saint Martin.

Accordingly, the commission to Benedict of Sainte-Maure must be regarded as a continuation of this Angevin genre of genealogical literature, which though still awkwardly mounted astride a latinate style, showed a clear penchant for the chivalrous cavalcade. Moving toward more forthright confrontation not only with Louis VII but also with the specter of Becket, Henry Plantagenet was casting about for a model both antiepiscopal and, to a certain extent, antiroyal, that could be fitted within the context of a panegyric to his maternal lineage (to which he owed the English throne) and that might prove useful for the edification of his household retainers. The faithful Benedict answered his master's call. Like the authors of the recent *Deeds of the Counts of Anjou,* he showed the dukes taking part in the

290

liturgies, just as the Capetians had done. But he placed the accent on the attribute that gave them the advantage over the rival dynasty: they were good knights. Did not Henry II owe it to his illustrious knighthood that he had been able to avenge his ancestor Fulk le Réchin on Philip I by seducing (*se-ducere*) Eleanor, the wife of the French king? To lend weight to his argument and bolster his patron's power, Benedict of Sainte-Maure reverted to the tripartite theory, which he may very well have borrowed from the kingdom across the Channel.

Such borrowing, moreover, if it took place, would have served a purpose similar to that of the tales of the Round Table: to lend weight to moralistic preachings directed against the "matter of France," against Charlemagne, against the incumbent king of the monks, of Gregorianism, and of the communes. Accordingly, when the model reappeared a century and half after the pro-Capetian, pro-Carolingian pronouncements of Adalbero and Gerard in its new anti-Capetian, anti-Carolingian guise, it was actually used to repudiate those earlier doctrines with which it had been associated. This was true to the extent that it served to endow knighthood with preeminence over "enlightenment"—over those attributes whose source lay in anointment and in an alliance between monarchical and sacerdotal power. Because the trifunctional figure was now incorporated in a quite different ideological system, it had taken on a wholly new aspect. New by comparison with its recent English forms: it in fact no longer served as the underpinning of a theory of the Church; snatched from the scholars at Canterbury—at that time the priests who administered the cult of St. Thomas Becket—it was spirited away to Winchester, to kings Alfred and Arthur. Even more clearcut was the difference between this latest and the earliest French (in the full sense of the word) forms, set forth in detail at Cambrai, Laon, Compiègne, and Saint-Denis. Benedict of Sainte-Maure may well have thrown off the influence of Dudo, combined clerks and monks, and set warriors apart from peasants, but his reason for doing so was by no means to revert to the configuration that certain bishops in *Francia* had used in the year 1000 in their efforts, *in extremis,* to consolidate the tottering power of the French king. Their model had been wholly in the thrall of the sacred; Benedict desacralized it. For Gerard and Adalbero, the *bellatores* had been the *nobiles*—lay princes, custodians of the *potestas,* judges, delegates of the king; what is more, they eliminated the knights from their picture, allowing to fall over the knightly order the shadow of the "potentates" whose underlings the knights were to remain. By contrast, Benedict of Sainte-Maure made the knights—all the knights, and the knights alone—responsible for the military and judicial function; i.e., he bestowed this function on all laymen who found themselves on the right side of the divide laid down by the seigniorial mode of production, and on the wrong side of the line earlier laid down by the peace of God. In the English manner, he took all the horsemen and made them into an order, which he exalted. Since the knightly order was the closest of the three to the prince, and since the prince ruled over all of them, the "order of knights" tacitly took precedence over the "order of clerks." This was a discreet but crucial change. Coming at just the right time and place, it restored to trifunctionality its ideological power.

22

KNIGHTHOOD

The fact is that the princes who wanted to contain-the steadily increasing pressure from the Capetians in the last third of the twelfth century had no surer rampart than the military order, more strictly defined than it had been, and cloaked in glistening robes. The meaning of the changes that the trifunctional image underwent when it came back into use can be fully understood only by considering the evolution of the lay aristocracy in the north of France, and its end result: in the eighth decade of the twelfth century, at the end of Louis VII's reign, as the plot that was to come undone at Bouvines was being hatched, knighthood became a genuine institution.[1]

This was the outcome of a long and obscure history, which exemplary research like Jean Flori's is beginning to bring to light. All of Latin Christendom was affected, even Latium, that rather exotic border region, where we now know that a feudal state was formed in the second half of the twelfth century. There the group of *milites castrorum* had been adopting ways of life and thought conveyed across the mountains by entertainment literature, whose models were accepted so readily because these small groups of knights were prepared to take them up, were awaiting their arrival.[2] Around 1170, Germany itself, long restive, suddenly opened up in response to two different sources of pressure, both impinging on the princes of the realm. Pressure came first of all from below, from the ministerial ranks, where there was a desire to win recognition of a status superior to that of the ordinary populace and to obliterate the servitude in which the *ministeriales* were kept by virtue of certain very old structures.[3] Pressure also came from the king, who was battling the Roman Church, adopting courtly values so as to improve his prospects for holding his own against the Capetians on the borders of Burgundy and the kingdom of Arles, and attempting to revive the Empire's prestige through the myth of the crusade and the ideal of knighthood.[4] To this end, Frederick Barbarossa staged a grandiose chivalric festival at Mainz in 1184, on the occasion of his son's dubbing.[5] Through the combined efforts of the Hohenstaufen and the Minnesinger, the mirages of the *militia* thus quickly conquered the Germanies. Nevertheless, they did not relegate the hierarchies to oblivion. There remained a gaping abyss in the Germanic aristocracy between the *Herr* and the *Ritter*. They were similar in that both practiced certain virtues, but clearly distinct in function, in the duties implicit in their respective functions, and in virtue of the very old customs which enforced a distinction between the *prelati* who lead and the *subditi* who serve.

Meanwhile, the knightly values spreading from France had there reached the point where they were beginning to reduce social distances to a considerable extent, uniting the lay ruling class in a single body. For the sake of illustration, I will consider the intermediary region between the kingdom and the area of Teutonic culture, Lorraine, the Romanized Lorraine up to the linguistic boundary, which is precisely the homeland of Adalbero and Gerard. Thanks to the vocabulary of the charters, we can fix two chronological markers in a very fluid evolution: beginning in 1025, the word *miles* slowly came into usage to distinguish the members of one social group from other men (whereas in German-speaking Lorraine, this term penetrated only after 1170 and really became established only after 1200). After 1175, the title *miles* regularly preceded the patronymic of all knights and was connected, as a rule, with another title: *dominus,* "messire." For centuries this term had been used to designate those in possession of a power considered to be a delegation of the might of Christ; in the year 1000, apart from the king, only bishops and counts, the *oratores* and *bellatores* of Adalbero and Gerard, were so designated. Then it was taken up by masters of castles and the ban. In the last quarter of the twelfth century, it was a title that adorned every knight—this was also the period when the use of coats of arms was vulgarized, passing from lords-banneret to their vassals; when village squires dug moats and raised towers to turn their residences into strong-houses, symbolic equivalents of the great castles; and when seigniorial taxation disintegrated as well, as ordinary knights began to levy *tallages* and exact *banalités* in the rural parishes. These simultaneous phenomena mark the end of the process of feudal decomposition. This was the culmination of the long decline which saw the various attributes of sovereignty come to be widely distributed, from the heights of the aristocracy down to its lowest levels, to the borders of that other social territory, the exploited masses.[6] During these same years, too, another term, "squire", *armiger*, insinuated itself into the formulas used to characterize men who by birth ought to have been called knights, but who could not be so designated, because they had not been inducted officially, according to the prescribed rites, into knighthood. They were a sort of reserve, awaiting their turn, and so another title was fashioned for them, using a word which had long served in noble households to designate apprentices or aspirants. This insured that they would not be confused with the common people.[7]

These changes in the legal vocabulary are significant in two ways. First, society officially recognized a superiority connected not with specialization in the military art but rather with birth; in other words, a hereditary caste took shape, juridically defining a nobility. Second, within this caste, a more limited group was singled out, whose membership included not all adult males but only knights, who were cloaked in a dignity assimilated to seigniorial authority, an authority evoked by the word "*messire.*" In the same period, this very title, "*messire,*" began to be taken up by priests as well—but only by priests, not by all the clergy. Like the priesthood, therefore, knighthood was subsequently viewed as an estate to which one acceded by ordination, a sort of *ordo,* in the sense that the Church, after the Roman Republic, gave to this term. Membership was gained by means of sacramental rites, the *adscriptio,* the *sacramentum militiae* of which John of Salisbury, imbued with the Latin classics, spoke in 1159. If we take account of the rigidity of the language of charters, which prevented them from quickly reflecting changes in behavior and mental representations, we can situate in the last third of the twelfth century, at the time Benedict of Sainte-Maure was reviving the trifunctional image, a major turning point in the history of the aristocracy, which appeared earlier and more prominently in northern France.

This change is inseparable from the history of the state: a political formation that was perfecting its administrative organs and needed more and more money had to be able to identify those of its subjects who were exempt from "ignoble" taxes: these favored subjects were soon to be called gentlemen, since their freedom, their "*franchise*" or tax-exempt status actually depended on their birth. This change is inseparable from the history of the army: in the late sixties of the twelfth century, there began to be a good deal of talk in northern France of the Brabantines, of swelling hordes of mercenaries who were very capable in battle but nevertheless contemptible, in the first place because they were low-born. It is also inseparable from the history of the economy: this was the time of the great shift in the north which saw the centers of growth move into the cities, with money taking the leading role, and the number of commercial fortunes increasing, creating competitors as formidable as the mercenaries for the pedigreed nobles, who consequently rejected as base and vile the newly rich merchants whom they saw elbowing their way into seigniorial positions in festivals and culture. Finally, the new forms in which the lay portion of the ruling class had shut itself up, as in a castle or a suit of armor, were associated with a more deep-seated evolution, that of kinship structures. What little we know of this evolution entitles us to believe that around 1175, in the north of France, the heads of aristocratic lineages no longer took care to see to it that only the eldest boy married. In giving wives to younger sons, they set them up as heads of small seigniories, for which purpose they assigned portions of the patrimony, building satellite houses around the ancestral residence. In this way, the powers of adjudication and taxation of the peasants were parceled out, and the might and dignity that properly belonged to the lord began to be distributed among many hands. There was a tendency for all gentlemen to become "sires." But most of them no longer reigned over anything more than a village or a parish. They were increasingly threatened by the rise of the state and of money. Aware of their increasing vulnerability, the group of old families, whose sons, when they reached majority and had not entered the Church, had long called themselves knights, coalesced, taking shelter behind the chivalric system of values. Even peasants were at this time buying seigniories. The boundary between the "powerful" and the "poor," established by the relations of production—the boundary between the classes—was displaced imperceptibly toward the lower end of the social spectrum. Where this frontier had been, the nobility erected a new rampart. It was like the shadow or ghost of the original fortification, its imaginary form. And it was built by ideology, by ritual.

This is where a history of dubbing should be included. Jean Flori is investigating it. His task is a difficult one, since it is the history of a meaning, a signification, and of the imperceptible changes it underwent. The formal setting, the gestures by which the completion of military apprenticeship was recognized and the initiation ceremony in which the young took their places alongside the old are, so to speak, outside time, or in any case much older than the documentation allows us to see. This was a profane ritual, a family ritual, on which Christianity left its imprint, as on all social rites. It thus became a "sacrament." Its meaning then began to change, under the influence of ecclesiastical ideology. This was a complex process, for which the impetus came in the first place both from Cluny and from the proponents of the peace of God, around the year 1000. To reestablish order and safeguard ecclesiastical interests, the *militia* had to be moralized. These unruly mobs were a stormy lot and had to be bridled and given duties—the duties of kings, of the *bellatores*—and called upon to protect the "poor," avenge injustice, and fight to extend the kingdom of God. Next, the clergy attempted to apply Gelasius' theory of two parallel *ordines,* one of which, that of the laymen, would be subordinate to the other, and thus "ordered" by it. Was it not the bishops who gave the king the symbols of his power? "Priests gird kings with their swords"—these very words were spoken by Gerard of Cambrai in his dissertation on the three functions. According to the *ordo* (the word here takes on its liturgical meaning, designating the ritual) of the coronation of the kings of France, the sovereign heard a prelate say the following words: "receive this sword." Endowing the sovereign with armed might, this was the first gesture in the ceremony, preceding the coronation and the bestowal of the scepter. And was it not the Church's role to institute the other *bellatores,* the possessors of temporal power, the "ministers of the lay order," in the same way, at each level of the hierarchy down to the lowest one, that of the knights? And did not the Church in this way spread the sacralized royal ritual of conferring the sword step by step down through the hierarchy, all the way to the inviolable barrier that separated those who did not work with their hands from the rest?

Traces of the progress of these practices are rare indeed, and all poorly dated. A few scarce and doubtful points of reference stand out of the thick obscurity in which the prehistory of dubbing is shrouded: these are contained in liturgical manuals. But all we have are scattered debris, tiny vestiges of some of the least well-preserved holdings of the episcopal libraries—and who can say where and when the prescriptions these *ordines* contain were really observed? I pass over the oldest testimony, provided by Egbert's *Pontifical,* written in the tenth century: it is Anglo-Saxon; moreover, the formula it prescribes for the benediction of arms, swords, lances, hauberks, and helmets is associated with prayers for the king and his accompanying soldiers; this was probably a special ritual intended to consecrate the royal army about to embark on a campaign, with the aim of infusing the entire troop with the charismas that in peacetime were the privilege of the sovereign. The study of texts that seem to have been concerned with northern France can help us to identify two periods that were particularly innovative in this field of liturgical practice.

The first of these is slightly prior to the first crusade. In the late eleventh century in Burgundy and Lotharingia, the text of pontificals used in the east Frankish kingdom, and particularly that of the *Romano-Germanic,* compiled at Mainz between 950 and 963,[8] ended with formulas for the "benediction of the newly girded sword." Then there is one from a manuscript said to have been written in the Besançon region in the second half of the eleventh century:[9] "When the young man [*juvenis,* i.e., the adult bachelor trained in the use of arms] wishes to buckle on the sword for the first time, benediction of the sword"; at this point in the officiant's invocation to God an allusion to trifunctionality slips in, which is fully consistent with the image in Gerard of Cambrai's mind: "God, who established three degrees [*gradus*—degrees, not functions; but clearly the latter are involved, the military taking up a position between the two others, with the mission of protecting the Christian people against the invisible enemy] of men after the sin of Adam, so that they faithful people may remain secure and peaceful, defended against any malicious attack. . . ." Another manuscript, written sometime around 1093 at Cambrai—yes, Cambrai[10]—includes a "ritual [*ordo*] for arming a defender [*defensor*] of the Church or other knight"—and there is reason to believe that these were actually rites undergone by those "knights of Lorraine" of whom Gerard had spoken: after the banner, lance, and sword, the warrior himself is blessed; just as he would ordain the clergy of the diocese, the bishop "ordains" the knights of the episcopal church and confers on them the cross-belt and the sword; he then pronounces words that are adapted from the royal rite; and, finally, he invokes the militant saints, Maurice, Sebastian, and George. With a ceremony created in the last decades of the eleventh century, on the strength of gestures and words, the functions and duties of kings were thus transferred to all sword-bearing men, to the entire body of knights. The specialists in war were, as a group, sacralized by rites of *consecratio*, which are clearly homologous with the rites of royal enthronement and sacerdotal ordination.

A second high-point occurred in the last third of the twelfth century. In the interim, knightly values had flourished, being magnified in the enthusiasm of expeditions to Jerusalem, while perfection of the techniques of mounted combat made the knights' manner of doing battle ever more distinctive. These values were heightened in the tournaments, for which the vogue reached such proportions in northern France that in 1130 the Church thought it well to condemn these mock-battles, occasions for intolerable displays of profane violence. In book 6 of the *Policraticus*, speaking of knights, who "in our day go to war as to weddings, dressed in white," John of Salisbury noted that they were doubly instituted, "corporally and spiritually," by a choice and by a sacrament: *electio, sacramentum*. In 1159, John was twisting the reality and adapting it to the shape of his dreams. When, like his fellow student, Otto of Freising, he evokes the "equestrian order," he has his eyes riveted on the fascinating models of Roman antiquity. In the theory of the state he constructs, he judges that it should be up to the sovereign to recruit those who will bear arms in his support; he imagines knights pledging themselves as legionnaires had done, "swearing by God, Christ, and the Holy Ghost, and by the majesty of the prince." Not all of this was a figment of his imagination, however. When he subsequently comes to define the function of knighthood thus institutionalized—or "of the order of knights" (*ordinata militia*)—he adds:[11] "It is now the solemn custom [or the rite: *consecratio* is the word used in connection with kings, as well as with spouses joined by the nuptial benediction] for the knight that on the day he receives the military cross-belt, he should enter the church solemnly, lay the sword on the altar, and, having thus made the offering as a sign of solemn profession, that he pledge himself to the service of the altar and promise God to place himself in the service of his sword, that is, of his function." The sword is the emblem of the knightly function—as the crown is of the royal function—and the knight swears to serve it. In the ritual as described here, which seems to have become more strict since the *ordines* of

Besançon and Cambrai were composed, this symbolic object plays a role analogous to that of the *schedula* in the consecration of the bishops. It bears witness to a pledge. It serves as a visible, tangible reference to the obligations undertaken. John of Salisbury considers it necessary, however, to note that this ceremony is subject to a different interpretation, a secular one, governed by an antagonistic ideological system: "some are seen, thus issuing a call to wrongdoing, protesting, when they place the cross-belt on the altar for military consecration, that they come with the intention of declaring war on the altar, on its ministers, and on God who is worshiped here. I shall believe that they are rather damned by malice [*malitia*] than consecrated in legitimate knighthood [*militia*]." [12]

It seems clear that during the twenty-five years following the publication of the *Policraticus,* i.e., in the period when the trifunctional schema once again appeared to buttress certain ideological pronouncements, in the period when the vocabulary of the charters attests that in social practice knighthood was indeed recognized as an order, the dubbing ceremony rapidly acquired new elements. In his treatise *On Correct Princely Conduct,* [13] the Cistercian Helinand of Froidmont adds a supplementary note to John of Salisbury's text to report a custom which he says was beginning to spread: the knight's vigil, a religious rite—consisting of nocturnal prayer, in the manner of monks—but also a test of physical endurance: "in some places, it is customary for the knight who is to be consecrated the following day to spend the whole night in vigil and prayer, not allowed to sit or lie down." The cited texts are authority enough, I think, for situating an essential phase of the history of dubbing in the seventh and eighth decades of the twelfth century. [14] The development of courtly culture solidified the moral edifice. Under the eye of the prince, the military order retrenched there as in a fortress. It was resigned—since it had to defend its privileges at all costs—to submitting at last to the admonitions of the clergy; resigned to lending an ear to sermons (modeled on those of Alan of Lille [15]) specially prepared for it, which consequently had the effect of distinguishing it from the rest of the faithful; resigned to discovering in each new romance of Chrétien de Troyes that the word "knighthood" was little by little acquiring a new meaning, which slowly effaced the original, quite concrete sense of military profession that it still had in Erec, coming insted to take on the idea of courtliness, of moral rigor and finally, in *Perceval,* becoming the verbal symbol for rejection of the world of flesh. [16] The vocabulary of the *chansons de geste*—that literary genre that reflects the semantic shift that took place in the area of social ritual all the better for having become common, banal, for having been forsaken by the inventions of genius—has been subjected to a remarkable study by Jean Flori, whose work has focussed on the level of language, "a good deal more revealing of behavior and the unconscious than the themes and motifs wittingly introduced by authors"; he puts the point appositely:[17] "after 1180, the knights no longer formed merely a professional or socio-professional body; they were tending rather to constitute a 'college,' recruiting members by cooptation, by ritual installation." Elsewhere he adds that knighthood "took up the ethic that had been offered to it for more than a century and adopted it as its own moral code, thus becoming an *ordo,* which justified its existence as such *a posteriori.*"[18]

Now it was in this same period that princes raised knighthood to the first rank among their dignities, that they began to give special commemoration to the ceremony of their own dubbing. Before the solemn ceremonials associated with the conferral of arms were simplified in connection with their adoption for the purpose of instituting knights in their order, it seems quite likely that they had long been used as public manifestations of the accession to the responsibilities of power of the heir of a king, a duke, or a count. We may refer to this original function, that of ritual celebration, to explain why the remembrance of dubbing came to occupy such a prominent place, from the end of the eleventh century on, in princely biography, in the autobiography of Fulk le Réchin, or in eulogies to William the Conqueror. It should be noted that quite early—as early as 1020 in the southern part of the kingdom, around 1100 in the Mâcon region[19]—powerful men thought it worthwhile to add the title *miles* to that of *dominus* in the charters granted in their name. But at the moment the custom of calling all knights *messire* took hold, princes took to celebrating their own knighthood more than ever. The counts of Guines, for instance: the priest Lambert, who wrote the history of their lineage in about 1200, was careful to gratify count Baldwin by noting that he had been dubbed by Thomas Becket around 1165; on the subject of the count's eldest son, the real hero of his tale, Lambert felt that the one event (which he describes at great length) worthy of being assigned a precise date—Pentecost, 1181—was the day of his dubbing. Henry II, too, expected to hear the initiation ceremony described at length when the life of his father, Geoffrey, written by John of Marmoutier, was read to him. For in his eyes, this was an essential rite of passage, set between the wedding feast and the marriage ceremony, i.e., at the heart of the two-part ritual that united the heir of the county of Anjou to the heiress of Normandy and the kingdom of England, preparing the way for the ascendancy of the Plantagenets over all other terrestrial powers. Henry was undoubtedly quite pleased that the docile writer depicted only the profane portion of this ceremony, speaking of the ritual bath as a mere preparation of the body, alluding to its sacred aspect only in recalling the day chosen: Pentecost, the moment the Holy Spirit spread over mankind. Finally, in 1184, the Emperor Frederick himself had the idea of staging the splendid celebration I mentioned earlier as a setting for the dubbing of his sons.

Bear in mind that at the end of the twelfth century dubbing was not an individual affair. It was a solemn ceremony of power, public and collective.

The prince was the master of ceremonies. The occasion was one for him to display his largesse. Along with his son—in the last days of his "childhood" preparing to leave home to embark on the grand sporting tour of "youth" (another ritual) in search of "glory"—the prince armed the boy's *commilitones,* comrades of the same age who had learned the profession with him and would follow him into battle. The "new knight" paraded before the court. At the head of a fresh crop of warriors marched the prince of youth, the prince of the generation making ready to carry the banner on. Heir apparent of the lord, he would lead the heirs apparent of all the vassals, in order, to adventure. On this vernal day of grace, the young men were "conscripts" in the true sense of the word, inscribed together in the *ordo.* Consecration confirmed in them the virtues they owed to their blood, to their gentle birth. On the occasion that marked their coming of age, the offspring of the "knights of the fatherland" promised to exemplify virtues that served to tighten the bonds that unified the new levy of recruits around the young man who would soon be prince, who would soon receive their homage and expect their loyal service. But on that particular day he would undergo the same ritual institution as the others, for the moment asking no more than to appear first among equals.

Thus on each successive Pentecost, the prince's proclaimed solidarity with his knights was reaffirmed. To him, its value was clear. The dubbing ceremony countered the tendency inherent in feudalism toward disintegration, at a time when the vulgarization of the emblems of sovereignty, henceforth the property of every knight, was reaching its peak; it also countered that other movement launched by the Church at the time of the Gregorian struggles, when it attempted to set the "knights of Christ" against the "schismatics," i.e., the simonist sovereigns; dubbing further helped to reconcile the *militia* with the prince (and at the same time briefly helped to alleviate the antagonism between the head of the family and his sons, particularly acute in the house of Plantagenet). It established indissoluble bonds between knighthood and the monarchy in northern France at the end of the twelfth century; when they took communion, all the members of the lay aristocracy shared respect for a common system of values, a common conception of merit, and a common duty, shouldered jointly by the first among the knights, who led, and the last, who served.

PREEMINENCE

The danger was that the prince would be lost among the knights. The table was round, and the knights were Arthur's peers, were they not? Was knighthood's dream—in his account of Bouvines, the Minstrel of Rheims was still poking up its ashes at the end of the thirteenth century—not to envelop the sovereign completely and absorb him into itself? To this threat there were two parries.

The first of these was the etiquette that governed court life. In the prince's household—which in northwestern France still sheltered a large company of domestic knights; which served as gathering place for the sons of vassals come to train in the use of arms; and which was used to receive traveling friends and to welcome the crowd of the faithful who came to mark the periodic ceremonies of suzerainty; but which housed a growing number of "masters," living on their patron's largesse, who were increasingly often not of noble but of "low" birth—the *senior* preferred to throw in his lot with the knightly portion of his entourage. With the knights he laughed at the others. Nevertheless, he meant to keep his distance, and no knight was supposed to entertain the slightest doubt that of the body of knights the prince was indeed the head. The master asserted his superiority by assuming the role of the generous purveyor of "pleasure." He kept the knights entertained by organizing their combats, and in the interim with court games. These games were played according to strict rules, respect for which was the backbone of what was properly speaking the courtly ethic. The play was presided over by a trinity. Another triad, closer, perhaps, than all the others to Dumézil's. Three persons. Three functions. Three moral requirements. The lord, seated, in the great hall or the chapel, praying, speaking, surrounded by clerics, laying down the law, paragon of justice and temperance; his wife, mistress of the interior, of provisions, of the bedchamber, always pregnant, begetting the progeny who would make the lineage illustrious, fecund, fertile, distributing abundance in careful measure: prudence was her virtue; the heir, finally, the "youth," whose province lay outside the house, a horseman destined for the tournament field or for battle, facing danger, reaping glory, throwing money about with abandon, of whom it was hoped that in default of other virtues he might possess the fourth cardinal one, strength. With this three-part bridle the prince held his knights in check.

The game was for the prince to control the knights' revels without arousing their suspicions, by using the two other persons as decoys. His son led the young warriors off to adventure, to wounds and woe, relieving the court of their boisterous presence. His wife was allowed to become the focus of their sham desires. In the forests and camps the youths dreamed of laying hands on her. Their elders chatted with her daily. In what is called "courtly" love—that joust, that succession of thrusts and withdrawals, analogous to the virtuosity of the tournament—the "lady," the master's wife, was the prize. Not the "maiden," silly little goose, who was taken at once, either by trickery or of her own free will. The lady. Her cunning prudence made her a worthy partner, because the outcome of the match had to be in doubt. So that the suitors could be locked tightly into a regime of obligations and services. Through the game of love, as much as by military exercises, the young man was initiated, learned to control his violence, to reduce it to order. In the game of love the knights claimed to be the sole participants—

and for the lord this offered another means of domesticating them, by surreptitiously bringing a few clerks or peasants from his court into the issue. From behind the scenes he manipulated the game. He refereed, from the sidelines, and in so doing clearly distinguished himself from the others. He, too, had been young in his time, and he clung to his youthful memories, which linked him to the knightly *ordo*. But he had lived life through. And life had taken him far, had made him *caput mansi*, "head of household." A father. Presiding over a fraternity, like an abbot over a monastery. And like the abbot, offering an example, exhibiting an "image"—that of God, or, at other times, that of the devil. In charge, in any case. Inspiring fear with his "ire"; administering discipline. Parading the mirror that he alone wielded constantly through the land, so that all might see the reflection of the three functions, perfectly fulfilled by the three persons of the domestic trinity.

The second of the two parries mentioned above was none other than the principle of social trifunctionality. The knights were not alone. Around the master were two other "kinds" of men, two other "orders." After his dubbing and marriage, and, later, at each summer's end, at the conclusion of his knightly adventures, the prince returned to his seat, to his household. The knights in his escort dismounted with him. It was essential that they get along with the clergy and the populace. In his wisdom, the master sought to maintain peace among the three orders, by making equitable distribution of his favors. Which is what Duke Robert is doing in Benedict of Sainte-Maure's *Estoire,* when he gives satisfaction first to the poor knight, but not only to him. He shows equal largesse to the clerk and the artisan. If the prince is a knight, he is not merely a knight. Knighthood was no longer the whole court. This is what the trifunctional figure asserted, for the purpose of augmenting the strength of the state. It was for this reason that it was revived: to place knighthood under the monarch's domination.

Because the monarch boasted of his knighthood, however, the knights were shown as surpassing the other orders in importance. Their preeminence had already been announced by Benedict of Sainte-Maure, not so much in his formulation of the tripartite schema as by the structure of the anecdotes he recounts. This became more apparent in the years subsequent to the completion of the *Estoire,* when every writer of the vulgar tongue gave expression to it, Chrétien de Troyes most clearly of all. In *Perceval* (1182–91), he describes the hero's dubbing, at the heart of the ritual:

> Et le prud'homme a pris l'épée
> L'en a ceint, et puis le baisa.
> Et dit que donné lui a
> Le plus haut ordre avec l'épée
> Que Dieu ait fait et commandé.
> C'est l'ordre de chevalerie,
> Qui doit être sans vilenie.[20]

[And the *prud'homme* took the sword, girded it on him [Perceval], and then kissed him. And said that with the sword had been given him the highest order that God had made and commanded. This is the order of knighthood, which must be without baseness.]

The only remaining problem was then to explain this priority. This was nowhere done with greater arrogance then in the continuation of *Perceval,* the vulgate *Lancelot* (written when? about 1215–25?).[21] In this text, too, the occasion for the discussion of the problem is provided by the account of the dubbing. Lancelot has just turned eighteen. The Lady of the Lake (note that the task of initiation now falls to a woman, another sign of the very rapid development of courtly values) reveals the meaning of "knighthood" to him, beginning with its origins, *ab initio*–like Gerard of Cambrai evoking the institution of the three functional categories. In the beginning the children of God were free and equal. But soon violence won out over righteousness. Then knighthood was established, to put an end to the chaos. "And when the weak could stand no more and could hold out no longer against the strong, they set above themselves [it is no longer God, but men who take the initiative; knighthood does not originate with a decision of the Creator, but is the result of a social contract; here we have complete desacralization, which leads straight to Jean de Meung and a good deal farther beyond] protectors and defenders to protect the weak and peaceful, to rule according to law, and to hold the strong responsible for the wrongs and offenses they commit [*debellare superbos,* to check the effrontery of the powerful, function of kings and of Geoffrey Plantagenet, the prince]. To provide this protection those whose worth exceeds that of the common run of men were established. These were the great, and the strong, and the handsome, and the fleet of foot, and the loyal, and the stout, and the hardy. Men full of goodness of heart and body. In the beginning, when the knightly order began, he who would be a knight, had the attributes, given him by direct election [John of Salisbury's *electio,* but here in the form of a gift of birth, a genetic quality], of compassion, of freedom from baseness, of compliance without treachery, of pity for the suffering, and of liberality [every word of this admirable prose strikes home, expressing the whole knightly ethic in perfectly concise form]. And ready to help the needy, ready and able to foil thieves and murderers. . . . Knights were also established to protect the Holy Church. For it ought not to avenge itself by arms, nor repay one wrong with another." The Lady then discloses the meaning of the emblematic attributes: the sword has two edges because "the knight is to be sergeant of our Lord and his people"; but its tip "is different, the tip of the sword signifies obedience, for all men must obey the knight" (here the major shift finds expression: recall that for Adalbero, all men, including kings, had to obey the clergy). The horse, for its part, symbolizes the people: "for, like the horse, the people must support the knight in all his needs . . . because the

304

knight guards and protects them night and day. And the knight is placed above the people. For just as whoever is seated on the horse guides it and leads it wherever he wants to go, the knight's will must guide the people justly made subject thereto, under him, as the people should be." But what about the Church? That is, "the clergy by which the Holy Church is to be served, and the widows, and orphans, and the tithe, and the alms that are established in the Holy Church"? "Just as the people uphold the knight on the land and provide him with what he needs, so must the Holy Church uphold him in the spirit, and provide him with eternal life. This it does by prayer and alms, so that God may eternally be his savior."

If trifunctionality is taken as the keystone of the ideological system, this, as can be seen clearly here, is to prove that knighthood is entitled to be "served" by the two other social categories, the people and the clergy. The whole ungainly edifice, with its two wings, corporeal and spiritual, was built for the needs of knighthood, the latter being clearly identified with royalty. With a slight shift in orientation, the model came to be used to celebrate chivalry's triumph. Did not its brilliant success in so doing threaten to destroy the hierarchies of the princely household, to invite the victory of the *imago juventutis* over *sapientia,* and of the sovereign's son over his father—i.e., the very subversion denounced by Adalbero, disorder, youth scoffing at its elders, Henry II dying naked, his sons risen against him? Perhaps. But the primary purpose of celebrating this triumph was to assert the preeminence of the knight-princes over the king of France.

When it returned to currency, the trifunctional figure initially served in the struggle against the Capetian revival being waged by the Plantagenets and the other heads of "feudal states," by the count of Champagne and by Philip of Alsace, count of Flanders, a direct descendant of the Carolingians who perhaps dreamed of one day inheriting the Frankish crown and for whom Chrétien de Troyes wrote *Perceval.* Bear in mind that the ideological system set forth in such splendid style by the Lady of the Lake reached the peak of its power when this rivalry was most acute, and, furthermore, that it was the largesse of the princes, not that of the king, that enabled that system to find its most substantial, and captivating, forms of expression, apt to strike roots in minds in every corner of the world, and enduringly. Its first champion was not Henry II, king of England, but rather Henry, duke of Normandy, descendant of Fulk the Good, count of Anjou—*strenuus miles* as the latter was said to have been, swaggering, seductive, eclipsing by the renown of his prowess and magnificence the *presbiter ordinatus,* Louis VII, of whom Eleanor, his wife, is supposed to have admitted—and she was no novice in these matters—that he behaved not like a king but like a monk. Forged along with the new etiquette in the eighth decade of the twelfth century, the notion of a knightly order securely paramount over the two others was the weapon with which a fierce ideological battle was waged on two fronts. First, against the ideology of the priests—and the situation was at that moment one of extreme tension between the two powers, spiritual and temporal, not only in England, but also in the Empire. Second, against the king (but was the enemy not actually the same?), against the powers of anointment, against the schools of Paris to which the English clergy were flocking in haste, and where the memory of Thomas Becket was venerated.

A fight of this kind was apt to attract the support of youth, of the new knights who in laying their swords on the altar were declaring war on God, who pretended not to understand Latin because it was the language of the confessors, who derided Cistercian preaching in their zest to enjoy life, and who were not unmindful of the fact that clerks were often proving more successful in winning the favors of the chosen lady than they were. This is why the superiority of knighthood and its efforts to lay claim to *clergie*—in the sense of learning, high culture—were so lavishly praised, far away from Paris. *Clergie* had the same value that Cicero attributed to rhetoric: it taught one to behave as an *honnête homme*. It involved a culture different, however, from that of the clerks—though it drew upon clerical culture, it was not dispensed directly by the school. *Clergie* was supposed to be the fruit of education of a different sort, imparted step by step, like scholastic knowledge, in the course of a long initiatory peregrination—albeit in this case secular and military, a "courtly" progress.

There were three stages. First came the dubbing at Pentecost, looked upon by the knights as the clerks looked upon the arts of the *trivium*. Then came adventure, forbidden to peasants, excluding the base—this was the equivalent of the clerical quest, wherein the clerk went from master to master, closeting himself away in a Cistercian cloister for a period of meditation. Adventure roved over a map whose two poles were the court and the forest—and whose imaginary topology deliberately omitted the intervening territory, the fields, the villages, the countryside that the knights laid waste as they galloped through abreast, flower in hand; churches, too, were omitted, both the Church and the peasantry being looked upon with contempt. The court was the zone governed by the laws of high society, in which the man of war was pleased to disport himself in the company of ladies and maids—the role attributed to seduction expressed the aggressive attitude of chivalrous ideology toward its Gregorian counterpart, its rejection of matrimonial confinement, and its taste for abduction and pleasure. The forest (in fact, the strip bordering the plains, the vast field of ambuscade, hunting, and tournaments) was the dominion of the wild, the untamed, of weird dangers that had to be faced alone (whereas in the realities of war and the hunt, the knight never dared abandon his group; why this dream of solitude? need for escape? remembrance of ancient rites of initiation? symbol of a search for perfection which, in the Cistercian manner, was little by little internalized, personalized?). The forest was an antiworld, good to immerse oneself in

306

periodically (the contacts between Cistercians and knights actually came about in the course of their comparable efforts to gain control over the disorder of the forest) a place where the strong might well catch a glimpse of what lay behind the gates of wisdom and the sacred. And here these gates were held ajar not by a clerk but by a hermit, one divinely deranged—in other words, disobedient, restive under the bishop's command—one who skirted heresy and was denounced by the canons (for Payen Bolotin, canon of Chartres, the hermit was merely a loutish upstart, respecting neither nobility nor valor) and yet was chosen by Chrétien in *Perceval* to give voice to the whole morality of the *miles Christi* in very simple terms: knighthood permitted none but the hermit to bring it any part of the message of the gospels. As for the third stage of the knight's education, it always lay in the future: it was the place of dreams, inaccessible, always receding, a mirage—did Saint Bernard not look upon this as the highest degree of love? It was the hoped-for end of the quest, where a man might lay hands on the object of that desire that drove him from the peaceful pleasures of the court to wander through the bush from ordeal to ordeal.

Such was the course of instruction which every prince in the late twelfth century took, in the company of his comrades, his knights, his vassals, and his fellow princes. The structure of a school of this kind encouraged the union of the two natures of which Adalbero spoke, the juvenile and the sober, the coupling of the two values, "youth" and "wisdom." It was vastly superior to the priestly school to which the king's sons were sent. It did not disparage the value of pleasure. All of this was first committed to writing by the court clergy in the service of Henry Plantagenet. But the echo of what they had to say could be heard within a generation reverberating through every court in northern France; around 1180 one might have encountered it in the courts of the counts of Flanders and Champagne, and ten years later in the minuscule court of the count of Guines.

This knightly education was warmly welcomed by what remained of the desire for feudal independence, sharpening resistance to the Capetian invasion. It sustained the latter as effectively as the casks of silver deniers sent by the king of England. Its success was responsible for that of the trifunctional figure in its new guises. But this success ran up against an obstacle. Paradoxically, what got in the way were the same deep structures that a century and half earlier had underpinned the original pronouncements of the theory of social trifunctionality in this region. The obstacle was royal France, that of Adalbero, of Saint-Denis—the pseudo-Dionysius the Areopagite—of Suger, of the new cathedrals, the France of the royal portals. The obstacle was Paris, treasure and symbol of a kingdom allied with the pope, with the bishops, with the reformed Church, with the school, with the communes, with the people.

23

PARISIAN RESISTANCE

Burgeoning to the full, the economy exhibited an ever increasing versatility, as did all forms of social relations. Men traveled about more easily than ever before, and tournament champions and enthusiasts for learning alike took to the highways in search of others of their ilk. This made possible an exclusive concentration of the most advanced scholarly work in Paris during the last third of the twelfth century. Both the French king and the pope wanted it thus, reckoning that if theological research was centered in one location, the work would be easier to control and the atmosphere more stimulating. Face-to-face rivalry would spur each scholar to outstrip the next, to labor with greater enthusiasm in honing the weaponry Christendom needed in its two great undertakings: the one external—the crusade; the other internal—the moral reformation of *societas christiana*. The clergy was responsible for both. As a result of its efforts to exert more effective control over the campaigns, clerical ideology had been strengthened, concurrently with the reinforcement of chivalrous ideology. The feudal princes collaborated in the efflorescence of the latter ideology. The former was aided by the king—sacred, he brought all his powers to bear on the task.

The ascetic imperative remained central to clerical ideology, but it had undergone two alterations. The first was due to Cistercian influence, whose effect was to shift the focus of concern from repression of the concupiscence of the body to stimulation of the concupiscence of the soul, i.e., the love of God. Second, moving from the monastery to the secular Church, asceticism contributed to the worldly activities of the reformed chapters, models of the "good life." In an air of heightened purity, the works of the "authors" were studied in pursuit of a single goal: the discovery of the ineffable. The rose window in Laon cathedral's north transept expressed this aim in distinctive fashion, exhibiting seven sources of light, each of them associated with one of the liberal arts, swirling around a central focus, wisdom, paying it court, setting it off, exalting it—encircling wisdom with a perfect crown consisting of the variegated jewels of learning; a splendid ornament, and yet discreet, no more obtrusive in the bare stone wall of perfectly cut Cistercian stone than were the sober initial letters on the austere pages of the great Clairvaux Bible.

The mission of the good clerks—analogous to that of the "good men" of Catharism—was to spread the Spirit among the Christian people. They made up several companies—the foremost of which took in the elements of monasticism that were most vital—upon which a magistracy was formally conferred by the pope and the king of France, allies, battling together against the "tyrants," heretics, schismatics, simoniacs, and the two fearsome rivals they shared: the kings of Germany and England. A clear-cut delegation of the real power, the disciplinary authority, was made to the heads of these *scholae*—the masters. Thereupon a new domination began: that of the doctors, knowledgeable, loquacious, and lording it over their students. Just as the prince tolerated an identification of his knights with himself, up to a point, emulating accordingly the bravery of the boldest of them, so the bishop allowed himself to become one of the *magistri,* trying to rival the most skilled preachers, and making a point of his preeminence only in exerting the sacramental powers that were his exclusively, while priding himself on his youthful accomplishments as a scholar much as the princes commemorated their dubbing. Before long the sculptors would be commissioned to work on an effigy of Christ intended for the pillar of the cathedral's central portal—a Christ no longer represented as a judge and not yet as an agonizing martyr, but rather as a doctor, serene, holding a book in his left hand: expressive of the ineluctable rise of the power of the intellectuals, of the association of masters and students and of the *universitas* they comprised.

This power was centered in Paris. Paris—the city in which the king had been born and which he cherished above all others, the city that in 1212 he decided to girdle with walls, ordering that the area within them be populated to the full.[1] In Paris was completed the "translation of studies" from Greece and Rome. Toward Paris hastened all the intellectual adventurers, all the young men eager to rise in the Church, all the would-be bishops and popes. And on Paris the Roman curia pinned its hopes, its major concern between the third Lateran council (1179) and the fourth (1215)—as it faced an increasingly worrisome onslaught of heresy—being to crown the Gregorian achievements with a regimentation of the lay populace intended to enforce doctrinal conformity and moral regularity. This was a pragmatic and clear-cut program, to the improvement of which all the Parisian masters, "artists" and scriptural commentators alike, were invited to contribute.

Accordingly, they were asked to focus more systematic attention on the social sphere. Which they did, thereby inaugurating that period in the history of scholasticism that fills the hiatus between the logical abstraction of the early twelfth century and the metaphysical abstraction of the thirteenth: the era of Peter the Chanter of Notre-Dame of Paris,[2] who worked in the company of a whole group of colleagues, including Robert of Courçon, Stephen Langton, and his students Fulk of Neuilly and James of Vitry. Motivated by a desire to see more clearly—the same desire that impelled others of their contemporaries to work at perfecting optical instruments—these scholars employed the same methods and pursued the same goals as their predecessors. Their investigations continued along the same lines as those whose first results had been divulged by Honorius Augustodunensis and that Hugh of Saint-Victor had carried on to new discoveries. Their efforts went toward refining their predecessor's ideas about social organization in order to make them more practicable and to bring them into line with the needs of the pastoral mission. Thus simultaneously, two imposing ideological structures were erected side by side: where the influence of Henry Plantagenet was paramount, the trifunctional schema molded a knightly version of society; at the same time the clergy produced its own version, based on clear-sighted observation of particulars. The latter, accordingly, was the less simple version. It dispensed with trifunctionality, which had just recently been set aside by the commentators on the Apocalypse.

Unlike its rival, this clerical version was not writ large and posted everywhere to attract the widest possible audience. It emerged slowly from painstaking research that might well be called sociological. Only rarely do the remnants of the writings of the schools permit us to glimpse its overall contours. More frequently its constituent parts come down to us dismembered, and depending on the case may appear in the context of a biblical commentary or transpire from the categories used in a typology of the sermon. John Baldwin has drawn my attention to one of the rare passages to divulge the whole rib-work over which the ideological veil has been cast: a page of James of Vitry's *History of the West*.[3] This work treats of the internal problems of Christendom. As mentioned above, the papacy was engaged in battle on two fronts. On one, the crusading spirit spearheaded the drive to Jerusalem; despite the discouraging failure of 1190, the great dream persisted tenaciously. On injunction from Rome, Fulk, curate of Neuilly, preached a pilgrimage to recapture the tomb of Christ, fallen into the hands of the infidels, first addressing his own flock and later, in 1195–96, exhorting the people of Paris; the masters all joined in the venture, moreover, urging Christendom to purify itself, since God, incensed, was refusing to lead his people to victory. Once again the air resounded with the words of the popular preachers of the eleventh century, men who had mobilized masses with talk of equality in poverty. James of Vitry reverted to their line of argument, glorifying Peter the Hermit in his *Historia orientalis*. Of later date (1223–25), the *History of the West* complements this earlier work. It pointed out what needed to be done on the second front, the home front, within Christendom itself, by way of reform.

The treatise consists of three parts. The first is a lament of corruption in the world, responsible for the defeat of the crusaders. Here James of Vitry tells his own story, recounting his erstwhile arrival in Paris—Babylon—and his amazement at the virulence of sin. Over the course of the twelfth century, the rift between urban and rural society had in fact widened. Shut up in the sprawling city, larger and denser with each passing day, the Parisian masters saw the countryside from a remote vantage point; they imagined it as a place where nature had not been adulterated by artifice, constantly purged by salutary labor, whereas they looked upon the city as a place of perdition. There evil was constantly being reborn, pullulating amidst the clatter of deniers on the benches of the money changers and in alleyways rife with bathhouses and brawls. Over the city reigned the *infelix ternarius*—the ternarity of misfortune—pride, cupidity, lasciviousness. Heresy, too, reigned supreme: it was said to be a creature of the forests, but everyone knew that in reality its lairs were urban. The *History of the West* opened with a brief—and urbane—treatise on lust, for good reason: it was essential to stake out claims to the rich vein waiting to be worked, where already eager prospectors—preachers of every sort following in the footsteps of Fulk of Neuilly and Peter the Chanter—were crowding in to claim their share in the redressment of morals. The work was hard. It took heart from the venerable ideal of *contemptus mundi,* the renunciation of worldly allures. Accordingly, the second part of the book was devoted entirely to monasticism, which offered logistical support for this kind of warfare. The third book, finally, considered the sacraments dispensed by the clergy, whose role was to do whatever could be done to restore to the perverted society of the streets and squares the radiant order of which monastic society was the most perfect exemplar. The portrait of the social order figures at the precise point where this final section is joined to the preceding one. What had been taught thirty years earlier in the schools of Notre-Dame was therein compiled and summarized (quite late in the game: Guillaume de Lorris may already have begun work on the *Roman de la Rose*).

The worldly needed guidance if they were to find their way to the good. Was not the best course of action to aid them in establishing lines of communication between the outer world and the purified confines of the cloister, by building bridges from the one to the other, and by fostering the slow osmosis whereby mankind made its way back to its original unity—back to paradise? Accordingly, was it not advisable, if not to eliminate, at least to lessen the height of the barriers that in the thought of Saint Jerome and Saint Augustine kept the three degrees of perfection—lay, clerical, and monastic—separate from one another? In order to eliminate the obstacles, as had been done in the interiors of the Gothic cathedrals, to the unimpeded passage of light, that Dionysian, life-giving, unifying light, whose earthly source was the righteous monastery. Listen to the words of James of Vitry: "We regard as regulars not only those who renounce the world and convert to religion, but all the faithful of Christ"; in effect, everyone followed a rule, namely, the Gospel (which was the only rule: so much had been said before by the author of the rule of Grandmont, and now the same message was being repeated by Francis of Assisi); by virtue of that rule, everyone was in holy orders, "ordained under one abbot superior and supreme, Jesus" (Christ as abbot rather than king or, as he would be later on, doctor: representing the triumph of Saint Benedict, at a time when only vestiges of Benedictine monasticism remained in a world that was rapidly losing its rural character); "hence we may also call them regulars." Unity was to come from the rule, from order, from discipline. The intention was not different from Gerard of Cambrai's. Nor was it different in any fundamental respect from the utopia of the heretics of Arras, from the hopes of Cluny, from the dreams of the crusade, nor from what the Cistercian Joachim of Flora was even then anticipating from a future age of mankind: that all Christian society would unite in brotherhood, under the paternal rule of a *magister,* whereupon the "orders" would be abolished. In like fashion, just after the year 1000, on the eve of the end of time, all differences had been seen to evaporate in that prefiguration of paradise, the Benedictine community, where one could feel the beat of angels' wings. And now in the fervent groups of scholars, too, all differences were being attenuated. At the time James of Vitry wrote this page, the school was brimming over with vitality, and the monastery was in decline. But the rule of life—which more and more clerks and laymen chose to impose upon themselves—was still comparable to a net that little by little caught imperfect, sinful, restive men in its toils and held them fast, as their flawed natures required, to be hauled off to the provinces of perfection where the monks were already stationed.

"Clerks and priests who remain in the world," James of Vitry continued, "also have their rules and their observances and institutions peculiar to their orders." The clergy, with its hierarchy and its ranks, was certainly an order. A more important point, however, was that "there is also a special order of married people, another of widows, and still another of virgins." Intent on passing a moral collar around the neck of all society, James reverted to the venerable ecclesiastical classification whereby men and women were grouped according to their merits, i.e., their sexual activity. It should be noted, moreover, that masculine continence was here accorded no place: the perfect order required that no adult male layman be celibate; the man who was not of the Church, whether regular or secular, had no value and no place in any *ordo* except through marriage.

So there were five "orders": three for men, two for women. James of Vitry did not stop at this, however. He was preoccupied with the needs of his fellow clerks, who would have to be supplied with the proper intellectual equipment for spreading the word of God. Sins and temptations were not uniformly distributed among the men and women in their audience. A skilled preacher needed to know his way around this varied terrain, needed to be able to tell one feature from another, so that he could sharpen his aim and ferret out the evil he was vilifying. Sex was, of course, the primary source of corruption—which meant that Jerome's orders of merit were the first to be invoked. But money, too, was a cause of decay, and in the city quite a virulent germ, which made a more minute classification imperative, a classification based in this case on occupation. Wage-earning was obviously intended here, and to this matter Peter the Chanter and his friends devoted much thought. Only men were involved: there was but one female "trade," prostitution, prostitutes being the only women paid for their physical labor. The sketch of the social organization drawn up by James of Vitry was thus extended by a further classification: "furthermore," he said, "knights, merchants, farmers, craftsmen, and other kinds of men, multifarious, also have their rules and institutions in accordance with the different varieties of talents [a reference to money] loaned by the Lord." "Multifarious": the word is indicative of an awareness of the diversity due to the division of labor, of the proliferation in the city of offices, functions, "crafts" that even as James of Vitry was writing were being institutionalized, as guilds, governed by prescribed regulations, by "rules." These, too, had their hierarchies, which Jacques was careful to observe, concluding his list with the workers of the *faubourgs*. Above them were the peasants (who usually went unmentioned, since they received no wages), then the merchants, and finally the knights. No sooner had this hierarchy been outlined, however, than it was subsumed in yet another bodily metaphor, which softened its impact. These various "kinds" of men were represented by the "several limbs," each assigned "particular functions," but united "in the body of the Church, under one head, Christ." Other images are brought in to add emphasis: the profusion of colors in Joseph's coat, the many stopping places along the road to the Promised Land. All evoke the idea of diversity—an attention-getting diversity. The danger of disintegration was warded off by the striving to achieve unanimity: to live, whatever the cost, in communion under one faith, to rally under the crozier of a single guide.

Such was society as James of Vitry imagined it. As we descend from its monastic heights to the bedrock of laymen, we pass from the simple to the diffuse, without ever departing from an order based on respect for a common rule, the rule laid down by the Gospel. Theory is central to this vision, but there is also a sense of concrete particulars. With the coming of the thirteenth century, the masters of Paris did not repudiate the vision of social perfection that Hugh of Saint-Victor had attempted to express. They kept the same pattern, but tightened the weave.

The schema they were elaborating was to serve for action. Standing midway between the monks and the populace, the clergy was charged with pragmatic responsibilities. Above all, such responsibilities fell to their leader, their "prelate," the bishop. During a period of forty crucial years between 1160 and 1208, two consecutive bishops of Paris, Maurice and Odo of Sully, devoted their efforts to putting the theoretical program into practice. The former (whose pride Peter the Chanter was unable to keep from criticizing; in the end, he withdrew to Saint-Victor to die) turned first to the task of shoring up the organizational structure: he rebuilt the cathedral, keystone of the whole system; he increased the number of parishes—and the question was raised in the chapter, among the masters, whether this move did not threaten to increase inordinately the burden imposed on the populace: the two goals of efficacious action and of poverty were contradictory and made consciences uneasy. Maurice also devoted attention to preaching, in both Latin and Romance. His message was addressed exclusively to the clerks of his diocese, to set an example for their own preaching to the laity—the good word filtered down by stages, from the bishop all the way to the dregs of society, from Latin to the dialect of the streets. Odo of Sully, for his part, made law, enacting synodal statutes which were supposed to serve as a basis for all future regulations. The two bishops thus molded society, but always respecting the duality of clergy and laity which the masters said was fundamental. Gathering together all the aides of the Lord and the confessors of the faithful, the "ecclesiastical order" was supposed to set an example. It was fitting that it should be the first to be taught: the sermons of Maurice and the ordinances of Odo were intended for its benefit. The clerk's duty was to practice "ecclesiastical honesty"—*honestas,* the Ciceronian notion, had at this time come to mean conformity, submission to the dictates of custom in a well-regulated society such as that of the city or the court. Guiot de Provins says it well:

> High church requires high nobility
> Honesty and gentility.

In particular, the clergyman, shunning sin, was obliged to do everything in his power to avoid scandal, which might harm the sacred trust that he administered. Fearlessly, he must also throw himself into "holy preaching" with the courage of a true soldier of Christ, and try hard to identify what sins were to be absolved and to whom absolution was to be granted—for pastoral activity was focussed on penitence (i.e., scrutiny), which was at that time rising to a paramount position among the sacraments.

Beyond the clear-cut boundaries of the ecclesiastical order, however, the battle lines were less clearly drawn. There the important thing was to root out sin, to wrest laymen from its clutches, and to unmask evil's multifarious disguises—without letup. This was the primary goal of preaching. The sixty-four sermons in the vernacular held out as models to curates by bishop Maurice of Sully all took as their point of departure a passage of the New Testament. The commentary disclosed the moral meaning of the passage, beginning with its teachings on the subject of sin. The point was to help the faithful uncover the lairs wherein misfortune lurked, and to involve the flock in the investigation, the inquisition, the hunt for heterodoxy—by delving into their own consciousnesses. This was followed by confession of weakness, whereupon pardon could be granted. The sections of Odo's statutes concerned with the laity focus on the two institutions on which social and moral order were ostensibly based: confession and marriage. Maurice's major concern was to insure that the priests know the proper procedure for classifying sins as venial, or excusable, and major, or "damnable"—sins that cut a man off from the company of God and the angels much as leprosy, heresy, false beliefs, and deicide isolated the Jews, the sick, and the "arrogant" poor from the rest of mankind in that time of banishment and exclusion. These "mortal" sins had by all means to be eradicated. Here, already, we meet with the obsession that Blanche of Castile was to pass on to her son, Saint Louis. Paramount among these major sins were "covetousness," lust, and the taste for money.

The Church—that state whose power grew along with that of kingdoms and principalities, a power symbolized by the cathedrals it raised up and by the polyphonic sounds that spilled forth from their naves—was bent on using the sentiment of sin to keep its subjects in bondage, with the threat of hell or purgatory. This explains the increasing prominence given to defining and classifying sinful intentions in clerical representations of the organization of society. Criteria of guilt very gradually supplanted functional criteria.

The prince of this state—the bishop—could not do the whole job alone, however. Like his fellow princes among the laity, he needed assistants, well-trained retainers. Accordingly, the work begun by Honorius Augustodunensis of providing the clergy with useful pragmatic manuals was intensified in the late twelfth century. Maurice of Sully personally took part in these efforts. The leading masters joined him in the traces. Incontestably, the most eminent among them was Alan of Lille, a magnificent writer and great thinker, standing head and shoulders above Honorius, devoted body and soul to reflective and hortatory labors alike—he preached personally against the Cathars in Languedoc before retiring to Cîteaux. He hoped to provide preachers and confessors with guidance. His *Summa of the Art of*

Preaching[4] taught that the content of the sermon should be selected in the light of the estate (*status*)—and not the *ordo* or the *conditio*—of the audience, and proposed exemplary models. To begin with, Alan discussed sermons intended for men of the knightly estate. His pedagogical technique is admirable: he first gives practical advice concerning what has to be said: "should he preach to knights, let him inspire them to content themselves with their pay, to refrain from issuing threats against other men, to molest no one, to defend the homeland, and to protect orphans and widows; just as outwardly they wield the weapons of the world, so inwardly shall they arm themselves with the armor of the faith" (Alan was here following tradition, the books of the *auctores*—reverting to the nineteenth homily of Saint Augustine, just as Abbo of Fleury did earlier in his *Collection of Canons*).[5] Next come examples: these are taken from the biographies of the militant saints. Finally, there is explanatory commentary: man consists of two parts, corporeal and spiritual; knights carry two swords: one outward, for securing peace in the world, the other inward, "for restoring peace in their own breast"; wielding the outward weapon, they stood under the threat of evil—and it was precisely this waywardness inherent in their action that the examination of their conscience must bring to light: "it is not knighthood they practice, but rapine; they not so much fight the enemy as batten themselves on the poor"; whereas wielding the inward sword was conducive to the good—internalization and sublimation giving a salutary fillip to an action which, if practiced in the context of their "craft," would tend towards evil: "the material knight lives in castles, deprived of his wife's embraces; he fasts, he keeps vigil; he bears arms, he withstands the enemy's onslaughts, he brings aid to his comrades." Let each Christian become a spiritual knight, by submitting to a life like that of the garrison "of a castle"; the social analysis makes it possible to use the *exemplum* metaphorically, as basic material for sermons covering the other "estates"—men of every sort. Alan next turns his attention to these other estates, passing them in review in the proper order: *oratores* (since this category occurs immediately after the specialists in warfare, does it perhaps refer to the specialists in the first function, so designated by Adalbero and Gerard? No: Alan makes clear that he means the *advocati*, specialists in the civic uses of oratory), followed by princes and judges, monks and priests, married couples, widows, virgins. Neither peasants, merchants, nor artisans figure in the list. Nor is anything said concerning the lower strata of society, except for their marital obligations and their duty of submission: "they shall obey like the men of the plebs."[6] They shall "comply with official orders" (*obtemperent*). For the principles of old are still paramount in the mind of Alan of Lille: to cure the body, treat the head. His preaching was intended exclusively for the ears of the *prelati*.

At the same time that he is explaining how to scold a prince, he adds a filigree to the lay ternary hierarchy—consisting of princes who give orders, knights who carry them out, "plebs" who obey—in the form of another ternary figure, this one cosmic: heaven, earth, and standing between, man, whose nature partakes of both the others. He thereby made his own the persistent notion of a close correspondence between heaven and earth brought about by the agency of man, which had earlier been expressed by Adalbero and Gerard. According to Alan, just as everything in the human body ("the land that we administer") has imposed upon it by an exchange of services—as in a seigniory or a state—an order, so the eternal goal ("the land for which we are searching," the land without evil) can be achieved only if, in the visible world ("the land in which we are paramount"), every man accepts his assigned condition and remains where God has placed him—unmoving, awaiting resurrection. The social and moral order that preaching was meant to reinforce was based on a myth: the reciprocity of the services rendered by the various organs of a body; and on a reality: power, power held by the prince, applied by the knights, and imposed on the "people," who had only to "obey orders." The need for this power was felt no less acutely in the late twelfth century than just after the year 1000, though now it was by no means faltering, but rather gaining new strength each day: the power of the state, served by intellectuals who trimmed their sails to each new wind, and yet deemed themselves free men.

Alan of Lille also wrote, in 1190, a *Penitential Book* that enjoyed an enormous success. It was dedicated to Henry of Sully, archbishop of Bourges. In substance it supplemented the synodal statutes of the bishop of Paris. Alan used its pages to teach that punishment should be apportioned to the seriousness of the offense. Accordingly, he urged the good confessor to evaluate the strength of the *impetus,* the malign aggression, to which guilt stood in inverse proportion. The "complexion" of the penitent was also to be taken into account. Alan of Lille had followed the rapid progress of the natural sciences closely; he was well aware that, since the human body was a microcosm, any study of man in the flesh, and accordingly of sin, must first take in the physical universe (the effects of the humors, counterparts of the four elements): if, because fire was paramount among the constituents of his organism, a man was naturally inclined to inflammation, or if he was inflamed by the fierce heat emitted by his partner, then he deserved greater indulgence for any sin of the flesh he might commit. So much for complexion: "condition," too, was to be taken into account. By this we understand—as Alan himself did—a greater or lesser degree of dependence on others.[7] Once a man had, as one says, "gone into service," he was no longer his own master, and responsibility for his sin was deflected onto the master. The old division between *servus* and *dominus,* between the instrument and the person who made use of it, was shifted within the social formation to a new position, now setting "men of the plebs" apart from knights and princes; the renaissance of the state caused this rift to widen, and the "masters" gazed across to the other side with condescension. But condition was not all—there was also "grade," or rank within the class, *minor ordo, major ordo:* sin was more serious among the great, for their inferiors looked to them as models. Finally, there was *status,* "estate"—that which depended neither on "order" nor on nature, and which was therefore far more variable than either, rising or falling with the turn of the wheel of fortune. It was also relative, like "nobility" and "poverty." Status took in everything that was changeable and ambiguous—the "play in the gears" of the social machine that resulted from economic growth—and everything that was multifarious. All these factors had to be taken into account in order to mete out a just "penitence"—so many counters to be thrown into the scales to balace the weight of the sin. To give an example of the way the system worked, consider a man who was undernourished or who ate less fancy fare than another man, and who suffered in toil; should that man commit the sin of fornication, he would deserve more severe punishment than the second man, since the fire permeating his body was not fanned as strongly as in the latter's case. By contrast, should he commit robbery, his claim to clemency would be the greater of the two.

The demands of the clerical office—preaching, confessing—required that an ever finer mesh be used in sifting through the substance of society, and accordingly that the clerks have recourse to the steadily improving creations of the art of making distinctions. Every day brought fresh evidence that society, that immense ungainly edifice, contained—like the stage scenery used in sacred plays—more and more *mansiones,* or places. No longer were there just three squares, but a whole checkerboard. Indeed, the symbolism of the chessboard—also used as a device for counting the pieces of silver that the prince took in—was at this time just beginning its slow penetration of the minds of Church thinkers.[8] On the chessboard, however, there were two opposed camps, and, whether they acknowledged it or not, the aim of the preacher and the confessor was to slow down social mobility, to soften the blows of fortune, to restore stability, and to establish institutions; in the end, accordingly, they balanced the increasing minuteness of their analyses by reverting to simpler images of order—seigniory, domination, the state. With stubborn determination, they thereby went back to the original distinction between the rulers—who cherished, or pretended to cherish, their inferiors—and the subjects, from whom reverence was demanded. They went back all the way to the system set forth by Gregory the Great. Accordingly, they began moving forward at the same time toward the system that would one day be proposed by Charles Loyseau.

How did the most perceptive doctors view the underlying architecture of society? Did they not see a binary plan? Did they not look upon order as having a dualist structure, built on an opposition more potent than the contrast between clerks and laymen or between city and countryside—namely, the opposition of two classes in direct conflict? In my view, such a view may be found in the thought of Stephen Langton, to whom I was led by the work of Father Carra de Vaux. An Englishman born in about 1155, Stephen arrived in Paris some fifteen years later, and there became first doctor of arts, then regent in the *divina pagina*. He was not a writer of manuals but a commentator on Scripture, from the 1180s until 1206. Designated archbishop of Canterbury by the pope, but against the wishes of the king of England, he bided his time in the Cistercian abbey at Pontigny, awaiting the moment when he might take up his post.

Virtually all the writings that he left us remain in manuscript: a few "lessons" that try to draw the moral significance, or "morality," out of the Bible, most useful to preachers and accordingly recopied with care. Of the commentaries on Isaiah and Hosea—one preserved in Vienne, the other in Paris in thirteenth-century manuscripts[9]—perhaps half the text is taken up with thoughts on the social categories and—sin still being the preoccupation—on their specific vices. To assist in the preparation of moralizing sermons, Stephen begins by distinguishing among five kinds of persons. The contemplatives were set apart, mingled indiscriminately, without regard to the color of their robe; though he has little to say about them—there being no reason to admonish penitents to repent—one feels that like James of Vitry he would have liked to have seen all sinners emulate their virtues. On the subject of his own circle, the schoolmen, he expostulates copiously, severely criticizing the legists and anyone else who abandoned the study of the Bible in favor of the profane sciences, and still more severely criticizing the "lettered" who traded on their knowledge at court. It was to the clerks, however, who made up the third group, that the essential portion of his thesis was addressed: devoted to preaching and confession, they were the men on whom the reformation of morals depended. The contemplatives set them an example of the perfect life; the masters imparted knowledge to them; their role was to make distribution of these riches: they were the "basin" or "channel" through which the word of God flowed. To enable them to carry out their mission, they were invested with authority: they were "regents," in a position "to rule over others" by virtue of their estate. The clergy dominated the laity. This marked one fundamental division. Stephen identified the location of a second rift. It ran through the laity, setting men who were "powerful, rich, princes" apart from those who were not. All things considered, the upshot was that in Stephen's view the order imposed on Christian society consisted in three tiers: the custodians of spiritual power, the custodians of temporal power, and the subjects. By way of Gregory the Great, whose authority he liked to invoke, Stephen Langton's thought thus harks back to that of Adalbero and

Gerard, and at the same time to Augustine and Dionysius. When, like so many other thinkers of his day he came to compare society to a body, this tripartition was not obliterated; at the eye and the heart were the "best," i.e., the priests and doctors; at the right hand that wielded the sword and distributed alms, the "powerful"; and at the "soles of the feet," the "lowliest, who work and toil [*laborant*] on the land to provide bodily nourishment to those who are at the heights, i.e., to the great [*majores*], so that the latter might supply them with spiritual nourishment."

In the course of his musings, however, ternarity takes on unmistakable overtones of conflict. Stephen indicates the "head" of this body[10]—unique, yet made up of three persons: the "prelate," the doctor, the prince. Leagued together, in collusion: the three kinds of leader were assigned the same duties: to defend their subjects by making wise use of their power, and to feed them by making judicious use of "abundance."[11] Power and plenty were concentrated around the rulers, in that closed group central to the state—the court. This was by no means a tranquil place. "Ambitious," the "men of the court," or *curiales*,[12] were riven by a deep-seated rivalry. The clerks were enemies of the laymen—the "rude, uncultivated" laymen. Here we see an instance of the "intense hatred that always exists between the clergy and the illiterate."[13] A split. Yet this conflict was less clear-cut than was the confrontation between those two hostile camps, the court and the people: physically separated, as they were in Paris, for example, with the populace ensconced on the right bank of the Seine. The fancier sections of town dueled with the suburbs, the virtuous with the suspect—reflected in the following chilling remark interpolated into a commentary on Christ's entry into Jerusalem on Palm Sunday: "the Lord does not like the mob." Is Langton to be regarded as having been more conservative than the others? Or more perceptive? In any case, he did take this split to be the most important, the primary one. It was unequivocal: there was no middle ground, no *mediocres*, not even among the clergy. The "plebs," the subjects (*subjecti*), the "abject" (*abjecti*), the poor, were bluntly set aside. And they were exploited: "the rich oppressing the poor," "the powerful afflicting the poor"—while the poor "adulated" the rich. The "blood of the poor" was "eaten,"[14] their labor was "stolen,"[15] thanks particularly to the efforts of the "lesser judicial officials," the agents of power, who played the part of the "millstone" in the great machine.[16]

Stephen Langton urged good clerks to wed the cause of the people, because according to him the blood of the poor was none other than the blood of Christ.[17] The time has come to give to the phenomenon whose mechanism he was attempting to explain to them its usual appellation: class struggle. For Langton, the society in whose midst he found himself, and that he was working with all his strength to deliver from evil, was a society of injustice, of oppression by the combined forces of power and money. Was

320

this pessimism, or was it a magisterial reformulation of rumblings that were in the air for anyone who cocked an ear to hear, and growing louder every day? His teachings throw a revealing light on the contradictions within feudal society, on the hatred between clerks and laymen, and on the subjugation of the workers, robbed of their life's blood. Hostility had two faces, since the dominant class was divided against itself by its hunger for power. Now, was the reason for the resurgence of the trifunctional figure not merely this: to explain these structural antagonisms within the context of knightly ideology? It was during the years that Benedict of Sainte-Maure was engaged in writing the *Estoire* that Stephen Langton crossed the Channel. What he preached at the very end of the twelfth century should be heard today as the Parisian antiphon to the melody that had rung in the ears of Henry Plantagenet some twenty years earlier, amid the pleasures of the courtly feast.

24

CONTRADICTIONS
OF FEUDALISM

MONEY

Asceticism, pessimism—these were the flotsam that remained as the great tide of *contemptus mundi* slowly ebbed away. Obsession with sin and damnation, an anxiety that fed on thoughts of the instability of "estates" and the unpredictable rotations of the wheel of fortune—this was the state of mind in the late twelfth century, after so many triumphs, as men became aware of the dark underside of expansion. True enough, trade of every variety was at that time on the rise in northern France, and the fairs of Champagne had known raging success, but this growing bustle was at the same time responsible for the rising cost of foodstuffs and the debasement of coinage. Silver pieces in small denominations were increasingly in demand, hence increasingly scarce, which accounts for the fact that we see *cupiditas* pushing its way to the forefront of the trinity of major vices, elbowing aside the two old demons of the Gregorian age, pride and lust. Scarcity of deniers: reason for that fever that set men to scouring the earth in the earnest hope of uncovering a new lode, and for the scandalous hoardings of the moneylenders, the usurers who earned the vituperation first of Guibert of Nogent and later of Maurice of Sully and Peter the Chanter. Money-fantasies obsessed lords fearful of never having enough cash on hand to maintain themselves in their rank, as well as peasants desperate to find hiding places for their meager hoards. It was an invasion, an infection of the body social by money.

To the prince money was indispensable. He had to have it first of all in order to give it away, as the *Dialogue on the Exchequer* makes clear. For generosity of whatever sort now required a treasury full of deniers. Money was also needed to wage war—by this time, going to war was no longer a simple matter: ramparts had to be reinforced; modern weaponry (alongside which the arms of bygone days looked ridiculous) had to be acquired, and its price was constantly on the rise; mercenaries had to be signed up, and they demanded ever higher wages; and the vassals had to be given fresh horses after each ambuscade. Nor could the ransoms of prisoners be paid without money. Still more was needed to bury the dead in a location propitious to their salvation, and to pay for prayers intended to save their souls. Money was needed for the dowries of daughters, and for the education of the eldest son so that he would not cut a sorry figure in those great fairs, the tournaments. The least political intrigue gave rise to excruciating financial concerns. The crusade? A cash affair, at the origin of the "Saladin tithe"—another scandal, thanks to the use made of the funds extracted on this pretext. With the expansion of the monetary economy, the places of the actors on the social stage gradually shifted. Growing steadily in importance was the third "pillar" of the state, the "villeins," whose role was neither to pray nor to fight but rather to provision the palace. But the latter was a business of sacks of grain; casks of wine; of the old "gifts" in kind brought by subjects of the rural seigniory. What was needed now was hard cash. The rift between the palace and the rural domains gradually widened. And the importance of agricultural tenants diminished, the cash prestations levied on them in the form of "customs" declining in value due to the erosion of money. Meanwhile, into the front ranks pushed the bourgeois, the "rich." At the end of the monetary circuit, it was in fact into their hands that the coin so necessary to power flowed. The pretense may have continued to be that the basis of power lay in all three functions; but in reality power was based on the efforts of a few men who would eventually give it the wherewithal to dispense with all the rest; of a few not altogether imposing types: paid mercenary captains skilled in storming fortresses; paid clerical retainers who kept the accounts; and last but not least, the merchants and money changers, who paid themselves, who lent a hand in the mint, who sold or loaned to the prince the precious metal he needed—those "prudent, legitimate [businessmen] of good repute" named special counselors in financial matters in each seigniorial unit of the royal domain by Philip Augustus as he departed for the Holy Land.[1] Standing alongside the prince, the third function underwent a change. No longer *labor,* it became primarily *negotium.* Trade: a kind of labor, antithetical to be sure to idleness and disinterest alike—the two qualities appropriate to nobility—and yet free of that curse that applied to physical toil, to manual and muscular effort. The commercial became the most useful of the three functions that now, thanks to economic growth, were more firmly than ever harnessed to the service of the state, domesticated by wages, interest, and money inside the palace itself.

Such was the reality that showed through the mists of the imaginary. The reality of the close of the twelfth century was first of all the court—a court alive with the din of jingling coins changing hands there: if the dreams dreamt at court were full of images of forests and greenery, the reason was perhaps that the court was now closeted away inside a city, cut off from the rural world by a screen of suburbs—places otherwise adventurous, plebeian and sordid, where the quarry of the hunt was profit. Reality was a court whose gates had been forced wide open by the ambitions of those ignoble men to whom the prince could refuse nothing, for the money he needed was in their hands. Also part of late twelfth-century reality were the knights, strutting about stiffly with their arms, armor, and armorial bearings—worried and threatened by the rise of the upstart commoners, as unmistakable in their eyes as was the collapse of the foundation on which their own superiority had rested. Gradually, they were being reduced to supplicants living by the good graces of the prince. Financial embarrassment beset the nobility, which had to spend more and more money, while their subjects in the villages were yielding less and less of it: for the provosts might seize livestock, wheat, and wine, but as for those easily hidden pieces of silver . . . They were the stakes in a war—an increasingly bitter war—against the peasantry, from which the tax collectors rarely emerged victorious. Accordingly, the nobility made prodigality and indebtedness caste virtues. Though knights were set at the pinnacle of the social pyramid in contemporary literature, in reality they were being reduced to beggary, to servitude, always on the lookout for gifts and benefices. How infuriating it must have been for the knights to find themselves forced to compete for handouts with sergeants at arms as stout-hearted as they pretended to be, with mercenaries capable of unhorsing and slaughtering them, with scholars who humiliated them, made them feel crude and uncultured and so inspired a hatred for the learned men whose knowledge the knights tried to assimilate bit by bit by ferreting out the secrets of the clerical libraries one by one. And worst of all the rivals were the bourgeois. The literature designed for courtly entertainments was thematically attuned to this torment: it projects the figure of the wicked prince, who paid too much attention to the "peasants," to the "serfs," rather than save, as he ought to have done, all his favors for the "poor" knights; the figure of the newly rich man, risen from the rabble, whose diligence in aping the manners of the well-born was mocked. As the thirteenth century got under way, the new romance—called realistic by literary historians because expressive in fact of disenchantment, an ironic self-image, and bitterness—gave the starkest description yet of the competition between the values of the aristocracy and the alien values promoted by the same ineluctable tendencies that were lifting up the bourgeoisie. The new romance depicted the triumph of the city over knighthood, noisily maintaining that birth was the be-all and the end-all—that "gentility" that Guiot of Provins implored from the high Church where it was no longer always to be found: were there not now bishops of very low origins, and what is more, who boasted of the fact? The nobility fled to what refuge it

324

thought there was: in etiquette, worldly pleasures, ideology—making its last stand on the ramparts of the imaginary.

The conjuncture provides the explanation for the destruction of the trifunctional theme, which fell to pieces under the penetrating gaze of the Parisian masters. It also provides the explanation for the fact that the theme should again have proved useful in the citadels of feudal pride, where it was adapted (with the connivance of the prince, for the adaptation amounted to paying lip service to knighthood while alienating it still further from the seat of power) in such a way as to denigrate the rivals of the nobility—relegating upstart plebeians to the vile depths, giving prominence to the blemish that tainted their very flesh, and ejecting them from the courtly feast into the midst of those who suffered in *labor* in the blustery out-of-doors. But hostility was not allowed to reach the point where commoners would have been expelled from the court in actual fact: the prince would never have consented to such a thing. His game required the presence of all three orders at the foot of his throne; besides, it would have been impossible to drive out the parvenus, impossible even to try. There was no way to quell the rising expectations engendered by the growth of the mercantile economy. Inevitably, the ranks of the dominant class swelled with men whose parents had worked with their hands, now rich enough not to follow the example of their forebears. Hence with each passing day the real dividing line, that between rich and poor, the inestimably tragic consequences of which Stephen Langton had understood—stood out in bolder relief. Thanks to the power invested in them by wealth, the rich were capable of surmounting the ritual obstacles placed in their way in order to worm their way into fashionable society. Thus they were able to amass even greater fortunes, since proximity to power made it easier to appropriate the surplus product of the laboring populace, whether directly through seigniorial confiscations, or indirectly through wages and benefices distributed by the rulers of the state.

On one side of the dividing line stood the poor, on the other, the "rich and powerful": wealth and power went together; let us admire Stephen Langton's lucid insight into the social infrastructure. Economic changes had reopened the old rift, the dualism on which Hincmar and the Carolingian bishops had built their civic morality. In the sweat of their brow the poor earned their few deniers, and grasping hands at once went to work to pry them from between callused fingers. "Ignoble" because they worked, they had to work because they were poor, or risk being accused of pride and consigned to eternal damnation. For this world—though in the throes of progress, and beginning gradually to avert its eyes from heaven so as to fix its gaze increasingly on earth, where the productive forces were the new preoccupation—still recognized only one value in manual labor: that of salutary punishment. Work was servitude. It debased, degraded. Everyone

325

with access to the resources of high culture—and we have no way of knowing what was on the mind of anyone without such access—remained convinced that labor should be shunned by men of quality, for whom the appropriate way of life was that of the lord, living on the sweat of others. Social conflict was not unknown in the circles that produced the ideological systems open to our scrutiny. But what interested the intellectuals was not the question of whether the workers should or should not be hauled out of the mire to which they had been consigned by general agreement. Debate centered on the following issue: to deserve the appellation "courtly" rather than "common," was nonproductiveness sufficient qualification? In fact, all of the intellectuals found themselves in the same camp, on the same side of the battle lines—across which the two armies took each other's measure, hurled challenges back and forth in mutual fear, and even at this early date hazarded a few skirmishes.

These were actually the warning signs of a "crisis" of feudalism. Just as they had done in the time of Adalbero and in the time of the great revolt of the Norman peasants (whose memory, kept alive in the courts, was reason enough for vigilance), so now, too, the people were making their demands heard. Protest came from the suburban zones where frustration was mounting. It came equally from the countryside. For the fields were ultimately the source of the money squandered in courtly festivities, even if most of it passed first through the coffers of the bourgeois. The fiscal burden fell on the peasants. Accordingly, they had to sell more of what they grew, to meet the city's new demands for good wine, meat, wood, and the wool that was spun by women. Some came to grief: they had to borrow. Others succeeded: they made loans. Thus in rural society, too, the gap between rich and poor was widening. We sense a worsening of the uneasy climate, of which the rapid wane of peasant conversions to the Cistercian order was one sign. The ranks of a proletariat swelled to accommodate people who earned their livelihoods in forest or pasture, "children" of all sorts—i.e., young men and women unable to find a place for themselves within the village household, an institution with its own imperatives. These early "stirrings" were at first disguised by the ideology of the crusade and the peace movement. In 1212, for example, the so-called children's crusade got under way.[2] *Pueri et puellae* set out without arms, marching behind the banners toward a Jerusalem of the imagination, led by clerks as poor as themselves. Holy innocents. The king saw them and sent them home. They had not yet turned to marauding. They were worrisome. Indeed, fear of the common man was on the rise—the real "villein," that is: the peasant, *horridus*, reduced to a near animal existence, like those shepherds evoked by Lambert of Ardres, who cursed their lord, the count of Guines, and hoped he would die a cruel death, because of the taxes he levied. This fear was implicit in the writings of Stephen of Fougères. Was it merely to deck out their residences

326

in the symbolic trappings of sovereignty that knights in the countryside began at this time to construct costly fortified dwelling-places? Or was it to protect themselves against possible *jacqueries?* To keep the peasantry at a distance, to command their respect? As the thirteenth century drew near, the rich joined together in appealing to the king for support against the poor, and against that misguided segment of the clergy that took their part. The atmosphere was therefore tense. A rather good account of the situation is provided, I think, by reports of two events of quite disparate importance.

William the Breton tells us that a papal legate, Robert of Courçon, was one of several men preaching the crusade in the French kingdom in 1215.[3] These preachers indiscriminately handed out the cross to the "very young, old men, women," and "seemingly wishing their preaching to please the people more than was necessary, they cast aspersions on the clergy, saying and inventing before the populace infamous things about the clerical life, thereby sowing the seeds of discord and schism between clergy and people." Inheritors of the tradition of Peter the Chanter and Fulk of Neuilly—not to mention Stephen Langton, who maintained that the blood of the workers was the blood of Christ himeslf—they went about praising poverty to the skies, reverting to the old myth from the time of Peter the Hermit; to insure that this campaign would be successful, like the first one, they mobilized women and the "unarmed populace." Their vituperation against the wealth of the Church did not, of course, fail to awaken echoes in cities ripe for "heresy." Virtually nothing is known of the Waldensian movement in its earliest days, other than that it denied that "order" or "function" had anything to do with salvation. In calling for brotherhood among the poor and for eradication of social distinctions, Robert of Courçon and his fellows were embarking upon a new pastoral mission whose aim was to blunt the cutting edge of heretical protest by going it one better. This new departure seemed fraught with danger in its day. Society defended itself. The rich— according to William the Breton, "many of the rich"—refused to take the cross, unwilling to throw in their lot with the great unwashed. "The king and all the clergy" complained to the pope. He silenced the preachers.

SOCIAL FEAR

The other matter was a far more serious one: sedition broke out in the southern part of the kingdom. Written accounts of this strife reveal a great deal about the mental attitudes of the dominant class. Serious trouble was then brewing in southern France in two areas at once, and in 1179 the Lateran council dealt with both together, the better to get a handle on them. These were the heretical sects and the bands of jobless mercenaries. To face up to this double threat, the peace movement was revived—along the lines of Bourges—and the entire populace was enlisted in the effort to aid the bishops by falling upon the two prongs of the enemy force, so as to impose a "sanctified" peace, the peace of "enthusiasm."[4] What actually happened was this: the tether holding the people in check was loosened, thereby raising the expectations of the "plebs" imprudently. The result was scandal—the affair of the White Capes.[5] Roughly contemporary with Benedict of Sainte-Maure's completion of the *Estoire of the Dukes of Normandy*, the agitation began in Le Puy in 1182. Thus the original impetus came from a city and subsequently spread to the countryside; it began with the ideology of peace and ended by attacking the seigniorial system and consequently the social order. The event had profound repercussions in high society, and was the subject of much talk. My intention is to examine that discussion as far as possible in order to trace the waves of fear and reprobation that for a considerable length of time swept over this part of the world, and within thirty years brought men of culture to a clear awareness of the stark reality, that society was divided into two antagonistic classes. There are seven principal witnesses, whom I shall call one by one into the dock.

The oldest report comes from a man of the region, Geoffrey, monk of Saint-Martial of Limoges and, since 1178, prior of Vigeois near Brive. He kept a chronicle in which he told of happenings in Limousin and La Marche, with particular emphasis on tales of mercenaries. He left off writing in 1183. His account is therefore limited to the beginnings of the movement.[6] Mention is made of it immediately after the report of a military victory: near Dun-le-Roi the peace-men of Berry had destroyed by fire a company of Brabantines, "robbers," together with the prostitutes they had brought with them. This gave rise to hopes that the earth could be purged of this particular infection. In the ensuing euphoria the sect of the White Capes was formed. To the consternation of the mighty, the Lord breathed his spirit into a most unworthy fellow; *vilissimus,* a manual laborer, an artisan, impure because he was married and the father of two children, and ugly besides—displeasing in every way. But he was a good pauper, a simple fellow, who feared God—a God who to make himself heard spoke through this man's mouth. The bishop of Le Puy was wary. A confraternity nevertheless gathered around their inspired brother: already some four or five hundred strong by Christmas, it soon numbered five thousand, which suggests that it spread very quickly beyond the walls of the tiny city. By Easter 1183—after the penitences of Lent—the followers were "innumerable." They were also organized: after confessing their sins—purified, freed of wrongdoing, hence restored to a condition of equality—they had sworn the oath of peace; all wore insignia: the white cape—emblem of purity, used to mask whatever differences might be indicated by clothing, hence to conceal, to deny the existence of the various "conditions"—and the image of the Virgin with Child in tin. These attributes had to be purchased by the brethren. Hence these were not wretched folk, not denizens of the lowest depths. In addition, they had to make a contribution of six deniers—not an insignificant sum—at Pentecost. When ordered to, they would take out after the war-mongers, all together, in unanimity, except for those compelled by a rule to remain in one place: the "regulars," monks and canons, and the contemplatives—the only group to which Geoffrey applied the word *ordo*—were not bound to engage the enemy, but were instead left behind to pray for victory. Alone, which proves that clerks not obliged to stay in one place might accompany the troops. On the occasion of the great pilgrimage of the Assumption, the bishop decided that he would preach, reservations notwithstanding. His voice was necessary: it induced knights, princes, ecclesiastical dignitaries and women—at any rate, those without husbands—to join the movement. Nothing indicates that Geoffrey con-demned his action: his chronicle ends before the bishop strayed into heterodoxy.

Another chronicle alludes briefly to the event. It was compiled over the years by another monk, Robert of Torigny or of Mont Saint-Michel—a fine, veracious observer.[7] His on-the-spot account, written in 1182, reveals nothing new, other than that the Virgin herself had appeared to the poor man, that he was a woodworker, and that against the enemies of the peace, against the outsiders, who were damned as they had been at Limoges in 1031, the sect rallied *milites*, "many bishops, counts, men of power [i.e., lords, custodians of the ban], men of middling rank, and poor men." Robert the monk saw society much as Raoul Glaber had seen it, paying no attention to "orders," showing no sign of reticence at the sight of bishops engaged in combat.

The third witness is again a monk: Rigord, of the abbey of Saint-Denis, where he wrote the *Deeds of Philip Augustus,* a work begun perhaps as early as 1186 but worked on and revised into the early thirteenth century. In this case the event is less faithfully reflected in the report, which is in-corporated into a royal panegyric. The writer allowed himself to make alterations and to twist the facts, particularly wherever his account touched on the subject of the mercenaries: they were said to have been in the pay of the Plantagenet, whereas the Capetian king, for his part, was bent on their extermination. Still, Rigord came from Languedoc; he knew the region, and he may even have written this portion of his narrative before he entered Saint-Denis in 1189.[8] Like Geoffrey of Vigeois, he moves without transition from the Dun affair—a victory he wrongly attributes to the royal army—to the White Capes. Towards this confraternity he seems to have harbored no greater disapprobation than his predecessors. He credits it with having brought the king of Aragon and the count of Toulouse to make peace. The text lavishes praise on the pacification efforts of which the sect was the instrument. It had been formed at the behest of one of the humblest of men: "the Lord, hearing the prayers of the poor, sent them as savior [the inspired artisan here takes the place of the infant Jesus] not the emperor, the king, or some prince of the Church, but a poor man." Rigord divulges his name: Durand, a "poor and humble" man, a "carpenter" by trade. With the evolution to this stage of the commemoration of the event, might we perhaps be witnessing one of the earliest symbolic celebrations of Joseph of Nazareth, father of the holy family? Rumor of the miracle spread widely in a society that even its official historian looked upon as similar in structure to the society of the crusade or of the peace assemblies—such was the continuity of traditional ways of envisaging the world, even in the cloisters on the wane: Rigord says that Durand was heeded by "princes, the greatest and the least, as well as by the whole of the populace" (princes, populace: the opposition derives directly from the terminology of the earliest directives relating to the institution of the peace of God; but comparatives are employed in connection with the aristocracy, which Rigord meant to depict as a hierarchy); on the occasion of the Assumption Day meeting, "the bishop with the clergy and the populace, and all the multitude" (*populus* here refers to secular high society, set above the faceless crowd) placed himself at the head of the whole undertaking.

Another echo—this one of later date (1205–10), secular, and in the vernacular—is audible in the *Bible* by Guiot of Provins. After submitting first the various religious orders and then the lay confraternities to a critical review, Guiot bitterly attacked Durand, characterizing him as a swindler and thief. This testimony gives us some idea of the view of the matter taken by the knightly order, which felt that the Church, proud and "honest," ought not to lower itself to the level of the mediocre, but rather ought to remain aloof from the populace. We also see that this was apparently the time that disapproval of the movement began to make itself felt—which disapprobation was no doubt responsible for the fact that when William the Breton made use of Rigord's writings, he omitted the material relating to the White Capes.

Unless—and who can say for sure?—the writings of Robert of Auxerre are of much earlier date. The *Universal Chronicle* kept by this Premonstratensian canon continues until 1211. Did he keep it up to date, recording what he knew of events year by year while they were still fresh in his mind? This is not out of the question: the complexion of his opinions changes utterly between his account of the events of 1183 and those of the following year. If he immediately recorded the news of what was happening as it reached him in Auxerre—where his convent was located—we should have to assign to his testimony a date close to Robert of Torigny, immediately after Geoffrey of Vigeois. Discreet, laconic, blunt, Robert of Auxerre shows himself to have been horrified, like everyone else, at the misdeeds of the impious "robbers," Christianity's outlaws. In this connection he refers to the efforts of the peace-men of Le Puy.[9] He says nothing of any apparition. A "humble" fellow received an order from on high; he called the people to rally round an image of Mary, symbol of peace. Soon the gathering grew to enormous proportions and was joined by "princes," who took charge of the military operations. While Philip Augustus was busy expelling the Jews, they were ridding Christendom of that other plague, the mercenaries. But when he comes to discuss the events of the following year, Robert shows the *Capuciati* sect gaining ground, reaching into "France" itself. There, transplanted into northern provinces where circumstances were different and no hordes of Brabantines were lurking about, the movement underwent a change of character. It became revolutionary. It was brutally put down. "Those people insolently rejected all subjugation, and the sect was destroyed by the reaction of the princes." That is all: heresy— not mentioned by anyone prior to Robert of Auxerre—insolence, refusal to obey, hence destruction of order—a natural order based on the distinction between princes and subjects. No allusion whatsoever is made to the clergy. Through the medium of the "humble," providence had roused the leaders—*principes, proceres*— from their torpor: they had done their duty, which was to maintain order by force. They annihilated all the troublemakers—first the "robbers," then the "insolent."

Also a Premonstratensian was the Anonymous of Laon, who may originally have been English. He was an excellent analyst—poorly understood by his editor, Waitz,[10] who accused him of spreading "fables": in fact, he tried to keep the event in critical perspective. His is the fullest account. it was certainly written after the sect had gone astray. But how long after? Was it prior to Rigord's text, or later? In any case, in discussing the noteworthy events of the year 1182, the Anonymous states that the uprising of the *Capuciati* or *Caperons* was due to a "mad frenzy." This, he explains, sprang from the "inflammation of summer"; here was a writer most attentive to cosmic disturbances and to their repercussions on the flow of the humors in man. But this explanation was insufficient. Why did these men lose their reason? Traditionally, a kind of fair was held at Le Puy on the fifteenth of August, a "gathering of princes" (the Anonymous pretends to see no relationship between the festivities and the Marian festival; by virtue of the habit he wore, he was defender of an austere religious life: any coincidence between the liturgies and worldly doings was repugnant to him). In behalf of their glory, their "honor," these princes gathered in the city in an ostentatious display of magnificence, a vain debauch of liberality. Clearly these parades of power and wealth were profitable to the merchants—the "multitude of merchants." At festival time they amassed a respectable hoard of deniers. The holiday also swelled the coffers of the cathedral, tied to the bourgeoisie in a myriad of ways. Greed—corruption. Because the mercenaries were abroad, scouring the countryside, the vitality of the Assumption festival was sapped, and accordingly business suffered terribly. At this point a canon took a hand in the matter, a canon who was not a regular like the Anonymous, but rather a "youth"—extravagant as were all the young, *ingeniosus,* clever enough to teach others. This canon employed a simple fellow, an artisan, as devout as he was stupid. The apparition was rigged up. The Virgin ordered the layman to speak. But because he was a layman, he was an "idiot." Hence it was the canon who spoke for him *(prolocutor),* behind him, just as he had spoken earlier in the guise of the Holy Virgin. He called for union to restore peace, denouncing violence while in reality establishing a tyranny. Anyone unfortunate enough to refuse to take part in the movement, or to oppose it, was threatened with a cruel death, a sudden death; and "any who might not wish to take the cape with the insignia" would be treated "as enemies of the peace." Whether willingly or by force, everyone was obliged to join. They were thereupon bound by a chain of interdictions, foreshadowing those that Saint Louis would one day decree: there were to be no more dice games, long robes, knives, taverns, or unseemly oaths (the Virgin Mary had made a special point of prohibiting oaths sworn by the limbs of God, his mother, or the saints, in any case those limbs situated *ab umbilico inferius,* below the belt). In such wise was the confraternity founded, with the intention that it would be a brotherhood of penitence, puritanical, whose members would refuse to take part in sexual relations or, at the outset, to use arms; there were to be processions in the streets, wearing the white cape, on Sundays and feast days, regular attendance at mass, chanting of psalms during the daylight hours. In its way the brotherhood was a prefiguration of the society of purity and equality—it was ready to enter into paradise. As the Anonymous saw the affair, nothing—apart from the initial subterfuges—was thus far very wicked. But the association turned into a "conjuration." As was mentioned earlier, the word was a foul one. At this point—nearly two centuries after Gerard of Cambrai, one century after Guibert of Nogent—the fear with which we have become so familiar became contagious once again; there was outrage at the sight of equals uniting for strength—strength which inevitably led to an attack on the established order in the form of a wholesale rejection of rank and of the necessary hierarchies. The parties to the conjuration were not proletarians, however. The Anonymous specifies the amount of their contribution. He doubles the previously cited figure: twelve deniers. This did not prevent the White Capes from attacking the "princes" at the same time as they attacked the mercenaries. Only those princes who failed to respect the peace were attacked, however—for the moment, at any rate.

The movement spread into Aquitaine, Gascony, and Provence, winning over bishops "and all those of the lower orders," meaning the whole of the clergy (not forbidden to engage in combat according to the Anonymous, either). In two months, four hundred thousand *livres* (money, again) were amassed in the coffers of the movement. This was an enormous sum, an incredible hoard of those little coins so much sought after in the world. Enough to frighten the princes. "They no longer dared make any unjust demands on their men"; an end was made of "exactions" and "tallages." Imperceptibly, the peace movement took a new turn: it was transformed into a movement against the fiscal regime of banal lordship, against excessive exploitation, against any attempt by powerful but hard-pressed lords to use their prerogatives to extract increased sums of cash. In 1184 this tendency took on a clear heading. Jealous of the victory over the mercenaries won by the great lords of Auvergne, the White Capes hunted down one of the captains, captured and killed him, and triumphantly carried his head back to Le Puy. From this point on they bore the stain of their sin. These petty men had dared lay hands on the body of a warrior, had impudently beheaded him. "Glory" and "pride" had deserted them by the time they returned. Evil had descended upon them, beyond the shadow of a doubt. Then came the outbreak of *vesana dementia,* madness, the rush of delirium. Or so the Anonymous dubbed what was really class war: the "stupid" *(stultus),* "rebellious" *(indisciplinatus)* populace had had the effrontery to "direct" (the verb was a very strong one: it was used in speaking of decisions taken by the sovereign) the "counts, viscounts, and other princes," all the possessors of power, and all who profited thereby, to take a more moderate line with their subjects, or risk provoking the redoubtable "indignation" of the parties to the conjuration. The "pacific" activities of the latter were from that time on aimed at establishing the *visio pacis,* i.e., paradise, from which inequality and exploitation were to be banished. But—it was a sign of their insanity—they wanted to see that paradise established then and there, on earth. And in truth it was mad to work for the abolition of seigniory. These were the men destined to work, and yet they fought and prayed. They refused to deliver up the surplus product of their toil. Hence they were threatening to undermine the righteous order, which depended on the power of the "masters." Worse still, these paupers had grown rich and vain, forgetting the humility appropriate to their station. Their attitude was that of the wealthy, and they shared the defect peculiar to wealth: arrogance. A perversion—an indubitable sign of which was the apparition of the Virgin, an out-and-out fraud. Having been deceived, the White Capes were destroyed, not by the princes, but by a mercenary captain: the kingdom was divided against itself.

To conclude this discussion, I shall turn to the *Deeds of the Bishops of Auxerre,* focussing in particular on the biography of Hugh of Noyers, who was bishop between 1181 and 1206.[11] The account of his doings may have been written, at least in part, during his lifetime, as was the eulogy of Gerard, bishop of Cambrai. In any case, it was certainly done well after the event that we are examining. In its pages an uneasy society, on the defensive, found the account of that occurrence that it was looking for. Of paramount interest here are wickedness, subversion, omens: the unknown canon of Auxerre who wrote this celebration of the bishop's glory deals exclusively with heresy and especially repression, with the forthright efforts to purge the diocese of the social pestilence that, after spreading through Berry, Nivernais, and along the ramparts of the Capetian realm, had come to infect it. The author of the *Deeds* did not trouble himself to say where all these "plebeians" whom he shows risen against "the superior powers" came from, but rather dissembles their rebellious spirit beneath the deceptive appearance of a "mutual charity." In fact, this was a conjuration, a detestable commune, in which a group of equals was joined together by an oath of mutual aid. By the time it reached these provinces, it seems, the movement had lost all trace of its original features: no one in an Auxerrois for the moment spared by the mercenaries appears to recall that the idea of the league at the outset was to secure peace. The symbols remained: the cape, the leaden image, the weapons—the sword that the conspirators had no right to possess, since by now the custom was for the sword to be blessed on the alter and girded in solemn ceremonial on men born to combat. Most important, it was this very usurped sword that gave substance to the demand for "freedom" (i.e., exemption from taxes)—"natural" freedom (meaning that it was a right derived from nature, from birth)—that continued to be characteristic of the movement. At this point, enter the devil, who figured in none of the earlier texts; "diabolical," the word Guibert of Nogent had shouted in the face of the communes, was the term used to characterize the audacity of this rabble, among whom "fear" and "reverence" had disappeared. Order had been definitively shattered. With an "insolent," a "lunatic presumption," the White Capes demanded freedom—not equality this time—invoking the *initium,* the origins, the earliest days of creation. Was it possible that these madmen were unaware that servitude was the wages of sin? Not to accept this point was to introduce confusion where scholasticism was attempting to make distinctions—to reject the division made between "lords" and power, on the one hand, and "serfs," "plebs," and abjection on the other. This accordingly, would lead to disarray among the "things" whose "whole" God had wished to see governed by the "moderating" power of superior men. Such confusion would destroy "political and catholic discipline"—meaning that discipline guaranteed by the two authorities, lay and ecclesiastical, acting in concert, according to the Gelasian principle—without which there could be no place for bodies, no salvation for souls. With the spine of Christian society thus broken, "carnal" heresy would triumph—carnal, i.e., social heresy: revolution. The hard-to-win victory of the true faith over the heretical infection; and the hard-to-maintain balance between the things of the flesh and those of the spirit; or, in a word, order (civil and religious) presupposed inequality—Gerard of Cambrai's word—and servitude—Adalbero's. Libertarian and egalitarian, the revolt was therefore damned, a "pestilence," something "fearsome." A malady that threatened the continued existence of society. On the threshold of the thirteenth century, people no longer looked upon evil as being incarnated in the warriors, nor even in the mercenaries, whose platoons had disappeared from the French kingdom. Evil lurked rather in the popular protests, because they called the seigniorial relations of production into question.

Against these protests, the bishop—the good bishop, defender of the faith, of discipline, of the established order—decided to act. To act, not by preaching, admonition or rhetoric—the time for oratory had passed—but rather by force of arms. Assisting him were not clerks but men of arms: *armati*. The author of this biography avoided the word *miles*. Nor is this term to be found in any other ecclesiastical accounts of the event in question—apart from the essay by Geoffrey of Vigeois, who was writing in the southern part of the kingdom. In northern France the notion of knighthood inevitably implicated trifunctionality—the subtle game whose play required the leisure of the court, the protection of high society with its isolating walls. Outside, however, where the struggle raging in society was reaching its peak, ternarity gave way to binarity. Under attack, the dominant groups did not want to give the enemy any reason to suspect division within their own ranks, and accordingly, at the height of the danger, the ideological representation they chose to put forward was simplified and toughened. Dualist, Manichaean, the new image was also logically composed, based on *discretio,* on a definition arrived at after laying down a series of distinctions familiar to functionaries trained in the schools. This image reflected the underlying structures of the state. To repress evil and to hold the "carnal" instincts in check, the "subjects" should obey the monarch, who was responsible for the *vigor ecclesiastica* and who consequently delegated his power to subordinates through a descending chain of command. These included the bishops, who, if needed, took a hand in running the repressive apparatus themselves—i.e., if their participation became imperative to insure the preservation of order, i.e., of seigniory and inequality. The White Capes, accordingly, were obliged to return to the fold. Their capes were taken away: as was befitting to commoners, they were once again exposed to the elements, their heads and shoulders bared to wind and sun, in order to inculcate the lesson that "serfs" ought not to display "insolence" toward their masters: hats off to lords. Their money was also taken from them. Indeed, their purses had not been empty. The point bears repeating: the rebels were not the poorest members of society. The bishop of Auxerre was acting in 1184 as the archbishop of Bourges had done in 1038, as a warrior captain. But this time God granted victory to the prelate. For his cause was just. He had not launched his attack against the powerful. His goal had rather been to cut down the arrogance of the populace, to bring the people to their knees in respect and obedience. A providential combat this time—the bishop had not made the mistake of enlisting on the wrong side. He had chosen the camp of the rich, of power—royal power.

For in the face of revolt by the exploited and powerless (who had managed, as we have seen, to find supporters among the clergy and in that segment of the bourgeoisie troubled by the words of the Gospel), fear—social fear—made men look to the king of France. From now on he alone, with the help of bishops and warriors, would have the capacity to maintain the social order as it should have been. It pleased him that his sycophants should depict him ridding his kingdom of the germs of corruption by fire and by the sword—expelling Jews (which was true), exterminating the mercenaries of Berry (which was false), and persecuting within the school of Paris itself that excess of intellectual temerity which deserved the appellation "heresy." He was also eager to let it be known by all that he was devoting painstaking efforts to the task of protecting good society against the intrusion of peasants and workers, including those known as "weavers"—wealthy people desperate to do penitence who joined pious brotherhoods and did degrading manual labor, like serfs. None of what the king did was surprising; it was expected that he would maintain the integrity of the boundary line setting apart those entitled to command because they were rich and did nothing from those obliged to obey because they worked; it was expected that he would keep intact the existing strict social divisions; and it was expected that in turn he would adopt the tripartite model.

25

THE ADOPTION

In 1184, the mortal remains of King Louis VII had been lying in a Cistercian monastery for four years. The power of the Capetian monarchy was just then changing rapidly in magnitude and gradually in nature. Thanks to the prosperity of the Ile-de-France—due to the exceptional vitality of its rich fields, its ever-growing vineyards, and its criss-crossing trade routes—the king was growing wealthy. A faithful ally of the Church—not only by reason of anointment, unction, and the promise he had made, but also because he and the Church had to confront the same enemies—the king was still leading an austere life. He did his part to encourage the role of the Church in high culture: the chapel was paramount among the departments of his household. As close as his ties were to the Church, however, the fourteen-year-old boy who had succeeded Louis VII to the throne in 1180 was just as closely bound by blood and marriage to the great princely courts of Champagne and Flanders. Plantagenet power was painted as his most dangerous adversary. He was advised to engage that enemy on its own terrain and with its own weapons—advised not to leave it to the aging Henry and to Richard the Lion-hearted to celebrate the values of knighthood, but rather to adopt them as his own. In order to win the allegiance of the lay aristocracy—and at the same time to throw off the tutelage of the Church (for King Philip had no intention of continuing to kneel, as his father was shown doing on the tympanum of Notre-Dame, before his bishops)—he had to show himself to be "courtly." In the thick wall that had been built up between the royal court and elegant society by the sacralization of the monarchy, cracks were beginning to appear. Profane fashions were even pushing their way into the chapel. Some of the clerks in Philip's entourage set themselves the task of incorporating into royal ideology what was most attractive in knighthood and courtly culture. One such was Andreas Capellanus.

THE ART OF LOVE

"Chaplain of the royal court," Andreas boasted of his position. Some think that he had been in the service of Marie of Champagne; he may have been raised up in those Champenois and Flemish surroundings that provided the adolescent Philip Augustus with his introduction to courtly manners. Therefore, this "art," this technical manual, designed according to the classroom model of the *artes disputandi,* sets out to justify love. The one fact of which we are certain is that Andreas somehow entered the domestic service of the king of France, and thereafter—as we sense clearly in the maliciously mocking touches he adds to his reports of the "sayings" of Eleanor and Marie— prudently held himself aloof from the extravagances of the world. His treatise *On Love*[1] was most likely written between 1186 and 1190 (just a very short time after the *Estoire* of Benedict of Sainte-Maure, but in Latin, the language of scholasticism), at which time he was an official in the royal chancellery, and there can be no doubt that his book was a product of the Capetian court. In fact, among the oldest registers collected in the Trésor des Chartes during the reign of King Philip, it is the only profane literary work. It was dedicated to Walter, son of the chamberlain in charge of that treasury, perhaps owing to the impossibility of dedicating it, without scandal to the king himself, who was then like Walter and Andreas a young man.

the rules laid down, once again, by the *Rhetorica ad Herennium.* It is a treatise on morals. The author says that he is writing at the behest of a "young" noble, not yet settled in life by virtue of marriage, still pursuing his education, his initiation—a man reminiscent of the hero of the early *Roman de la Rose.* Andreas saw—or pretended to see, for a smile plays over the entire work, and the problem is to avoid being taken in by the irony— Andreas saw his work as a teaching aid to be used in Paris to help restore order, "honesty," Ciceronian *honestas,* i.e., morality, to amorous fashions that clearly could no longer be condemned. Accordingly, the major concern was to overcome the reticence as to the games of love that remained prevalent in the entourage of the new sovereign for some years following the death of the puritanical king, Louis VII; and, to that end, to moralize the love-play. Consider, for example, one of the "disputes," or dialogues, of which Andreas' work was made up.[2] To the assertion that "love is offensive to God," three answers are given. The first is highly pragmatic: once "youth" has passed, in latter years through penitence "one can purify what one has done under the impetus of nature" (with the veiled underlying question: can what is natural really be wicked? Was nature not, as Jean de Meung would say, "God's constable," or, as Dante would say,

"God's art"?). To back this up were two further statements contradicting the original assertion: love did no harm to one's neighbor; it was the "origin of the supreme good"—a notion deriving directly from Cistercian preaching, from Bernard of Clairvaux, who maintained that carnal love was the first and necessary stage of divine love. This whole line of reasoning was based on the idea that there existed two categories of phenomena, two orders (the two spheres said by Adalbero to be governed by two distinct laws), the natural and the supernatural; each, moreover, had its own values, and "in the world" love represented the highest value of all.[3] This, it is worth emphasizing, was the idea that legitimated the desacralization of the trifunctional schema, restoring the three "orders" of society to the sphere of the carnal, wherein they came under the sway of the independent system of values on which the natural order was based. Now, was it not the case that the controlling principle of this order—of which the secular prince was the defender—was love, profane love, the linchpin around which other distinctions—political, social—were arranged? Whence the necessity of an art of love.

The work consisted of three books: how to attract love, how to increase it, and finally how to extricate oneself from its toils. It ended with a *reprobatio amoris,* which counseled men to show contempt for this worldly vanity of vanities. An ending of this sort is usually regarded as hypocritical. I do not think that this one was. To progress, in the course of a lifetime's learning, from youth to wisdom, to pass from the one realm to the other, to raise oneself a step above "nature," was to put love in its proper place relative to life's other experiences and to the global order of things. It was a way—a most clever way—of establishing the credentials of love in a royal court whose morals were severe. I have already spoken of the critical irony so evident in this Parisian work. Its style was light, playful—and so only the more audacious, making bold as it did to argue under the watchful eye of the prelates at the highest levels the most serious problems with which the Church moralists, Peter the Chanter and his friends, were then faced. Problems of sex, marriage, and relations between classes within courtly society were treated by Andreas in a very free manner, and at great length in the sixth chapter of book 1, which takes up two thirds of the work: "how does one acquire love, and in what way." This consists of eight dialogues between a man and a woman, the couple assuming eight different positions on the chessboard of social conditions. Looked at from the standpoint of Latin literary conventions, the major innovation here is that women are allowed to speak, allowed to declare that the feminine has its place—an essential place—in the game of love, in the stable and stabilizing amorous contest, and therefore in the larger society as well. Make no mistake about it: good society is what was meant here.

For love, if it was to be "honest," must not step outside a narrow field, enclosed within high walls—the very same walls that Guillaume de Lorris would soon raise up around the Garden and his Rose. Hence the peasant and the prostitute find themselves cast out of the bower, forbidden to enter inside—their expulsion is set forth tersely and unequivocally in two very brief chapters, the ninth and the eleventh. I have here translated *rusticus* as "peasant." In fact the line circumscribing the outcasts ran through the city. This point is made in unmistakable terms by the "noble" lady in the second dialogue in her reply to the "plebeian":[4] if anyone who wanted to participate in the game were allowed to do so without regard to social distinctions, "all manner of horrid, hirsute men who pass their lives in agriculture [the rustics], and not only they, but also every beggar in the public square, would be able to vie for the love of a queen." Thus not only was the beggar excluded, but with him all men whose hands were callused but empty, cast out together among the beasts: these were men who made love in the manner of horses and mules, unable to dominate the *impetus*. Why? Because they were poor. Physical suffering made them alien, kept them from sufficiently extricating themselves from the clutches of the carnal. Beauteous love was denied to any slave of labor. Hence it was denied also to prostitutes: they turned love into work.

The exclusion was more far-reaching than that, however. It also covered (chapters 7 and 8) the clerk and the nun (note the place reserved for femininity within ecclesiastical society—reserved, however, by men, misogynists, who were contemptuous of women because they were frightened of them: the advice given here was by no means to show respect for the nuns or to refrain from provoking them, but rather to be wary of them, to resist their advances). Facing heavenwards, this second barrier enclosed another domain, wherein the supernatural order was paramount. For Andreas, the clerk, *nobilissimus,* had a place in a higher echelon of nobility, a nobility "that he held not of his ancestors and of which the secular power could not deprive him." This nobility was not of this world, it did not originate with "nature." Divine law—as Adalbero of Laon had said—instituted the *ordo sacratus,*[5] which demanded sexual purity of its members: if a priest should allow himself to be sullied by carnal sin, he thereby became "ignoble"—the word is again Adalbero's. Here we catch an echo of the great rivalry that divided the court (by this date the French royal court, too, along with the others)—the rivalry between the clerks and the knights: the emphasis on a nobility of soul that arose out of the spiritual and was better than, superior to, the nobility of the body stemmed from rapidly swelling ranks of men who had risen through the Church hierarchy. But other men, who owed their rise to money, were making demands of their own. "You belong to a superior nobility," said the plebeian woman to the plebeian man, "for it is a nobility that stems not from your birth or your blood, but from your virtues and your moral character."[6] Such antagonisms, which the head of the

340

household took pains to foster by making careful distribution of his favors, assured him of power over court society. Andreas, for his part, refrains from considering love among the clergy, which would have been indecent—this despite the fact that clerks did have a nature of their own. In fact, they usually ate rather well and did not suffer greatly from the effects of fatigue, which made them more vulnerable to bodily instincts. And the following question arose: "why should a clerk be required to remain more chaste than a layman?[7] Should not both alike shun the besmirchments of sex?" The case of the clerk is in fact broached in one of the dialogues, in the conversation between the "more noble" pair—to whom virtually anything was permitted: the lady imagines herself with a clerical lover. A clergyman, she points out, would make a better lover than other men, because he would be more clever, circumspect, reserved, and temperate in behavior—all qualities that would one day bring the curate Clergue of Montaillou the many successes that we know he enjoyed. Andreas concludes the debate in the following way:[8] if the clerk wants to make love, if he enters into the game, then let him choose his place carefully, "according to the rank of his parents."

For thus delimited from above as well as from below, the protected zone within which affairs could be played out according to the rules was not homogeneous, but comprised three ranks, or echelons. The representatives of these hierarchized estates were designated by three different terms: *plebeius, nobilis, nobilior,* "plebeian," "noble," "more noble"—the "very noble" being the clerk. The absence of the word *miles* is again to be noted. The reason for this may have been that this term, like its vernacular equivalent, had no common feminine form. For the classification actually began with women: "among women," Andreas says, "I distinguish the *plebeia,* the *nobilis,* the *nobilior.* The same holds for man."[9] "You know very well what I mean by *nobilis.* I call *nobilis* any woman who is descended from a rearvassal or a lord, who is the wife of one of the two [as Gilbert of Limerick had maintained, a woman takes the estate of the man she "serves," of her "master"]; the *nobilior* is descended from great lords." Thus Andreas, familiar with his society, arranged the dignities within the aristocracy in accordance with the feudal hierarchy on which the monarchical state then relied for support. He adds that "the man does not change rank, regardless of the rank of his wife [marriage practices were in fact threatening to cause a breakdown of order, because at this time the nobleman usually married a woman of higher station than his own, and especially because for some time now knights hard-pressed for cash had been forced to give daughters without dowry to "plebeians": was not the great danger the prospect of seeing one of these Georges Dandins ennobled?]. By marriage a man can never change title. In addition, there is an extra category among men, for more noble than anyone else is the clerk." Outside the clergy, therefore, birth determined a man's rank. The order we see here was indeed natural. But

341

nobility of blood was justified only by primordial virtues. The opening speech of chapter 6 of the first book prefigures the speech made by the Lady of the Lake: "we are all offshoots of a single trunk, and by nature we have the same origin"; but moral qualities have "engendered an elite which is the nobility" (of blood).[10]

In fact, the noble and the more noble speak the same language. The most elaborate dialogues involve these characters and are given over entirely to discussions of love. The plebeian man and woman play mere secondary roles, the purpose of their presence being to make it possible to expand on the theme of social differences. Yet their inclusion in the scene and the words that they speak attest to the fact that good society, though pruned down, shorn of manual laborers, did not consist solely of clerks and nobles. Access was afforded to men and women from the third zone. Andreas had difficulty finding a suitable name for these intruders. The pedantic words that he chooses (*plebeius, plebeia*) are suggestive of the "populace," the "plebs." They are disparaging, but not because these outsiders were unarmed. In this world of mundane amusements, reference to military activity would have been out of place. The contest considered here was the opposite of the tournament. It was a linguistic joust. No knight figures in the *Art of Loving*, any more than in the *Roman de la Rose*. "Trade" is what is *déclassé*. Though not manual labor, commerce was nevertheless an activity antithetical to leisure: "throughout the week," it is said of the plebeian, "he applies all the strength of his intelligence [not of his arms] to various affairs of trade and profit; on the seventh day, resting, he would like to immerse himself in affairs of love."[11] Sunday. The pleasure of love is gratuitous and can blossom only in idle moments. Because the plebeian was unusually busy, because he was bedeviled by concern for profit, because he earned money, he lacked nobility of bodily form: "you aspire to a place among the knights; but look at your fat legs, your huge feet." Not that he was "horrible," repugnant, as those who suffered in their toil were. Trade nevertheless did debase the body to some degree. The tradesman was thus a misfit among the idle. The merchant was not of pure stock.

Yet he was not a figure of ridicule. The countess agrees to hear him out, deigns to teach him ethics and the ways of love. This, it seems to me, is of major importance. He is granted the right, moreover, to ask for even greater things: for equality, for freedom to love. In the name of the common ancestry, of the brotherhood of the sons of Adam. The song, the subversive song of our common ancestors here makes its furtive appearance. In the name of the "prowess of morals," of "culture," I am, he maintains, a virtuous, a "*prud'homme*," hence I am noble, or in any case "more so than my parents." For this man belonged to a type of family that was gradually rising to prominence in urban society. He claimed not to resemble his father. Did "virtue" not transform the features, did it not clear accounts of old black

342

marks? His legs and feet, he is sure, will before long reveal a greater delicacy of shape. Then, too, we are left with the clear impression that in celebrating that true nobility inherent in the soul, the clerk Andreas is speaking for himself and his friends. In that other "trade," the Church, men climbed more rapidly than elsewhere. The third and final argument was that if the plebeian had the temerity to try to force his way into the nobility, his prodigal nature was responsible. His profits were "honorable." They came not from toil but from trade. More than that, this was not money that he kept locked up in his coffers. Rather than save, he spent, *largissime,* as lavishly as a knight, hoping to appear through generosity as noble as a man of high rank. Original equality, high cultural attainments, and open-handed generosity spreading deniers right and left seemed to him ample justification for knocking down the hedgerows, the trellis-work (*saepta*) that kept him an outsider: "my race is too cramped within the space afforded it," he admits to the "more noble" lady, "our instincts push us to transgression." The desire for social advancement is here depicted as a manifestation of *impetus,* of the instincts of nature, a nature called upon for support by an ideology that can only be termed bourgeois, whose earliest expression we may be reading here. "It was not nature's will that I be confined within the bounds set for my class. Since I am the victim of no vice [as a clever lawyer might do, he capitalizes on his adversary's own argument: if inequality was the price of sin, why should he, who sinned no more than others, be sub-jugated?], do you think you have the right to lay down immovable obstacles in my path? These distinctions, which date from antiquity [rather than 'from the beginning of time' in this instance, for the classification in question here was not a product of mythic times, but a historical fact, hence open to modification], are imposed only on those who show themselves unworthy: the law [the *lex,* the law of interdiction, the human law whereby the serfs, according to Adalbero, were relegated to a position of inferiority] is not made for the just, but for the sinners." Yes, but what about order, *ordo?* The answer: nobility is an "order." "The orders were instituted among men *ab antiquo,*" his female companion replies. They must not be mixed to-gether. "A distinction of orders has existed among men since the beginning of time [*ab aevi primordio:* the noble lady casts social division out of the realm of historical time, to a place among the inviolable structures of crea-tion]. I do not reproach you for conducting your business 'honestly,' as your condition would have it, but rather for seeking the love of a woman of the nobility, while you are very busy with your trade. As for the generosity you display in spending what your occupation brings you, it makes you eminently worthy of the love of a woman of your own kind." Let every man keep "therefore within the limits of his kind [*genus*]," like with like. Just as Nature herself has laid it down that buzzards do not mingle with nobler birds of prey. Thereby reaffirmed was the following obvious truth: social differences were in conformity with the laws of the natural order, which made for stability. It was in the nature of the *ordo major* not to change, just as the animal species did not change.

But to make the imperatives according to which society was ordered dependent on nature was at the same time to remove that order from the jurisdiction of supernatural law—bringing it down to earth, desacralizing it. Not the priest but the prince was responsible for its vigilant defense. Only princes had the right to modify those imperatives. This fact is pointed out to the "plebeian" by the "more noble" lady—by virtue of her birth a member of the ruling order, far better versed in these matters than the mere "nobles" and accordingly equipped to give instruction to others: "although prowess [*probitas:* which gives us *'prud'homme'*] can ennoble [*nobilitare*], it cannot alter the order, to make the plebeian a baron [*procer*], or even a rear-vassal [*vavassor*], unless appeal is made to the power of the prince, who may confer nobility upon anyone of good moral character." This art of love actually celebrates the authority of the monarch. Quite clearly, the world in which one behaved "honestly" and from which all baseness was banished, a world kept scrupulously distinct from the fields of the countryside and the evil quarters of the city, was organized for the advantage of the state. In this select sphere one learned to behave properly, without coarseness, and to assume an assigned place in the ranks. This took place either within one of the two orders, clergy or nobility—the latter itself subdivided as in Loyseau—or else in that third category, specifically tailored for people who though certainly not idle were nevertheless not immersed in their work up their elbows, who lived in comfort and in the knowledge of how things were done at court, and who by condescension were allowed a place below that afforded to persons of quality.

Thus there were three categories, the three functional categories, in fact; the servants of God, the specialists in warfare who off the battlefield did nothing, and finally those who busied themselves with "trade," whose role was to supply the court with the goods it needed. But within the court, inside that zone of courtliness whose topology is set forth in Andreas' treatise, these three categories had ceased to fulfill any functions. For this closed society that power actually shaped to its own ends was reduced thereby to *otium*—indolence that needed to be furnished with amusing diversions, the more enthralling the more their rules were complex. This was in fact what defined the elite and insured its subjugation: respect for the rules of the game—good manners, etiquette, the strict ordinances of a code that was not moral, but entirely a matter of propriety: "a nobleman may sit down next to a plebeian woman without asking her permission; a nobleman may ask a noblewoman permission to sit down next to her . . . a man of lesser rank may ask a woman of superior rank to sit at her feet; she may perhaps grant him the right to sit beside her." Derisory, this power imputed to the female. The real power lay with the king, reinforced by whatever contributed to the diversion of the idle pastimes of the dominant class towards futile games of love.

A scholastic work, the treatise *De amore* laid out the parts of a complex whole with great care. The picture it painted was identical with the one earlier set down by Benedict of Sainte-Maure, but far more clear, elucidated with the aid of techniques made available by the Parisian art of distinction. It met with immediate success: before the end of the century, the name of "Andreas the Parisian," specialist in matters of love, was known in the tiny court of the count of Guines.[12] It is also clear that the book vanquished long-standing opposition in the Capetian entourage. From this point on, the theme of the three orders wasted no time making itself ubiquitous in the vernacular literature of northern France. It was woven into the little works that the knights with their new-found sobriety all dreamed of writing—for the knightly order now presumed to administer its own admonitions and to get on quite well without the preaching of the clergy. In 1205–10 or so, a "converted" Guiot of Provins claims to have written his *Bible* at Cluny; Hugh of Berzé, a vassal of the king, wrote yet another ten years later, having reached the age of maturity and wisdom; still others donned the guise of hermits, like the Recluse of Mollien, for instance, for whose *Roman de Carité* and *Miserere* we have no precise date—1185? 1225?[13] These elders all took it upon themselves to give instruction to the young, in reality adopting the tone, the bittersweet preachiness of the hermits who populated the forests of courtly literature. Like those hermits, they were quick to denounce the failings of the established Church. Piece by piece they laid out the system, incorporating the principle of trifunctionality and the complementary principle of a balanced exchange of services. Did not the "*carité*" of the *Roman* consist in mutual support? The reversion to ternarity was due to the fascination exerted on men's minds by the trinitarian image (long before Loyseau, Thomasin of Zerclaere confessed that he "understood that all perfection lay in the number three"). Thus the notions of function and reciprocity were once again made central—but not because the moralists meant to advise each individual to increase his own merit by practicing the virtues peculiar to his estate. It was rather to insure the stability of society, to preserve that "admirable ordainment," to secure peace, and to strengthen the state that "the man who does manual labor," "the man who provides food, the man who prays, the man who defends" had "to help one another on the field [of battle], in the city, in the church."

Guiot and Hugh considered the number of the "orders" to be three, whereas the Recluse applied the word "order" only to the knights and the monks. Both these groups were in fact more stringently ordered and observed more explicit rules than the rest of society, for which they set an example of regularity, the knights for the laity and the monks for the clergy; society ranged itself in several "pews" behind these two models of perfection. The essential feature of this picture is that once again the focus is exclusively on high society, on the rich; as Jean Batany has aptly put it, these minor writers looked upon the populace as an "antigroup"—a subjugated class used by the dominant classes (which, being responsible for the whole of society, absorbed the full attention of the highest authorities) as a sort of foil to reinforce their sense of their own internal order. The game that grew up between the "orders" was indeed a peaceable contest, because the common fear and hatred of the serfs enforced a closing of ranks around the sovereign. The royal presence was another essential feature. In the work of the Recluse, perhaps the most recent of the several in question, that presence was most prominent. The *Roman de carité* was dedicated to the king. His place was in the first pew. He was responsible for putting right (*aroyer*) the disarray (*desroi*), the disorder. He himself sat enthroned above order, i.e., above the three orders that made up court society. In the material sphere he carried out the work of God. His proper function was to insure an equitable distribution of well-being among the several "kinds." This was a role of such great importance—particularly for the lords, all of whom, whether noble clerks or otherwise, were well aware of the precariousness of their "wealth"—that there would have been no reason for them to stint in their assistance to the monarchy. Without so much as a murmur of protest, the throne occupied a paramount position as the keystone of the trifunctional system—an ideology that admirably served the interests of the dominant class.

BOUVINES

I have chosen to conclude this study with Bouvines: this was not a choice made out of force of habit, nor was it made because I overestimate the importance of the event. I am convinced that 1214 was the year in which the primitive history of the trifunctional figure came to an end. By that date—its form crystallized and superimposed upon the French kingdom as a whole—that figure was ready to emerge from the realm of the imaginary, ripe for embodiment in an institution. Bouvines, moreover, is more than a symbolic landmark. As the sun set on the field of battle, Philip truly became Augustus, the real Caesar, who may have scoffed at the idea of donning the imperial insignia found among the spoils of victory but who was nonetheless assured from that day on of presiding along with the pope over the destiny of Christendom. Augustus—the appellation means conqueror as well. Philip had defeated the count of Flanders. The count of Champagne shared his blood and was his subject. He had conquered Normandy and Anjou, provinces in which trifunctional ideology had been brandished against his father and himself. From the Plantagenet legacy he had seized whatever might serve his own glory, in particular the theme of the three orders. And we do in fact see trifunctionality incorporated in the commemorative literature designed to glorify the sovereign whose legitimate right God had just confirmed in the ordeal of battle.

I have already had several occasions to cite William the Breton, one of those *litterati* against whom Stephen Langton fulminated: schoolmate of James of Vitry at Paris, he used his knowledge not to preach but to make a career for himself, like Andreas entering the service of the royal chapel. At Bouvines he stuck close to the king in the thick of battle; he made the event his own, and virtually on the spot wrote a brief account of it in Latin prose. The trifunctional theme was already present then, but only on the side of right—in the Capetian camp. On the enemy side lay evil, disorder. Lustful, greedy, proud, its captains were prey to the *infelix ternarius,* its troops madmen or mercenaries. The ranks of the routed army could boast neither good men of the people nor good clerks. The emperor Otto was an excommunicate, and his followers were the enemies of the pope, the friends of the heretics. By contrast, behind Philip Augustus—forced against his will to engage in combat on a proscribed day, whereupon his first act was to kneel in prayer to Saint Peter—the entire army was sanctified, and righteous order governed the deployment of its ranks. The king flaunted the oriflamme, the banner of pacification blessed by the Gregorian Church. Saint Dionysius was on his side. And his host in fact embraced the three orders of the nation. First and foremost, of course, were the knights, pressed close around the body of the king, his strong right arm, his last resort when danger threatened, and his salvation. But the knights did not stand alone at the king's right hand. Other warriors helped them, ones who did not belong to the evil, opposing side: taking part in the first skirmishes, rivaling the nobles in virtue and loyal service, these were the "good sergeants of the Soissonais"—sons of the people: the abject, loyal people, as distinct from those putrefying dregs of the "plebs" from which the mercenaries were recruited. Next to be placed on the stage by William the Breton as accompaniment for the cavalry, which for Suger was the army, the army of the peace of God, whose ranks were drawn from the populace and led by the parish curates—similar to the army of the White Capes before it was led astray by pride and greed: rushed to the front from the wine-growing cities and towns of northern France, these men of the communes were a worker elite, and to them the mission of guarding the oriflamme was entrusted. Last to appear on the scene are the men of prayer: chanting psalms near the king were his chaplains, followed by the man responsible for planning the victorious strategy, Brother Guerin, a Templar, bishop-elect, not yet consecrated but soon to be, a man who combined the charisms of the episcopate with those of that "new," improved knighthood extolled by Saint Bernard for purifying physical valor in a bath of monastic rigor.

347

In disarray, in disorder, the wicked and the damned took flight on July 27, 1214, driven from the field by tripartite society, which under the king's command had formed up in ranks, respecting the hierarchies, to wage the war of God the avenger. But the clearest statement of the imperatives for ordering the good society to be found in this early account of the battle is saved for after the victory, coming in the description of the triumphal feast (*festum*) laid on to celebrate the marriage, as it were, of the victorious king with the kingdom just delivered by the might of his right arm.[14] From the ritual site of tournaments and battles on the borders of the realm, the sovereign made his way back to his domicile, carrying with him the booty that he would soon parcel out among his men—with the vanquished prisoners herded behind him, and Satan prostrate, chained to a cart. The king himself rode on horseback, among his comrades, the knights, displaying his "image of youth," *strenuus miles* for all that he was sacred—as a stout-hearted horseman he was the equal of Fulk the Good, of Henry II when he seduced Eleanor, of Richard the Lion-hearted parading in the shadow of Saint John of Acre. This homeward march—very much like a nuptial procession, but even more reminiscent of the new knight's joyous return from the tournament field, on which he displayed his prowess after the dubbing ceremony, to the abode of peace, the house in which the *senior* prayed, delivered judgment, and learnedly held forth, where he provided lavishly for his faithful retainers and fathered his children out of concern for the future of his line—this homeward march glorified only one of the three functions, that of the warrior—swaggering, overpowering, masculine. In the narrative account of Bouvines, this procession is shown passing through the body social, through the *inermes* submitted to the protection of God and king— the grateful society of noncombatants applauding its guardians. Respecting a hierarchy, the march proceeds through three locales one after another: first, the churches, lavishly embellished both outside and in, reverberating with "triumphal hymns"—encomiums of the king customarily sung by the clerks during coronation ceremonies while the people danced; next, the cities, "all the boroughs and towns," in whose main streets, draped with wall hangings and strewn with flowers, the parade took on the aspect of a Palm Sunday procession, prefiguring the processions of Corpus Christi, the festival of Christ the King—amid "the gathering of his people," unanimous in joyful celebration, came the king-Christ on horseback, "acclaimed by the people of every kind, of every sex, of every age"; and finally, the countryside. There the marchers met with the last group to be invited to join in the festivities, the "peasants and reapers"—workers, shouldering their scythes and rakes: of all the people, these were the weakest and poorest, most needful of royal solicitude. "Peasants, old women, and children," reads the text: *rustici, vetule et pueri*. Audible in these words are overtones of the ancient formula whereby the monarch was implored to bestow his protection on widows and orphans above all others. Here the peasants are classed together with the dispossessed, stripped by misfortune of the means of defending themselves. Perhaps the point of this was to belittle the rustic populace by depicting it as childish and helpless, whereby ultimately the germs of rebellion that it was known to carry might be exorcised. Feeble of mind and dead with exhaustion, the peasants did not join with the others in singing the praise of the victor, but merely derided the vanquished count of Flanders. But the count was a prince—and this malicious laughter from the peasantry was therefore an outrage, even a danger, for it might lead to disorderly behavior. William the Breton takes pains to drive this point home: *nec verecundabuntur:* "they had a lot of nerve," he says, to taunt the prisoner. Even so, for a short while they were allowed to indulge themselves. During a brief period the collective exuberance broke through the social carapace. An ephemeral equality blossomed with the license made legitimate by the festival atmosphere. The made-up account of the events ensuing upon victory gave prominence to the virtue and strength of the king, obscuring the customary hierarchies. But what emerges even more clearly is the henceforth fundamental antagonism of two worlds, urban and rural: the peasants—those imbeciles, those lummoxes—are too stupid to applaud or even dance; all they can do is laugh hysterically.

The marching column at length reaches its destination, which is triply symbolic: it is the *domus,* the palace of the prince; the capital, the Capitol—William the Breton had read the Latin classics, and his imagined triumph may be the ghost of Caesar's; and it is also Jerusalem. In actuality the destination was Paris. To meet the king, a cortège—a second procession—advanced along the rue Saint-Denis towards the savior. This procession consisted of two parts, in keeping with the dualist order of Gelasius. For it was not organized according to courtly conceptions, but rather reflected the Church liturgies—the clergy stood apart from the "people," chanting hymns and canticles as during the solemn observances of the rites of the faith within the walls of the cathedral. William the Breton names the principal officiants: represented were the most prominent figures in the Parisian *clerus* and *populus*—the "multitude of schoolmen" stood on one side, the "citizens" on the other. *Cives*—also suggestive of Roman antiquity, given the climate of the twelfth-century renaissance. The term was one of greater esteem than "bourgeois" and did not altogether rule out nobility.[15] It was evocative of the preponderant forces in the sprawling city. As we have seen, there were three Parises: commerce on one bank, studies on the other, and in between, the island, wherein lay the seat of power—the palace that housed chapel and court. It was to this central location that the king returned, hemmed in on one side by the tradesmen, on the other by the scholars. There he dismounted and struck his other pose, that of the old man, the sage, taking his place in the pew, putting off the military function and turning to the judicial, which henceforth would be paramount, for with the military victory began the time of peace and parley. The feasting, however, was not yet over; it continued for seven full days, and seven nights—illuminated "so that night seemed as bright as day." Indeed, the unifying victory—which mingled ages, sexes, and "kinds" in the common jubilation—also did away, for a time, with the frontier between light and darkness. After Palm Sunday came Easter and the gleam of a new flame in the heart of darkness, obliterating the night, sweeping evil away. And yet the chronicle makes not the slightest allusion to an action of grace, to anything like a *Te Deum,* a gesture of thanks to God. The whole ceremonial centered on the royal person. A liturgy—albeit monarchical, profane—the celebration culminated in the pleasures of the body: the ball, the banquet, and a spendthrift rivalry of wastrels from which the schoolmen emerged victorious.

William went immediately to work on a revision of his first draft, and put in ten years of hard labor before offering in 1224 to Louis VIII and to the glorious memory of his father his *Philippiad*—a poem in twelve cantos, a pretentious rival of the *Aeneid,* puffed-up, pompous, monumental: the earliest monument to the French state, already chauvinistic. The evocation of Bouvines comes at the conclusion of the work, the first ten cantos serving merely as prelude to this stupendous finale. In it we see the sovereign laying the groundwork for the victory by striving to eliminate corruption from his kingdom, to establish order everywhere, and to carry out slowly and laboriously the task to which Adalbero had implored Robert the Pious to harness himself: the forceful restoration of the social forms and organization envisaged by God. In the hundred and fifty verses into which the thirty-four lines of the initial version are recast and amplified in the twelfth canto's depiction of the victory feast, we notice that some of the pleats in the ideological mantle have taken on a new prominence over the years, while new ones now appear. This is the real advantage in having a two-part report of a single event, spanning a decade-long period: the changes that have occurred in the ideology of power are made manifest.

Most of the original chronicle was taken up with the description of the procession. In the later version it has been abridged considerably, to a scant few words: count Ferrand is turned over to the "citizens of Paris." The peasants have totally vanished from sight. Their jokes (considered shocking, as we have seen) are no longer heard: to give vent to plebeian sarcasms was deemed inappropriate for so magnificent a panegyric. Attention is focussed entirely on the triumph, which has taken on truly imperial trappings. The poet begins with an evocation of the triumphs of Pompey, Caesar, and especially Titus and Vespasian: this was a way of showing Philip Augustus as the destroyer of the Jews, a way of praising him for having had the wisdom to purify the kingdom—and the city of Paris—of that primordial taint before proceeding to the battlefield. At the same time, William the Breton wanted to show that the triumphal festival of the king of France was superior to those of the Roman emperors. For unlike theirs his was not confined to a single city. Of course its high point did take place in the city of Paris, and the Parisian schoolmen, "whom the king cherished above all," were the principal sponsors of the games, of the eight days of candlelit celebration. But the festivities were held throughout the kingdom. "Through the cities, towns, and burgs"—these being the main subsidiary strongholds of the royal power (the countryside goes unmentioned)—glory and glad tidings flowed to the four corners of the realm, irrigating the entire body social, and at a time when the myth of national unity was first coming into flower. Indeed, this communion *was* the festival:[17] it was as if "a single victory had engendered a thousand triumphal celebrations."[18] The military procession had simply dissolved in this exaltation, this "common" rejoicing. No line of demarcation now set the warriors apart from those whom they protected. To their king—as to Christ on Palm Sunday—all the subjects brought "glory, praise, and honor,"[19] in the form of chanting and singing (the clerks) and jigging and dancing (the people).[20] Stated more forthrightly in the *Philippiad* than it had been was the idea that the victory—that judgment rendered on high, reaffirming the alliance between God and the king he had chosen to represent him on earth—marked the beginning of an abnormal period (an octave, a span of time comparable with the week subsequent to each of the major holidays of the Trinity: Christmas, Easter, and Pentecost) during which were celebrated rites signifying the return of light—an interlude during which mankind was allowed to behave as though it were living in the age of equality before the Fall. The blood spilt at Bouvines, like a new baptism, had cleansed the people of their sin.[21] It had returned them to a state of innocence, had draped over all the subjects of the realm a cape beneath which—as beneath the White Capes—all distinctions stemming from the relations of domination vanished. But this tunic was not white. It was purple—like blood, like the oriflamme, like the triumphant emperor. Resolved in a chord, in a harmonious mingling of voices as in Gregorian plainsong or in the angelic choir of the highest heavens, all dissonance vanished—gone were differences of sex and age, as well as of "condition," "fortune," and "profession."[22] These three words replaced the one—*genus*, or "kind"—used in the original version. They explain its meaning. *Conditio* (according to both Adalbero and the Anonymous of Laon) referred to the degree of dependence. *Fortuna* occurs here no doubt because William the Breton was aware that Cicero usually linked it to *conditio,* but it was surely also suggestive of that unpredictable excitement in the air in this tumultuous period of urban economic growth that constantly threatened to undermine hierarchies based on birth. *Professio* indicated a chosen way of life. All these differences were concealed beneath

351

the festive garb, the same for everyone. It was splendid: "knight," "citizen," and "peasant" were all "radiant,"[23] each reflecting the life-giving light, alluded to by the pseudo-Dionysius, according to his rank—but now the source of this light was not God: it emanated instead from the king. Victorious, the king had drawn the triumphal mantle around his shoulders; its ample skirts enveloped the whole of the people—his mystical body. On this day Philip Augustus replaced the wicked emperor Otto IV, whom his knights had been unable to kill, but whom they had driven from the field of battle in defeat. He prepared himself to take his place at the head of purified Christian society, to lead it toward the end of time and eternal glory.

As was fitting, the grateful populace was intent on giving the king something in return for the boons it owed to his strength, eager to add another ornament to his robes. In fact it was the people—France itself—who offered "their Philip" the solemn feast as a token of their appreciation.[24] No effort was spared to render it magnificent. No one worried about the expense.[25] To the purple of the *Aeneid,* the generous subjects added the *samit* of the crusading princes from the banks of the Orontes. The triumphal cape and the crusader's robe thus came to resemble that marvelous garb worn at court revels—those feasts at which each guest wanted to outshine all the others. Yet throughout the period of rejoicing, the rivalry pitted equal against equal. Divisions between estates were forgotten. They were four in number: the clergy stood on one side; on the other were the people, divided into three factions—the knights first, the cityfolk next, and then the countryfolk. The latter were really outsiders. This point is unmistakable in William the Breton: of the four types, only the "rustic" was "stupefied"— *stupet:* as in Virgil, the word indicated bedazzlement at the sight of the miraculous.[26] Whereas the other groups—clerk, knight, and bourgeois— had their appointed places in court ceremony and so were accustomed to the magnificence, the rustic could not get over the fact of being present at the festivities. He "dared" (*audet*) conceive of himself as "raised up to the level" (*componi*) of the greatest kings—he, the peasant, that hairy creature: that was what was so unimaginable. It was tantamount to daring to ask for the love of a queen, as Andreas the Chaplain would say. We may rest assured: it was only a game, the game of victory. At the end of the octave, on the following Monday, the mask would have to be removed, the costume put aside, and everyone would have to go back to work. For eight days people went through the motions of communion, leveling, equality. But nothing changed. Only a peasant could have dreamed otherwise, could have believed that clothes could change the man, that "in changing suits, one could change minds." Only the peasant was taken in. With consummate unsophistication, he believed in the revolution, like his predecessors, the White Capes. Only he forgot the continued existence of sin and the curse of toil; only he forgot that once the lanterns had been put out, hierarchy would be reinstated, whereupon the power that stood behind it would reappear, in the shape of the king, to enforce the distinctions between orders, to preserve order, and to see to it that the manual laborer was sent back to his manure pile.

And so it was; after a time of tribulation, the aging Philip resumed his office and reigned in peace for many years after the great victory. Equitable,[27] a protector, he punished wrongdoers and lavished affection on the upholders of order. His fondest wish was to be seen as "king of the clergy," as a "pillar of the church."[28] To the people he was the king-father, the "father of his country."[29] His "affection" was "paternal."[30] This *dilectio* was the compensation offered by the master of every well-run seigniory in exchange for the *reverentia* owed him by the subjects. The stability of the state, like that of the household and the court, was based on the myth of an exchange of love between the ruler and his underlings and on the reality of a power that supplied the family with food and occasionally with pleasure, preached to it, and maintained harmony by force in its own best interest. For the festival of Bouvines, as it is depicted so admirably in this document, with its liturgies borrowed both from the Church and from the revived memories of the splendors of imperial Rome—an extraordinary, gratuitous moment symbolizing egalitarian hopes but revealing, beneath the illusions of community, in its orderly and regular structure, the resilience of the unshakable distinctions—was at bottom nothing other than a domestic ceremony. Under the gaze of a master identified with the king of the heavens, with God the Father, it ranged in proper order the male retainers of the household—those who prayed, those who fought, those who through trade provided the goods indispensable to survival. In a place apart, women and young children had their private quarters. And last of all, outside the stalwart ramparts, relegated to their workshops and fields, were the workers—those who suffer, those who sweat, those who "toil."

EPILOGUE

I shall end here. After Bouvines. Where William the Breton placed the last full stop of the *Philippiad*. At a time when the theme of the three orders has become a commonplace in everything being written in the French dialect. On November 29, 1226, the day of the anointment of the young man who would one day become Saint Louis, a day on which he promised to defend the clergy, by seeing to it that "all the Christian people through [their] will secure for the Church of God a true and lasting peace"; to check the greed of the powerful, by "forbidding all rapine and iniquity"; and to secure a right-eous, compassionate justice for the poor, by "preserving in all judgments equity and mercy" [1]—whereby the sovereign placed himself outside the social triangle, in a position to insure its stability as Christ's vicar on earth, in God's own image, through the steady flow of his benevolence—the veritable creator of the natural order. I end here, because at this point the trifunc-tional postulate has come full circle back to its origins. In this same region, the land of the Franks of old, it had been set forth by the bishops of the year 1000, who—in those troubled times that I have called the age of feudal revolution—had looked to heaven in defiance of heretics, monks, knights, and the welter of disruptive forces that surged forth from the southern part of the realm. Later, the lay aristocracy adopted it as a defense first against the morality of the Church and afterwards against the claims of the monar-chy, the competition of the newly rich, and the intractability of the peasant-ry. And finally, once the Capetian king had succeeded in bringing feudalism to heel, the clerks in his entourage, trained in Parisian schools where Saint Augustine and Dionysius the Areopagite were being read more closely than ever, once again incorporated the postulate into the ideological system as-sociated with sacred kingship. This system was founded on the principle of inequality and obedience, on the necessarily hierarchical relationship between those who, under obligation to "cherish," set the example and gave the orders, and those who, under obligation to "show reverence," carried them out. Within this hierarchy functional triparition once again found a natural place. But now it was fitted into the breach between monarch and "plebs," and helped the former hold the latter in check.

The history that I have attempted to trace is that of a figment of the imagination. It was drawing to a close. For as early as the first quarter of the thirteenth century, trifunctionality had ceased to be one of those categories of the imagination that "exist in no definite place."[2] This was well before the representatives of the three estates of the realm were called together by the counselors of Philip the Fair, who faced problems of government too serious to be resolved by himself alone, paternally, within his own household, and accordingly had to turn to the nation to win approval of fiscal machinery of a quite novel kind, and to resist the arrogant demands of a pope who, in bulls addressed to the French king, evoked—as Stephen Langton had done—"the inveterate hostility of laymen toward clerks," and who maintained—invoking the authority of Dionysius—that "the law of divinity is that inferior things are connected to superior things through intermediaries." The trifunctional figure was beginning to find embodiment in the institutional machinery and organizations of the society of orders, the form in which "society was to become standardized" "on the model of the royal domicile."[3] After Bouvines, another history begins: the history of an institution of the monarchical state.

In the words of Charles Loyseau, "these are our three orders or estates general of France": the clergy, the nobility, and that "negative order defined only in terms of that from which it was excluded: not privileges, to be sure, but blue blood and the service of God."[4] This latter order did not embrace the entire populace, but remained confined to an elite—an urban elite, based on the wealth of the city, blessed like the other two orders with privileges, and like them dominating the rest of society. For institutionalization brought to light the reality that there were actually four "estates." In 1567, Du Bellay stated as much in unmistakable terms in his *Lengthy Discourse to the King Concerning the Actuality of the Four Estates of the Kingdom of France,* in which the "popular rabble," i.e., the workers, were opposed to the three "idle" estates, and work was said to be "vile and abject." Of this everyone in the entourage of Philip Augustus and Louis VIII was convinced: at the beginning of the *Roman de la Rose,* it is Indolence who keeps sharp watch over the gate of the Garden—i.e., the court, high society, ordered society.

But had not feudal society's imaginings in reality harbored this quadripartition for a long while, beneath the veil of ternarity? The number three focussed thought on heavenly perfection. The number four drew attention to earthly materiality. When cultivated men first noticed—as early as the

355

eleventh century—that the cities were beginning to stir from their torpor, and that cityfolk were becoming rivals to be reckoned with, not to be underestimated in struggles over power; when the class lines laid down by the mode of production began slowly to shift, making it necessary to distinguish within the populace between the men of "trade" and the men of "toil"; and when the monarchy turned into something more than a myth; at that time what seemed to have been divided "since the beginning" into three functional categories was no longer "mankind," but rather an intermediary body, an elite. The three estates already sat high above an enormous mass of men bowed down in silence—forgotten.

In the hall of the Tennis Court, in 1789, three arms were raised for the oath. These were not the arms of workers. Nor were the deputies of the Third Estate—those well-appointed men then busily engaged in the destruction of "feudalism"—peasants, but rather the "plebeians" of the treatise *On Love*. No more proletarian than the White Capes, they, too, demanded their *natural* liberty and equality. But they demanded these things for themselves, for the dominant class to which they belonged, and whose dominance they by no means intended to see abolished. The original rift, accordingly, continued to gape as large as ever—a moat beyond which, as though under guard, the "toiling classes" had been corralled. I do not see that this moat has even today been entirely filled in. Nor has the immemorial image of utopia—the mirage—ceased to obsess the minds of men: the image of a society no longer riven by class distinctions, and yet still ordered. The dream . . .

ABBREVIATIONS

BEC	*Bibliothèque de l'École des Chartes*
BN	Bibliothèque Nationale (Paris)
c.	*capitulum* (chapter)
MGH	*Monumenta Germaniae Historica* (1826 to date). See also *SRM, SS*.
MS lat.	Latin manuscript
PL	*Patrologiae cursus completus . . . series latina,* ed. J.-P. Migne, 221 vols. (Paris, 1844–64).
RHC	*Recueil des historiens des croisades. Historiens occidentaux,* 5 vols. (Paris, 1844–95).
RHF	*Recueil des historiens des Gaules et de la France,* ed. Martin Bouquet et al., 24 vols. (Paris, 1738–1904).
SHF	Société de l'Histoire de France
SRM	*Scriptores rerum merovingicarum* (of *MGH*)
SS	*Scriptores* (of *MGH*)
v.	verse

NOTES

PART 1. THE FIELD OF INQUIRY

1. *Ep. 54, PL* 77:785–87.

2. Georges Dumézil, *Mythe et epopée,* 3 vols. (Paris, 1968–73) 1:15.

3. G. Baechler, *Qu'est-ce que l'idéologie?* (Paris, 1976).

4. Georges Dumézil, *Les Dieux souverains des Indo-Européens* (Paris, 1977), p. 210.

5. Marc Bloch, *La Société Féodale,* 2nd ed., (Paris, 1966), p. 406 (trans. by L. A. Manyon, *Feudal Society* [Chicago, 1961], p. 291).

6. Jacques Le Goff, *La Civilisation de l'Occident médiéval* (Paris, 1964), p. 319.

7. D. Dubuisson, "L'Irlande et la théorie médiévale des trois ordres," *Revue de l'Histoire des Religions* 190 (1975):61, n. 3, is justified, in correcting me, to assert that the theory of the three orders was not constructed, but merely, as he puts it, "brought up to date."

8. W. H. Sewell, "Etats, Corps et Ordres: Some Notes on the Social Vocabulary of the French Old Regime," *Sozialgeschichte Heute: (Festschrift für Hans Rosenberg zum 70. Geburtstag)* (Göttingen, 1974), pp. 49–68.

1. FIRST FORMULATIONS

1. R. T. Coolidge, "Adalbero, Bishop of Laon," *Studies in Medieval and Renaissance History* 2 (1965):1–114; C. Carozzi, *Le "Carmen ad Rodbertum regem" d'Adalbéron de Laon. Edition, traduction et essai d'explication,* thesis defended in 1973 at the University of Paris IV and unfortunately not yet published; T. Schieffer, "Ein deutscher Bischof des 11. Jahrhunderts: Gerard I von Cambrai (1012–1051)," *Deutsches Archiv* 1 (1937):323–60; H. Sproemberg, "Gerhardt I, Bischof von Cambrai (1012–1051)," *Mittelalter und demokratische Geschichtsschreibung* (Berlin, 1971).

2. The following chart, based on M. Bur, *La Formation du Comté de Champagne, v. 950–v. 1150,* (Nancy, 1977), pp. 128, 204, traces the relationship between Gerard and Adalbero.

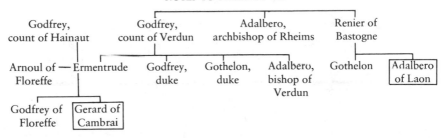

Concerning this genealogy, see: E. Hlawitschka, *Die Anfänge des Hauses Habsburg-Lothringen. Genealogische Untersuchungen zur Geschichte Lothringens und des Reiches im 9., 10. und 11. Jahrhundert* (Sarrebruck, 1969).

3. Concerning the place of the *princeps,* see now K. F. Werner, "Westfranken-Frankreich unter den Spätkarolingern und frühen Kapetingern (888–1060)," *Handbuch der europäischen Geschichte,* ed. T. Schieder, in progress, 1 (Stuttgart, 1976):731–83.

4. Jean Batany, *Approches du Roman de la Rose* (Paris, 1973).

5. P. E. Schramm, *Der König von Frankreich. Das Wesen der Monarchie vom 9. bis zum 16. Jahrhundert* 2nd ed. (Weimar, 1960) chs. 1, 2, 4.

6. *Carmen,* v. 366 (all references are to the edition prepared by C. Carozzi, currently in press).

7. *Carmen,* v. 258–59.

8. L. Wallach, *Alcuin and Charlemagne,* (Ithaca, 1959). (Thus Alcuin's *Disputatio de Rhetorica* is a treatise on kingship: see W. Ullmann, *The Carolingian Renaissance and the Idea of Kingship,* [London, 1969]).

9. *MGH, SS,* 7; the sentence appears on page 485.

10. E. Van Mingroot, "Kritisch onderzoek omtrent de datering van de *Gesta episcoporum Cameracensium,*" *Revue belge de Philologie et d'Histoire* 53 (1975):281–332.

11. Georges Duby, "Gérard de Cambrai, la paix et les trois fonctions sociales. 1024," *Compte rendu des séances de l'Académie des Inscriptions et Belles-Lettres,* 1976, pp. 136–46.

2. GERARD OF CAMBRAI AND THE PEACE

1. *Gesta* 3, c. 52 (*MGH, SS* 7:486).

2. O. Köhler, *Das Bild des geistlichen Fürsten in den Viten des 10, 11, 12 Jahrhunderts* (Berlin, 1935).

3. *Gesta* 3, c. 44 (*MGH, SS* 7:482).

4. *Gesta* 37 (*MGH, SS* 7:480).

5. G. de Smet, *De paces Dei der bisdommen van het graafschap Vlaanderen (1024–1119). Kritische studie en tekstvitgave,* thesis, Louvain, 1956, unpublished; H. Platelle, "La violence et ses remèdes en Flandre au XIe siècle," *Sacris Erudiri* 20 (1971):101–73; J.-F. Lemarignier, "Paix et réforme monastique en Flandre et en Normandie autour de l'année 1023. Quelques observations," *Droit privé et institutions régionales. Études historiques offertes à Jean Yver* (Paris, 1976), pp. 443–68.

6. For the most recent consideration of this text, see E. Van Mingroot, "Acta synodi Attrebatiensis (1025): problèmes de critiques de provenance," *Studia Gratiana* 20 (*Mélanges G. Fransen,* 1976), pp. 201–29.

7. *Gesta* 3, c. 27 (*MGH, SS* 7:474).

8. R. Bonnaud-Delamare, "Les institutions de paix dans la province eccléiastique de Reims au XI⁰ siècle," *Bulletin philologique et historique, années 1955–1956* (1957), pp. 148–53, has published these two texts side by side.

9. *PL* 142:1294.

10. *PL* 142:1289.

11. *PL* 142:1294.

12. *PL* 142:1307–9.

13. *PL* 142:1307.

14. *PL* 142:1307.

15. *PL* 142:1307.

16. *PL* 142:1308.

17. *PL* 142:1308.

18. *PL* 77:34.

19. F. Cabrol and H. Leclercq, *Dictionnaire d'archéologie et de liturgie,* 15 vols. (Paris, 1907–53), 3:1534–36, article "Christ (letter from)."

20. He thought it best to join the latter portion of the speech to the earlier part at the end of 3, c. 52, *MGH, SS* 7:486.

21. *MGH, SS* 7: 485, lines 48–49.

22. Ibid., 486 line 11.

23. *MGH, SS* 7:485.

24. *Gesta* 1, c. 115 (*MGH, SS* 7:452).

25. *Gesta* 3, cc. 40, 43, 48 (*MGH, SS* 7:481–83).

26. *Gesta* 2, c. 4 (*MGH, SS* 7:456).

27. *Gesta* 2, c. 19 (*MGH, SS* 7:460).

28. *Gesta* 1, cc. 117, 120.

29. *Gesta* 3, c. 52 (*MGH, SS* 7:486, l. 2).

30. *Gesta* 3, c. 52 (*MGH, SS* 7:486, l. 17).

3. ADALBERO OF LAON AND THE ROYAL MISSION

1. See also the brief study by E. Hegener, "Hagen, Politik und Heilsgeschichte: 'Carmen ad Robertum regem.' Zur 'zweiten Sprache' in der politischen Dichtung des Mittelalters," *Mittellateinisches Jahrbuch* 9 (1973):31–38.

2. *Carmen*, v. 191–92.

3. *Carmen*, v. 189.

4. Georges Dumézil, *L'Idéologie tripartie des Indo-Européens,* (Brussels, 1958), pp. 62–67.

5. *Carmen*, v. 424.

6. *Carmen*, v. 366.

7. *Carmen*, v. 361, *legibus edocti;* this expression echoes the *per sanctos patres edocti* of Gerard of Cambrai's last speech (*Gesta* 3, c. 52), which strengthens the feeling that this passage belongs to the first draft of the *Gesta,* that it was written in 1025, and that Adalbero was familiar with it before writing his poem.

8. Still another echo of the *Gesta;* in opposition to his confrères, who were asking that one penitence be imposed on all, Gerard left it to the wisdom of the bishops to decide what sanctions were to be meted out.

9. *Carmen*, v. 367.

10. *Carmen*, v. 312.

11. R. W. Southern, *The Making of the Middle Ages* (New Haven, 1953), ch. 4.

12. *Carmen*, v. 193.

13. *Carmen*, v. 196–97.

14. *Carmen*, v. 203.

15. *Carmen*, v. 204.

16. *Carmen*, v. 209–10.

17. *Carmen*, v. 214.

18. *Carmen*, v. 217.

19. *Carmen*, v. 218–23.

20. *Carmen*, v. 229–36.

21. *Carmen*, v. 240.

22. *Carmen*, v. 257–58.

23. *Carmen*, v. 260–73.

24. *Carmen*, v. 274.

25. *Carmen*, v. 275.

26. *Carmen*, v. 288, 291.

27. *Carmen*, v. 282.

28. It is important to translate such a text as directly as possible, even at the cost of sacrificing elegance. D. Dubuisson's errors of interpretation are due largely to his use of an imperfect translation of the *Carmen*.

29. Concerning this point, reference should be made to another poem versified in the same mode by Adalbero, the *De Summa Fidei*, ed. G. A. Hückel, "Les poèmes satiriques d'Adalbéron, *Université de Paris: Bibliothéque de la Faculté des Lettres* 13 (1901):168—77; certain of its verses echo those of the *Carmen:*

> Tres in personis quorum substantia simplex
> Est natura trium simplex, nati quoque bina
> Nam Christi natura duas se dividit in res.

30. *Carmen*, v. 56.

31. *Carmen*, v. 59: again the expression comes from the *Libellus of Arras*.

32. *Carmen*, v. 69–76.

33. *Carmen*, v. 155.

34. *Carmen*, v. 156.

35. *Carmen*, v. 167.

36. This was indeed Cluny's outlook, formulated notably by abbot Odo of Cluny; is he not the subject of the allusion in v. 127–28 to Saint-Martin of Tours, of which he was canon before becoming a monk?

37. *Carmen*, v. 112.

38. *Carmen*, v. 95–117.

39. H. Platelle, "Le problème du scandale: les nouvelles modes masculines aux XIe et XIIe siècles," *Revue belge de Philologie et d'Histoire* 53 (1975):1071–96.

40. Verse 118 of the *Carmen* begins a parody of the crusade in which monks, young and old alike, are shown grotesquely being put to rout by the infidels.

41. *Carmen*, v. 177.

42. *Carmen*, v. 412–16.

4. THE SYSTEM

1. H. Courbin, *L'Imagination créatrice dans le soufisme d'Ibn Arabi* (Paris, 1977), p. 19.

2. As was clearly seen by Sewell with regard to the society of the ancien régime and the first of the orders, the clergy.

3. *Carmen*, v. 302–3.

4. Claude Lévi-Strauss, *Anthropologie structurale* (Paris, 1958), p. 58 (trans. C. Jacobson and B. G. Schoepf, *Structural Anthropology* [New York, 1967], p. 158).

5. Robert Fossier, *Histoire sociale de l'Occident médiéval* (Paris, 1970), p. 144.

PART 2. GENESIS

1. É. Lesne, *Histoire de la propriété ecclésiastique en France*, 6 vols., (Paris, 1910–43) 4:635–36.

2. B. Merlette, "Écoles et bibliothèques à Laon du déclin de l'Antiquité au développement de l'université," *95ᵉ Congrès des sociétés savantes, Reims 1970, Section philologique et historique* (1975) 1:275–99.

3. *Gesta* 3, c. 52.

4. A few preliminary works facilitate this exploration. In particular, L. Manz, *Die Ordo-Gedanke. Ein Beitrag zur Frage des mittelalterlichen Ständegedankens* (Stuttgart-Berlin, 1937); H. Krings, *Ordo. Philosophisch-historisch Grundlegung einer abendländischen Idee* (Halle, 1941); Heinemann, "Zur Ständedidaxe in der deutschen Literatur des 13–15. Jhd," *Theodor Frings zum 80. Geburtstag* (Berlin, 1973); Y. Congar, "Les laïcs et l'ecclésiologie des *ordines* chez les théologiens des XIᵉ–XIIᵉ siècles," *I laici nella societas christiana dei secoli XI e XII* (Milan: Atti della terza Settimana internazionale di studio. Mendola, 21–27 agosto 1965; 1968).

5. HIERARCHY

1. J. Paul, *Histoire intellectuelle de l'Occident médiéval* (Paris, 1973), p. 101.

2. *PL* 77:34, "As I recall having said in books on morality"; *PL* 76:203.

3. *Sentences* 3, c. 47, *PL* 83:717

4. See the Variant, *PL* 76:203.

5. *Enarratio in psalmis*, 39, c. 6 (*PL* 36:436).

6. 1 Cor. 15:22–23.

7. *PL* 2:864.

8. *Jonas d'Orléans et son "De institutione regia." Étude et texte critique*, ed. J. Reviron (Paris, 1930), chap. 10, p. 164.

9. *Capitularia regum Francorum*, ed. A. Boretius, V. Krause, 2 vols. (Hanover: MGH, *Legum Sectio II*, 1883–97), 1, no. 33 (92).

6. CONCORD

1. *Sermo* IX, *PL* 89:860.

2. *Libellus de exordiis et incrementis quarundam in observationibus ecclesiasticarum rerum*, *Capitularia* 2:516.

3. C. Carozzi, *Le "Carmen."*

4. *The Letters and Poems of Fulbert of Chartres*, ed. F. Behrends (Oxford, 1976), no. 51 (= *RHF* 10:463).

5. *Manuel* 10, c. 3 (ed. Pierre Riché, *Dhuoda. Manuel pour mon fils* [Paris, 1975], pp. 346–48).

7. ORDERS

1. C. Nicolet, "Essai d'histoire sociale: l'ordre équestre à la fin de la république romaine," *Ordres et Classes* (Saint-Cloud social history colloquium), 1973.

2. B. Kübler, "Ordo," in *Paulys Real-Encyclopädie der classischen Altertumswissenschaft*, new ed. E. Kroll, 18 (Stuttgart, 1939): 930–34.

3. *De Officiis* 1, cc. 4, 5.

4. *De civitate Dei* 19, c. 13.

5. *De exhortatione castitatis*, *PL* 2:971.

6. *Ad uxorem* 1. c. 7 (*PL* 1:1398); *De monogamia*, c. 12 (*PL* 2:997).

8. FUNCTIONS: TO PRAY AND TO FIGHT

1. Schwanz, *Publizistische Sammlung zum acacianischen Schisma* (Munich, 1934), p. 7 ff.

2. *MGH, Epistolae merowingici et Karolini aevi* 1:56 (p. 310).

3. *Tusculan Disputations* 4, c. 24.

4. Whereas the word *ordo* does not appear therein, contrary to what is implied by E. Delaruelle, "Essai sur la formation de l'idée de croisade," *Bulletin de littérature ecclésiastique*, 1944; "En relisant le *De institutione regia* de Jonas d'Orléans," *Mélanges d'histoire du moyen âge dédiés à la mémoire de Louis Halphen* (Paris, 1951), pp. 185–92.

5. *Codex Carolinus, MGH, Ep. Karolini aevi* 1:480.

6. *MGH, Legum Sectio III, Concilia aevi Karolini* 2:610, c. 3.

7. Reported by Paschase Radbert in his biography, *PL* 120:1609.

8. *Libellus de exordiis* (841), *Capitularia* 2:516.

9. *MGH, Ep. Karolini aevi* 3:226.

10. W. Ullmann, *The Growth of Papal Government in the Middle Ages*, (London, 1955), p. 143.

11. M. Avery, *The Exultet Rolls of South Italy*, 2 vols. (Princeton, 1936) 2, plate 169.

12. *MGH, Ep. Karolini aevi* 4:191–92.

13. Theodore Caplow, *Two Against One: Coalitions in Triads* (Englewood Cliffs, 1969).

9. TERNARITY

1. *PL* 23:225; cf 213–16.

2. G. Folliet, "Les trois catégories de chrétiens. Survie d'un thème augustinien," *Année théologique augustinienne* 14 (1954):81–96.

3. *PL* 75:535.

4. *PL* 76:976–77.

5. *Vita Burchardi*, written at the same time as the *Gesta, MGH, SS* 4:840, cited by J. Batany, "Abbon de Fleury et les théories des structures sociales vers l'an mil," *Etudes ligériennes d'Histoire et d'Archéologie médiévales* (Auxerre: Semaine d'études médievales, Saint-Benoît-sur-Loire, 1969; 1975).

6. *De moribus et actis primorum Normanniae ducum*, ed. Jules Lair, *Mémoires de la Société des Antiquaires de Normandie*, 3d series, 23 (Caen, 1865).

7. Georges Duby, "L'image du prince en France au début du XIe siècle," *Cahiers d'Histoire* 17 (1972):211–16.

8. H. Prentout, *Étude critique sur Dudon de Saint-Quentin* (Paris, 1916).

9. L. Musset, "Le satiriste Garnier de Rouen et son milieu," *Revue de Moyen Age latin* 10 (1954):240–41.

10. K. F. Werner, "Quelques observations au sujet des débuts du 'duché de Normandie,'" *Droit privé . . . Etudes . . . offertes à Jean Yver*, pp. 691–709.

11. Ed. Lair, p. 201.

12. J.-F. Lemarignier, "Autour de la royauté française du IXe au XIIIe siècle," *BEC* 108 (1956):5–36.

13. A. Vidier, *L'Historiographie à Saint-Benoît-sur-Loire et les miracles de Saint Benoît* (Paris, 1965), pp. 104–5; J.-F. Lemarignier, "L'exemption monastique et les origines de la réforme grégorienne," *A Cluny, congrès scientifique . . . 9–11* juillet 1949 (Dijon, 1950), pp. 301–15.

14. Jean Batany, "Abbon de Fleury," p. 107.

15. *PL* 139:471–72.

16. *PL* 139:464.

17. *PL* 139:463.

18. *PL* 139:464.

19. Carl Erdmann, *Die Entstehung des Kreuzzugsgedankens* (Stuttgart, 1935), pp. 86–87 (trans. M. W. Baldwin and W. Goffart, *The Origin of the Idea of Crusade* [Princeton, 1977], p. 96).

20. *Histoire des fils de Louis le Pieux*, ed. P. Lauer (Paris, 1926) 4, c.2, p. 120.

21. *Ep.* 18 (793), *MGH, Ep. Karolini aevi* 4:51.

22. *Capitularia* 1:303–7.

23. *Poème sur Louis le Pieux*, ed. E. Faral (Paris, 1932) 2, vv. 954–57.

24. Ibid., 1, v. 151.

25. *MGH, SS* 15:512–13.

26. See *Collationes* 2, c.7 (*PL* 133:554).

27. *Vita Geraldi* 2, c. 8. (*PL* 133:675; trans. G. Sitwell, *St. Odo of Cluny* [London, 1958], p. 139).

28. "All religion lies in the rejection [of the world]." *Collationes* 3, c. 23 (*PL* 133:607).

29. *Vita Geraldi* 2, c. 16 (*PL* 133:679; Sitwell p. 145).

30. *Vita Geraldi* 1, c. 32 (*PL* 133:660; Sitwell p. 121).

31. *Vita Geraldi* 1, c. 8 (*PL* 133:647; Sitwell p. 101).

32. *King Alfred's Old English Version of Boethius' De Consolatione Philosophiae*, ed. W. J. Sedgefield (Oxford, 1899), pp. 40–41.

33. E. S. Duckett, *Alfred the Great* (Chicago, 1957).

34. Grierson, "Grimbald of St. Bertin's," *English Historical Review* 55 (1940):529–61.

35. B. S. Donaghey, "The Sources of King Alfred's Translation of Boethius *De Consolatione Philosophiae*," *Anglia* 82 (1964):23–57; K. Otten, *König Alfreds Boethius* (Tübingen, 1964); F. A. Payne, *King Alfred and Boethius* (Madison, 1968).

36. In the phrase of Wendy Davies, who dealt with these subjects in my seminar in 1972.

37. And more recently his student Dubuisson, "L'Irlande et la théorie médiévale des trois ordres," *Revue de l'histoire des religions* 190 (1975). It should be noted that Dubuisson's study in fact shows quite different intellectual models: society is conceived more readily in quaternary than in ternary form; the life of Saint Patrick, on which he comments (pp. 54–55), declares that the king engenders other kings, warriors, and priests; but the people are a wholly separate category.

38. G. Lanoë, "Approche de quelques évêques-moines en Angleterre au Xe siècle," *Cahiers de civilisation médiévale* 19 (1976):135–50.

39. M. M. Dubois, *Aelfric, sermonnaire, docteur et grammairien. Contribution à l'étude de la vie et de l'action bénédictines en Angleterre au Xe siècle* (Paris, 1943).

40. *Aelfric's Lives of the Saints being a Set of Sermons on Saints' Days*, ed. W. W. Skeat, 2 vols. (London, 1881–1900) 2:120–24.

41. *Pseudo Egberti Exceptiones* 161, ed. B. Thorpe, *Ancient Laws and Institutes of England* (London, 1840) 2:126.

42. *De vetero et novo testamento*, ed. S. J. Crawford, *The Old English Version of the Heptateuch, Aelfric's Treatise on the Old and New Testament and His Preface to Genesis* (London, 1922), p. 71.

43. The most recent edition is that of K. Jost, *Die "Institutes of Polity, civil and ecclesiastical": Ein Werk Erzbischofs Wulfstans von York* (Berne, 1959).

44. Ed. Jost, pp. 55–58.

45. Wendy Davies.

46. *PL* 117:953.

47. A monk of the nearby abbey of Vauclair was still doing so in about 1160, MS Laon 85, f° 81.

10. THE HEAVENLY EXAMPLE

1. *Monuments Historiques* (Cartons des rois), ed. Jules Tardif (Paris, 1866), no. 250.

2. B. de Montfaucon, *Bibliotheca bibliothecarum manuscriptorum nova*, 2 vols. (Paris, 1739) 2:1296.

3. *BN*, MS lat. 1141; M. T. Gousset, "La représentation de la Jérusalem céleste à l'époque carolingienne" *Cahiers archéologiques* 33 (1974):47–60.

4. The theories that Suger attempted to implement through a hierarchization of feudal services, for instance, derive directly therefrom.

5. *Celestial Hierarchy*, §165 (trans. M. de Gandillac, *Oeuvres complètes du Pseudo-Denys l'Aréopagite* [Paris, 1943], p. 197).

6. In the second half of the seventeenth century, bishops from Bérulle on invoked the pseudo-Dionysius to justify social inequality.

7. *Celestial Hierarchy*, §165 (*Oeuvres*, p. 196).

8. *Celestial Hierarchy*, §273 (*Oeuvres*, p. 222).

9. *Treatise on the Names of God*, §729 (*Oeuvres*, pp. 121–23).

10. *Celestial Hierarchy*, §164 (*Oeuvres*, p. 196).

11. Letter 9, §1108 (*Oeuvres*, p. 354).

12. *Ecclesiastical Hierarchy*, c. 1.

13. *Ecclesiastical Hierarchy*, c. 1.

14. *Celestial Hierarchy*, §200, c.6 (*Oeuvres*, pp. 205–6).

15. *Celestial Hierarchy*, §257, 260, 261, c. 9 (*Oeuvres*, pp. 217–21); B. Vallentin, "Der Engelstaat, Zur mittelalterlichen Anschauung vom Staat (bis auf Thomas von Aquino)," *Grundrisse und Bausteine zur Staats- und zur Geschichtslehre, zusammengetragen zu den Ehren Gustav Schmollers* (Berlin, 1908).

16. *Ecclesiastical Hierarchy*, §505 (*Oeuvres*, pp. 297–98).

17. *Manuel* 9, c. 3 (ed. Riché, pp. 330–32); *Capitularia* 2:451, c. 3.

18. In particular in the Missal of Saint-Denis, BN, MS lat. 9436, f° 15.

19. O. Guillot, "La consécration de l'abbaye de Beaulieu-les-Loches," *Actes du Colloque médiéval de Loches* (1973). (*Mémoires de la Société archéologique de Touraine* 9, 1975).

20. R. Roques, *L'Univers dionysien. Structure hiérarchique du monde selon le pseudo-Denys* (Paris, 1954), p. 174.

21. *Ecclesiastical Hierarchy*, §501 (*Oeuvres*, p. 294).

11. THE POLITICAL CRISIS

1. These documents have been newly exploited by J.-F. Lemarignier, *Le Gouvernement royal aux premiers temps capétiens (987–1108)* (Paris, 1965).

12. THE COMPETING SYSTEMS

1. As is done by R. H. Bautier, "L'hérésie d'Orléans et le mouvement intellectuel au début du XIe siècle. Documents et hypothèses," *95e Congrès des Sociétés savantes, Reims 1970, Section philologique et historique* (1975) 1:63–88.

2. H. Taviani, "Naissance d'une hérésie en Italie du Nord au XIe siècle" *Annales E.S.C.* 29 (1974):1224–52.

3. C. Castoriadis, *L'Institution Imaginaire de la Société* (Paris, 1975), p. 218.

4. H. Taviani, "Le mariage dans l'hérésie de l'an mil," *Annales E.S.C.* 32 (1977):1074–89.

5. Most recent contributions to the question: B. Töpfer, *Volk und Kirche zur Zeit der beginnenden Gottesfriedensbewegung in Frankreich* (Berlin, 1957); H. Hoffmann, *Gottesfriede und Treuga Dei* (Stuttgart, 1964); H. E. J. Cowdrey, "The Peace and the Truce of God in the Eleventh Century," *Past and Present* 46 (1970):42–67.

6. Georges Duby, "La diffusion du titre chevaleresque sur le versant meditérranéen de la Chrétienté latine," *La Noblesse au Moyen Age, XIe-XVe siècles,* ed. P. Contamine (Paris, 1976), pp. 39–70.

7. *Historia episcoporum autissiodorensium, RHF* 10:172.

8. D. F. Callahan, "Adhémar de Chabanne et la paix de Dieu," *Annales du Midi* 89 (1972):21–43.

9. H. Clastres, *La Terre sans mal. Le prophétisme Tupi-Guarani* (Paris, 1975), p. 120.

10. Ibid, p. 141.

13. THE FEUDAL REVOLUTION

1. Pierre Bonnassie, *La Catalogne du milieu du Xᵉ à la fin du XIᵉ siècle. Croissance et mutations d'une société,* 2 vols. (Toulouse, 1975–76).

2. J. Johrendt, *"Milites" und "Militia" in 11. Jahrhundert. Untersuchung zur Frühgeschichte des Rittertums in Frankreich und Deutschland* (Erlangen, 1971).

3. As Jacques Le Goff thinks, *L'Europe aux IXᵉ-XIᵉ siècles. Aux origines des états nationaux* (Warsaw, 1968), p. 69, n. 14.

4. Devereux, in A. Besançon, *L'Histoire psychanalytique. Une anthologie* (Paris, 1974), p. 138.

5. *Carmen,* v. 197.

6. C. Castoriadis, *L'Institution imaginaire,* p. 112.

7. The letter *De episcopis ad bella procedentibus* of Fulbert of Chartres, *PL* 141:255–60, echoes on the French side of the Channel the propositions of Aelfric and Wulfstan.

14. THE AGE OF THE MONKS

1. *MGH, SRM* 2:509–24.

2. R. Folz, "Tradition hagiographique et culte de Saint Dagobert, roi des Francs," *Le Moyen Age* 69 (1963):17–35; F. Graus, *Volk, Herrscher und Heiligen,* 1965, p. 403, n. 604; K. H. Krüger, *Königsgrabkirchen der Franken* (Munich, 1971), pp. 190–93. These historians agree in dating this text from the last third of the eleventh century. I join them in their hypothesis, remaining unconvinced by that of C. Carozzi (*Congrès des Sociétés savantes,* Lille, 1976). Carozzi believes that the *Vita* was written much earlier, prior to 1040; otherwise, he says, the hagiographer would not have failed to bestow upon his royal hero the thaumaturgic power that Helgaud attributed to Robert the Pious. Is this really a proof? What the pilgrims of Stenay hoped for from Saint Dagobert was not healing of their bodies but fertility of their lands, much as other peasants hoped to be healed by king Henry IV of Germany when they pressed forward to touch the fringes of his cloak. Be that as it may, C. Carozzi still maintains that the text is prior to 1069, basing his judgment on the fact that no mention is made therein of monks. True—but the *Vita*'s intention was to speak only of potential pilgrims, of people who could move, seculars. There is I think another indication which might incline one to date the writing of

the life of Dagobert to the decades prior to 1100. In one of the manuscripts in which it is contained, the text is followed by a royal genealogy. In this C. Carozzi sees a sign, and surely he is not wrong, that the dukes of Lower Lorraine wished both to bring out the connections between their line and that of the Frankish kings and, by glorifying Dagobert, to give themselves a saint for an ancestor. But it seems unlikely that the dukes wanted to exalt a sovereign in the third or fourth decade of the eleventh century. Indeed, at that time, as shown by the *Deeds of the Bishops of Cambrai*, the house of Ardennes was in violent conflict with the king of Germany as well as the *Carlenses*. By contrast, it would have been natural for the duke to have the virtues of the *rex pacificus* celebrated either in 1069, when a sanctuary with relics was being restored on his domain, or else after 1087, when Lorraine had devolved upon Godfrey of Bouillon, grandson of Godfrey the Bearded, an authentic descendant of the Carolingians, who was quite concerned that his ancestry be known (see the study of the *Genealogia comitum Bulloniensium* by L. Génicot, *Etudes sur les principautés lotharingiennes*, [Louvain, 1975]). I do not therefore regard the *Vita Dagoberti* as contemporary with the proclamations of Adalbero and Gerard.

3. *MGH, SRM* 2:515, 521.

4. *MGH, SRM* 2:515.

5. *Vita Trudonis*, c. 4 (*MGM, SRM* 6:278): "ut mos est regiis pueris, venandi exerceret ritum"; *Gesta Dagoberti*, c. 2 (*MGH, SRM* 2:401): "cum autem adolescentiae aetatem ut genti Francorum moris est venationibus exerceret."

6. J. Leclercq, *L'Amour des lettres et le désir de Dieu. Initiation aux auteurs monastiques du Moyen Age*, (Paris, 1957).

15. FLEURY

1. Helgaud de Fleury, *Vie de Robert le Pieux*, ed. R. H. Bautier and G. Labory (Paris, 1965).

2. Ibid., c. 30, p. 138.

3. Ibid., p. 140.

4. Ibid., p. 136.

5. Ibid., p. 138.

7. *Vie de Robert de Pieux*, c. 27, p. 126.

8. Eudes de Saint-Maur, *Vie de Bouchard le vénérable, comte de Vendôme, de Corbeil, de Melun et de Paris*, ed. C. Bourel de la Roncière (Paris, 1892).

9. Very poorly edited by E. de Certain, *Les Miracles de Saint Benoît* (Paris, 1858), corrected by A. Vidier, *L'Historiographie à Saint-Benoît-sur-Loire*.

10. *Miracles* 5, cc. 1–4, pp. 192–98.

11. *RHF* 11:387.

12. *Miracles* 5, c. 2, p. 193.

13. Ibid., c. 4, p. 196.

14. Ibid., c. 2, p. 194.

15. *Pedites* 5, c. 4, p. 196.

16. Ibid., c. 2, p. 194.

17. *Clerici* 5, c. 2, p. 193.

18. Ibid., c. 2, p. 193; c. 4, p. 196.

19. Ibid., c. 2, pp. 193–94.

20. Ibid., p. 194

21. Ibid., c. 4, p. 196.

22. Ibid., c. 2, v. 194.

16. CLUNY

1. *"Utriusque sexus et ordinis,"* Raoul Glaber, *Les cinq livres de ses histoires (900–1024),* ed. M. Prou (Paris, 1886) 4, c. 13; see also 2, cc. 4, 15.

2. Ibid., 3, c. 8, 26; 4, c. 1, 4.

3. Ibid., 5, c. 1, 13.

4. Ibid., 2, c. 9, 18.

5. Ibid., 3, c. 4, 15.

6. See 4, c. 5, 15.

7. Ibid., 4, c. 4, 10; c. 5, 14; 5, c. 1, 16.

8. Ibid., 4, c. 6, 18.

9. *Ep.* 4, c. 21, *PL* 157:162.

10. *Gesta Francorum, RHC* 3:324.

11. *Historia hierosolymitana, PL* 166:1068.

12. Roman synodal statutes of 1096, T. N. Bisson, "The Organized Peace in Southern France and Catalonia, ca. 1150–ca. 1233" *American Historical Review* 82 (1977):295.

13. Raymond d'Aguilhers, *Historia francorum, RHC* 3:254.

14. *PL* 159:916.

15. A. L'Huillier, *Vie de Saint Hugues, abbé de Cluny, 1024–1109* (Solesmes, 1888), p. 610.

16. *Bibliotheca cluniacensis,* ed. M. Marrier (Paris, 1614 [Mâcon, 1915]), pp. 439–40.

17. NEW TIMES

1. 3, c. 9, *PL* 143:1153.

2. Causa 12, quaestio 1, c. 7.

3. O. Lottin, "Nouveaux fragments théologiques de l'École d'Anselme de Laon," *Recherches de théologie ancienne et médiévale* 13 (1946):206.

4. Y. Labande-Maillefert, in *I laici nella societas chrisitana* (Milan, 1966), plate XII, pp. 519–20.

5. I am citing documents from Mâcon: *Cartulaire de Saint-Vincent-de-Mâcon,* ed. C. Ragut (Mâcon, 1864), nos. 548 (1079–96) and 598 (1096–1124; *Recueil des chartes de l'abbaye de Cluny,* ed. A. Bernard and A. Bruel, 6 vols. (Paris, 1876–1903) 5, no. 3726 (1097).

6. J. Batany, *Approches du Roman de la Rose,* p. 85.

18. MONASTICISM'S LAST LUSTER

1. See J. F. Benton, *Self and Society in Medieval France: The Memoirs of Abbot Guibert of Nogent* (New York, 1970), p. 11.

2. Guibert de Nogent, *Histoire de sa vie (1053–1124),* ed. G. Bourgin (Paris, 1907) 3, c. 14, p. 203 (Benton trans. p. 204).

3. Ibid., c. 10 (Benton, p. 183).

4. Causa 17, quaestio 4, c. 38.

5. Guibert, *Histoire* 1, c. 6 (Benton, p. 50).

6. *Gesta dei per Francos* 5 (*RHC* 4).

7. Guibert, *Histoire* 1, c. 21 (Benton, p. 104).

8. Ibid., cc. 21, 22 (Benton, pp. 102–5).

9. Ibid., 3, c. 19 (Benton, pp. 221–22).

10. Ibid., c. 7 (Benton, pp. 166, 172).

11. *Gesta* 1 (*RHC* 4).

12. *Gesta* 7 (*RHC* 4).
13. Ibid.
14. *Gesta* 2 (*RHC* 4).
15. *Sermones de diversis* 9, cc. 2, 3 (*PL* 183:566); 35 (*PL* 183:634).
16. Geoffroy de Saint-Blaise-d'Amont, *Homiliae in scripturam* 12 (*PL* 174:1112–13).
17. Idung de Prüfening, *Argumentum super quatuor questionibus* 3, ed. R. B. C. Huyens, "Le moine Idung et ses deux ouvrages," *Studi medievali* (1972).
18. *Ep.* 365 (*PL* 182:570).
19. Note reported by his companion Geoffrey of Auxerre, *Declamationes ex sancti Bernardi sermonibus* 10 (*PL* 184:444).
20. *Statuta capitulorum generalium cisterciensis* 1 (Louvain, 1933):108.
21. *Ep.*116 (*PL* 197:338).
22. J. Leclercq, "Un document sur les débuts des Templiers" *Revue d'Histoire ecclésiastique* 52 (1957):81–91.
23. *PL* 182:924.
24. Suger, *Vie de Louis VI le Gros*, ed. H. Waquet (Paris, 1929), c. 2, p. 14.
25. Ibid., c. 24, pp. 172–74.
26. Ibid., c. 30, p. 250.
27. *Historia ecclesiastica*, ed. A. Le Prevost, 5 vols. (Paris, 1838–55) 3:125.
28. Ibid., 11, c. 34 (4:285).
29. Ibid., 12, c. 19 (4:364).

19. IN THE SCHOOL

1. *PL* 172:1081, 1590.
2. M. Zink, *La prédication en langue romane avant 1300* (Paris, 1976), p. 130 ff.
3. M. Durliat, "La tribune de Serrabone et le jubé de Vezzolano," *Monuments et Mémoires de la Fondation Piot* (Académie des Inscriptions et Belles-Lettres) 60 (1977).
4. *MS* of Bruges, f° 55.
5. Laon, MS 85, f° 94.
6. *BN*, MS lat. 8865, f° 102.
7. See above, p. 109.
8. The latest occurrence may be found in the writing of the Englishman, Stephen Langton.
9. D. E. Luscombe, *The School of Peter Abelard* (Cambridge, 1964).
10. This ternary image, also hierarchized, accounts equally for the organization of power in Christian society. *Caritas* (the Holy Spirit, but also the lay populace, the seemingly natural beneficiary of the imperative of charity) was subordinated to *sapientia* (Christ, but also the clergy), with laymen and clerks remaining subject to the power of the Father: unconsciously, the secular Church in the Ile-de-France was preparing to recognize the paternal power of the Capetian king.
11. *PL* 176:966. Note the metaphor: the earnest-money sealed the matrimonial contract; here the soul is the bride of Christ; Hugh reflected on marriage at length, for in the twelfth century it was one of the tasks of clerks—who in this way were carrying through to completion once again the work of Hincmar of Rheims and Gerard of Cambrai—to strengthen by making sacred what they deemed the basic framework of lay society: conjugality.
12. *PL* 171:630.
13. *PL* 176:417–18.
14. *De sacramentis*, II: 2, c. 3 (*PL* 176:418).

15. W. Cahn, "The Tympanum of the Portal of Saint Anne at Notre Dame of Paris and the Iconography of the Division of Powers in the Middle Ages," *Journal of the Warburg and Courtauld Institute* 32 (1969).

16. *PL* 176:417–18.

17. See above, p. 70.

18. Even after so much research, including that of Y. Lefèvre, and of R. D. Crouse and M. O. Garrigues. "Quelques recherches sur l'oeuvre d'Honorius Augustodunensis" *Revue d'histoire de l'Eglise de France* (1975).

19. *PL* 172:1147–49.

20. *PL* 172:828–29.

21. Bonizo of Sutri (in about 1090–99) in the *Liber de vita christiana,* ed. E. Perels (Berlin, 1930) also divided men in the Gregorian manner: subjects, prelates; clerical order and lay order. The responsibility of the sinner, according to him, depended as much on the rank he occupied as on the nature of the sin; for him the important breach fell between the "plebs" and the potentates. Among the latter were the knights, for whom he constructed (7, c. 28) a particular moral code, cast in a royal mold. In book 8. Bonizo divided the "subjects of the lay order" into three groups, the artisans, the merchants, and the peasants "whose *labor* is without sin." But he took his inspiration from Ratherius of Verona (C. Leonardi. "Raterio e Marziano Capella," *Italia medioevale e umanistica* 2 (1959): 73–102; and the proceedings of the recent colloquium, *Raterio di Verona,* Todi, 1970–71) who, in the *Praeloquia.* pushed to considerable lengths the dissection of the social body, carefully examining, below the level of princes and nobles, the various estates (or, rather, the various domestic services, for the overall model is that of the princely household, that of God, that of the king), including *milites, artifices, negociatores, mercenarii.*

22. *Liber duodecim quaestionum* (before 1115), *PL* 172:1177–86.

23. One came directly from Dionysius: *perfecti, imperfecti, ypocrite, PL* 172:1011.

24. *PL* 172:166.

25. *PL* 172:1260.

26. See *PL* 172:586.

27. *PL* 172:1128 and 874.

28. *PL* 172:361.

29. *PL* 172:357 ff.

30. H. Weisweiler, *Das Schriftum der Schule Anselms von Laon und Wilhelms von Champeaux in deutschen Bibliotheken* (Munich, 1936), p. 153.

31. Georges Duby, *Medieval Marriage: Two Models from Twelfth-century France* (Baltimore, 1978).

20. IN THE SERVICE OF PRINCES

1. *Histoire du meurtre de Charles le Bon, comte de Flandre (1127–1128),* ed. H. Pirenne (Paris, 1891); trans. James Bruce Ross, *The Murder of Charles the Good* (New York: 1967).

2. Maurice Godelier, "Infrastructure, société, histoire" *Dialectiques,* 1977.

3. *Ep.* 179, *PL* 190:652.

4. *Ioannis Saresberiensis episcopi Carnotensis Policratici,* ed. C. C. J. Webb. 2 vols. (Oxford, 1909) 5, c. 2 (1:282).

5. Ibid., 6, cc. 19–20 (Webb, 2:58).

6. Ibid., 8. c. 17 (2:348).

7. Ibid., 6, c. 25 (2:73–77).

8. Ibid., 5, c. 10 (1:325).

9. Ibid., 6, c. 3 (2:11–13).
10. Ibid., 6, cc. 20, 25; 1, c. 3 (2:58–59, 73–77; 1:20).

21. THE TRUE DEPARTURE

1. *Chronique des ducs de Normandie par Benoît,* ed. C. Fahlin, 3 vols. (Upsala, 1951–67) 1, vv. 13,242–43.
2. Ibid., vv. 13,251–53.
3. Ibid., v. 13,254.
4. Ibid., vv. 13,247–48.
5. This excerpt and the six following taken from vv. 13,257–301.
6. Ibid., 2,368–69 (vv. 34,885 ff.).
7. Ibid., vv. 32,273 and 32,314.
8. D. Rocher, *Thomasin von Zerklaere: der Wälsche Gast (1215–1216)* (Paris-Lille, 1977).
9. *Chronique des ducs* 2, vv. 32,268–69.
10. *Chroniques des comtes d'Anjou et des seigneurs d'Amboise,* ed. L. Halphen and R. Poupardin (Paris, 1913).
11. Ibid., pp. 183–84.
12. Ibid., pp. 191–92.
13. Ibid., pp. 195–96.
14. Ed. J. Kremer, (Marburg, 1887). Cf. Hard af Segerstad, *Quelques commentaires sur les plus anciennes chansons d'état françaises: le Livre des manières d'Etienne de Fougères* (Upsala, 1906). Professor Köpezy of Budapest has prepared a new edition of this text.
15. *Livre des manières,* vv. 673–76.
16. Ibid., vv. 677–80.
17. Ibid., vv. 681–84.
18. Ibid., vv. 705–6.
19. Ibid., v. 711.
20. Ibid., vv. 707–10.
21. *PL* 159:679.
22. *PL* 159:997.
23. Of which the manuscript in the cathedral library at Durham gives, from the late twelfth century, in folio 36, an extraordinary graphic reproduction (R. A. B. Mynors, *Durham Cathedral Manuscripts to the End of the Twelfth Century* [Oxford, 1939]).
24. The manuscript illustration is reproduced by Jacques Le Goff, *La Civilisation de l'Occident médiéval,* p. 344, nos. 117–18.
25. J. Leclercq, "Les *Distinctiones super cantica* de Guillaume de Ramsey" *Sacris Eruditi* 10 (1958):345.
26. *Chroniques des comtes d'Anjou,* p. 35.
27. Ibid., pp. 140–42.

22. KNIGHTHOOD

1. The current state of the question is examined in F. Cardini, "La tradizione cavalleresca nell'Occidente medievale. Un tema di ricerca tra storia e 'tentazioni' antropologiche," *Quaderni medievali* 2 (1976): 125–42.
2. P. Toubert, *Les structures du Latium médiéval,* 2 vols. (Rome, 1973) 2, c. 10.
3. See for example the Alsatian chronicles cited by Karl Bosl, "Caste, ordre et classe en Allemagne (d'après un choix d'exemples allemands)." *Problèmes de stratification sociale, actes du colloque internationale, 1966,* ed R. Mousnier (Paris, 1968): the

chronicle of Etichon: "the group (*familia*) of ministerials known as military (or knightly), i.e., noble and warlike"; the chronicle of Ebersheim, reporting that after the conquest Caesar supposedly recommended to the *principes* not to treat the *milites* as *servi* or *famuli*, but as *defensores* and lords. requiring them to carry out no servile labors but only the practice of their own "profession."

4. Cf. E. Otto, "Von der Abschliessung des Ritterstandes," *Historische Zeitschrift,* (1940) which considers the Constitution against the incendiaries, excluding from knighthood, so that it might remain pure, the peasants because they were serfs, and the sons of priests because they were bastards, i.e., excluding men born into the two other orders, workers and *oratores.*

5. J. Fleckenstein. "Friedrich Barbarossa und das Rittertum. Zur Bedeutung der grossen Mainzer Hoftage von 1184 und 1188," *Festschrift für Hermann Heimpel,* 2 vols. (Göttingen, 1972) 2; "Die Entstehung des niederen Adels und das Rittertum," *Herrschaft und Stand,* ed. J. Fleckensteim (Göttingen, 1977), pp. 17–39.

6. M. Parisse. *La noblesse Lorraine, XIe–XIIIe siècles,* 2 vols. (Lille-Paris. 1976). The evolution in northern France appears to have been similar. In the Mâcon region, it was slightly later (first indication, 1188, *Recueil des chartes de Cluny* 5, no. 4331) that the term "messire" was applied to all the knights, and to the knights alone.

7. In charters from Lorraine, the term *armiger* appeared in 1176; the equivalent term *domicellus* entered around 1220 into documents of this kind originating in the Mâcon region.

8. C. Vogel and R. Elze, *Le Pontifical romano-germanique au Xe siècle* (Vatican City, 1963).

9. Manuscript of Wolfenbüttel, Andrieu. *Les Ordines romani du haut moyen âge,* 5 vols. (Louvain, 1931–61) 2:445.

10. Edited in the sixteenth century by M. Hittorp, following a lost twelfth century manuscript. Andrieu. *Ordines* 1:188, 509, C. Vogel and R. Elze, *Pontifical* 3, p. 45, no. 74.

11. 6, c. 10 (*PL* 199:602).

12. 6. v. 13, (*PL* 199:608).

13. *PL* 212:743–44.

14. Also writing in about 1185, Peter of Blois (*Ep.* 94, *PL* 207:294) spoke of these rites as of something recent: "today the young knights receive their sword from the altar, thus declaring themselves sons of the Church."

15. *Summa de arte predicandi, PL* 210:185–87.

16. L. Maranini, "Cavaleria e cavalieri nel mondo di Chrétien de Troyes." *Mélanges offerts à Frappier,* 2 vols. (Geneva, 1970) 2:737–55; P. Le Rider, *La Chevalerie dans le Conte du Graal de Chrétien de Troyes* (Paris, 1977).

17. Jean Flori, "Sémantique et société médiévale. Le verbe adouber et son évolution au XIIe siècle," *Annales E.S.C.* 31 (1976):915–40.

18. Jean Flori, "La notion de chevalerie dans les chansons de geste du XIIe siècle. Etude historique du vocabulaire" *Le Moyen Age,* 1975.

19. Georges Duby, "Diffusion du titre chevaleresque," *La noblesse,* pp. 44–48.

20. V. 16,032 ff.

21. *The Vulgate Version of Arthurian Romance,* ed. O. Sommer (Washington, 1910) 3:113 ff.

23. PARISIAN RESISTANCE

1. This was the only deliberate effort to develop Paris prior to those of 1820 and 1870; B. Rouleau, *Le Tracé des rues de Paris* (1976), p. 48.

2. An eminent figure, certainly better known thanks to the work of J. W. Baldwin. *Masters, Princes and Merchants. The Social Views of Peter the Chanter and His Circle,* 2 vols. (Princeton, 1970).

3. *The Historia occidentalis of Jacques de Vitry,* ed. J. F. Hinnesbusch (Fribourg: *Spicilegium friburgense* 17, 1972).

4. *PL* 210:184–98.

5. *PL* 139:506.

6. *PL* 210:188.

7. P. Michaud-Quantin, "Le vocabulaire des catégories sociales chez les canonistes et les moralistes du XIIIe siècle," *Ordres et classes.*

8. E.g., the mind of Alexander Neckham, another Parisian master, who began his treatise *On Nature* with a chapter on the exchequer.

9. Vienne, MS 1395, *BN,* MS lat. 505.

10. Isaiah, f° 4.

11. Isaiah, f° 8.

12. Isaiah, f° 10.

13. Hosea, f° 24.

14. Hosea, f° 23.

15. Isaiah, f° 8.

16. Isaiah, f° 8.

17. Isaiah, f° 8.

24. CONTRADICTIONS OF FEUDALISM

1. *Recueil des actes de Philippe Auguste, roi de France,* ed. H. F. Delaborde et al., 3 vol. to date (Paris. 1916–66) 1, no. 345 (417).

2. P. Raedts. "The Children's Crusade of 1212," *Journal of Medieval History* 3 (1977): 279–323.

3. *Oeuvres de Rigord et de Guillaume le Breton,* ed. H. F. Delaborde, 2 vols. (Paris: *SHF,* 1882–85) 1:303–4.

4. T. Bisson, "The Organized Peace," *American Historical Review* 82, pp. 293, 304–5.

5. Studied long since by historians of the bourgeoisie: H. Géraud, "Les routiers au XIIe siècle," *BEC* 3 (1841–42): 125–47; A. Luchaire, "Un essai de révolution sociale sous Philippe Auguste" *Grande Revue,* 1900.

6. *Pars altera chronici lemovicensis,* c. 22, *RHF* 18:219.

7. *MGH, SS* 7:534.

8. *Oeuvres de Rigord et Guillaume le Breton* 1:38–39.

9. *RHF* 18:251.

10. *MGH, SS* 26:443.

11. *RHF* 18:729–30.

25. THE ADOPTION

1. André le Chapelain, *Traité de l'amour courtois,* trans. C. Buridant (Paris, 1974). On the text and its author, see the recent decisive contribution by A. Karnein, "Auf der Suche nach einem Autor: Andreas, Verfasser von *De amore*" *Germanisch-romanische Monatschrift* (1978).

2. Ibid., 1, c. 1 (Buridant, p. 115).

3. J. Batany. *Approches du Roman de la Rose,* p. 18.

4. Buridant, p. 62.

5. Buridant, p. 141.

6. Buridant, p. 55.

7. Buridant, p. 126.

8. Buridant. p. 141.

9. Buridant, p. 54.

10. Buridant, p. 53.

11. Buridant, pp. 64–65.

12. Lambert of Ardres, in evoking in his *Historia comitum Ghisnensium,* c. 11, *MGH, SS* 24:568, the dynasty's ancestor Siegfried, dying of love, calls him "alterum Andream exhibens Parisiensem."

13. J. Batany, "Le vocabulaire des catégories sociales dans quelques moralistes français vers 1200," *Ordres et classes,* and "Un prédicateur sémiologue: l'apostrophe au roi du Roman du carité," *Mélanges Le Gentil* (Paris, 1973).

14. *Gesta Philippi Augusti,* c. 203 (*Oeuvres de Rigord et Guillaume le Breton* 1:296–97).

15. T. Zotz, "Bischöfliche Herrschaft. Adel, Ministerialität und Burgentum in Stadt und Bistum Worms (11.-14. Jahrhundert) *Herrschaft und Stand* (Göttingen, 1977), pp. 98–99.

16. *Philippide,* in *Oeuvres de Rigord et Guillaume le Breton* 2, vv. 190–245.

17. Ibid., vv. 236, 237.

18. Ibid., v. 239.1

19. Ibid., v. 243.

20. Ibid., vv. 243–44.

21. Ibid., v. 241.

22. Ibid.

23. Ibid., v. 248–49.

24. Ibid., vv. 200–201.

25. Ibid., v. 248.

26. Ibid., vv. 251–52.

27. Ibid., v. 283.

28. Ibid., v. 288.

29. Ibid.

30. Ibid., vv. 281–82.

EPILOGUE

1. P. E. Schramm, *Der König von Frankreich,* 2nd ed., p. 198.

2. C. Castoriadis, *L'Institution imaginaire de la société,* (Paris, 1975), p. 200.

3. M. de Certeau. *L'Ecriture de l'Histoire* (Paris, 1975), p. 165.

4. D. Richet, "Autour des origines lointaines de la Révolution française, élite et despotisme," *Die französische Revolution* (Darmstadt, 1973).

INDEX